HISTORIC PRESERVATION

Curatorial Management of the Built World

HISTORIC PRESERVATION

Curatorial Management of the Built World

JAMES MARSTON FITCH

University Press of Virginia
Charlottesville and London

THE UNIVERSITY PRESS OF VIRGINIA
Copyright © 1990 by the Rector and Visitors
of the University of Virginia

This edition first published 1990

Originally published by McGraw-Hill, Inc., 1982

Library of Congress Cataloging-in-Publication Data

Fitch, James Marston.
    Historic preservation : curatorial management of the build world /
James Marston Fitch.
        p. cm.
    Includes bibliographical references.
    ISBN 0-8139-1272-5
    1. Architecture—Conservation and restoration. 2. Historic
buildings—Conservation and restoration. I. Title.
NA105.F47 1990
363.6'9—dc20   89-22641
                                                                      CIP

Printed in the United States of America

Contents

List of Illustrations

Preface to the Paperback Edition

The maturation of historic preservation in America has been a cultural process, decades in the making. It might be said to have begun, as a conscious organized movement, when Ann Pamela Cunningham met with a group of Virginia gentlewomen to form the Mt. Vernon Ladies Association in 1859. And it might be said to have come of age a century later, during the 1960s, when the first national legislation in support of historic preservation was passed by the U.S. Congress and when the nation's first academic program in historic preservation was established at Columbia University's Graduate School of Architecture and Planning.

During that period, preservation has grown from the activity of a few upper-class antiquarians, organized to save a few monumental works of architecture, to a broad mass movement engaged in battles to preserve urban districts, "Main Street," and indeed whole historic cities and towns. As the scale and complexity of preservationists' work has expanded, so too has their understanding of the built world they have been struggling to save. Thus, from concentrating upon the cosmopolitan structures of the powerful and wealthy, the preservationists have come to appreciate their interconnectedness with the vernacular and folkloristic fabric of which they are a part. The preservationists' exclusive attention to urban buildings has broadened to include farm and village architecture and the countryside generally. And from an emphasis on buildings, they have come to understand the equal importance of the gardens, open spaces, and streets around them—that is, of the connective tissue that binds the built world into an organic, life-sustaining whole.

The most recent period has been significant in another respect since it marks the entry of professionals (architects, landscape architects, art historians, archaeologists) into the field which hitherto had been filled almost exclusively by antiquarians: that is, by laymen who, whatever their training or erudition in other fields, were usually amateurs in architecture and building. (We use the term *amateur* in its original signification, as one who does the work for love of it and not for pay.) It is this participatory aspect of the field which has always given historic preservation its power and which, in the last decade or so, has enabled it to become a dominant force in architecture and urbanism.

As a matter of fact, the success of the historic preservation movement has had quite unanticipated consequences for the practice of architecture itself. More than any other factor, it has made the styles of the past respectable in a profession in which, for over half a century, they had been in disrepute. It has thus created a climate of opinion in which historicizing eclecticism (now called Postmodernism) became a fashionable mode of design. It is ironic indeed that the preservationists have contributed, however unwittingly, to a movement like Postmodernism, which advocates the purely decorative use of past styles of architectural expression in new construction. Whatever errors the preservationists may have made in the past, the deliberate fabrication of facsimiles and reproductions of historic artifacts has never been part of their program. To the contrary, their battle has always been to save the original, the authentic, the prototypical so that future generations would be able to see what the past was *really like*. No one could have put it more succinctly than Anne Pamela Cunningham in her farewell address on June 1, 1874, to the Mt. Vernon Ladies Association: "Those who go to the house in which [Washington] lived and died wish to see in what he lived and died. . . . See to it that you keep it that way."

But the restoration of old buildings for their historical associations and aesthetic value has also had unanticipated consequences of another and higher order. For the restored buildings have demonstrated a regenerative impact upon their immediate environs, similar to that of healthy cells when new skin is grafted on to damaged or distressed tissue. This effect can be observed in many cities where extensive historic restoration has occurred. For example, in Boston and Seattle, where comparatively modest schemes for the restoration of old public markets have broadened spectacularly into the regeneration of the entire urban fabric surrounding them. And this has included not merely additional old buildings not originally scheduled for rehabilitation, but also the construction of many new ones. In the case of Boston, one can say that a scheme that began with the restoration of the old Quincy Market has initiated a process of urban regeneration that now extends across the whole northeastern quadrant of the central city. In the case of Seattle, the successful battle to save and restore a popular market has similarly led to regeneration of the largely abandoned waterfront behind and below it.

This phenomenon, which can now be seen across all America, occurs at the same time—often in the same cities—in which ambitious urban renewal plans have failed. And it suggests a fundamental weakness in city-planning theory, which often tends to regard the past, as represented by existing urban fabric, as merely an obstacle to future growth. This attitude was epitomized at the beginning of this century by Daniel Burnham's famous dictate: "Make no little plans, they have no magic to stir men's blood." Under this philosophy, Burnham and his Beaux Arts colleagues produced schemes that not only called for a very large, but also an entirely new, urban fabric. Thus, one would never guess, from the great bird's-eye perspectives of Burnham's Chicago Plan of 1909, that we are looking at a scheme for a built-up and highly structured site *already* occupied by a quarter-million Chicagoans. The same must be said of Otto Wagner's 1910–11 scheme for the rebuilding of the XXII district in Vienna or (for that matter) of LeCorbusier's 1922 scheme for the rebuilding of central Paris.

This formalist philosophy in city planning remained dominant throughout the first half of this century and indeed dictated the reconstruction of many of Europe's war-damaged cities—though, fortunately, not all of them. Many of these were so savagely and repeatedly bombed that, at war's end, few traces of the prewar urban form were visible beneath the rubble. Indeed, so mountainous was the rubble in cities like Rotterdam, Dresden, Berlin, and Warsaw that its disposal constituted a logistical problem in itself. Under such conditions, it was all too easy to conclude that the best solution was to clear it all away and start over, beginning with adoption of a completely "rational" new street plan designed first of all to facilitate motor traffic. Such was the decision made in LeHavre, Rotterdam, and Dresden. In other towns, often after much discussion, a contrary policy was adopted. In Nuremberg, Warsaw, and Leningrad the decision was made to preserve the historic footprint of the streets in the historic core and to restore all its significant buildings, no matter how badly damaged.

Today, three of four decades later, it is easy to see which of these two policies led to the most satisfactory urban form—one dominated by rationalist city-planning theory, the other by the need to restore (and, where necessary, reconstruct) historically determined urban form. As examples of the first, the radically remodeled centers of LeHavre, Rotterdam, and Dresden are dull, monotonous, auto-dominated cityscapes, with scarcely a visual hint to indicate their points of origin in space and time. In Nuremberg, Warsaw, and Leningrad the reverse is true: their visual specificity has been maintained for the pleasure of visitor and resident alike. Merely to *be* in their dazzling panoramas of Gothic, Renaissance, Baroque, Roccoco, and Art Nouveau is an unforgettable experience.

These case histories demonstrate that the preservationists have been correct, for reasons perhaps even more profound than they had realized. For the historically evolved urban fabric offers a critically important life-support system to everyone who is sheltered there—whether temporarily as the tourist or permanently as the resident. This support is complex and multiform. It is first of all supremely physical—indeed physiological. But it goes beyond that to offer psychic shelter as well. The city has been correctly defined as the theater of memory: that is, as the cumulative scene of past actions. The impact of this scene upon us occurs across the two interconnected faces of consciousness: direct sensuous perception ("I saw it with my own eyes") and intellectual cognition ("Everyone knows that this is where the Declaration of Independence was signed"). Thus the foreign visitor to Leningrad, ignorant of its history, may be overwhelmed by the baroque splendor of the palaces along the River Neva, while the native-born Leningrader—knowing little about Czarist palaces—may nevertheless be brought to tears by the restored scenes of the heroic resistance of the city to Nazi armies during World War II.

Moreover, it is clear that this historically determined city form presents a picture for whose complexity it is impossible to fabricate convincing replicas or facsimiles. The historic city is a visible record of an endless chain of human responses to both the ongoing need for change and to such periodic cataclysms as fires, floods, and war. This is a process that cannot be simulated, either in the sanitizing of old urban forms purged of all "accidental" intrusions of history (as in the restoration of Carcassonne and Colonial Williamsburg) or in candid efforts to replicate the past de novo (as at Disneyland and Disneyworld).

In defending the wholeness of central Charleston and Savannah with all its imperfections or the integrity of Warsaw and Leningrad, no matter how savagely mauled by war, the preservationists have proved to be correct. In their practice, if not yet in their theoretical formulations, one can discover an incrementalist approach to urban development that closely parallels the theories of such iconoclastic planners as Jane Jacobs and Christopher Alexander.* These theoreticians of urban development have argued persuasively that the city is a living organism. That, like all organisms, it grows by cellular incrementation and that this growth should be genetically programmed, not designed merely in a formal, city-planning sense. Though neither Jacobs nor Alexander has shown any interest in historic architecture per se, both take the position that the *whole* built world is our primary resource, to be managed most conservatively.

In light of such developments as these, historic preservation is emerging into a centrally important role in the future of American architecture and urbanism. And this suggests that the thesis of this book, as outlined in the original Preface, is, if anything, more relevant than ever.

---

*Jane Jacobs, *The Death and Life of Great American Cities*, Random House, New York, 1961, and *The Economy of Cities*, Random House, New York, 1970; Christopher Alexander, *The Oregon Experiment*, Oxford University Press, New York, 1975, and *A New Theory of Urban Design*, Oxford University Press, New York, 1987.

Preface to the First Edition

This book aims to provide an overview of the urgent problems connected with the management of the built world, as well as to offer a holistic theoretical apparatus for a wise and civilized system of solving them. The book itself is a consequence of my efforts, beginning in the early 1960s, to develop an academic program for formal training in the field of historic preservation (the generic term in America for this form of activity).

Such a program appeared mandatory in the light of several factors: the rapid quantitative expansion in the field since 1945; the resultant need for an increased number of trained preservationists; and the complete lack of any structured form for training them in the United States. This paradoxical state of affairs derives from the fact that we have never had in the United States any government institution comparable to the French Service des Monuments Historiques, with its wide powers over the national historic and artistic heritage. Because of this lack of a comprehensive custodial agency, the task of managing the American heritage had originally fallen, *faute de mieux,* to the citizenry at large, especially to that small and heroic band of amateurs (to use the term in its original connotation of one who does the work for love and not for pay) without whom there would have been no historic preservation movement at all.

But as an expression of the rising concern of the American people over what was happening to their native habitat, there have developed an ever-increasing number of preservationist activities. These have ranged from battles to save a single *Magnolia grandiflora* tree in Brooklyn to the successful campaign to designate an entire island, Nantucket, as a historic district. For such rapidly expanding activities, an increasing cadre of trained personnel was required. The old autodidactic method of training, so successful in earlier years, was simply no longer adequate. Under such circumstances, the emergence of university training programs became inevitable.

Such academic programs have not been necessary in European countries, most of which have national agencies like the French Service, which have evolved their own systems of in-house training. Under this system, any young architect, art historian, or archaeologist desiring to specialize in preservation can enroll in a structured work-and-study program which, when successfully completed, leads to the diploma in the subject. But academic training in historic preservation must necessarily reflect the special characteristics of the field in America. It must, on the one hand, train young professionals to collaborate actively with the army of amateurs in the field. And it must, on the other, produce professionals equipped to deal with the scope and complexity of the projects generated precisely by those amateurs.

The standard pattern of specialized graduate education is one in which the student is led into increasingly deep but increasingly narrow areas of concentration. Such specialization is obviously essential for many discrete areas of activity, e.g., embryology, astronomy, and nuclear engineering. But the task of retrieving, recycling, and curating the built world is, by its very nature, synoptic and cross-disciplinary. Above and beyond their specialized undergraduate training (architecture, art history, chemistry, engineering, urban planning), preservationists must also be generalists. That is, they must see their own special area of expertise as being only one strand in a larger fabric, the warp and woof of which consist of many other coequal and coexistent specialities. To work together effectively, preservationists require common concepts of their curatorial task, shared methods and technologies for dealing with it, and a common language for describing it.

For such reasons, the formal graduate education of preservationists must be an unorthodox mix of the general and the specific, the comprehensive and the definitive. They must, on the one hand, be encouraged to develop the application of their own specialized skills and training while, at the same time, they are learning the interfaces between them and those of other specialists working alongside them in office, field, and laboratory. They must be literate in the design fields: architecture, landscape architecture, and the decorative arts. They must understand the basic methods of research and documentation of historic artifacts and the means of recording, drafting, and delineating. They must understand the general methodology of scientific artifactual conservation, if only to know when, where, and to whom they must turn for collaboration in such matters. And increasingly they must understand current economic, legal, and legislative forces acting upon historic district planning, since this is the context in which most projects must be analyzed.

In short, their education should give students a firm conceptual armature around which to organize their professional activities when they enter the field. What they do with such conceptual equipment will depend partly upon their own interests and capacities and partly upon how they apply them, in light of their widened comprehension of this growing and immensely important area of human activity. If this book aids that process, it will have served its purpose well.

1

Why Preserve the Prototype?

Prototype: An original type, form, or instance that serves as a model on which later stages are based or judged

Replica: A copy or reproduction of a work of art, especially one made by the original artist

Duplicate: An identical copy . . . anything that corresponds exactly to something else, especially an original

Facsimile: An exact copy or reproduction, as of a document

Reproduction: That which is reproduced [a counterpart, image, or copy]*

The outstanding accomplishment of modern industrial technology has been what we may call the democratization of material culture. It goes without saying that the consumption or enjoyment of a given cultural artifact—a book, a picture, a chair, a sherbet—by the masses of the people awaited the technical means for multiplying that artifact; only then could there be wider access to the forms of material culture. Depending upon the artifact in question, this multiplication has been achieved by replica, duplicate, or facsimile. Generally speaking, the replica, an expression of handicraft production, has disappeared. The duplicate and the facsimile have, therefore, become the standard expressions of modern industrial production.

In the United States, the classic instances of the duplicate would be the production of textiles in volume and the serial production of firearms made of interchangeable parts. In these instances, the new artifact has been the literal double of its prototype. And the availability of cheap cloth and cheap guns had a direct and immediate effect on the conditions of life and the material well-being of Americans during the late eighteenth and early nineteenth centuries. The printing press, on the other hand, made dramatically

*The American Heritage Dictionary of the English Language, William Morris, ed., American Heritage Publishing Co., Inc., and Houghton Mifflin Company, New York, 1969.

clear the power of the facsimile, enormously extending the general accessibility of formal knowledge through the printed page. And the subsequent development of engraving, photography, motion picture film, phonograph, radio, and television have made possible the instantaneous and worldwide distribution of visual and sonic facsimile.

It is equally clear that this new capacity to multiply and distribute material culture makes possible its introduction into places, times, and circumstances where hitherto it would have been inconceivable. Thus, today, even isolated persons of moderate means can participate in a range of sensual and aesthetic experience which would have been at one time available only to the urban rich. In either duplicate or facsimile form, they can enjoy theater, ballet, opera, and concert; sculpture and painting; poetry, novel, and essay; *haute couture* and *haute cuisine*; luxurious architecture and speedy, comfortable transport.

Moreover, they can enjoy such urbane artifacts under quite new conditions of privacy or isolation. Historically, the circumstances under which these artifacts might have been either produced or consumed would have been largely *public* circumstances, and they would have been available only in an urban context. Today Beethoven is accessible to the loneliest cowboy or forester with a transistor radio. But in Beethoven's own day it needed a cosmopolitan audience to sustain the hall and the orchestra by which, alone, such compositions could be transposed to sense experience. Moreover, the event was both discrete and unique. It could not be multiplied, stored, or distributed (the printed sheet of music was only the schema of the form, not the form itself). In short, under these circumstances, access to the performing artist was limited to a specific audience at a specific time and place. Modern technology, via the electronic facsimile, has removed nearly all these preindustrial limits. And what has happened in music has its analogues in the other performing arts, as well as in painting and sculpture: the works of Shakespeare and Verdi, Michelangelo and Picasso, have become ubiquitous in our consciousness.

Through the industrially produced duplicate, other forms of urbane material culture—pineapple in Alaska and strawberries in January; warm baths in winter and cooled rooms in summer; urbane clothing and luxurious private transport—are becoming commonplace. The airplane, carrying people halfway around the world in a day, exposes them to stimuli of exotic cultures that a lifetime of earlier travel could not have encompassed.

This quantitative multiplication of the artifact represents an enormous extension of individual experience. And the value of it is both concrete and demonstrable, for we have been describing nothing less than the aesthetic equivalent of intellectual literacy—surely a logical extension of political democracy. But it is imperative that we also recognize that this new capacity to mass-produce the artifacts of material culture has had a profoundly disturbing effect upon culture itself. On the one hand, it has altered both the condition of the artist and artisan and their relationship with their audience or clients. On the other hand, it has modified the very properties of the artifact, as well as the circumstances under which it is enjoyed or consumed. All of these changed relationships have implications for the future of art which, to say the least, have scarcely begun to be explored.

THE "PRIVATIZATION" OF THE CULTURAL ARTIFACT

Among the most striking results of the application of modern technology to the production of the cultural form is the bias toward the *privatization* of the form itself. To repeat: before modern times, the enjoyment and consumption of most cultural artifacts were public acts. It was not only that the city offered the most fertile seedbed for artistic and social creativity. It was also that the created forms were deliberately designed for public exposure and public enjoyment there. Museums and libraries, restaurants and theaters, salons and publishing houses, universities and laboratories were, one and all, both urban and public institutions. Nor was the public aspect peripheral to the intrinsic quality of the cultural form itself. On the contrary, physical proximity between artist and audience stimulated both: the one to more intense creativity, the other to a heightened response. A first night, a vernissage, a new publication, a great dinner, a brilliant salon, or a public debate—all these events drew much of their luster from the fact that they were public occasions in which the line of communication between artist and audience was short and incandescent.

It is true that modern communication media, carrying visual and sonic facsimiles, make possible the sharing of such events with incomparably larger audiences than ever before—but not without profound attenuation of that very line of communication. The American critic Gilbert Seldes has dubbed these new media (press, radio, movies, television) the "public arts." But this is a misnomer. What we have invented is in fact a new "privatized" cultural form and a new kind of audience that is public only in a statistical sense. It is an audience of isolated individuals, thinly scattered before living-room TV screens, or listening to radio broadcasts on beaches and ski runs, or watching distant cinema screens through the windshields of parked cars in drive-in movies. Here every dimension of the traditional relationship between artist and audience, audience and cultural artifact, has been seriously distorted. It may be open to discussion whether the cultural value of the form has been heightened or lowered in the process; but that it has been altered is beyond dispute.

The greatest danger is, of course, the most familiar. In preparing the form for mass distribution, the entrepreneur inevitably modifies the form itself. The motive for this intervention may be either valid or venal, but it is usually altogether extraneous to the aesthetic requirements of the form itself and, consequently, hostile to its aesthetic integrity. Thus stage plays are "cut" to meet the time modules of broadcasting, or "adapted" to form movies and musicals. Books are "digested" for quick reading and easy carrying. Great paintings are used to "illustrate" magazine articles and advertisements. Musical compositions are "excerpted" to serve as "theme songs" for movies and "signatures" for television serials, or cut up into easily digestible bits to form "mood music" for dining, dancing, "dreaming."

Even when the mass production of the facsimile leaves the prototype unaltered and intact, mass distribution confronts it with another danger. Heedless repetition of the form ends by emptying it of emotional force: overfamiliarity reduces its cultural potency and ends by destroying its capacity to move us. There is an upper limit to the multiplications that Michelangelo's *David* or Van Gogh's *Sunflowers* or Washington's Mount Vernon can survive. Tchaikovsky's poignant melodies have already been reduced to soiled clichés. The "great books" have been made into mail-order merchandise. Even the vocabulary of cultural discussion is robbed of its original significance; "tragic" has come to mean merely "sad" (fallen breasts, a lost pet) while "comic" has come to describe the witless violence of Orphan Annie and Steve Roper.

THEATER: INSTANTANEOUS AND INCANDESCENT COMMUNICATION

It is in the very nature of mass production to attenuate the line of communication between artists and audience and to make private the circumstances under which it is experienced. No cultural form suffers from this sort of attrition so severely as the performing arts, for when living actors, dancers, and singers confront the living audience across the proscenium, action and reaction are to all intents and purposes simultaneous, and contact is instantaneous. The specific emotional temperature of the theater is the result of a triangular current: the actor's effect upon the audience; the audience's collective response to the actor; the effect of the audience upon its individual members. This is the reason that the theater is the most electrifying of all cultural forms. When the Greek city-state of Euboean Eretria made theater attendance compulsory on certain high holidays, it was merely acknowledging this potency. The theater was the instrument whereby citizens were inculcated with Greek values—where, in sober fact, they were taught to be Greek! Recognizing this, the Greeks took great care with the ambience and circumstances under which the play was to be experienced. Sight lines and acoustics were exactly calculated; every member of the audience could hear and see the actors at all times. The identifying feature of this Greek design for communication is, as everyone knows, the chorus, which acted both as interlocutor for the audience (Why, oh why, must Oedipus kill his father at the crossroads?) and as interpreter for the playwright (Patience, patience, you will see, the Fates have willed it so!). Its words pulsing back and forth between cast and audience, the chorus joined the two in one selfless communion. Catharsis through pity and terror was the result of this intricate relation.

It should be apparent, then, that any departure from this prototype, from this organic trinity of actors, audience, and individual spectator, implies a qualitative drop in the potency of the form. When the play is transposed to the movie screen, it has already been divested of one of its most electrifying aspects: the feedback between actor and audience. Nevertheless, the cinema still retains a portion of the theatrical equation: the living audience that heightens the individual spectator's response to the action on the screen. But when this same cinematic facsimile is transposed to the television screen in the living room, the experience has been reduced from three dimensions to one. Privatization is complete. With the alteration of both the intrinsic properties of the form and the extrinsic circumstances of participation, the experience has been converted into a pale and impoverished reflection of its original quality.

Nor does the creation of a new dramatic literature, especially written for radio and television, surmount the inherent limits of the media. At its best, the new form can be very good; at its most usual, it is aesthetically disastrous. And of course, the usual cause of failure is the common compulsion of producer and author to win the largest possible audience. Motives may vary: the producer may simply require the largest possible return on an investment, and thus demand a plot that, if it cannot please everyone, should at least offend nobody; the author, on the other hand, may aspire to the loftiest creation, but the highest taste common to a public spanning New York, Tokyo, and Istanbul is low indeed. Technology here confronts the author with an "audience" such as he or she never faced before—a statistical entity defined by access to an electronic receiver. It seems improbable that a high art form can develop from facsimile; it is more suited to the informing than to the aesthetic function.

It is probably true that the fine arts and the performing arts have been peculiarly susceptible to multiplication in visual and sonic facsimile—so much so that recordings of the symphony, telecasts of the stage play, colored prints of the painting, and casts of the sculpture threaten to supplant the prototype. Unfortunately, we can see the same processes at work, the same dangers inherent, in other areas of the material culture. For example, all of the artifacts of the personal environment—food, clothing, furniture, housing—were formerly handmade prototypes, that is, folk art and *artiginato*. Today the prototype disappears before the remorseless advance of the industrially produced duplicate. The prototype was never plentiful or equally accessible to all, and today it is more expensive than the duplicate.

5

Yet quantity and cost are purely descriptive aspects of an object. From a qualitative point of view, the handmade prototype is often superior to its machine-made duplicate. Both practically and aesthetically, it once met the needs of the personal environment in all particulars, as prosperous farm and city houses in preindustrial Europe, North America, and Japan show very clearly. The machine has yet to weave a better carpet, bake a better loaf of bread, or build a better table than the artisan.

FOOD: QUANTITY UP, QUALITY DOWN

We now know the astonishing extent to which all artifacts can be manipulated by modern technology. In regard to food, we find a vast entrepreneurial apparatus interposed between producer and consumer; a lengthening separation in time and space between fabrication and consumption; and the interjection of a series of processing and packaging techniques that are extraneous (where they are not actually hostile) to the intrinsic quality of the food itself.

And here, of course, we meet a confounding paradox. It is obvious that the techniques of modern science and technology, applied to the growing, processing, and distribution of foodstuffs, have disclosed the prospect, for the first time in history, of an adequate and balanced diet for all mankind. Productivity has been greatly increased, nutritional and sanitary problems are understood, putrescence and infection can be controlled, techniques for storage and preservation are perfected. All of this must be reckoned an epochal accomplishment—but in the countries of the West, where this process is most fully realized, it is increasingly clear that the "solution" raises its own new problems. An adequate diet is no guarantee of good food; indeed, it often seems as if a rise in the quantity of mass-produced foodstuffs is matched by a qualitative decline in the public cuisine.

Here, again, we should contemplate the difference between prototype and duplicate, for all national and regional cuisines are inheritances from our preindustrial past. Modern technology has yet to discover a single new food source or to invent an essentially new recipe. Most of the exotic "new" foodstuffs that now enrich the Western diet are simply the inventions of the folk cultures of Asia, Africa, and South America. But regardless of their point of origin, we find these foodstuffs and recipes being subjected in due course to the exigencies of mass production. Here the reasons for entrepreneurial intervention may range widely. At one extreme we have gross venality, as in the past Italian scandals of food "sophistication." At the other extreme is simple technological necessity. Manipulation may take the form of pasteurizing or irradiating for sanitation, or it may introduce chemical additives that make the product look better, remain soft longer, ship more easily. But whatever the reason for the intervention, it is extraneous to the culinary, that is, aesthetic, integrity of the form itself.

6

And here again we find that the audiences, the consumers, are statistical. In prepared foods (cooked, canned, quick-frozen) the recipe is manipulated to meet the norms of "average" or "national" taste. The inevitable result is vulgarization of the prototype, a vitiating of the distinctive taste, texture, or appearance of the original. Traditionally, culinary art was regional and exclusive, conditioned by local custom and resources. The most complex and sophisticated cuisines were understandably the urban, products of palace and town, of the greatest resources and most demanding audiences. By the same token, the best urban food has usually been prepared and eaten in public company, whether in the great dining rooms of the palazzi or in the restaurants and cookshops of the city. Such, at least, has been the case in France and Italy in the West, China and Japan in the East—the points of origin of the world's *haute cuisine*.

Further analogies between theater and restaurant are inescapable. The best food, like the best acting, is found where the line of communication between artist and audience is shortest. The reasons for this are at once psychological and chemical. That cook is happiest who works directly for a clientele that share his tastes and enthusiasms; and that diner is happiest who shares a piping-hot meal with friends. The sheer chemistry of cooking, on the other hand, establishes certain limits of time and space. The lapsed time between preparation and consumption is critically important in the aesthetic quality of cooked foods. Though their nutritional properties may be unaffected, their taste deteriorates rapidly on a steam table or refrigerated tray. They suffer even more through the techniques of the mass canning and freezing industries. Thus, in food as in theater, technical multiplication leads to a measurable drop in the quality of the artifact. Mass cookery may indeed be an essential part of modern life. But it can only approximate, never match, the hand-crafted prototype.

ARCHITECTURE: THE PARADOX OF PLENTY

In no other sector of material culture, however, has the means of replicating a prototype—and replicating it anywhere in the world—been as pervasive as in architecture. Earlier European conquerors of Asia, Africa, and the Americas had, of course, brought with them their own vocabulary of architectural forms. But the extent to which they were able to apply them in the new environment was sharply limited by their own relatively primitive preindustrial technologies. All this is quite changed today. The great prototypical forms of contemporary architecture—the mass-housing projects of Gropius, the skyscrapers of Le Corbusier, the glass pavilions of Mies van der Rohe—have been endlessly replicated around the world. In this proliferation of a few basic prototypes, we face in microcosm all the paradoxes of modern industrialized mass production. The ability to produce a 40-story high-rise office building as easily in Lagos as in Los Angeles is, in abstract terms, a remarkable accomplishment. Such an exportation of exotic architectural forms would have been inconceivable a century ago. Moreover, it can be argued that the need for multistory construction in a rapidly growing city like Lagos may be quite as justifiable there as in American cities where the type was invented.

Nevertheless, the efflorescence of these internationalized prototypes has serious consequences. In the first place, the artifact itself is usually ill-adapted to the foreign environment. Its construction and maintenance depend upon the importation of the high technology of the West, itself a very expensive operation. Moreover, the buildings themselves can be kept habitable only by the massive application of mechanical energy.

But there is another and perhaps more serious cultural consequence. The imported artifact—skyscraper, suburban house, automobile—by its sheer prestige of being new, modern, cosmopolitan, tends to discredit and then replace the older local forms and concepts. These precedent life-styles, which have evolved across centuries or millennia of experimentation, often offer much higher levels of environmental response than the international replacements. This will be stunningly apparent to anyone who compares the overall amenity of the colonial centers of Quito or Lima with that of the new urban sprawl which surrounds them.

Here in America, substantially the same paradox confronts us in the endless replication of a handful of discredited clichés: the ranch-type house, the "colonial" shopping center. It may be argued that the industrialized multiplication of this limited range of artifacts has brought a higher level of privatized comfort to middle-class American families than ever before. But it can scarcely be denied that it has been accompanied by the degradation of the style itself. It is probably an instinctive response to this vulgarization that the same middle-class families visit in increasing numbers such historic sites as Deerfield, Williamsburg, and Savannah, for there they can experience the original, the prototype, in all its sensuous and associational appeal.

It is not easy to imagine how or if this particular form of American replication can ever be halted. The most that might be hoped for is that it be slowed down and modified. This is not at all impossible, given the profound changes now occurring in the economy as a result of the shortage and high cost of energy. The construction of new houses on new land has been dropping for several years, whereas the retrieval and recycling of older urban districts has been growing apace. From San Francisco and Seattle to Charleston and Boston, we can see encouraging evidence of this new potentiality.

For middle-class citizens of the urbane Western world, the essential characteristic of their life-style is the way in which all the constituent parts of their material culture—instruments, tools, goods, and services—have been unitized and packaged for privatized consumption. This has been accomplished by the massive application of science and technology to most of the processes of living: housing, toileting, laundering; cooking and eating; shopping, entertainment, transportation, even leisure itself.

Simultaneously, the application of this same technology to other areas of activity has had the opposite effect of transferring them from the private to the public world. Almost all productive work has been moved from its preindustrial habitat—the kitchen, the farm, cottage industry, and the craftsman's kilns and forges—into the centralized mill and factory. Other areas of activity have been similarly transformed. The most important of all forms of education—that of being taught a trade or craft by working alongside one's elders in its daily pursuit—has all but completely disappeared from the Western world. In transferring formal education from the one-room schoolhouse to the huge centralized schools, the process of cultural homogenization has been accelerated. At the same time, ambulance and hospital have changed the locus of birth, illness, aging, and death from the "borning rooms" of the preindustrial home to the huge, impersonal institution.

Another consequence of this mechanization of goods and services is that they seem increasingly to exacerbate those class and ethnic divisions which already exist in a given society. Although widely hailed for their "democratizing" cultural effect, these privatized amenities are becoming increasingly expensive to buy and consume. This leads to that urban condition, so disturbingly apparent in the Western world today, of private well-being in the midst of public squalor. It also leads to an unprecedented physical segregation of classes and ethnic groups. This is tragically clear in most North and South American cities. In the United States, technology has generated a double migration which permits the well-to-do to flee to the suburbs while the disadvantaged, displaced by mechanized agriculture, flood into the central city. In great cities on other continents, the same process is at work but in reverse: in Mexico City, Lima, and São Paulo, the rich are concentrated in the central city while the poor are relegated to the squatters' towns and *favelas* around the perimeter.* The irony of all this is that it leads inexorably to the impoverishment of urban life for everyone,

*Brasilia, the 30-year-old capital of Brazil, was conceived along Utopian lines to demonstrate the democratic application of modern technology to architecture and town planning. Laid out as a linear city along an arc of superhighways 25 kilometers long, it has no mass transit system at all, relying upon private autos and buses exclusively. The consequences are socially disastrous. Advanced technology (in the form of private autos) benefits only the bureaucrats. The working people, relegated to the jerry-built shantytowns on the perimeter, depend upon the totally inadequate privately owned bus system. The result is a rigid segregation of classes, perhaps the most severe anywhere outside South Africa.

advantaged and disadvantaged alike. As Charles Dickens once observed, in connection with the institution of human slavery, it is as disastrous for the owner as the owned: the moral damage differs in kind, not in severity.

THE NOT UNMIXED BLESSINGS OF INDUSTRIALIZATION

The dilemma is clear enough; yet we scarcely admit it to thought. Modern industrial technology constitutes the indispensable agent of material abundance and hence of political democracy. But in the very process of mass-producing the artifacts of material culture, it subjects the prototypes of these artifacts to remorseless attrition. The industrial duplicate or facsimile cannot, under any circumstances, be the qualitative equal of its prototype, no matter how socially useful it may be. Yet, under the dominant materialistic impetus, the prototype is placed at the mercy of social and economic forces it was never designed to resist. It is not that entrepreneurs are more venal than they were in Vergil's or Shakespeare's day; it is rather that they are incomparably more strong. Their capacity to manipulate the form in all of its qualitative and quantitative dimensions has been enormously extended by technology. Both the uniqueness and the integrity of the artifact are in jeopardy because, left to itself, the facsimile tends to supplant and then to destroy the original. Already, in the highly developed countries of the West, this process has advanced far enough that a new generation is among us whose aesthetic experience and hence aesthetic judgment are based upon private contact with duplicate and facsimile, rather than upon public participation in the exposure to great originals. Such a development, indefinitely extended, can lead only to the impoverishment of the sensual and aesthetic life of each individual and a drastic alteration in the tone of the entire culture.

The paradox of our impoverishing wealth hinges upon the new position of the common man under the new system. For his taste is the product of his experience both as consumer *and* as producer. The good taste he once displayed in what he bought under earlier systems of handicraft production was of a piece with the good sense required of him in what he made: indeed, the two are only different aspects of the same thing, as is clear enough in folk art. Here the confrontation of man the consumer with man the producer is of the most direct sort. The folk artist works by himself and for himself, on artifacts of his own design, intended for his own use.

The industrial system of serial production acts in precisely contrary fashion: industrial workers labor with others, for others, on artifacts designed by professionals with whom they have no contact, for ultimate uses of which they often have no comprehension. Divided and particular production on the assembly line robs the work of either significance or intelligibility for the individual workers placed somewhere along it. That good sense which is the basis of good taste cannot derive, as it always had before, from the world of work. And any specialized knowledge or skills will have very little application to the act of consuming, in which the worker as consumer is forced to judge the values of artifacts of increasing complexity. The result for the common man—each of us—is a steadily declining capacity for mature and satisfying aesthetic decisions.

No one who believes in raising the material well-being of mankind will propose that the world return to a preindustrial state. But no one who cares for full human emotional and intellectual development can remain indifferent to the general degradation of popular taste which has been, to date, the concomitant of modern industrial technology. The central factor in this paradox is the role which the prototype plays in the evolution of both our material culture and our philosophical attitudes toward it. The absolute and unique value which our society accords the prototype is simultaneously a function of our individual sensuous perception of the artifact itself *and* the intellectual understanding of its provenience which we bring to that experience. Thus there will be measurable, tangible differences between the original Rembrandt and even the best facsimile. If the copy is skillful enough, these differences may be apparent only to the expert. But the ultimate response of expert and layman alike will be conditioned by the extra-sensuous cognitive understanding that one of them *is* an original, the other a fake. In this sense, all our aesthetic judgements are preconditioned by the culture of which we are a part.

Under such circumstances as those described above, three distinct levels of cultural action are implied: intervention in defense of (1) the prototypical artifact itself; (2) of the artist or craftsperson who creates it; (3) of the métier or specialized skills which are generated in the very act of handcrafting and which are lost when it ceases. For Americans this will certainly not be an easy task; and it will not come about automatically. On the contrary, such a national intervention implies a conscious sociocultural program for which our only precedent would be the great WPA arts program of the 1930s and 1940s. The fructifying impact of this program, in the fields of painting and sculpture, literature and music, theater and dance, is still apparent, decades later. A comparable energizing impact is to be seen today in the national ateliers for traditional building crafts in Czechoslovakia (pp. 361–375) and the Polish programs for resuscitation of that nation's folk arts (pp. 375–390).

In any case, such a program implies the creation of new national institutions and agencies and the establishment of new relationships among the old institutions of classroom, workshop, and marketplace. The field of historic preservation, for all its pragmatic, ad hoc development up to date, already displays a high order of social innovation and invention. These activities already display many of the elements of a comprehensive national program by which we shall be able to preserve the prototypical forms— settlements, districts, individual buildings, and gardens—against which all material culture must be judged.

2

The Heritage as Cultural Resource

HISTORIC ATTITUDES TOWARD THE ARTISTIC PAST

Americans are inclined to think of the historic preservation movement as being a phenomenon of the past 50 years or so. Actually, as we shall see, conscious intervention in the defense of the national historic and artistic heritage began at least as long ago as the formation of the Mount Vernon Ladies Association in 1859. And even this was tardy: in Britain the movement for preservation of historic buildings was well under way by the 1770s; and France had created its national preservation agency, the Commission des Monuments Historiques, in 1831.

Indeed, an appreciation of the material culture of preindustrial societies has grown in the Western world in almost exact proportion to the ever-intensifying industrialization of the West itself. For centuries, this interest has been so powerful and persistent that it would be a serious mistake to dismiss its motive forces as being merely sentimental, romantic, or obscur-antist. There have always been good and evident reasons for this ever-growing concern on the part of some of the best-informed and most sensitive sectors of Western society; and these apply with especial force today.

As a conscious act of exploration, the discovery by the West of its architectural past involved the progressive liquidation of all the concentric shells of self-centeredness and parochialism which had encapsulated European thought since late Roman times. The first aspect of the past which the West began deliberately to explore was, of course, its own: classical antiquity—first the Roman, because that was closest in time and space; then the Greek. Architectural response to these investigations was prompt (ideed, many of the investigators were themselves architects). Brunelleschi's Ospedale degl' Innocenti, begun in Florence in 1421, is commonly regarded as the first expression of a passionate interest in the past, an interest which was to extend through 5 centuries and spread across the whole Western world. The

rediscovery of classical architecture gave the Western world its basic alpha-
bet and grammar of the idioms of the Renaissance, baroque, rococo, and
neoclassic revivals. Its prestige was so great, and its ideological utility so
apparent, that it was adopted by Peter the Great, who, with great difficulty,
employed it to extirpate precedent idioms and to remold at least urban Russia into a facsimile of the classicized West.

AESTHETIC CONSEQUENCES OF
WESTERN EXPANSIONISM

The discovery by the West of cultures foreign or eccentric to its own course
of development—Near Eastern, Far Eastern, New World, and Egypto-
African—came as the direct consequence of European imperialist implosion
into those continents from the fifteenth century on. The stimulating effect
of these extra-European cultures can be directly traced in Western art and
architecture. The discovery of Chinese culture is expressed in the popularity
of Chinese motifs in rococo design (Chinoiserie). A little later, Chinese and
Japanese landscape painting played a decisive role in the development of the
English naturalistic garden. English penetration of India and the Near East
led to such "Hindoo" styles as that of the Royal Pavilion at Brighton by the
court favorite John Nash.

Naturally, the first information brought back to Western designers
from these early voyages of discovery was inexact and garbled. But new
concepts of historical development and new techniques of investigation
were developed with surprising speed. In exploring its own past, Europe
perfected new methods of analyzing documentary materials (art historical)
and artifacts (archaeological). Both had reached essentially modern forms
by the latter half of the eighteenth century, when Johann Joachim Winckelmann published his famous *History of Ancient Art*.[1] This book was a
pioneer effort to apply to the fields of art and architecture the already well
developed historiographical methods of the day. An immensely influential
work, it brought to public attention the first real information on the current
excavations at Pompeii and Herculaneum, where the basis was being laid
for modern archaeology. In Athens, meanwhile, the Englishmen James
Stuart and Nicholas Revett were using modern methods of surveying and
drafting to prepare accurate measured drawings of the Acropolis.[2] These
works were to be but the first rather crude beginnings of what has since
become an enormous corpus of literature and a rich tradition of professional
expertise on the art and architecture of classical antiquity.

But in exploring the material culture of the outside world, the Europeans had necessarily to develop other techniques for observing and recording what was found. Peoples, customs, and terrains were strange, their lan-

2.1. ***Echoes of European penetration of the exotic lands of China and Arabia*** were quickly felt in English and American architecture. Thus the English landscape architect Humphry Repton could propose converting a classical *tempietto* at Brighton into a more fashionable Chinese pagoda *(above)*. In America, the Napoleonic conquest of Egypt led to the "Hindoo" style of Longwood, near Natchez, designed in 1859 by the architect Samuel Sloan for a dealer in Egyptian cotton *(below)*.

1

2.2. Europe's exploration of its own classical origins, initiated by connoisseurs in Rome, later spread to Greece. Modern art history began with Winckelmann's book on ancient art, while the basis was laid for modern archaeology by such studies as those by Stuart and Revett on the Acropolis. Less than accurate by today's standards, these engravings gave Europeans their first images of Periclean *(above)* or Etruscan art *(below)*.

2

16

guages (at least at first) incomprehensible. The early explorers therefore prepared illustrated reports of what they found, laying the base, thereby, for cultural anthropology. The need for such reports was understood quite early on. Spanish officials reported with tolerable accuracy the magnificent cultures they were extirpating in Mexico; these reports began to be published in Spain as early as 1517. The French expedition of 1564 to Florida included what today would be called a staff artist, Jacques Le Moyne. Even allowing for the liberties the engravers later took with them, his drawings of the Indians, their customs, architecture, and agriculture, must have been models of careful observation.[3] And John White, head of the English expedition of 1585–1587 to Virginia, returned with a remarkably broad and accurate set of drawings of the people, flora, and fauna of the Virginia seacoast.[4] French and Portuguese missionaries to the Far East published many volumes on the customs, art, and architecture of the Orientals.[5] And, of course, the French were to be much later the authors of that paradigm of scientific reports on a foreign culture, the many-volume study of Egypt commissioned by Napoleon.[6]

From the conceptual point of view of the Western metropolis, *all* of the peoples, customs, and artifacts uncovered by the explorers were more or less historical oddities—eccentric, that is, to the main orbits of European ambitions. Whether they represented contemporaneous societies (e.g., the Aztecs and the Chinese mandarins) or societies from the historical past (e.g., the Egyptians and the Sumerians), they were assumed to be, by definition, inferior to the West: slated, as we would say today, for "modernization," for being "brought up to date." It is not until the very end of the nineteenth century that Europe is able to break through the last shell of cultural chauvinism and bring itself to face the possibility that many other cultures might well be qualitatively the equal of its own.[7]

And yet, with the exception of aboriginal peoples like the North American Indians or the South Sea islanders, the newly discovered societies were complex, class-structured, and urbane. Their architecture and gardens reflected this fact: urbanized, high-style, the idiom of palace and temple. The vernacular or folk building of these societies went almost unnoticed by early European reporters, who, apparently because it was rural, modest, and impermanent, dismissed it as of no more significance than their own peasant building at home.*

---

*This bias in favor of upper-class, urbane, and permanent artifacts has persisted in art history and archaeology up until the very recent past. Even epigraphy consolidated this bias: illiterate peasants could leave no written record of their contribution to culture. Only recently have archaeologists begun to pay as much attention to rural or pastoral sites as to the great urban centers of wealth and power.

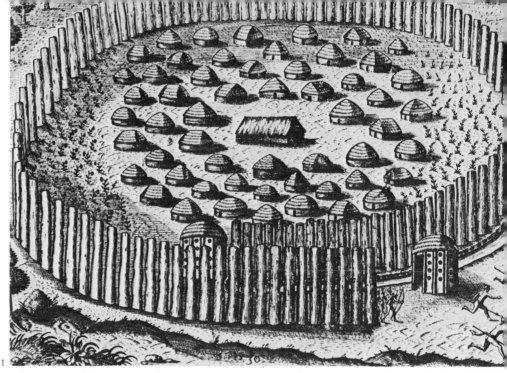

1

2

2.3. *In their contacts with aboriginal peoples* whose customs and languages were completely strange, Europeans were compelled to develop new techniques for recording and describing their discoveries. Thus, though conquest was their objective, their expeditions were organized along quasi-scientific lines, with specialists for recording the flora, fauna, and customs of the terrain. The basis was laid for the new science of anthropology. Jacques Lemoyne, staff artist for the French expedition of 1564, recorded the Timicuan Indians *(above)*; an Englishman made a comparable report on the Secoton tribe of North Carolina for the British expedition of 1585–1587.

2.4. *At the very moment when aristocratic taste* in the French court had reached a pinnacle of rococo frivolity, this facsimile of a peasant house was commissioned by the queen. A new fascination with the simple and unadorned represented a rediscovery of an autochthonous vernacular idiom which, unremarked by urbane circles, had survived almost three centuries of historicizing classicism which had begun with the Renaissance.

THE DISCOVERY OF FOLK AND
PRIMITIVE ARTS

The first indication of an upper-class interest in folk or vernacular architecture appears, paradoxically, in the most aristocratic circles of European absolutism: the court of Louis XVI. In the 1780s, Marie Antoinette commissioned the architect Robert Mique to build a little retreat in a corner of the palace grounds at Versailles. It took the form of a three-dimensional facsimile of a Normandy farm group. One of the buildings was actually habitable and here, in warm weather, the Queen could dally with her intimates. The motivation is sufficiently clear: escape from the boredom and rigid protocol of the court to a putatively "simpler" life. But why specif-

ically that of a Norman peasant? We know, of course, that rising dissatisfaction with life under the monarchy took many forms. Rousseau had
already published his prize-winning essay on the noble savage in 1750; Abbé
Laugier, in his *Essai sur l'Architecture* of 1753, had formulated his functionalist credo, *"Tenons-nous au simple et au naturel"*; and painters like Chardin
had already turned away from the frivolity of court life to celebrate sober,
middle-class virtues. Such new conceptualizations must have penetrated
even Versailles, thus making acceptable the folk art of the noble peasant, if
not yet that of Rousseau's noble savage.

One of the very earliest evidences of an educated understanding of the
aesthetic quality and functional significance of primitive art comes from the
American sculptor Horatio Greenough. While on a visit to Washington in
1842, he visited an exhibition at the Patent Office of "curios" brought back
from the South Seas by American whalers. He admired these artifacts for
the formal elegance with which they met the demands of functional necessity. He recognized this aesthetic quality as resembling that of archaic Greek
and Etruscan sculpture; and then, in a brilliant leap of intuition, he saw its
extension in the design and craftsmanship of the American clipper ship. In
all three aesthetic idioms, drawn from such widely disparate climes and
cultures, he saw the common thread of functionalism and saw, moreover,
that they are the end result of evolutionary process.[8]

However, Greenough's most pregnant intuitions were to have no
immediate impact upon American architectural theory. It would be half a
century before Louis Sullivan postulated his theorem *form follows function*,
and even longer before Western artists began to discover the aesthetic merits
of primitive art. There was, of course, an enormous expansion of ethnographic and anthropological work on primitive societies. Americans could
read a remarkable series of papers by Lewis H. Morgan on the domestic
architecture of the North and Central American Indians during the 1870s—
papers which are supposed to have had a profound effect on Marx and
Engels, among others.[9] Simultaneously, the great French architectural theoretician E. E. Viollet-le-Duc published his *Histoire de l'habitation Humaine,
depuis les temps historiques jusque à nos jours*.[10] Responding to the new concepts of evolution propounded with such stunning effect by Charles Darwin, Viollet-le-Duc applied evolutionary theory to architecture. He not
only attempted to trace historic architecture back to its prehistoric roots.
He also took the position that the contradiction between formal and functional elements, always immanent in man's constructions, was best resolved
by primitive societies, i.e., when stern necessity restrained and disciplined
formalistic conceits.

Of course, the grandest and most sustained polemic in favor of preindustrial handicraft production was that carried on during the last three-
quarters of the nineteenth century by an English trio, A. W. N. Pugin, John
Ruskin, and William Morris. Their field of interest was, however, almost

1

2.5. *Darwin's theory of the evolutionary development of organisms* led Viollet-le-Duc to propound an analogous theory of architectural evolution. "The First Hut" *(above)* is assumed to precede a "Primitive House for the Upper Indus" *(below)*. Inadequate in the light of modern knowledge, they anticipate current evolutionary concepts.

2

completely ethnocentric, seldom extending beyond medieval England and never beyond Western Europe. Nor did they often make any clear distinction between the art of usually literate and always highly skilled guildsmen, working for urbane ruling-class institutions, and that of the illiterate peasantry, working only for itself. Nevertheless, they contributed mightily to the growing European interest in folklore, especially folk song and folk dance. And they certainly helped to prepare the way for the contemporary prestige, throughout the Western world, of every facet of preindustrial art and architecture, whether it be of vernacular, folk, or authentically primitive origin.[11]

It is thus apparent that the changing perspectives through which the Western world viewed the artistic past sprang from diverse and often contradictory motivations. Although in early Renaissance times, and again in the epoch of Jefferson and the French Revolution, antique idioms were put to progressive or even revolutionary uses, they served quite other interests, too.[12] For the true keepers of the past, from classic antiquity onward, have often represented the most conservative interests of their society. Their motivations were either pietistic or patriotic, and they employed art and architecture to buttress the institutions of church and state. This was true in Pausanias's day, as is clear from his *Tour of Greece*, with its endless lists of graves, shrines, and temples to be visited.[13] It is equally true today: when if the DAR acts at all, artistically, it acts to preserve the shrines of its own eponymous heroes.

THE WEST'S INTEREST IN ITS PAST BEGINS TO WANE

It is not surprising, then, to find that the West's inexhaustible fascination with its own and other peoples' pasts gave rise to many and contradictory attitudes among artists and architects themselves. In fact, by 1875, after 4½ centuries of artistic exploration, it might have been argued that any further fruitful studies were impossible. And this was just the way it appeared to the radical artists and intellectuals of the times. Painters, poets, musicians, and architects felt themselves being suffocated by the sheer massive presence of the past, everywhere—in the landscape around them, in the attitudes of institutions and individuals who peopled it. That generation demanded that the way be cleared for wholly new artistic idioms that would be congruent with the new potentials which seemed to be promised by science, industry, political democracy. If architecture lagged a few years behind painting or poesy, it was only because it was an incomparably more costly and obdurate medium of expression. But from the Chicago of Louis Sullivan right on down to the Weimar Republic of Walter Gropius, the battle was on to liberate building and landscape alike from aesthetic thrall-dom to what seemed to them a corrupt and ineffectual past.[14]

It was historically a development long overdue, but it had implications which the radical architects of the Bauhaus generation were unable to antic-ipate. (Who could have dreamed, in 1925, that the time would come when *old* buildings would be in short supply?) As it turned out, their attack on the eclectic use of historic idioms did not occur in "normal" times. On the contrary, it began just when science and technology were accelerating along an exponential curve; when absolutely unprecedented technical means of construction and destruction were beginning to appear; and when even popular taste, historically so fundamentally conservative, was being radi-calized by planned obsolescence and the annual model. As a consequence of such developments, especially since World War II, we now run the literal risk of losing *all* the past, man-made and natural—either piecemeal, to the bulldozer, or instantaneously, to nuclear weapons.

NEW PERSPECTIVES OF THE VALUE OF THE PAST

This revolutionary reversal of man's historic relationship to the environ-ment suddenly imbues all material evidence of the human past with new significance. It is the cause of legitimate concern to all environmental sci-entists—ethologists, ecologists, conservationists, public health specialists, and so forth; but it is an issue of special poignancy to those who are entrusted with the care of the artistic heritage. The frantic efforts of archae-ologists, anthropologists, and art historians to keep ahead of the technolog-ical manipulation of the landscape is unfortunately a worldwide phenome-non. The great monuments at Abu-Simbel may have been saved, thanks to an international campaign. Here and there, an occasional monument or set-tlement is being, if not saved, at least recorded before it disappears forever. But the general tendency of urban redevelopment authorities, as of dam and highway engineers, has been to dismiss as romantic or sentimental the efforts to protect historical impediments to their special brand of "prog-ress." The comprehensive protection of such monuments and artifacts, and the scholarly examination of the theories and techniques which produced them, is of central importance to our cultural future.

THE SOCIAL CONSEQUENCES OF HISTORIC PRESERVATION

Until very recently, most national preservation programs have been pre-ponderantly upper-class and urbane in their emphasis. Because of this inher-ent bias, most of the artifacts studied and conserved have been monumental—palaces, castles, cathedrals, and parliaments: the seats of the powerful and famous. This bias has, in a sense, been almost accidental, the natural outgrowth of the historical origins of the field. The written record has always dealt at length with the activities of the literate ruling classes (e.g., Washington, Jefferson, and the Tidewater plantation aristocracy) while it has neglected entirely the experiences of the submerged illiterate majority (e.g., black slaves, poor white tenant farmers, mountaineers of Appalachia). Thus, in even the highly developed nations of Western Europe and America, much the largest portion of the nation's historical experience has gone unobserved and unrecorded. As a consequence of this blind spot, vernacular architecture, whether urban or rural, went unnoticed, which meant among other things that the contextual settings of the monuments themselves were ignored. Primitive settlements, whether extant or prehistoric, were either ignored or considered as of only archaeological or anthropological interest.

This narrow and compartmentalized attitude toward the artistic and historic heritage has had a stultifying effect at several different levels. One consequence has been that whole categories of artifacts—from entire villages down to isolated farmhouses and parish churches—have been excluded from national inventories and hence from any prospect of preservation. (The French, for example, with Europe's oldest preservation agency, have only recently begun to list vernacular buildings, whether in urban or rural locations). Another consequence of even more serious nature has been to cut contemporary design professionals (architects, landscape architects, planners) completely off from any contact with the conventional wisdom of their preindustrial past. Yet this past is by no means dead. Even in highly industrialized nations, it survives in the traditional crafts, folklore, and folk practice for farm and village life. And in third world countries such as Egypt, Mexico, and Peru it is still the dominant mode of behavior in architecture and related fields.

In fact, the survival of preindustrial forms confronts developing countries with a paradox of agonizing acuteness. Such countries as Peru, Ecuador, and Guatemala have an immensely rich heritage of historic cities, villages, and individual monuments. These are not only valuable for broad cultural reasons; they are also of steadily increasing touristic significance. Thus their preservation and display are of real importance to the national economies. In this context, the preservation of the great colonial centers of cities such as Lima, Quito, and Antigua (not to mention hundreds of charming villages and their rural countrysides) is an urgent matter.

But a broad program of restoration and preservation confronts a dismaying range of obstacles, ideological, economic, and technological. In all developing countries the sheer prestige of the new, the machine-made, the technically "advanced" is enormous; and the parallel disrepute of the old, the handmade, the traditional is profound. But beyond that, there are purely technical problems. All three cities sit astride one of the most active earthquake zones on earth, as recent disastrous tremors in Peru (1971) and Guatemala (1975) have demonstrated. At the same time, the historic centers of these cities are built almost exclusively of mud masonry—mud brick, adobe, or *terra pisé*. Such structures proved to be vulnerable in the recent tremors (even though, statistically, an astonishing percentage of the old buildings have survived for centuries!).

As a result of the recent seismic disasters, some of these countries have enacted national building codes which require earthquake-resistant structures of either steel or reinforced concrete. These new codes apply especially to public buildings—hotels, hospitals, theaters, schools, and the like. But such sophisticated structures will obviously be too expensive for the countryside in general, where the peasant will perforce be compelled to continue to build with traditional materials of mud and straw. And even in the cities, it is difficult to see how existing monumental structures can be effectively reinforced with concrete or steel armatures even if expense were no problem.★

What seems indicated in such a dilemma is the application of modern research methods to traditional folk practice: in this case, the development of mud masonry reinforced with vegetable fibers. Traditional construction in Peru has always employed some versions of this. For example, many of the great town houses of old Lima, for all their monumental masonry appearance, actually have lightweight, flexible walls. These consist of a wooden skeleton of upright peeled poles supporting a woven mesh of vegetable fibers (wattle) onto which are applied successive coats of plaster (daub). Modern chemicals could certainly be experimented with to give greater strength and homogeneity of mud masonry in all its forms, as well as to render the vegetal material fireproof, rotproof, and insect-resistant. Such research is all the more important because mud masonry remains environmentally the optimal material for hot, dry climates and requires no cash outlay for raw materials.

THE NEW SIGNIFICANCE OF PREINDUSTRIAL PRACTICE

We have seen that the material culture of the past has been useful to the West for a wide spectrum of reasons, ideological, aesthetic, and technical.

★Seismic threats to historic structure are by no means limited to third world countries. In California, from San Francisco down to Los Angeles, earthquakes threaten many important twentieth-century structures, and building codes are being redrafted to require their structural stabilization. This raises serious problems, not only for the few historic adobe and *terra pisé* buildings in the area, but also for the far more numerous examples of Spanish colonial and art deco of the teens and twenties. Their exuberant sculptural ornamentation of terra-cotta and cast concrete is highly vulnerable to seismic shock and constitutes a serious hazard to passing pedestrians and motorists. Stabilization will be neither simple nor inexpensive.

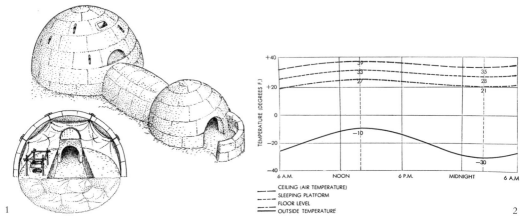

CEILING (AIR TEMPERATURE)
SLEEPING PLATFORM
FLOOR LEVEL
OUTSIDE TEMPERATURE

1

2

2.6. *The cultures of those primitive peoples* whom the Europeans held so long in contempt are now being reassessed. The fundamental sagacity of their folk practice, as revealed in their architecture, is now quite apparent. Given the limits of their technology and material resources, the folk builders of desert and tundra achieve high levels of energy efficiency. They have little to build of beyond snow and mud: paradoxically these materials turn out to be excellent thermal insulators for their respective environments. Note how the Eskimos, confronting a steady deficit in environmental heat, maintain an even temperature inside their shell of snow (*2*). The desert builders face an equally stressful thermal regime: here the problem is an excess of environmental heat but with great diurnal variations. Note how the mud shell slows down transmission of heat through the walls, lowering and flattening the temperatures inside the mud-built structure (*4*).

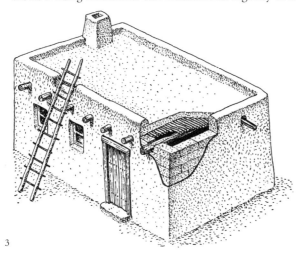

3

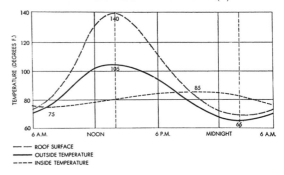

ROOF SURFACE
OUTSIDE TEMPERATURE
INSIDE TEMPERATURE

But the past now has a significance of quite a new and different order. This can be demonstrated very readily in architecture and urbanism: a broad, truly scientific examination of traditional building—and especially of folk and primitive building—is one of the field's most urgent tasks. Such a program should proceed at two levels, one rather narrowly technical and professional, the other broadly cultural. The first would involve an *intensive study of the theories and practices* of the past, with special emphasis on folk and primitive cultures. The second would imply the development of a comprehensive system for the *protection of the forms* of the entire artistic heritage, with special attention to folk and vernacular forms (if for no other reason than that they have been the most neglected to date). The first program would be international in scope, i.e., covering all building technologies whether extant or historical. The second would presumably be built up of national or regional components—e.g., New England folklore would be best preserved and enjoyed in its native habitat; Cajun and Creole, in Lower Louisiana; Navajo, in the Southwest. Many projects of this latter type are of course in operation in Europe and the Americas.

3

The Economic Sense of Retrieval and Recycling

Throughout history, the cost of making anything—a city, a house, even a quilt—has been high in terms of both labor and materials. Thus every artifact was used and reused until it "wore out" or "fell apart." Final dissolution was postponed as long as possible by patching, remodeling, and repair. And often, dissolution was not absolute even then: the artifact was cannibalized, every possible bit and piece being salvaged for reuse in new combinations. This sort of conservation of energy cut across every level of preindustrial societies. In Periclean Athens the columns of earlier temples were used in the retaining walls of the modernized Acropolis; and down at the foot of the hill, other column drums were used in the construction of a new road in front of the Stoa of Attalos. Builders of the noblest Romanesque churches were not above recycling whole columns from the ruins of nearby Roman temples, even where the columns did not always match in style or size. And the very aesthetics of Orthodox churches in the Eastern Mediterranean derived from the use of brick and stone scraps salvaged from pagan sites (with pagan inscriptions and bas-reliefs turned upside down to empty them of their original iconographic significance).

And if such cheeseparing practices were common among the rich and mighty, they were universal among the common people, urban and rural alike. Some building materials were so valuable that inordinate amounts of energy were expended in salvage. Bronze and iron pins and tenons which held classic masonry together offered sufficient incentive for the local peasants to pull down entire temples; the same marble blocks were then burned to make lime. Similarly, many an American frontier family, forced by circumstances to move on, would burn down the cabin it was abandoning so as to recover iron nails, straps, hinges, and hardware. And houses that were not abandoned went through a never-ending process of alterations, with the same bits and pieces of wood being cut, patched, refitted to serve in another function.*

Of course, wholly new artifacts have been continuously produced throughout history, often of brand-new materials. Khufu, the Fourth Dynasty pharaoh who built the Pyramid of Cheops c. 2700 B.C. could scarcely have used recycled materials even had he wanted to (though the pharaohs were not above reusing old stone blocks, turned with inside facing out to conceal earlier bas-reliefs, in constructing the new Temple of Amun at Thebes). The Roman highway system was wholly new in both concept and construction, as was the Great Wall of China. But the high costs of making anything placed severe restraints on even the mightiest of monarchs. The palace complex of the Roman Palantine was continuously reworked for centuries; never once was it completely remade. Louis XIV could build brand-new gardens at Versailles so huge that their axes disappeared in the curve of the earth. But he was working on open farmland. When the English crown decided to mimic Louis XIV at Whitehall in London, Inigo Jones got no further along than constructing his Banqueting Hall, one small module of a huge complex larger than Bernini's unrealized design for the Louvre. And with London in ashes after the Great Fire of 1666, even English wealth could not afford to rebuild London along the lines proposed by Christopher Wren.

TECHNOLOGICAL OBSOLESCENCE: A NEW CONCEPT

In short, until a century or so ago, obsolescence was a purely physical phenomenon. The physical processes of aging determined quite literally the useful life of the artifact. Current concepts of technological obsolescence, of objects becoming useless *economically* without reference to any residual *physical* utility, are modern inventions, the result of the industrial revolution. But once unleashed by this revolution, science and technology began to develop at an exponential rate. Under these new circumstances, the old artifact (tool, factory, town) began to be regarded as an intolerable restriction upon increased productivity. It seemed increasingly that it was "cheaper to throw the old one away and get a new one." This tendency was

---

*Such scraps are often very important to restorationists; it was one newel post, reused elsewhere in the house, which enabled National Park Service architects to reconstruct completely the original stairway in the house of President Andrew Johnson in Johnson City, Tennessee. One of the country's most significant collection of samples of eighteenth-century textiles comes from a single quilt belonging to the Smithsonian Institute. This family quilt incorporates half a century of clothing, bedding, and upholstery textiles, offering important data on the spinning, weaving, and dyeing technologies of the period.

apparent everywhere in the industrializing West, but it reached its most exaggerated expression in the United States, gathering velocity ever since the 1840s. Thus a huge new canal system along the Atlantic Seaboard was abandoned before it was even finished, victim of the even newer railroads. Similarly, steamboats replaced sails and oars along American rivers; but this great riverine transportation system was also thrown away in favor of the railroads. And in this century, we have seen the world's greatest mass-transit system junked in favor of much less energy-efficient highways and airports built with billions of taxpayer dollars.

Rapid and uncontrolled technological evolution has become so institutionalized that change is now seen as synonymous with progress. The annual model, the disposable container, the throw-away city have become the norms; the sheer prestige of the new has suffocated the old tool, the traditional craft, conventional wisdom in general. Only in the very recent past, in the decade between Rachel Carson's epochal book, *The Silent Spring,* and the Arab oil embargo 1973–1974, are we being compelled to reexamine the ultimate cost of this new attitude toward the making and using of artifacts. And the more soberly we begin to examine it, the more it becomes apparent that the real costs will prove to be insupportably high, even for the rich and industrialized West.

There is, of course, no doubt about the vastly increased productive capacity of mechanized mass production over earlier modes of production. The qualitative leap is dramatically clear in American agriculture, where in 1880, 43.8 percent of the population was needed to feed the nation as a whole: by 1970 the farm population had dropped to a mere 4.8 percent. But it seems increasingly clear that such dazzling gains in one area may conceal staggering losses in another. This is certainly the case in architecture and urbanism, where true societal costs are hidden in three ways:

1. The true cost is shifted from the individual entrepreneur to the community in general. Thus the developers of huge housing projects assume no responsibility for providing schools, hospitals, fire and police protection; water, power, and sewerage systems; and all the rest of the complex infrastructure without which no settlement is ultimately viable. Such costs are absorbed by the municipality.

2. Ultimate costs of new developments can be hidden by shifting them from the rich industrialized nations to the poor, which are producers of raw materials. This hidden transfer enables the average middle-class American family to consume 3500 times as much energy per annum as the peasant family of India which supplies it with such raw materials as oil, jute, and bauxite.

3. Finally, ultimate costs of high rates of technological obsolescence can be transferred from the present to the future. Thus urban sprawl today exists at the price of depletion of absolutely limited supplies of land, forests, coal, and oil—not to mention the often irreversible pollution of air, land, and water.

But phrased in these terms, the costs are societal, not personal: such a formulation is therefore useful only at a theoretical level. The fact is that, until very recently, individual entrepreneurs have usually found it immediately more profitable to "tear it down and start over," no matter what the putative value was of the demolished building. It has been all but impossible to quantify the actual value of the built world. Recently, however, and especially since the international oil crisis of 1973–1974, it it has become increasingly clear that we must develop the means for doing just this. Harry M. Weese, the Chicago architect who restored Sullivan's Auditorium Theater, has put it this way:

> In these times, one valid case for preservation is economic. Can we afford to rebuild the environment every generation? With the doubling of construction costs in the last five years, new construction is pricing itself out of many markets, making recycling not a sentimental exercise but a necessity.
>
> Another case for preservation is energy: important in the decision to recycle instead of rebuild. The residual value of energy built into old cities is enormous, packed into streets, utilities, and buildings: 1) time energy—manifold individual decisions over a period of development and use; 2) natural and human energy invested in materials and artisanship; 3) kinetic energy of construction and the fuel required.
>
> This is the energy content of a city. Energy is wasted when any old building is pulled down.[1]

QUANTIFYING THE ENERGY IN THE BUILT WORLD

Here Weese employs a new and significant concept: the "residual value of energy" in the built world. The key word is "energy." And the moment that we begin to appraise the value of this built world in terms of units of energy (rather than the conventional dollar unit), we transfer the whole discussion to a much more fundamental plane. For the British thermal unit (Btu), as a measure of energy, has an absolute, not relative, value. If we could quantify all the energy which went into the production of a cubic foot of brick wall, from the moment the clay was dug and the limestone quarried up to the finished product, we could for the first time put the appraisal of old buildings and proposed new ones on an exactly comparable basis.

Now, thanks to computer technology, such a methodology has been established in an important study, *Energy Uses for Building Construction*.[2] Using an energy input/output model, the study develops a unit of measurement called "embodied energy," which can be expressed in Btu per cubic foot or Btu per square foot for all building types and structural systems. When buildings are analyzed by the Stein/CAC methodology, surprising new relationships are revealed. For example, the study compares three 30-foot bays using three standard systems of high-rise building construction: all-steel, steel and concrete, reinforced concrete. Although the dollar costs are found to be approximately the same for all three, the embodied energy is vastly different.[3]

Structural system	Btu/sq ft	Energy embodiment index (for this comparison)
Standard steel	293,187	100.0
Composite steel	251,206	85.5
Reinforced concrete	172,021	58.5

In a later study (fall 1977),[4] the authors extend their methodology to the adaptive use of historic buildings:

> There are a favorable set of interconnected benefits to be gained from the intelligent reuse of historic buildings. In addition to the important cultural benefits derived from the preservation and extended life of historical buildings, they are repositories of large expenditures of energy and materials. The fact that their rehabilitation for extended use is a labor intensive activity rather than an energy intensive one, and will probably be at a lower dollar cost than new work, supports the desirability of restoration for new adaptive use. The further consequence of the sociological changes triggered by restoration will, of course, vary in relation to a complex set of circumstances. In general, however, there is a contextural pattern that is affected by whether a building is restored to use or allowed to deteriorate and eventually be demolished. In the latter case it often happens that other buildings nearby also deteriorate, resulting in high social costs in combatting crime, in fire prevention, and in the gradual erosion of the community's tax base.

In the light of this, the new Stein study proposes to formulate the following methodologies:

A. Tables of energy for construction per square foot of building described by building use (residential, commercial, etc.) and by type of construction (high rise, single family detached, etc.). These tables will be further detailed to reflect modifying factors of local distribution or climatic patterns.

B. Energy required for demolition of existing buildings will be described in terms of BTU per SF of building scheduled for demolition. Consideration given to type of construction, height of building, immediate surrounding environment (determining demolition technique applicable). Energy requirements for site preparation will be described in terms of BTU per SF of site as modified by geological conditions and disruptions resulting from the previous building. In addition, consideration will be given to requirements for reconnection to site utilities and restoration of paving and landscaping.

C. The energy content of existing buildings will be determined based on gross take-offs of the materials contained in those buildings. The energy content of basic building components will be identified in terms which will readily permit their application. Examples of this would be stone exterior walls with plaster interior finish, wood joist floor systems with plaster ceiling, plaster partition on wood studs, etc. The material will be arranged in a format similar to a cost estimating format to facilitate its use by personnel familiar with building material take-offs.

D. Energy required for the restoration and rehabilitation of existing structures will be identified in an estimating format similar to that described above. In this way, for a project under consideration, the energy values for work to be performed can be estimated at the same time as the cost since cost estimating also requires take-offs of removals, the energy required to execute these removals as well as the embodied energy in the material to be removed can be accounted for as part of the estimating process.

E. A format for comparing the energy efficiency of new buildings with that of existing or rehabilitated buildings will be developed which combines the energy required for construction with the energy required for operation, viewed over the projected useful life of the building.[4]

It is obvious that, with the perfection of such analytical methods, preservationists will have important new tools for the defense of the built environment.

The very necessity for the intensive application of the most advanced technology to every aspect of human affairs is being increasingly challenged—and not only for the ineluctable technological obsolescence which it brings in its wake. It is also being challenged as fundamentally uneconomical and wasteful. This is the substance of the arguments of such theoreticians as L. S. Stavrianos in his *Promise of the Coming Dark Age*[5] and of E. F. Schumacher in his *Small Is Beautiful*.[6] The one argues for the need for labor-intensive modes of production rather than energy-intensive, whereas the latter argues for an "intermediate technology" as being inherently a more suitable scale for most forms of production.

ORGANIC GROWTH: PROGRAMMED, NOT PLANNED

The environmental consequences of the massive application of technology to the construction of human settlements has been criticized with devastating effect by Christopher Alexander and his associates. In a recent study, *The Oregon Experiment,* they draw the analogy between any living organism and the human settlement: any living system must repair itself constantly in order to maintain its balance and coordination, its quality as a whole. In the case of an organism, it is only the constant repair, the adjustment of chemical fields, the replacement of cells, and the healing of damaged tissues which maintain the basic morphology of the organism.

"In the case of the environment, the process of growth and repair that is required to maintain morphological integration is far more complex," the authors point out. Repair not only has to conserve a preordained order, as it does in an organism, but also must adapt continuously to changing uses and activities, at every level of the scale. For environments, therefore, an organic process of growth and repair must create a gradual sequence of changes, and these changes must be distributed evenly across every level of scale. There must be as much attention to the repair of details—rooms, wings of buildings, windows, paths—as to the creation of brand-new buildings. Only then can an environment stay balanced both as a whole and in its parts, at every moment of its history.

"All the good environments that we know have this in common," says Alexander. They are whole and alive because they have grown slowly over long periods of time, piece by piece. The pieces are small—and there are always a balanced number of projects going forward at every scale. If one large building is being built, there are, simultaneously, many repairs and changes going forward at smaller scales all around the building; and each new building is not a "finished" thing but brings in its train a long series of smaller repair projects. In such a way, buildings adapt to changing users and changing needs. They are never torn down, never erased; instead they are always embellished, modified, reduced, enlarged, improved. This attitude to the repair of the environment has been commonplace for thousands of years in traditional cultures.

"But in modern urban developments, the environment grows in massive chunks. Now pieces are often more than three to four stories high and more than 10 to 20,000 square feet in area." Once a building is built, says Alexander, it is considered finished; it is not part of a long sequence of repair projects. These "finished" buildings are assumed to have a certain finite lifetime; the process of environmental growth is seen as a process in which those buildings which have reached the end of their lifetime are torn down and replaced by new large buildings, again assumed to have a certain lifetime. The fundamental assumption is that it is better to be in a new building than in an old building: and the money spent on the environment is concentrated in the huge new projects, while the money spent maintaining old buildings is reduced to the bare minimum.[7]

The evisceration of the built-up urban core by uncontrolled urban sprawl around its periphery is more and more being challenged. The question is more and more being raised as to whether these urban cores, now being "thrown away like Kleenex," should not be viewed as resources rather than impediments. The massive application of technology, whether to wholesale urban renewal in the center or to the construction of new satellite communities, such as Levittown on Long Island and Reston and Columbia outside Washington, is viewed as impermissibly wasteful precisely because of the hidden costs cited above. The total environmental costs of constructing and operating any settlement are, of course, complex and hence difficult to calculate. Only now are attempts being made systematically to isolate and investigate them. A most impressive effort along these lines is a recent study, *The Costs of Urban Sprawl,* prepared for the National Environmental Protection Agency.[8] This study compares overall costs of various types of development on open land. It does not deal with the retrieval and recycling of built urban tissue such as makes up the inner cores of all large American cities. Nevertheless, this study does afford a pattern or template for analysis of all costs of any type of settlement. The sheer complexity of the problem is staggering, as even the table of contents of the study will show. The picture which emerges from this study, says *The New York Times,*

> . . . is of a country on a disaster course of spread city and urban sprawl, eating up its natural resources in speculative, unplanned development, putting a higher and higher price on the provision of scattered utilities and services. At the same time, financial resources, leadership and vitality are drawn from the cities as the rural areas to which the urbanites have fled become increasingly urbanized.
>
> To a large extent, the destructive pattern is set by Government policy, as much by spasmodic legislation and funding practices as by any pronouncement of national intent.
>
> The Federal Government has virtually ordained the expansion and form of suburbia, and now of exurbia, through FHA rules and supports and the funding of highways in preference to mass transit. Federal spending has discriminated against the urban areas that need it most. This Administration has declared the urban crisis over, withdrawing national attention and necessary focus from the problems of the cities. [But] that this is a national crisis is clear from debates that currently rage about the right of communities to limit growth and the sociological and environmental use of zoning law, from open housing to ecology.[9]

Stated in its most general form, the major conclusion of *The Costs of Urban Sprawl* is that, for a given number of households, "sprawl is the most expensive form of residential development in terms of economic costs, environmental costs, natural resource consumption and many types of personal costs. . . . This cost difference is particularly significant for *that proportion of total costs which is likely to be borne by local government* [italics added]."[10] If all these hidden costs are to be truly expressed in the balance sheet, then the retrieval and recycling of the built environment will once again seem a rational means of managing the materials resources of the nation. Then the huge areas of semiabandoned urban tissue which characterize cities such as New York, Detroit, and Chicago will be seen as resources, not obstacles, to future growth.

As we shall see in more detail (Chapter 5), the recognition is growing that the old cores of central cities, with all their huge investment in infrastructure, are to be regarded as assets, not liabilities. Abroad, this recognition is exemplified in the complete rehabilitation of the centers of Leningrad and Avignon, in the Marais district in Paris, and the Barbican in London. In the United States, one sees the same growing understanding in cities across the land: the Boston waterfront; College Hill in Providence; SoHo in New York City; Philadelphia's Society Hill; the regeneration of downtown in Annapolis, Charleston, and Savannah; and the prototypical historic district, the Vieux Carré in New Orleans. In every one of these cases, orthodox economic wisdom—that the only way to save them is "to tear 'em down and start over"—is being disproved. By every accepted index, including increased tax revenues, increased business activity, increased downtown residential use, these areas are proving their astonishing viability.

4

Conceptual Parameters
of Historic Preservation

The rapid expansion of the field of historic preservation is marked by the need for more precise definitions and terminology. Indeed, were it not for the fact that the term has become generic, it might well be replaced by one more accurately descriptive, e.g., retrieval and recycling of the historic environment, or—even more comprehensively—the curatorial management of the built world. However, in the United States, the term will continue to serve as the umbrella name for the field for the simple reason that it has become institutionalized, e.g., the National Trust for *Historic Preservation;* the Association for *Preservation* Technology; the societies for the *Preservation* of New England, Virginia, and Long Island Antiquities; national legislation entitled *Historic Preservation* Act of 1966; and courses in some 90 universities classed as *preservation*-oriented. It is true that somewhat different terms are employed abroad. The concept of *protection* of the historic and artistic patrimony is embedded in European practice, while the term *conservation* is standard in Great Britain. In the United States, however, this term already belongs to a highly structured field of expertise, the conservation of works of art, with its own specialized profession in being. For such reasons as these, it would therefore be a fruitless semantic exercise to propose abandoning the present nomenclature.

THE MATTER OF SIZE, SCALE, AND TYPE

One of the most characteristic aspects of historic preservation today is that its domain is being constantly extended in two distinct ways. On the one hand, the *scale* of the artifact being considered as requiring preservation is being pushed upward to include very large ones (e.g., the entire island of Nantucket) as well as downward, to include very small ones (e.g., historic rooms or fragments thereof installed in art museums).

On the other hand, the domain is being enlarged by a radical increase in the *types* of artifacts being considered worthy of preservation. Thus, in addition to monumental high-style architecture—traditionally the concern of the preservationist—whole new categories of structures are now recognized as equally meritorious: vernacular, folkloristic, and industrial structures. In a parallel fashion, the time scale of historicity is being extended to include pre-Columbian settlements at one end and Art Deco skyscrapers at the other.

In terms of artifactual size, the expansion of the domain has been greater with large objects than with small ones. This is because of the discovery that the future of the individual site or monument cannot be isolated from that of its environmental context. This can be clearly seen in the experience of cities like Charleston and Savannah, where in the past decades, battles to save individual buildings have inevitably been enlarged to include the surrounding district. Similarly, in New York City, the Landmarks Commission has been compelled, by the sheer logic of its assignment, to extend its jurisdiction from individual monuments to the creation of entire historic districts.

This shift of concern from the isolated artifact to concern for its context has had far-reaching consequences, some of which are only now beginning to be understood. When we undertake the rehabilitation or regeneration of an entire historic district, as opposed to that of an isolated building, we are immediately confronted with the responsibility for the indigenous population of that district. Should it be rehoused in the recycled structures? The historic cores of old cities have long ago lost much or all of their original populations. Instead of the rich and mighty who once lived there, they are more and more occupied by working people, especially the elderly, the poor, and ethnic minorities. By the same token, the housing stock of these districts, whatever its historic associations or aesthetic potentials, is usually substandard by today's standards. Hence restoration involves a large investment in basic amenities—new kitchens and baths, new heating and lighting, fireproof halls, and so on—investments which inevitably mean increased rents or sales prices. In practice, this has meant that higher-income populations replace low-income people in the rehabilitated housing, while the displaced population is compelled to find new accommodations as best it can.

This internal migration, popularly termed "gentrification," has a number of unfortunate consequences. It alienates the displaced population even farther from its urban base, transposing the slum and ghetto instead of eliminating it. It has the effect of pushing a wide range of small stores, workshops, and ateliers either into bankruptcy (because they cannot survive forced transplantation) or out of the central city altogether. Thus, while the physical fabric of the heritage may be preserved and enhanced, the life-styles it has generated and supported may be impoverished.

Minimizing or preventing these disruptive effects of retrieval and recycling of historic districts clearly calls for new levels of sociocultural engineering—levels which in the United States we are only beginning to explore. In a number of European cities, where experience is more extensive (Paris, Bologna) or legal and financial resources greater (Prague, Split), the process of preserving *both* the historic district *and* the traditional population is well under way. These cities merit the attention of Americans as prototypical examples of how this can be achieved.

SCALE OF ARTIFACT TO BE PRESERVED

The largest artifact which the preservationist is apt to be called upon to manage in a curatorial sense will be a *historic spatial module*. This might be an entire *historic town or village* (Telč, Czechoslovakia; Sveti Stefan, Yugoslavia; Deerfield, Massachusetts; or Williamsburg, Virgina). It might be the *historic core* of a large and still-growing modern city (Bologna, Italy; Split, Yugoslavia; or Savannah or Charleston in the U.S.A.). Typically, it will be the *historic district* in a modern city—the ancient nucleus which is no longer the functional center (Malá Strana in Prague; Le Marais in Paris; Vieux Carré in New Orleans). The formulation of a correct preservation policy for the module will necessarily be derived from an analysis of local conditions. It may be a viable community inhabited by an indigenous population going about its regular daily life (Annapolis, Maryland). It may be a module still physically intact but given over to a tourist population (Sveti Stefan). It may be a straight museum operation with little or no permanent nighttime population (Williamsburg, Deerfield). Whatever the circumstances, the objective of preservation policy should be to maintain the physical and aesthetic integrity of the module, on the one hand, *and* the well-being of the resident population, on the other.

Historic Town: The largest preservable unit would be the entire settlement. Some American cities have historic districts which include most of all of the territory of the original settlement (New Orleans, Savannah, Santa Fe), which are today embedded in the fabric of the much larger modern city. The Williamsburg Restoration stands almost complete in its original colonial configuration, with the modern town tangent only along the eastern boundary. A few smaller American villages and settlements have survived intact the accidents of history, and are now preserved in their unspoiled rural context; e.g., Harrisburg, Vermont; Deerfield Village, Massachusetts. Two Shaker settlements survive intact: Hancock Village, near Pittsfield, Massachusetts, and Pleasant Hill, near Lexington, Kentucky. Generally, however, the urbanization of North America has been so complete that few such urban modules survive in pure, undamaged form. When they do, they are uniquely valuable.

Historic District: This is currently the most active module of preservation activity. Classic examples are the Vieux Carré in New Orleans, Society Hill in Philadelphia, and College Hill in Providence. The original historic preservation districts of Savannah, Charleston, and Annapolis have by degrees been extended to encompass almost the entire central business districts of these cities. There are now dozens of such districts across the country, and their number is rapidly growing. Despite the demographic imbalances already referred to, historic district preservations have established their economic viability. Not only have they brought new vigor to downtown districts (Boston, Philadelphia, Annapolis, San Francisco): in Savannah, Charleston, and New Orleans, they furnish the base for the new industry of tourism.

Outdoor Architectural Museum: The concept of exhibiting whole buildings in the open air (*plein air* in French, *Freiluft* in German) is analogous to the display of small artifacts in the controlled environment of the museum. Although fairly new in the United States, it is a well-established type in Europe, the first, Skansen, having been established in Stockholm in the 1890s. The curatorial principles are the same as those of the orthodox museum: to preserve, protect, display, and interpret the artifacts of material culture which might otherwise be lost. Of course, a critical difference between works of art and works of architecture is that the latter are containers of human life and social process. Hence the process "contained" is of equal or greater importance than the buildings which contained it. This principle was recognized at Skansen, which is dedicated to the display and interpretation of preindustrial Swedish folk life, activities, and artifacts. The Danish National Folk Museum near Copenhagen, a more up-to-date example of this type, reflects contemporary expertise in archaeology, art history, and ethnography. It constitutes an authoritative collection of farm settlements from all the regions of the country, each set in a landscape which replicates the original topography, botany, and agricultural activity.

The "Skansen Principle" has been generally accepted in the United States. However, most of our open-air museums were initially launched by private individuals or local groups of amateurs and history buffs. They tend to reflect the perspectives of their founders. Three prototypical examples of this type are Henry Ford's Greenfield Village in Dearborn; Electra Webb's Shelburne Village near Burlington, Vermont; and Old Sturbridge Village in Massachusetts, the creation of two wealthy collectors, Albert and Cheney Wells. These institutions tend to be idiosyncratic both in their collections and in the way in which these collections are organized and interpreted. They have all been institutionalized in recent years, with professional staffs which are reorganizing both plant and program along modern museological lines.

Like art museums generally, the new architectural museums have mostly followed a policy of including only authenticated artifacts ("genuine antiques") in their collections. Everything on display, from entire buildings to small artifacts, is guaranteed to be the "real thing." There is, however, a small group of these museums whose collections are largely or wholly of replicas or duplicates. Old Salem in Massachusetts, New Salem in Illinois, and Plimoth Plantation in Massachusetts are typical of this new subtype. Plimoth Plantation is the most radically innovative of this new type of outdoor museum (Fig. 10.9). Here *nothing* is original (not even the site of the original village, since that has been preempted by the modern city). Instead, as a matter of policy, *everything* at the Plantation is a facsimile, from the largest house to the smallest teaspoon. Every one of these facsimiles is as accurate as modern research and scholarship can make it. But the main didactic emphasis here is on the processes and life-styles that these artifacts made possible, not on the connoisseurship which is encouraged by the "genuine antiques" of Williamsburg.

Historic House Museum: This has been the basic module of historic preservation, acting as the nursery for the entire movement. Today there are hundreds, if not thousands, of such establishments, operated by a wide gamut of institutions and individuals. Generally, they are detached, single-family houses; and generally, they have been preserved because of some association with famous personages or historical events. Less commonly, they have been preserved for their sheer artistic or historic merit. Mount Vernon and Monticello are prototypical examples of the first type: indeed, because of its age (begun in 1859), the Mount Vernon Restoration encapsulates the whole experience of the American preservation movement. The entertainment and educational value of these houses is obvious from the enormous number of visitors they annually attract. Their main deficiency, in the light of contemporary knowledge and cultural attitudes, is the elitist, upper-class bias of their interpretation, educational programs, and publications.

Historic Rooms in Art Museums: These are the smallest artifactual module of the preservationist. Historic rooms, like the decorative arts collections of which they are usually a part, often serve as the custodians of artifacts which otherwise would be literally homeless. In addition to preserving an important segment of the national artistic heritage, they are also critically important teaching tools in both art history and connoisseurship generally.

The heyday of the isolated historic room has, however, almost certainly passed, largely because of a fundamental change in museological attitudes toward the proper handling of cultural properties. Internationally, there is a growing demand that all such properties be kept in situ, and a growing resistance to the gravitation of all artifacts to urban centers, especially of wealthier nations. Nationally, this sentiment is expressed in the now general agreement that the cannibalizing of older houses for choice bits and pieces—a common practice in earlier decades—is no longer permissible. Most museums today will accept historic buildings or rooms only if there is no possibility of their remaining in situ. Thus, Old Bethpage Village Museum on Long Island accepts only Long Island buildings which are doomed by "progress" (urban renewal, highway construction, and so on) on their original sites. Thus, too, the Metropolitan Museum accepted the living room of Frank Lloyd Wright's Frank Little House in Wisconsin only after all efforts to save the house in situ had failed.

Adaptive Use: Most old buildings whose future is at risk are in danger precisely because the original tenants for whom they were designed no longer inhabit them. Since these buildings will often have neither important historical associations nor exceptional artistic merit, it will be difficult to save them for purely museological purposes. Hence new uses must be found for them; and adapting them to new uses may involve fairly radical physical interventions of one sort or another. Aside from the fact that such buildings will often be quite sound and viable as *built space,* their main aesthetic value will be in the role they play in the streetscape (*le tout ensemble,* as it is defined in New Orleans). While their retrieval involves many of the procedures which used to be called "remodeling," there are subtle but important differences. Now we recognize that there is a visual identity which must be preserved and celebrated rather than concealed. The new use is to be inserted into the old container with the minimum visual dislocation. Subtle though it may appear, this shift in emphasis involves a profound revolution in taste and underlies the rehabilitation of the waterfront in South Boston, of the riverfronts in Paterson, Georgetown, and San Antonio, and in the whole of downtown San Francisco.

Moving to Save: Many an old building, no matter how culturally significant or physically viable, can be preserved only by moving it from its present site to one more suitable. Actually, moving buildings—often for considerable distances—is an old American tradition, largely because the buildings themselves were light, wood-framed, and structurally integral. (Charles Dickens remarked on this practice during his visit to America. One should never be surprised, he wrote in 1842, to meet a house coming down the street in Boston or even sailing across the bay!) Fortunately, the same technology which makes it possible to demolish old structures so quickly and easily also makes it possible to move them. The structure can be moved intact, e.g., Church of the Virgin Mary in the town of Most, Czechoslovakia, cut up into manageable pieces or completely disassembled, and moved piecemeal to the new site and reassembled there, e.g., Old Bethpage Village (Fig. 10.8).

PROFUNDITY OF INTERVENTION

Because of the greatly increased activity in preservation, it becomes both necessary and possible to establish a broader and more precise nomenclature

1

4.1. *Contemporary in-fill in the historic core of Bologna* consists of simplified and modernized versions of historic house types (*1*). They are built only in small groups to replace units too deteriorated for restoration. In its policy of preserving both historic habitats and indigenous population, the city government completes new housing units before demolition of the old (*2*) to permit transfer of inhabitants with minimum dislocation. All rents are subsidized and controlled to prevent gentrification.

2

to accommodate both the immensely broadened scope of the field and the various types and levels of intervention. We must think of the artifacts with which we deal—cities, districts, individual buildings—as living organisms. Then it becomes apparent that they display all the pathological processes of life, including that of simple aging, and that therapeutic interventions will necessarily cover a wide spectrum of treatments, from the conservative to the radical. The medical analogies are not at all farfetched. Specialized problem areas are already being described as "stone disease," "glass diseases," "diseases of timber structures." Such terms describe syndromes of cause and effect which must be understood before a successful therapy can be undertaken. And again, as in medicine, the most conservative treatment possible in any given case is usually the wisest, if for no other reason than that it is most easily reversed: least done, soonest mended. Reversability is a criterion which has developed from a century's experience in archaeology and art conservation, where radical interventions employing the "latest thing" in science and technology have often led to the irreversible degradation of the artifact in question. We can therefore classify levels of intervention according to a scale of increasing radicality, thus: (1) preservation; (2) restoration; (3) conservation and consolidation; (4) reconstitution; (5) adaptive reuse; (6) reconstruction; (7) replication.

Preservation   implies the maintenance of the artifact in the same physical condition as when it was received by the curatorial agency. Nothing is added to or subtracted from the aesthetic corpus of the artifact. Any interventions necessary to preserve its physical integrity (e.g., protection against fire, theft, or intrusion; heating, cooling, lighting) are to be cosmetically unobtrusive. Examples: FDR Home, Hyde Park, New York; Royal Pavilion, Brighton, England; Wavel Palace, Warsaw, Poland.

Restoration   describes the process of returning the artifact to the physical condition in which it would have been at some previous stage of its morphological development. The precise stage is determined either by historical association (the way it was when Washington slept there) or aesthetic integrity (the portico at Mount Vernon must have *all* its columns). Intervention at this level is more radical than simple preservation. Examples: Mount Vernon; Monticello.

Conservation and Consolidation   describes physical intervention in the actual fabric of the building to ensure its continued structural integrity. Such measures can range from relatively minor therapies (fumigation against termites, Royal Palace, Honolulu (Fig. 6.10); stone cleaning, Notre Dame, Paris) to very radical ones (consolidation of desiccated wood, *Vasa* warship, Stockholm (Fig. 7.7); insertion of new foundations, York Minster, England) (Fig. 7.2).

Reconstitution   is a more radical version of the above, in which the building can be saved only by piece-by-piece reassembly, either in situ or on a new site. Reconstitution in situ is ordinarily the consequence of disasters such as war or earthquakes, where most of the original constituent parts remain in being but *disjecta,* or scattered (Cathedral of Antigua, Guatemala; Bridge of Santa Trinita, Florence). On occasion, it may be necessary to dismantle a building and reassemble it on the same site (Old Stage Capitol, Springfield, Illinois, Fig. 7.3). Reconstitution on new sites is much more familiar, usually the consequence of the transplanted structure being too big or bulky to have been moved intact. Examples: Old Bethpage Village; London Bridge, Lake Havasu, Arizona.

Adaptive Use is often the only economic way in which old buildings can be saved, by adapting them to the requirements of new tenants. This can sometimes involve fairly radical interventions, especially in the internal organization of space, in which any or all of the above levels of intervention may be called for. Examples: Castello Sforzesco, Milan; Old City Hall, Boston; "Chattanooga Choo-Choo," Chattanooga (Fig. 8.5).

Reconstruction describes the re-creation of vanished buildings on their original site. The reconstructed building acts as the tangible, three-dimensional surrogate of the original structure, its physical form being established by archaeological, archival, and literary evidence. This is one of the most radical levels of intervention. It is also one of the most hazardous culturally: all attempts to reconstruct the past, no matter what academic and scientific resources are available to the preservationist, necessarily involve subjective hypotheses. In historiography, such hypotheses can be (and indeed are) constantly revised; in architecture, the hypothesis is obdurate, intractable and not easily modified. Examples: Royal Palace, Warsaw, Poland; Governor's Palace and House of Burgesses, Williamsburg (Fig. 6.6); Stoa of Attalos, Athens; Iwo Treasure Houses, Japan.

Replication in the art field implies the creation of a mirror image of an *extant* artifact; in the case of architecture, it implies the construction of an exact copy of a still-standing building on a site removed from the prototype. In other words, the replica *coexists* with the original. Physically, the replica can be more accurate than the reconstruction, since the prototype is available as a control for proportion, polychromy, texture. It is at once the most radical and the most hazardous of all forms of intervention; nevertheless, it has specific utility in certain situations, e.g., to stand in the open air as a surrogate for an original which must be moved to the controlled environment of a museum. Examples: the Acropolis, Athens, Greece; Plimoth Plantation, Massachusetts; Getty Museum, Malibu.

Even such a summary description of the parameters of physical intervention in the built world as this has its utility. It suggests that, despite the size and complexity of the field, it is yet susceptible to rational quantification, description, and analysis. In view of the novelty of our task, that of the curatorial management of this built world, some such conceptual system as outlined here will be essential to future progress.

5

Regeneration of Historic Urban Cores

The rehabilitation of the world's cities confronts municipal administrators, architects, and planners with very difficult problems; for these centers are also the nexus of a complex system of forces, economic, cultural, and artistic. Criteria which normally apply to the development of peripheral communities or wholly new settlements in open land must be modified to meet the special complexities of the central districts of large cities. Here, a new man-made environment has almost completely supplanted the preexisting natural environment of the site. And the marked deterioration of this urban environment is the cause of rising concern everywhere.

Plans to raise the environmental quality of central-city districts must therefore manipulate not merely meteorological, geographic, and botanical factors but social and cultural, physiological and psychological factors as well. For example, the most valuable buildings in the nation, from a historical and artistic point of view, are usually concentrated in these central districts. But many of these same buildings may be either physically or technologically obsolete. Characteristically, some of the worst housing conditions in the city may obtain there. The rehabilitation of such areas therefore cannot be regarded as a simple matter either of historic preservation or of slum clearance.

Venice is today the prototypal example of this environmental paradox. Whole sections of the city are in a stage of advanced physical deterioration; much of its housing is substandard—some of it actually uninhabitable. Yet this same urban tissue constitutes one of the world's rarest architectural heritages. Moreover, it is the basis of Venice's largest industry, tourism. The environmental causes of its degradation are partly natural, partly induced by human beings. The sea level is rising and the land simultaneously sinking: these geological forces conspire to erode building foundations. But this process is aggravated by the wave action generated in the canals by hundreds of motor-powered boats. Atmospheric pollution resulting from industries on the mainland and domestic heating in the city is corroding the stone and marble; and this chemical attrition is aggravated by the feces of millions of pigeons. Clearly, the salvation of Venice will require a broad and sophisticated program of environmental manipulation.

But dramatic as are the problems of Venice, they are by no means unique. Few of the world's cities have a historic core as valuable, as extensive, and as undisturbed as that of Venice. But in varying degrees, they share many of Venice's problems and will require much the same types of intervention. Thus, the next stage of central-city regeneration will be one in which the massive "slum clearance" of recent decades will be replaced by the discriminating insertion of new buildings and facilities to reinforce desirable neighborhood patterns and life-styles; where wholly degenerated urban tissue is surgically removed or, if artistically and historically significant, carefully restored; where old buildings are rehabilitated for new uses not envisioned by the original owners; where the existing infrastructure of services and utilities is modernized; and where transportation systems are strengthened, with special reference to the pedestrian scale of the central city.

THE FALLACY: CITIES ARE OBSOLETE

But we cannot discuss the conservation and rehabilitation of the central city without confronting the problem of the city itself. Perhaps one of the most serious problems before us, especially in Western Europe and North and South America, is psychological: the feeling in many important circles that the city itself may be historically doomed. In previous ages, it would never have been necessary to justify the existence of the city, since it was so obviously the source of all the things which made civilized existence attractive. The technological revolution of the last century and a half has served to obscure this central fact. Today, the mechanization of life in the technically advanced countries has gone far toward equalizing the historic disparity between the material conditions of urban and rural life. A whole range of amenities which had thitherto been the monopoly of the city has been extended into the countryside—amenities of which the public school, the paved road, the ambulance, and the power line are merely symbols. Mechanization has also made possible the decentralization of manufacturing, thereby introducing new modes of work and thought into the rural hinterland. Thus the countryside has been opened up to become the theater of much wider and more varied life-styles than were conceivable in preindustrial times.

These same developments have, of course, affected the function and the form of the metropolis. Mechanization makes possible the unprecedentedly fluid movement of people and goods. This has meant that many of the commercial and industrial activities historically concentrated in the city could be moved out of it; with those activities could go the populations connected with them. These shifting populations and processes have, especially in recent decades, left ugly vacuums and imposed dreadful strains upon the physical and social fabric of the central city. The resulting confusion and squalor have driven further sectors of the population out to the suburbs, even though their economic and cultural focus remained in the city.

The result of all this has been the blurring of the physical and cultural distinction between the city and the countryside. Indeed, urban amenities have become so widely distributed beyond the urban area that a whole new set of misconceptions, as well intentioned as they are misinformed, has come into being about the city. Not only is the countryside now described as a more pleasant place in which to live (the urban elite, Vergil no less than Vanderbilt, have often felt this way during epochs of social peace). Now, for the first time in Western history, it is seriously being argued that the city itself is no longer viable. A whole literature on the "disappearing city" has appeared. Following that special brand of social Darwinism which is endemic in so many technical and academic circles, it is argued that the central city is "doomed" and "obsolete," its disappearance from the stage of history ineluctable. According to this interpretation of the "law" of survival of the fittest, the city is destined simply to dissolve, distributing its amenities in a thin film of suburban houses, shopping centers, and country day schools across the landscape.

THE CITY AS GENERATOR OF CULTURE

This is a grotesque misreading of the city's historic function. As the etymology of the word suggests, the city has always been not merely the vessel but the actual generator of civilization. It is not at all accidental that such words and concepts as "civil," "civilized," "citizen," and "urbane" and "urbanity" cluster around the word and concept of the city. Urban experience with the city as a special instrument of social organization is the basis for all such concepts. It has always been the lodestar of farmer, herder, hunter, sailor. It offered them paved streets, lighted taverns, and buzzing markets instead of barnyard mud or storm-tossed ocean nights. It promised them music, dancing, theater, and spectacle. Even more precious, it gave them relative safety from war, a place of sanctuary, an asylum for dissent. But beneath all of these was the city's most splendid gift: a *range of choice,* an entire spectrum of possible lines of action.

This attractive power of the city is somewhat obscured in the technically advanced countries by the surface glitter of universal mechanization. But even in many such countries (e.g., in the North of England and the American Prairie states) the steady attrition of villages and small towns con-

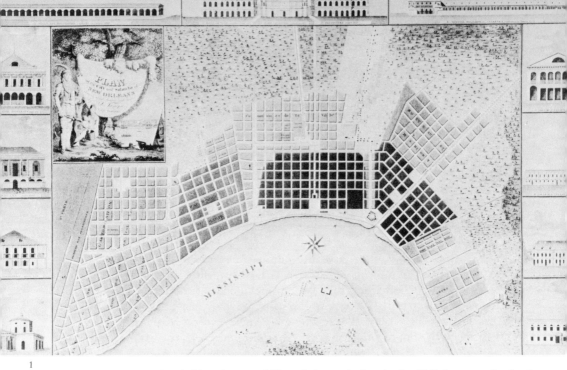

1

5.1. The Vieux Carré, historic core of New Orleans, is first in the U.S.A. to receive landmark preservation designation. Originally forming the whole of the city laid out in 1717—center of map (*1*)—the Vieux Carré had a remarkably consistent urban fabric that remained largely intact until the 1940s. Designation as a protected district in 1932 has preserved this character. But its successful preservation has generated a large tourist industry which, in turn, exerts great pressures on its aesthetic integrity—a common plight in many historic cities.

2

tinues apace. In such underindustrialized countries as Egypt or Greece, the centripetal pull of the city is even more marked. The peasantry flees the stupefying poverty and monotony of a countryside ravished by centuries of ignorance and neglect. This instinct is correct, however inadequately or unevenly Cairo or Athens may live up to its promises, for the amelioration of the material conditions of life can be accomplished only by the science and technology of the city. Even the regeneration of agriculture and the countryside is, culturally, the task of such urbane institutions as the universities and research laboratories.

TECHNOLOGY AND URBAN MIGRATIONS

For the last century, technology has served to accelerate two superficially contradictory tendencies in the cities of the world, one centrifugal, the other centripetal. These two tendencies—made possible above all by the development of mechanical transport and rapid communications—have altered both the form and the function of central urban districts. Commercial, cultural, and governmental functions are still concentrated in the center. In fact, in cities where a wide use has been made of skyscrapers (São Paulo, Chicago, Moscow), they are probably more concentrated than ever before in history. But the populations which use and support these centers are now widely distributed in space, since home and workplace need no longer be close together. Thus, while the city has grown enormously in size and spatial extension, its overall density has often diminished (Los Angeles, Houston).

This process of decentralization has been made possible by the technological development of a whole succession of transportation forms, all of them based on a mechanical prime mover: steam commuting trains, steam ferries, electric trolleys, elevated railways, and subway systems. Though these systems accelerated the centrifugal dispersion of the city, they were confined to the fixed trajectories of rail lines; and this set rational (or at least comprehensible) parameters to the process of expansion. But the scale of this process was altered by the introduction of the auto bus, the auto truck, and, most of all, the private automobile. This new means of moving people and things across the landscape has acted like a powerful acid, dissolving the very tissue of the historic city.

The result of this shift has been to alter the life-styles of the central city. The residential component has been almost everywhere reduced. Many of the older European metropolises continue to have sizable residential populations at or near the center (London, Paris, Rome). But in many cities where there has been extensive modernization, especially as a result of World War II, there has been a deliberate policy of shifting residential func-

5.2. *The historic core of Prague* escaped radical nineteenth-century "improvements" when the Austro-Hungarian monarchy shifted its second capital to Vienna, thus dooming Prague to economic stagnation. Unlike most European capitals, it escaped damage in both world wars. Hence, with its fabric intact, the Old Town requires only conservation of street façades, although there is considerable interior modification for new uses.

tions to newly created microcommunities and satellite towns around the periphery (Moscow, Warsaw, Stockholm, London). The most characteristic pattern has, however, been the steady centrifugal spread of suburbia. This evisceration of the central city of a large part of its resident population varies, of course, from country to country. It is much less evident in densely built-up countries such as Holland or Portugal than in the western United States or South America. It is even affected by local geography: cities located on islands or peninsulas (Stockholm, New Orleans, San Francisco) show a tendency to maintain a much firmer central district than cities in which such constraints do not occur (Detroit, Mexico City, São Paulo). Finally, the tendency is most marked in newer cities where mass-transit systems were never fully developed (Houston, Los Angeles, Brasília). In its most extreme cases, it has left a still-viable central business district surrounded by a widening ring of no-man's-land of abandoned buildings and empty lots (South Bronx district in New York City; Chicago's South Side).

Nevertheless, and despite these profound changes, the central urban districts, by definition, are the nuclei of the city. They all share certain characteristics, irrespective of climate, culture, or age:

54

1

2

5.3. Nationalistic motivations are explicit in current restoration activities in the Canadian city of Quebec. A direct expression of the Quebecois' determination to reassert the presence of French culture in contemporary Canada, the Place Royale is being radically restored. Most physical evidences of the original town site of the earliest seventeenth-century settlement under the cliffs on the St. Lawrence, had been blurred or destroyed by subsequent development. The current campaign involves a hard-edged mix of demolition, restoration, and sometimes complete reconstruction of the oldest buildings to re-create the appearance of Place Royale before the British conquest.

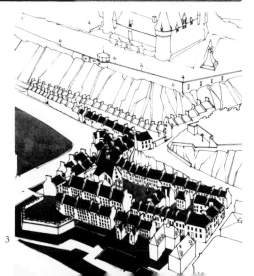

3

55

1. They remain the locus of finance and banking, of nationally significant businesses; centers of communication, publication, and mass media.

2. They tend to be densely built-up and densely populated, at least during working hours.

3. They are the site of the most important secular and religious institutions—castles, parliaments, city halls; cathedrals, monasteries, universities.

4. Most cultural institutions are central-city-based: opera, ballet, symphony, theaters; museums and art galleries; libraries.

5. Finally, central cities tend to be the locus of most monuments and districts of artistic and historic significance; because of this, they are also the center of tourism.

Because of their historic development, all central urban areas also display a characteristic range of idiosyncrasies. These include:

1. There is an intricate, random, and complex physical structure. They show both vertical and horizontal discontinuities due to such cataclysmic events as war (Warsaw), earthquake (Lisbon), fire (London).

2. Land costs are highest, though not necessarily equally distributed throughout.

3. Ownership of land and buildings is highly diversified and complex.

4. The infrastructure is complete (paved streets, sidewalks, squares; sewers, water systems, streetlighting; fire-fighting and waste-disposal systems, and so on), but because of its evolution across time, much of the infrastructure may be redundant, obsolete, or irrational.

5. Municipal services (hospitals, clinics, morgues; police, fire fighting and waste disposal; educational facilities at all levels) are densely textured and complex. Again, individual components may be obsolete or redundant.

6. Transportation systems, both intra- and intercity, were typically better than adequate until after World War II. In most European cities, the system is intact and functioning; in North and South American cities, it has been largely demolished.

7. The physical condition of many old buildings, especially if they are privately owned, may be very unsatisfactory (structurally unsound, not fire-safe, inadequate sanitary facilities, lack of light and air). This becomes especially serious when buildings are used as housing.

Such a list as this suggests both the urgency and the difficulties of any program for the regeneration of the total physical environment of central urban districts.

Ironically, modern technology is often used as the argument for abandoning completely the central city. It is declared to be "obsolete": the only "progressive" response is held to be either (1) complete redevelopment or (2) extra-urban development in the form of endless suburban sprawl (Los Angeles, Detroit, Rome); or the creation of New Towns (England; Washington, D.C.); or microcommunities (Moscow, Bucharest, Warsaw). There are, of course, many situations in which the creation of brand-new urban tissue on raw land is justified. But the same technical expertise can be fruitfully applied to the regeneration of central-city districts.

The basic argument to justify the decision to abandon the central city is usually based upon conventional economic factors: "It's cheaper to start from scratch." While it may often be more expensive to modernize an individual building than to construct the same cubage on raw land, such costs take no account of the life-support systems, the infrastructure of institutions, services, and utilities without which no building could operate at all. Missing from such arguments about the "economy" of building anew are such hidden costs as loss of arable land to agriculture; costs of installing new highways, streets, sidewalks, streetlighting, sewer and water systems; cost of new health, hospital, educational, and governmental facilities, etc., etc.

If, however, such hidden costs are properly taken into account, then the expediency of retrieving and recycling the central city with its huge infrastructure, in being and paid for, becomes much more attractive. Of course, in many of the world's older cities, elements of this infrastructure are often archaic, fragmentary, and confused. In the rehabilitation of such areas, if may often be advisable to bypass an existing system altogether. For example, to eliminate the atmospheric pollution caused by the burning of brown coal in Middle Europe (Cracow, Prague, Budapest) it might be advisable to install district heating and relinquish any effort to modernize individual heating systems. This has been done in central Warsaw. The installation of such new heating mains might be integrated with the rationalization of water, gas, electric, and sewers. Again, it seems probable in most cities with centers of ancient or medieval origin, where the street pattern is too small and irrational for any rational organization of surface traffic, that subways will in the long run be the most economical—as they are certainly the most efficient—means of diurnal movement into and out of the center. That such subways can also furnish extremely pleasant transportation is amply demonstrated by the new lines in Mexico City, Montreal, and Leningrad.

URBAN ORGANISMS HAVE SPECIAL METABOLISMS

Concretely, the regeneration of the city must necessarily involve coming to grips with the following factors:

1. Environmental pollution or degradation

    a. Atmospheric: pollution due to emission of noxious wastes from factories, power stations, heating plants, automobiles

    b. Thermal: due to heat-holding characteristics of urban tissue; inefficient heating and cooling systems; inefficient thermal insulation of buildings; "haze hood" over cities from atmospheric pollutants

    c. Aqueous: due to discharge of fluid wastes into water bodies and underground streams

    d. Sonic: due to wasteful energy conversion in manufacturing and transportation

    e. Luminous: due to wasted light from signs, autos, street lights, etc.

2. Substandard performance of individual buildings

    a. Overcrowding—lack of sunshine, ventilation, privacy

    b. Inadequate or obsolete sanitation (bacteria, insects, vermin)

    c. Inadequate or obsolete heating

    d. Structural instability

    e. Lack of fireproofness

    3. Inadequate, obsolete, or unevenly distributed amenities and services—schools, playgrounds, parks, markets, etc.

Physically, cities should be regarded as organisms with their own special metabolism. This special metabolism has two origins: structurally, it has heat-holding capacities without parallel in surrounding nature; functionally, it concentrates and consumes unprecedented amounts of energy (fuel, food) in small areas. According to Abel Wolman, the input-output energy ratios per 1,000,000 urban inhabitants are as follows:[1]

Input (fuel)	Tons per day	Output (waste)	Tons per day
Water	625,000	Sewage	500,000
Food	2,000	Solid wastes	2,000
Fuel		Particles	150
Coal	3,000	Sulfur dioxides	100
Oil	2,800	Nitrogen oxides	100
Gas	2,700	Carbon monoxide	450
Motor	1,000		

All cities create their own microclimate; and this climate is always hotter and drier than the natural climate which it displaces. This effect is due to three causes:

1. Cities, by definition, replace the natural ground cover by masonry and cementatious and bituminous surfaces. These surfaces, because of their tendency to absorb solar energy and only slowly to release it back to the environment, create a desertlike thermal regime. This is the opposite consequence of the thermal behavior of plant materials, which absorb solar energy and convert its sensible heat into other forms of energy.

2. All cities generate immense amounts of heat. This is more marked in the upper latitudes, where buildings must be heated to be habitable. But it is also true of cities in the lower latitudes, where almost any process, from cooking a meal to smelting steel, generates a waste product of excess heat.

3. All cities generate a haze hood—an umbrella of the waste products of the combustion of fossil fuels discharged into the atmosphere. This hood acts to trap both solar and man-made heat, slowing down its escape by either convection to the upper atmosphere or reradiation to outer space.

From a purely thermal point of view, this tendency of cities to create a warmer microclimate might be considered as advantageous in the high latitudes, where an absolute shortage of environmental heat is basic; and as disadvantageous in the lower latitudes, where an absolute surplus of environmental heat is very stressful.

Unfortunately, however, the environmental problem is not exclusively thermal; it is also (and increasingly) atmospheric. For the by-products of the combustion of all forms of fossil fuel, from wood fires to automobiles to thermal power plants, constitute a grave threat to the environment. These waste products are themselves directly hazardous to health (e.g., the carcinogenic and pulmonary disorders of automobile exhausts). Also, as particulates suspended in the atmosphere, they set in motion another level of environmental disturbances, typified by the smogs which are becoming endemic in cities in all latitudes.

Thus, effects no. 1 and no. 2 could presumably be considered as potential assets in cities in the high latitudes. That is to say, far northern or far southern cities could be considered as thermal megastructures in which heat-holding and heat-generating capacities could become a *planned* aspect of their design rather than (as today in Moscow or Calgary) *accidental*.

The reverse would be true of cities in the low latitudes (Miami, Cairo, Bombay), where effects no. 1 and no. 2 are largely or wholly negative. Here the heat-holding and heat-generating characteristics of cities should be minimized in every possible way, from the design of the individual building to the design of the whole city. Here again, the city should be regarded as a thermal megastructure but with the fundamental task of rejecting solar energy, minimizing the production of heat, and maximizing its dispersal. It is worth noting that devices for minimizing heat gain are a feature of traditional low-latitude architecture and urbanism, either architectural (e.g., the white walls, narrow streets, and dense self-shading compartmentalization of space which mark most Mediterranean cities); or botanical (e.g., the continuous canopy of eucalyptus trees in Addis Ababa, the parasol of spreading banyan in many Caribbean towns, and the nut palms of the Egyptian Delta).

In cities where a surplus of solar energy is a major environmental problem, a whole series of regulations governing architectural and landscaping plans could be written into zoning law. Small in themselves, their cumulative impact on urban microclimate would be very large. For example:

1.   The planting of deciduous trees along all streets

2.   Stringent control of quantity and shading of paved surfaces, especially of asphalt

3.   Encouragement of continuously canopied sidewalks (Modena, Bologna, Torino)

4.   Compulsory shading of all open-air parking lots (deciduous vines on stainless-steel net trellises would be relatively light, low-cost, maintenance-free)

5.   Encouragement of rooftop landscaping, especially turf

6.   Wall and room colors could be controlled (dark for colder climates, light for hotter ones)

7.   Prohibition of unshaded glass walls (to cut down on air-conditioning loads at peak overheating periods)

It is obvious that the third effect, atmospheric pollution, threatens the continuing viability of all cities in all latitudes. It can be considered as absolutely negative, and every step should be taken to eliminate it. These steps should cover every activity or process which involves the combustion of fossil fuels: the heating of residential, commercial, and industrial buildings; all industrial processes; traffic and transportation and, above all, the use of the internal combustion engine. The success of London in its antismoke campaign or of rebuilt Warsaw, with its central thermoelectric plants, demonstrates the feasibility of reducing pollution from heating sources. Success in reducing industrial smoke and gases has been more erratic, though for economic rather than technical reasons. But the latest, largest, and by now gravest source of atmospheric pollution, the automobile, has yet to be faced. Even at this late date, when the environmental hazards of the automobile have been documented beyond any possibility of doubt, most of the world's largest cities will be found to be still at work on highway schemes which can only result in more cars being introduced into the central city. The almost universal corollary is the decline of mass transit either relatively (as in Moscow or London) or absolutely (New York, Rome, and Paris).

Coextensive with atmospheric pollution, and often generated by the same processes and activities, is the phenomenon of sonic pollution. All mechanical work involves the incomplete conversion of energy; and noise (counterproductive sound) is one characteristic expression of this inefficiency. The deleterious effects of noise upon health and efficiency are fairly well established. For example, Rosen and his colleagues, in comparing the health and hearing of certain "primitive" African people with contemporary Americans, discovered a startling correlation between good hearing and good health.[2] But the epidemiological aspects of urban noise have not received anything like the same attention in the mass media as has the connection between atmospheric pollution and morbidity. Since the factors which produce atmospheric pollutants (industry, aviation, railroads, trucking, automobiles) are the same as those which produce noise, it follows that steps taken to ameliorate one condition are apt to be helpful in the other. (Thus the atrocious custom of removing auto mufflers and gunning the motor which makes Italian streets a nightmare could be controlled either by making muffler removal a legal offense or by excluding all cars from those streets.) Today, air-pollution control measures are beginning to be recognized as necessary: but noise-abatement criteria are fragmentary and incomplete and legislation often nonexistent.

Another great area of environmental pollution which threatens the welfare not merely of cities but of entire regions is the dumping of wastes into the water bodies on which most cities stand (and on whose continuing viability they still largely depend). The "death" of the Great Lakes and the catastrophic decline of the Rhine are merely among the most spectacular examples of such pollution; we can assume that most of the same processes are at work wherever urbanization and industrialization occur. On the other hand, London's reclamation of the Thames, where fish are now swimming again for the first time in a century, is a spectacular demonstration of how comparatively simple measures have effected a reversal of this trend.

Generally speaking, two broad categories of wastes imply different methodologies of disposal and/or conversion:

1. *Industrial wastes:* These are of such increasing complexity, with such unpredictable environmental consequences, that they must be controlled at the point of origin, i.e., the industrial plant itself. This certainly implies a new criterion for industrial plant design: the so-called closed production cycle in which all waste products are either fed back into the cycle or completely "disarmed" to prevent atmospheric, thermal, aqueous, or nuclear pollutants being discharged into the local environment.

2. *Sewerage, garbage:* Many of the world's great cities have inadequate waste-disposal systems (New York still dumps some of its raw sewage into the Hudson: Miami Beach pumps all of its a mile out to sea). Some cities have none at all (Addis Ababa). But even those cities which have "up-to-date" systems, including sewage treatment plants and garbage incinerators or sanitary dumps, are merely disarming wastes. None of these systems

make any effort to conserve the enormous amounts of organic materials and hence potential energy sources which they contain. Here and there, one hears of isolated experiments aimed at one or another form of conservation: the use of methane from sewage to power electric generators (New York); the use of sewage solids as fertilizer and humus (Milwaukee); the use of heat from decaying garbage to heat greenhouses (Moscow). Such piecemeal experiments at least suggest the enormous potentials inherent in municipal waste-disposal systems which are also closed-cycle, where the aim is not merely to neutralize waste materials but to return them to productive use. Fortunately, facilities for such types of conservation and energy conversion could be regarded as discrete elements in citywide collection systems. Even such equipment as garbage grinders in apartment houses could be used to enrich the sewage for generation of methane gas for power.

THE AUTO, ENEMY OF URBANITY

In addition to the well-documented threat of the auto to life and limb (as a result of sheer physical impact and well-established causal link between its exhausts and lung cancer, emphysema, and respiratory ailments generally) the auto is responsible for another form of environmental pollution: that of the sheer degradation and wasteful use of urban space. Since the automobile occupies exactly the same life zone as the human being—i.e., the first 6 feet above the earth's surface—it is in constant, irreconcilable kinesthetic and aesthetic conflict with pedestrians. When moving, it displaces some 600 cubic feet, as opposed to some 12 cubic feet for a standing human being. When parked, it occupies 120 square feet (a reclining human being is comfortable in under 20); the parking and unparking process requires three times that much area. Because it occupies precisely the same zone as pedestrians, it is a constant obstacle to their movement. It is even an obstacle to the free movement of their vision when standing still. Anyone who compares the Italian piazzas, for example, in the years before World War II and their present state as traffic circles and carparks can only be appalled at the qualitative drop in amenity.

But the aspect of the private automobile which is perhaps most destructive to urban experience (and the one which has been least studied) is its absolute lack of capacity for autonomous movement. Every other form of transport, including bus and taxi, has the capacity to deliver its passengers or freight and *then take itself away under its own power*. But the private car is tied to its owner like the tail of a dinosaur: by its very nature, it is compelled to occupy the same space as its owner. To try to escape this paradox, Americans have lavished ingenuity and funds on parking schemes: but no parking system (vertical or horizontal, automatic or chauffeur-operated) escapes this fundamental limitation. The result of this "foreign body" in the pedestrian zone is radically to reduce the pedestrian population per square foot of urban earth surface. This in turn lowers the whole richness, intensity, and diversity of the urban experience: the very quality of urban life is impoverished and degraded.

All of this suggests still another reason why the regeneration of the physical environment of the central cities will be to a large extent dependent upon the way in which the internal combustion engine, and above all the private automobile, is handled in the future. It may be possible to design completely new human settlements in such a way as to minimize the severe spatial dislocation caused by the automobile (provided, of course, that the internal combustion engine has been replaced by other motive power, such as electricity or steam).

But most central-city districts, in their basic street patterns, predate modern vehicular traffic by centuries. Even when large in extent, they are small in scale, fundamentally designed to facilitate pedestrian movement. This scale becomes absolutely critical when a historic district is to be developed for touristic purposes. Such areas can be enjoyed only on foot. This suggests that a policy of permitting no wheeled traffic in such areas (except for fire, ambulance, waste removal, and so on) is the correct one. Though merchants in such areas are often initially skeptical of the impact of such measures on retail trade, they have proved to be successful in certain cities (Piazza Navona in Rome, the New Precinct in Coventry). As we have said, the subway is unquestionably the most rational means of moving people into and around such districts. In cities where many tourists arrive by bus or private car, parking facilities should be provided around the periphery—preferably underground and in small, dispersed units to avoid peak-hour traffic jams.

WHEN IS THE OLD BUILDING REALLY OBSOLETE?

Old buildings and old neighborhoods are often declared "slums" on the basis of quite superficial examination and inadequate data. Actually, many factors enter into the viability (or lack thereof) of any old urban tissue. These factors may be listed under four headings: *microclimatic response; structural stability; sanitary levels; historic and artistic significance.* No truly effective rehabilitation program can be evolved without due consideration of all four.

1. Microclimatic response: Most old urban areas, especially if they predate the nineteenth century, represent an adroit manipulation of climatic and topographic factors—maximizing the positive aspects and minimizing the negative. This is very evident around the entire littoral of the Mediterranean, where both town planning and architecture are aimed at minimizing the impact of excessive heat, light, and glare; or along the Baltic and North Seas, where the aim is the reverse: maximum exploitation of the winter sun. From this point of view, many old town centers incorporate environmental principles which ought to be extended to the design of brand-new neighborhoods and settlements.

Negative environmental factors—such as rooms without adequate light or ventilation, or lack of visual and aural privacy—are usually due to alterations over the years, especially the tendency to build over former yards, courts, and patios. Correcting such conditions usually means the removal of such appendages, thus restoring light and air and reducing overcrowding.

2. The structural stability of old buildings is too often judged on the basis of cosmetic effects (peeling paint, stained stucco, rusted gutters). In most cities, masonry construction is predominant; in many parts of the world, where wood has long been in short supply or nonexistent, floors and roofs, as well as walls, will be of masonry. New techniques for consolidating old masonry (injection of mortar under pressure, insertion of reinforced concrete members), as well as the availability of prefabricated concrete beams and columns and lightweight floor and roof slabs, make the rehabilitation of old masonry buildings much more feasible than hitherto. In those areas where the cost of labor is low relative to materials, the balance is especially favorable.

3. Sanitary levels in central-city housing will almost always be deficient relative to contemporary standards. Inadequate cooking and bathing facilities; inadequate or environmentally defective heating equipment; lack of fire-safeness; overcrowding: all are typical of such districts. In view of the difficulty of inserting new plumbing into old buildings, efforts should be concentrated on perfecting lightweight, prefabricated kitchen and bathroom units. A central steam and hot water supply from district plants, or from local boilers in each building, is efficient but difficult to install in old buildings. Unit heaters are simpler to install but raise serious problems of local asphyxiation or area pollution. Electric radiant heating is optimal, architecturally and environmentally, but too expensive to be practical in most parts of the world.

Overcrowding is a social, not an architectural, phenomenon: it can be corrected only by broad programs of housing construction and rental subsidies.

4. The historic and artistic significance of old districts must be judged by quite different criteria than no. 2 and no. 3 above. Some of the most deteriorated sections may well have the greatest value and offer the largest touristic potentials for restoration and preservation.

PRESERVATION OF HABITAT AND
INHABITANT

From one point of view, cities can be regarded as vessels or containers in which a number of complementary processes are simultaneously occurring. But because of their development across time, both vessel and process change—and often along accidental or unanticipated lines. As a consequence, uses often conflict and functions overlap, because they occur in buildings and districts which might have been designed originally to house quite different activities. The older the urban district in question, the most pronounced such contradictions are apt to be. The consequences are, however, by no means wholly negative. On the contrary, the very intricacy of old urban centers is precisely what nourishes the urbane activities of the regular population, on the one hand, and makes the centers so attractive to visitors and tourists, on the other.[3]

The rehabilitation of such centers confronts architects and planners with problems of unprecedented intricacy. Yet Vienna inside the Ringstrasse or Split inside the Diocletian precinct afford excellent examples of how these problems can be met. Both areas have been rehabilitated in such a way as to strengthen their central business district function. At the same time, old buildings have been refurbished; substandard housing either improved or eliminated; monumental complexes restored and adapted to new users.

Of course, as we have suggested, the oldest and historically most significant districts in many cities which seem so romantic to the tourist (Venice, central Rome, East London) will often appear as offering intolerably poor living conditions to the people who live there. Thus, the regeneration of such districts involves meeting simultaneously two quite different sets of the requirements: the conservation of the physical fabric of the quarter (i.e., the container) and the protection of the interests of the population (i.e., the contained).

It should be remembered that, in many cities, the worst living conditions occur precisely in these historic districts; but these are often also the areas of lowest rents. Thus, while slum dwellers may identify old buildings with low living standards (and new ones with high standards), plans for restoration and rehabilitation will often seem to them to run against their most fundamental short-range interests. That is, they will see programs for area restoration as merely a pretext for evicting them from the only housing they can afford without providing new housing within their means. This has proved to be the case in several American cities (Charleston, Savannah, Providence) where very successful restoration projects have been carried out. These projects, which have been executed by private nonprofit institutions, were unfortunately not matched by any complementary public programs for rehousing the evicted poor, either in new buildings elsewhere or in rehabilitated housing in their old neighborhoods. The antagonism resulting from such errors of policy is often serious.

All too often, the rehabilitation of historic inner-city districts are subjected to a process which the British have dubbed "gentrification"—i.e., the poorer, working-class populations are "decanted" and the historic container is filled with a new, upper-class population. This process of gentrification has not been studied systematically. Indeed, it is only now beginning to be recognized as an international phenomenon, especially in the great cities of Western Europe and North America. Donald Appleyard, in a recent study of the phenomenon, has described it quite succinctly:

> Most commonly it is a private process, with a chain of gentrifiers. Those who spearhead invasions of lower income districts are often students, artists, and design professionals looking for cheap accommodation and interested in living in mixed neighborhoods. They are often single people or couples without children. From the Trastevere to Telegraph Hill, Chelsea to Greenwich Village, this process has inexorably transformed the character of these places. It appears to take place in some Eastern European cities too.
>
> Ironically many of the complaints about gentrification come from the first groups who enter. Jane Jacobs' famous book described the same richness of life in Greenwich Village that used to attract artists to Trastevere. The pioneer migrants are usually welcome and only marginally affect the quality of life in such an area. However, they usually do not wish to live under the same conditions as the inhabitants and therefore improve their dwellings. As more are attracted, the neighborhood becomes mixed, still retaining much of its original character but now acquiring the status of being "chic," and relatively safe even for more conventional young executives, professionals, secretaries, and the like. By this time real estate speculators are actively buying, converting, and selling. The first wave of gentrifiers resents the destruction of character caused by the second wave, sometimes even more than the original working class population. The area loses its "life" and "integrity." The old bars or wine shops fold. Boutiques, art galleries, specialty shops take their place.[1]

As a consequence of this paradoxical state of affairs, preservationists are now beginning to demand that the existing population (or at least that portion of it which wishes to remain) be maintained in situ. This is, of course, no easy problem either economically or sociologically. In theory, at least, housing in recycled historic buildings could be subsidized for low-income families as easily as new construction in the suburbs. But in many cities around the world today, this population has a large component of migrants—foreigners who either cannot or do not wish to remain permanently. *Urban Conservation,* for example, points out that most Western European cities have large populations of Turks, Yugoslavs, Spanish, and

Portuguese migrant workers who are not true residents. Grenoble has a large district populated by Algerians. Typically, these migrants are single men who leave their families in their native land and return there as soon as they have accumulated sufficient funds. Thus, while their housing needs should be met with facilities which meet acceptable norms of amenity and economy, there is no reason per se that they should be housed in the historic central city.

Surprisingly few historic centers have today a historically indigenous population, i.e., families which have lived there continuously for a century or more. All the major cities of the world have been inundated by peasants fleeing the intolerable conditions of the hinterland. This is as true for Chicago or New York as for Cairo or Caracas. But except for the United States, this peasantry has settled in a ring of ad hoc suburbs around the city. Only in the United States have the peculiar conditions of upper- and middle-class flight to the suburbs left a void which has been filled with native-born American blacks and, more recently, Latin Americans from the Caribbean basin and Mexico. Thus there seem to be few cities in which a conscious effort has been made to retrieve and recycle both the historic center and its contemporary population. Among them are the Marais district of Paris (Fig. 5.4); the ancient center of Split in Yugoslavia, built in and around the fourth-century Palace of Diocletian (Fig. 5.5); and the historic medieval and Renaissance core of Bologna, Italy.

A PARISIAN EXPERIMENT IN DISTRICT PRESERVATION

Le Marais holds many of Paris's most significant architectural monuments, including libraries, churches, palaces, and town houses. Its population has, even today, something of the same demographic composition that it has maintained for centuries—a mix of aristocratic wealth, intelligentsia, craftsmen, artists, and artisans. It has always been and still is a center of highly specialized skills: jewelers, clock smiths, gunmakers; the special crafts associated with haute couture; lace, ribbons, buttons, artificial flowers, etc.; fine hardware; etc., etc. Many of these specialists still work in the area; their shops, workrooms, and studios still line the streets of the quarter. Formerly, these same people lived there also. But increased prosperity is permitting them to abandon the substandard housing accommodations of the district and move their families to modern housing in the suburbs. The danger is very real that, sooner or later, they will also move their workplaces out of the Marais.

To forestall this development and to preserve the population mix which makes the quarter so attractive, the national government and the municipality have joined in a comprehensive, long-range program of restoration

67

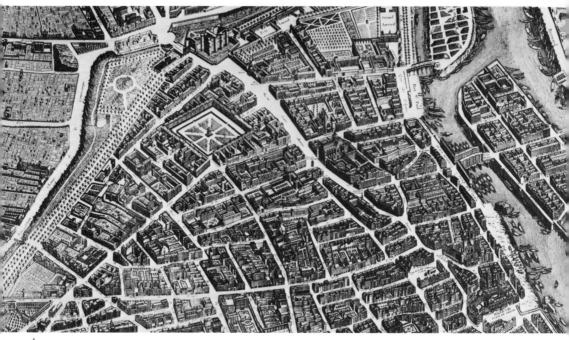

5.4. *To save both habitat and inhabitant is the ambitious goal of a current program in Paris.* Le Marais, one of the oldest and least disturbed quarters of the city, is the scene of a long-range cooperative effort on the part of the national government, the municipality, and private landlords. The aim is not merely to rehabilitate thousands of old buildings, many of them

dating from medieval times, but also to stabilize and preserve the traditional demographic mix of the area, which boasts a wealth of historically and artistically important buildings—churches, palaces, and the first of the great formal squares, the sixteenth-century Place des Vosges—map (*1*), and view of loggia (*2*). The plan envisages the restoration and adaptive use of the Hôtel de Sully as headquarters for the Service des Monuments Historiques (*3*) and the Hôtel de Sens as a library-museum of music (*4*). But the Marais has another great resource, its working population of artisans and craftsmen. They have been for centuries the base of such important Parisian industries as jewelry, clockmaking, gunsmithery (in medieval times, swords and armor), and *haute couture*. Because of substandard housing facilities, this population was moving to modern housing in the suburbs. The fear was that they would ultimately take their shops and ateliers with them. Hence old multistory tenements are being retrofitted (new kitchens, baths, heating, elevators) and new housing infill being constructed (*5*), (*6*). Rental subsidies for such housing are aimed at keeping it within reach of the present inhabitants.

3

4

5

5.4 *(Continued). A demographic experiment: in an effort to maintain traditional Parisian mix* of working class and haute bourgeoisie, the Marais plan calls for mixed housing types. In this single large block, old five- and six-story walk-ups are being completely retrofitted, including new lobbies, elevators, and underground garages. These units will have subsidized rentals (5). Opposite, new single-family maisonettes have been built *(left, below)* and an eighteenth-century town house has been restored. An underground garage will be topped with a landscaped, tree-planted courtyard.

6

1

5.5. Huddling within the confines of Diocletian's Palace, begun in the northeast corner of the Adriatic in A.D. 300, the medieval town of Split became in time the historic core of the modern city of 250,000: it remains even now its social center. Because of its international significance as one of the greatest late-Roman monuments, the Yugoslav government some years ago initiated a long-range plan of development. But because it was very much an inhabited site, a complex strategy was adopted: (a) a definitive archaeological investigation of the entire enclave within the walls; (b) the restoration and touristic interpretation of all Roman remains; (c) the rehabilitation for alternate use of all significant Romanesque and Venetian structures; and (d) the upgrading of all housing, by either retrofitting or the insertion of new infill. No demolition would occur except with buildings that were structurally at risk or those that occupied critically important Roman discoveries. All of this complex operation was to be accomplished without "closing the city down." Thanks to this strategy, the Roman origins of this palace town are now more intelligible to the tourists and it is more livable for its citizens than ever before.

2

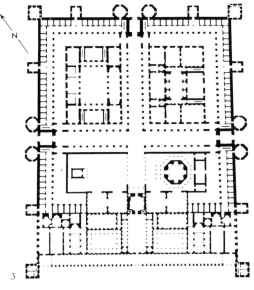

3

5.5 (Continued). *Although it had been studied for centuries,* the palace had never been systematically excavated before the present campaign. Thus many internal relationships had never before been fully understood, viz., the precise connection between the southern sea-level gate and the imperial living quarters above. Now that relationship is clear: a great vaulted corridor led from the quays (6), under the imperial apartments, and up to the peristylium (2). Another puzzle has been unlocked: it had been assumed that the vaulted crypto-portico on which the palace stands had been used for stables, warehouses, or workshops. Excavation of these vaults, filled with the midden heaps of 1,500 years, reveals that they had only one function: to furnish a stylobate, or platform, from which the emperor could enjoy an optimum southern exposure and ocean view, safe from either unruly barbarians or stormy seas— plan (3).

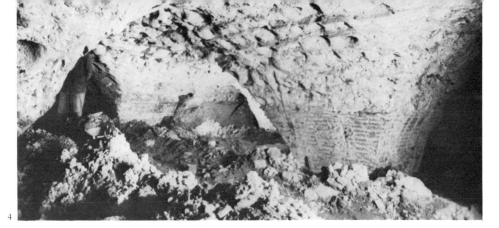

4

Some of the grandest Roman masonry still extant, and in excellent condition because it was used only as a cesspit and midden (*4*), has now been revealed. The entire crypto-portico, now cleaned and restored, will house a whole complex of tourist-related shops and offices as well as a department store for the citizens. Especially important for scholars is the superb condition of cut stone paving and piers and brick masonry vaulting: few comparably pristine examples remain.

Before Excavation

5   **Conjectural Restoration of Peristyle**

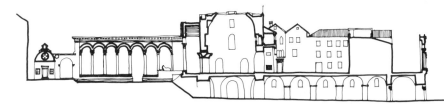

6   After Excavation

73

7

8

9

5.5 *(Continued). Two populations—touristic and "native"—inhabit the same terrain* in modern Split. The conflicts arising from such dual occupancy is often stressful for both. Luckily for Split, most tourist-support facilities (hotels, restaurants, beaches) lie well outside the historic core. Thus tourists tend to leave at nightfall. But the enclave within the walls remains the effective center of modern Split. Much of the commercial activity is centered here; and here every evening occurs a local event—the *passeggiata*—which brings out the entire younger population (*8*). To minimize interruptions in everyone's life, archaeology has been carefully phased in time and place; all demolition and new construction are similarly phased. Several thousand people lived within the enclave in hopelessly substandard housing. If historically or artistically significant, old buildings are rehabilitated, either for dwellings or for other uses. Otherwise, they are demolished and replaced by new housing infill. All new construction is designed to be congruent with the old in terms of size, mass, materials, etc. New apartments (*12*) are typical.

10

11

12

and preservation, with special emphasis on upgrading the housing stock of the entire quarter. Rents will be subsidized where necessary to hold the present population. The results of the program are already physically most impressive, though it is too early to tell if the gentrification process described by Appleyard can be wholly avoided in the Marais.

The regeneration of the core of Split was an incomparably more complex task, since it involved intervention in an urban container which has been continuously occupied since the time of Emperor Diocletian, in the early fourth century. A comprehensive and far-reaching program, facilitated by the socialist regime of Yugoslavia, includes definitive archaeology; restoration of all significant monuments of all periods; rehabilitation of the housing stock (including insertion of new units wherever possible); and installation of facilities for a large and growing tourist industry. The notable aspect of the Split plan is its commitment to maintaining the current population of the center and consolidating its function as the commercial and social nucleus of the modern town. Although the program is far from complete, enough has already been accomplished to demonstrate that radical intervention into the physical fabric of a historical center *can* be accomplished without destroying extant populations and the network of sociocultural activities which supports them.[5]

Bologna is a city whose historic center, dating from medieval and Renaissance times, is still largely intact. Like those of many old Italian cities of its type, this center is in bad physical condition: for all its romantic streetscapes, most of the housing is sadly substandard. The working-class population of this district is, like that of Marais in Paris, largely indigenous; many families have lived here for generations. Yet, largely because of poor living conditions, the younger members of the community have been leaving it in increasing numbers. The municipal government, which has been Communist-controlled almost continuously since World War II, took the position that both the historic center *and* its inhabitants constituted resources of the first order: and that it was the city's obligation to intervene to preserve *both,* the container and the contained, by improving the physical environment, increasing the level of services and amenities, and promoting democratic participation in all decision-making. Therefore, in 1969, it adopted an overall, long-range program of development with the following objectives:

1. Stopping speculation in the periphery and limiting growth, generally through implementation of the city's new master plan.

2. Improving services and recreational space in the center.

3. Financing housing rehabilitation.

4. Restricting growth of tertiary activities in the center and decentralizing commercial and administrative functions.

5. Improving transport links between the center and other parts of the region.

6. Facilitating pedestrian movement in the center.

7. Maintaining a stable, socially mixed population.[6]

The Bologna Plan is unique in Western Europe, according to Angotti and Dale.[7] It takes the position that the city had no justification for continued expansion if it threatened the human quality of urban life. Hence a moratorium was declared on all new construction. The citizens, however, had the right and the need for improved housing. Improved housing had to come from existing housing stock. Since this was concentrated in the historic center, public investment could fulfill a dual task of conserving an artistic and historical heritage of inestimable value and providing improved housing for the working-class population. Publicly financed renovation of old buildings, with a minimum infill of aesthetically congruent new construction, was seen as the best means of accomplishing this. The plan did not go into full effect until 1975, by which time many of its proposals had already been initiated. Whatever the obvious political limitations of the Bologna Plan for the capitalist West, it nevertheless incorporates many architectural and cultural features which merit Western attention.

TOURISM: ASSET AND THREAT TO PRESERVATION

For millennia, the urban rich have been tourists, leaving home to visit the shrines of potent dieties, to take the waters at famous spas, or merely, like Pausanias or Pliny the Elder, to see how foreigners lived. In Europe, cultural tourism has been commonplace among wealthy cognoscenti since the beginning of the seventeenth century. As a matter of fact, it was these cultural tourists—and above all the English, the Russian, and the American—who established the typical travel itineraries of today: Alhambra, Florence, Venice, Rome, Athens. Cultural tourism had already reached such proportions by the end of the eighteenth century as to constitute an important factor in the economic life of these cities. Nevertheless, the volume of such tourist traffic never reached a stage where it posed any serious threat to the continued survival of those centers themselves. It remained for modern life to raise that problem.

People travel today in order to enjoy two broad types of environment:

1. *Natural scenery*—mountains, beaches, fjords, waterfalls, and so on

2. *Man-made scenery*—cities, castles, gardens, churches, museums, galleries, zoos, theaters, operas, concerts, restaurants

Tourism in its broadest sense is one of the major industries of the contemporary world. Certainly it is the major industry of many of the world's largest cities, which are focuses for local, regional, national, and international tourism. By definition, this activity is concentrated in the historic urban core. Here are found structures and complexes which are famous either in their own right (the Louvre, the Hermitage, the Uffizi) or because of the institutions they house (opera houses in Vienna, Milan, Paris, London). The world's greatest religious shrines are almost without exception urbane (Hagia Sophia, Mosque of al-Akbar, Notre Dame, Westminster Abbey), as are the seats of national power (the White House, Westminster, the Kremlin).

These centers have become the generators of the international enterprise of mass cultural tourism. On the one hand, it produces important economic aid to the preservation of the historic and artistic heritages: but, on the other, it has become the greatest single threat to their survival. The paradox is compounded, as we have said, by the fact that the very means of transport which we so deplore are precisely what make mass tourism possible and without which it could not survive.

The objective basis of this new phenomenon is an increasing interest on the part of the citizens of the more advanced countries in the artistic and historic past of their own and other cultures. The increasing leisure in these countries makes it possible for their citizens to indulge this interest by visiting the relics of the past; and since these sites and monuments are overwhelmingly urbane, the new tourism tends to agglutinate in the historic cities of the world—Kyoto, New Orleans, Paris, Leningrad. But in these centers, the sheer volume of visitors during the height of the tourist season begins to threaten their actual physical fabric.

Thus London, with a shortage of low-cost hotels, tried the experiment of allowing young tourists to sleep in its parks; but the wear and tear on the landscaping was so severe that this permission had to be rescinded. In many famous individual monuments, tourist traffic has reached its absolute limits: at Mount Vernon, George Washington's residence, stairs and floors have had to be reinforced to carry the weight of the visitors; and the abrasion of flooring surfaces is so severe that protective membranes must be replaced in a matter of weeks. Faced with the noise, confusion, and downright squalor which such overcrowding often produces, it would be all too easy to reject the whole concept of mass tourism and yearn for a return to the good old days of aristocratic travel.

But as the Second General Assembly of ICOMOS at Oxford in July, 1969, correctly resolved:

> . . . cultural tourism, by creating the conditions for a new humanism, must henceforth be one of the fundamental means, on a universal level, of insuring man's equilibrium and the enrichment of his personality, in a civ-

ilization which, owing to the ever more rapid development of technical progress, may now be daily directed towards the intelligent use of its leisure.[8]

The assembly resolution takes the position that the complex and unprecedented problems posed by mass cultural tourism can be resolved only by comprehensive management programs, tailored to fit local conditions. Mass tourism has been made possible by developments in transportation technology: above all, the large jet plane, the tourist bus, and the private automobile. Without their high-speed, low-cost transportation, the great mass of vacationers would have neither the time nor the money to travel during their limited vacations. But here again, another paradox: the very machines which make these sites and monuments accessible to a mass public jeopardize their continued existence—directly, by their noxious wastes and vibration and now sonic boom; and indirectly, by their tendency to inundate a given area or monument with spectators beyond its physical capacity to support. (The daily summer attendance at the Roman Forum, for example, is physically destroying the footpaths, benches, and landscaping, not to mention the monuments themselves.)

The physical attrition caused by automotive invasion of urban cores, whether historic or contemporary, has reached a degree of urgency which can no longer be met with palliative measures. The crisis is as obvious in Addis Ababa or Lagos as it is in Paris or Rome; but it has reached the most acute stage in the United States, where the almost complete collapse of public transport has paralleled an increasing dependence upon the private automobile. Architects and planners from countries with as yet low per capita ownership of automobiles should study American experience particularly as a guide to what not to do.

Each of the above problems is intricately related to the others; and all are encapsulated in the economic and political structure of each country. Means of effecting a comprehensive program for the preservation of the artistic-historical heritage must therefore extend across a wide range of legislative, institutional, and financial measures.

SPECIAL PROBLEMS OF HISTORIC DISTRICT PRESERVATION

Because of the immense prestige which attaches nowadays to the new, to the technologically advanced, to progress, real or putative, many people tend to regard organized intervention in defense of historic buildings and districts as sentimental or antiquarian—an "unnatural" policy which runs counter to "common sense." Such suppositions often lead people to consider historic preservation as being somehow artificial. The facts of modern life no longer permit such a narrow, mechanically functionalist view of urban development. The sheer volume of tourists who now flock to such centers all over the world is proof of the great hunger of modern people for first-hand contact with the physical evidence of their history. We are beginning to see that the protection of the artistic and historic heritage against the ravages of uncontrolled technology is a fundamental aspect of the curatorial management of the environment as a whole. *The two environments, natural and artificial, are actually complementary halves of the human biosphere.* ★

There is also no denying that these new conceptual approaches to the past imply new tasks of unprecedented complexity for both architect and planner. Historic centers will have to be handled like valuable artifacts, deserving the sort of care and expertise which we have hitherto associated with art museums and galleries. The entire urban tissue is to be placed upon display, and all the devices of modern museology brought to bear upon it. We must recognize that the curatorial approach has inherent limitations when applied to artifacts like buildings or cities. One is the tendency to "prettify" the past. Any museological or curatorial function involves selection and interpretation. The *whole* past could never be displayed, if only for reasons of space and budget. There are also many aspects which could not be replicated or exhibited for reasons of convention and taste: the smell of the burned flesh of the branded slave at Williamsburg or the blood on the headsman's ax at the Tower of London; the mud and garbage of eighteenth-century streets; the flies and ordure (not to mention the truculent bull) of the farmyard. Sanitary and safety regulations would, in any case, prohibit such realistic details.

The restoration of historic urban districts presents aesthetic problems which are not found in the isolated villa or village church. In such cases, the monument still stands in its original visual environment. In some old cities, such as Prague or Vienna, the historic core remains largely intact, undestroyed by nineteenth- and twentieth-century interventions. In such cases, the restoration of old buildings or the insertion of new ones is largely a matter of discretion and good taste. But most of the world's great cities have seen a continuous process of urbanization: here the historic cores have been fragmented (Mexico City, Milan). Formerly uniform streetscapes of

---

★There is, of course, a sense in which such a curatorial function might be called artificial: but so, too, could museums, art galleries, libraries—indeed, the whole apparatus of formal education. In each case, the artifact or theory has been removed from its life context in order to study it. This is in contrast to preliterate societies, where all wisdom is conventional, transmitted either orally or by apprenticeship. But in such societies there is no sense of time or change: each individual thinks of himself or herself as being embedded in the only cultural matrix that ever was. Modern people, on the other hand, need fixed points in their physical environment, landmarks which afford intellectual and emotional orientation in a world of terrifyingly rapid change.

3- and 4-story houses have been interrupted with incongruous replacements, ranging from single-story filling stations to multistory skyscrapers. In many cities, the resulting distortion in scale takes on surrealist proportions, contrasts without precedence in the whole history of architecture.

Yet no one can seriously visualize a return of these urban cores to the small-scaled, low-profiled cityscape of the past. For better or worse, this is the condition the preservationist must face. In such circumstances, many contemporary architects have argued that it is too late to save anything. Or, applying some metaphysical criterion of "consistency," they will argue that the historic fragments which have survived cannot be successfully reintegrated into the changed city. Admittedly, the problem is not without its difficulties, but the fact that such juxtapositions are without historic precedent is not especially relevant. Building and zoning ordinances should be stiffened to prevent the future intrusion of large-scale buildings (such as the skyscrapers around Westminster in London or the cathedral complex in Milan). But the juxtaposition of old and new buildings can often lead to exhilarating new passages in the cityscape—as is obvious in the current redevelopment of Faneuil Hall Square in Boston (Fig. 8.4) or the precincts around St. Paul's in London.

As a result of more than a century's professional activity in the field of historic preservation, it is both necessary and possible to define with precision the various scales and types of technical intervention which are possible—and also to establish norms or criteria for estimating the putative desirability of each. The famous Venice Charter of 1964 made a historic beginning along these lines.[9] While accepting without reservation the general conceptual attitudes embodied in the charter, it is necessary to define the parameters of available measures and techniques in more detail. International experience seems to indicate that the more conservative the intervention, the safer in the long run. But it is obvious that any or all of these techniques will be employed, especially in complex preservation projects such as the rehabilitation of historic urban cores.

6

Preservation, Restoration, Conservation

In the field of historic preservation we confront an entire spectrum of physical intervention in the life of an extant building, with many gradations. To decide upon the precise policy to be followed in curatorial work on any given project therefore depends upon a balanced analysis of several distinct (even if umbilically connected) considerations:

1. *The present physiognomy of the building,* which can be seen as the visual record of everything which has happened to it across time. This accumulated physical evidence—this "track" of additions, deletions, and mutilations—can be viewed as a prime historical resource.

2. *The architectonic or aesthetic integrity of the building in purely formal terms.* Here the present physiognomy is compared to its initial state to determine if its appearance has been strengthened or weakened by "the slings and arrows of outrageous fortune": in other words, whether its current state helps or hinders our comprehension of the aesthetic intentions of the original builders.

3. *The philogeny and morphogenetic development of the artifact across time,* in response to earlier interventions by historically significant events or personalities (e.g., the radical conversion of New York's City Hall into Federal Hall in preparation for Washington's First Inaugural). Such an examination necessarily includes an evaluation of the original significance of the artifact (e.g., "first of its kind") and its contemporary uniqueness (e.g., "last surviving example").

At the level of theory, all three considerations are equally important. In actual practice, a balanced decision is often difficult—the more so because the first two value judgments are sensual or at least based upon sensory perception, while the last is purely cognitive, i.e., knowledge derived from the historical record. The difficulty is reconciling their often contradictory conclusions, which is at the heart of the perennial controversy around such restoration projects as the Capitol and Governor's Palace at Williamsburg

(Fig. 6.6) or the current one around Schermerhorn Row in New York City (Fig. 6.2).

Until recently, the terms "preservation" and "restoration" have been used almost interchangeably. Thus, for example, the Society for the Preservation of New England Antiquities, although founded in 1910, did not find it necessary to make any distinction between these two quite different levels of intervention until recently, when it had become obvious that the ambiguity of terms was much more than a mere problem in semantics. It had led to confusion in the policies followed in the management of the society's properties. In earlier years, there had been the assumption that (funds permitting) each property should be restored to some putatively golden period in its history. This had sometimes led to radical and, as is now all too often apparent, historically inaccurate manipulation of the fabric. Such manipulations have proved to be undesirable in several respects. Not only were many elements of the building removed and discarded, without their having been properly photographed, measured, and cataloged; also, by the same token, the changes became irreversible. As a result of its reexamination of this problem, the SPNEA has recently reformulated its policy toward its holdings and especially toward new acquisitions. This policy calls for keeping any newly acquired properties in precisely the condition in which they are received. The only physical intervention will be those necessary to preserve and maintain the physical integrity of the artifact.

Whether or not one agrees with the society's new policy, one cannot fault the definition of the term "preservation." As can be seen, it coincides with that given in a preceding chapter, "the maintenance of the artifact in the same physical condition as when it was received by the curatorial agency. Nothing is added to or subtracted from the aesthetic corpus. . . ." When analyzed from this point of view, it will be apparent that few of the nation's thousands of historic sites and monuments are simon-pure preservation projects. Upon closer examination, it becomes apparent that many of them will have been altered to meet local (and often amateurish) concepts of "making it look the way it *really* was."

PRESERVATION: THE "SIMPLEST" COURSE OF ACTION

Simple preservation is the most conservative of all levels of curatorial intervention. It is also the safest in the sense of "least done, soonest mended." Of course, even the simplest preservation can involve substantial interventions in the fabric. Fire and security alarm systems may have to be installed. The project's program of interpretation may require the installation of new mechanical systems, e.g., summer cooling. The sheer weight and vibration

6.1. *The world's oldest continuous preservation project,* the Japanese temple complex of Ise Naiku in Honshu Province has been replicated every twenty years since the reign of Emperor Temmu (673–686). Actually a treasure house of the Shinto religion, Ise is built of a pale yellow local cypress. In the humid climate of Japan, untreated timbers sawn of such soft woods have a very short life. Immortality could be won only by periodic replication. On adjacent sites, the new temple *(right, above)* stands ready for dedication, after which the old one will be disassembled to make way for the next.

6.2. *Preservation versus Restoration: the dilemma at New York's Schermerhorn Row.*
Because it represents a radical and irreversible intervention in the life of an old building, restoration is less desirable than preservation. However, there are circumstances in which it might be advisable to return an old building to some specific stage in its morphological development. One might be that it was the scene of a unique historical event; another, that the building is a very rare survivor of a once avant-garde type. Against such museological criteria, Schermerhorn should probably have been restored to its original configuration: instead, an 1869 remodeling into a hotel will be preserved while the remainder of the block will be returned to a status c. 1840.

Schermerhorn Row was begun before 1820 as a part of the new Fulton Street Market (*1*). Although built in increments of ordinary countinghouses for merchants and importers, the row was unprecedented because it was visualized, when finished, as becoming a monumental presence. This ambition on the part of its builders—that of giving a commercial building the urban importance hitherto reserved for churches and palaces—was unique for its time. (Boston's Quincy Market, with much the same ambitions, appeared a few years later: see Fig. 8.4.) As such, Schermerhorn was the precursor of that American institution the "Cathedral of Commerce"—Woolworth, Wrigley, Rockefeller Center. Under such circumstances (first of its type, last of its kind), the architects Jan Pokorny and Robert Burley recommended restoration (*3*): they were overruled; Schermerhorn Row (*4*) was preserved in its 1980's aspect.

1   Schermerhorn Row c. 1825 with new Fulton Market at right.

Schermerhorn Row as it appeared in 1980.

3

Schermerhorn Row: rejected restoration *(above)* and accepted preservation schemes *(below)*.

4

6.3. *The curatorial assignment at the Roosevelt home at Hyde Park* is nominally simple, i.e., to preserve it forever in the same visual condition as when FDR last saw it. In reality, the task is enormously complex. Thus the artifacts in his bedroom—dressing gown, bedspread, photographs, telephone—must be protected from slow and ineluctable attrition due to fading, soiling, and cleaning—not to mention protection against fire, theft, and vandalism. Such curatorial intervention requires every resource of modern conservational science and technology.

of tourists passing through the building may demand structural reinforcing at strategic spots. Such interventions will naturally be kept as nearly invisible as possible. Necessary tubes and wires, ducts and reinforcements will be buried in the fabric so that its aesthetic integrity is as little disturbed as possible.

The Franklin Delano Roosevelt Homesite at Hyde Park, New York, conforms fairly closely to this definition. Given to the nation by the late President's family shortly after his death and managed by the National Park Service ever since, the house, furnishings, and grounds are kept as nearly as possible in their condition at the time of the President's death in April 1945.

George Washington's home, Mount Vernon, today is America's prototypical example of historic preservation (Fig. 6.4). It is by far our oldest continuously operated museum house, the Mount Vernon Ladies' Association having taken possession of it in 1859. After more than a century of operation, it offers a history of changing American attitudes toward the field of historic preservation. It was already one of the best-documented properties in the nation when the association took it over. Washington was himself a very careful manager of the mansion and its farms, taking a personal interest in the day-to-day management and keeping diaries, records, and surveys throughout his life. Moreover, the house was fundamentally intact when the Ladies started work (except for the ravages of weather and the vandalism of early pilgrims to the shrine after the Washington family had ceased to live there).

Anne Pamela Cunningham, that remarkably prescient woman who was the driving force in saving Mount Vernon for posterity, had a very clear understanding of the task. Her policy, clearly formulated in her farewell address, was explicit ("Let no irreverent hands change it; no vandal fingers desecrate it with the touch of progress"), and it has been followed as closely as possible. Thus the mansion had reached its present stage of preservation decades ago. Some of the outbuildings have been restored, as have been the gardens. The greenhouse, which had been burned in 1835, was completely reconstructed in 1930 on the basis of archaeological explorations and documentary research. There have, of course, been subtle shifts across the years in the interpretation of Anne Pamela Cunningham's final abjurations. These are most apparent in the decorative schemes followed in the mansion. An ongoing policy of acquisition aims at returning to the house every artifact which can be surely identified with Washington's tenancy. Most changes in the property as a whole have been due to increased knowledge of the morphological development of the house and its contents. Other modifications have been required by environmental attrition and the sheer wear and tear of over 1 million visitors annually. But generally speaking, the curatorial policy followed at Mount Vernon has been one of astonishing consistency.

The Mount Vernon formula has been followed in a number of other preservation projects, most notably at Monticello, Thomas Jefferson's home near Charlottesville, Virginia (Fig. 6.5), and the Hermitage, Andrew Jackson's home near Nashville, Tennessee. It is significant that all three of these monuments have been preserved by private organizations of women, without any assistance from governmental agencies.

TWO "CLASSICAL" RESTORATIONS: WILLIAMSBURG AND INDEPENDENCE HALL

The most significant American restoration project is Colonial Williamsburg in Virginia: not only because it is the largest but also because it has been, from the start, the best-financed and most professionally staffed operation

6.4. *Mount Vernon, the nation's oldest preservation project,* began in 1858, when a group of farsighted women led by Ann Pamela Cunningham—despairing of being able to persuade either the Congress or the state of Virginia to save the mansion—decided to do it themselves. Thus the Mount Vernon Ladies' Association has become itself a historical phenomenon, meriting study by today's preservationists. Its 130-year history reflects quite accurately the nation's changing attitudes toward its historic and artistic heritage and a growing understanding of what must be done to save it.

The association has adhered quite literally to Ann Cunningham's parting admonition that "those who go to the home in which [Washington] lived and died, wish to see in what he lived and died." But, as the pioneer in the field, the association had to develop pragmatically its own methodology for meeting Ann Cunningham's admonition. For to preserve this old wood-framed mansion in the exact visual condition in which Washington saw it has required radical interventions into the fabric itself. They had neccessarily to be invisible. Thus the main stairway had to be strengthened with a hidden steel armature to carry the thousands who climb it daily instead of the twenty or thirty persons who would have used it in Washington's time.

As a basis for its restoration, Mount Vernon offered the best documentation of any building in America. Washington himself was a voluminous correspondent, inveterate diarist, and careful record keeper. Thousands of visitors, during his lifetime and afterward, painted, photographed, and described the house and grounds (2 to 7).Out of such materials, the association has built up an impressive archive. At first largely antiquarian in emphasis, these data have increasingly become the basis for scientific curatorial policies—enabling the association, for example, to know which of the eleven trees in the Oval (1) survive from Washington's day. The same policies have led to the creation of a definitive collection of Washingtoniana inside the mansion. If it has not yet retrieved every letter, candlestick, or china teacup known to have been owned by Washington, it knows where they are and hopes eventually to acquire them by purchase or gift.

2 West Front c. 1792. Painting by unknown artist.

3 East Front, 1796. Watercolor by Benjamin Latrobe.

4 East Front, c. 1830. Sketch by A. J. Davis.

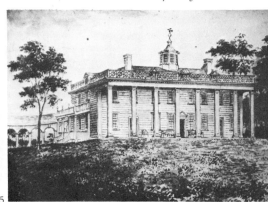

5 East Front, 1858. Painting by Ferdinand Richardt.

6 East Front, c. 1858. Photographer unknown.

7 East Front, 1861. Lithograph by J. Kern.

Conjectural development of mansion, 1757–1787, by Norman W. Isham.

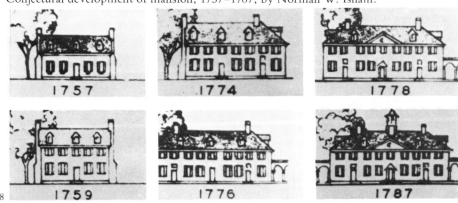

8 1757   1774   1778
  1759   1776   1787

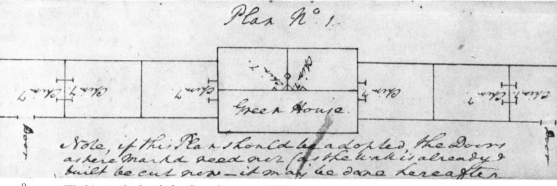

9   Washington's sketch for Greenhouse, c. 1785.

10

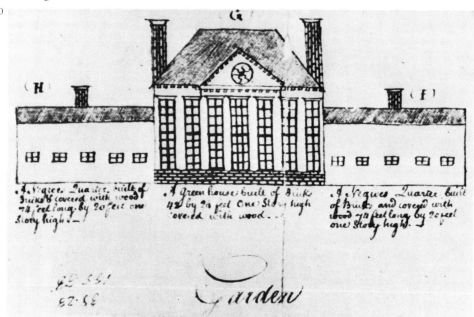

Sketch for fire insurance policy, 1803 *(above)*.

Sketch of ruins by Benson J. Lossing, 1835.

11

6.4 (Continued). *Reconstruction of the long-vanished Greenhouse* at Mount Vernon was also based on extensive documentation. An advanced horticulturist as well as a progressive gardener and farmer, Washington was well read on developments at home and abroad. (He had purchased Batty Langley's *Principles of Gardening* as early as 1759.) He himself sketched the plan for the Greenhouse (*9*). One of the first in the country, it employed both south-facing glass for passive solar heating and a wood-fired furnace and hypocaust. The reconstruction was completed in 1952 after extensive archaeology. (For details on flower and vegetable gardens, see Figs. 13.11.1, 13.11.2.)

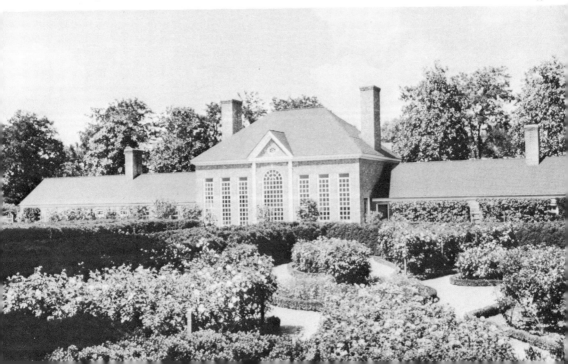

6.4 (Continued). *Changing concepts of "what the past was really like"* are very striking in the archives of as old an institution as the Mount Vernon Restoration. Thus an 1860 engraving of the Banquet Hall *(above)* tells us more about Victorian taste than Washington's. Developments in both scholarly and scientific research make possible a more accurate understanding of the past and putatively a more "accurate" re-creation of it *(below)*. But it must be assumed that the subjective factor can never be fully eliminated from curatorial decisions, now or in the future.

of its kind. At its half-century mark (it was begun in 1927), the Colonial Williamsburg Restoration constitutes a kind of paradigm of American experience because it has incorporated every level of curatorial intervention, from preservation of extant buildings to outright reconstruction of long-vanished monuments.

As is well known, a cutoff date for the restoration of Williamsburg was established, early on, at 1775—that being the year in which the town ceased to be the capital of Virginia, the seat being transferred to Richmond. That date is also the reason for the use of the word "Colonial" in the official name. This programmatic decision was interpreted to mean that all buildings or changes in buildings which were post-1775 were to be excised. It was interpreted to mean that all pre-1775 buildings were to be returned to their prerevolutionary status. And finally, it was interpreted to mean that vanished pre-1775 buildings which would be important to the scenographic or historical interpretation of the town were to be reconstructed.

The rationale for this policy of preservation-restoration-reconstruction was entirely plausible. For example, the long-lost Capitol and the Governor's Palace, together with the still-extant if badly mutilated William and Mary College, formed the monumental finials to the T-shaped system of axes around which the town plan was organized. It was a typical baroque conception in which the seats of secular power and academic learning acted as endpieces to the two avenues, whose intersection was appropriately monitored by the parish church (religious authority) and garrison headquarters (military power). The founders of the Williamsburg Restoration felt that the town would not have been intelligible, either visually or conceptually, without these monumental termini. On this rationale, the Governor's Palace and the Capitol were totally reconstructed. The college was radically altered to restore its pre-1775 appearance.

But the arguments against these reconstructed facsimiles were also substantial. The first, most obvious, was that no one knew what these long-vanished buildings had looked like: the palace was destroyed by fire in 1781, the Capitol in 1832.[1] There was massive archival material, but it was textual, not pictorial. Archaeology quickly established the siting and spatial organization of the buildings. But it was not until 1929 that a researcher in the Bodleian Library in Oxford discovered a single engraving on which the façades of all three buildings were depicted. This was to be the only pictorial documentation uncovered;[2] none was ever found for the monumental interiors. Hence a large proportion of the fabric of both the palace and the Capitol is a completely hypothetical infill of the scaffolding furnished by the foundation walls and the Bodleian print. Many critics have continued to feel that this was an inadequate basis for the reconstruction of such complex and visually important monuments.

Through the historical accident of having been abandoned by the state government, Williamsburg became a backwater southern village for a century and a half, far removed from the vertiginous impact of urban expansion which largely destroyed so much colonial urban tissue. In 1927, nearly 100 buildings dating from prerevolutionary times were still standing. Some of them—including the James City County Courthouse (also known as the court of hustings)—were in such sound and unmutilated condition that only simple preservation was required. The majority of the houses, however, required varying degrees of restoration—e.g., removal of post-1775 porches, re-creation of pre-1775 chimneys—to return them to their prerevolutionary appearance. The gardens, grounds, and urban landscape generally are almost wholly hypothetical reconstructions.

The Williamsburg we see today is a beguiling mixture of the preserved, the restored, and the reconstructed. And this confronts us with the first paradox: the fact that today's town, for all its sensuous verisimilitude, never existed at any given point in time or space. Its historical evolution has been telescoped, large portions have been excised, and the balance has been frozen. The present-day streetscapes—even though they are composed of authentic antiques, excellently restored and excellently conserved—are in one sense fictitious. There are other anomalies: the relative absence of workaday activities and artifacts; the improbably high level of maintenance and housekeeping; the snobbish connoisseurship of much of the interpretive program.

Yet it must be remembered that many of Williamsburg's problems are endemic to the museological process itself. The whole concept of the outdoor architectural museum is a relatively new one, as we shall see in Chapter 10; and the current interest in active, working demonstrations of process rather than inert displays of artifacts is an even later development. There is nowadays a new emphasis on this aspect of interpretation at Williamsburg. There is, for example, a working brick kiln. But considerations of public health and hygiene prevent many eighteenth-century processes from being revived, e.g., the sale of flour from demonstration mills or of butter and milk from cow barns. Problems of safety limit the extent to which domestic animals could be used to lend verisimilitude to the streetscapes. The droves of cattle, sheep, and geese which in prerevolutionary days were permitted to graze freely in the town would offer real hazards to children unaccustomed to contact with animals outside of the zoo.

But the most egregious didactic error of the Colonial Williamsburg Restoration has been its evasion of a crucial aspect of its history: the fact that its culture and economy alike were based upon the institution of human slavery. The reasons for ignoring the "peculiar institution" are readily apparent, since black slavery stands in such squalid contradiction to the upper-class white urbanity celebrated in this provincial capital. Many of the routine incidents of slavery—slave markets and slave snaffles, chain gangs and brandings, not to mention miscegenation and lynching—are too ugly to be recreated or displayed by normal museological techniques. In the con-

6.5. *The struggle to save Thomas Jefferson's beloved Monticello* repeated almost verbatim the earlier battles for Mount Vernon. After years of unsuccessful efforts to persuade either the U.S. Congress or the Virginia state Legislature to intervene, a small band of citizens finally raised the necessary funds to take title in 1923. In subsequent years the Thomas Jefferson Memorial Foundation has completed the structural renovation of the mansion and the restoration of its interiors, gardens, and grounds, bringing them up to a level of technical perfection unsurpassed in the nation.

Unlike most historic house museums, Monticello has in recent years paid its own way. In fact, the foundation found itself with surplus funds above those required to maintain and operate the house. It therefore decided to apply these funds to support a broad program of Jeffersonian studies. Working with the University of Virginia—housed in Jefferson's other architectural masterpiece, the campus at Charlottesville—the foundation now supports fellowships in history, political science, and architecture. Working with the University, it has established new professorships in both history and architecture. Since 1959 it has annually funded the purchase of manuscripts dealing with Jefferson and Monticello. It has assisted in the acquisition of more than three-quarters of the books in Jefferson's own library. More recently the foundation has established the Thomas Jefferson Memorial Medal for distinguished contemporary work. Thus, in a highly innovative manner, the foundation has used Monticello to cultivate two distinct constituencies: the many tourists who visit the mansion annually, and the smaller but culturally important circles of scholars interested in studying Jefferson both as architect and statesman. By such activities, the foundation has extended its sphere of influence far beyond the usual reach of the historic house museum.

1

6.6. The return of an entire town to an earlier stage in its historical development has not been accomplished anywhere more completely, and with more competence and skill, than in Williamsburg, Virginia. In the half century since the project began in 1929, it has become the paradigm of American restoration—a project whose most beguiling aspects are, at the same time, its most controversial. The initial decision to restore the town to its pre-1776 state seemed logical, since that was the date when it ceased to be the state capital. (It was this sudden loss of political function that was to preserve it, like a fly in amber, and make its restoration so much easier 150 years later!)

As the largest, best-funded, and most professional project of its kind, Williamsburg has an impressive record of archival and archaeological research. Thus the present condition of the intersection of Palace Green and Duke of Gloucester Street *(above)* is based on such documents as the 1753 map *(below)*, showing most of today's features.

2

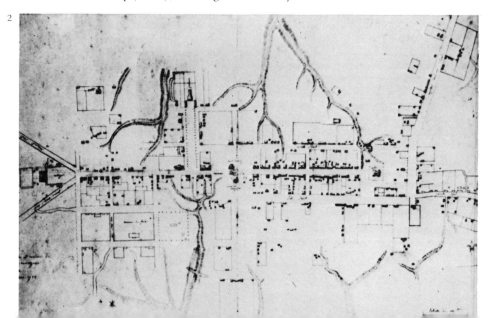

3

4

Two views of Duke of Gloucester Street in Williamsburg—one made c. 1929, the other c. 1965—clearly show the transmutation from a seedy little backwater town into a wealthy provincial capital. The results are physically most attractive, as millions of tourists will testify. But a troubling question remains: Did the street ever look like this at any given point in time? Today's streetscape is composed of buildings and gardens, all of which have been carefully researched and conserved or reconstructed. They are also furnished and maintained in first-class condition—all of which suggests a simultaneity of well-being that would seldom if ever have occurred. This tendency to purify and telescope historic processes is a paradox that no outdoor architectural museum can ever fully escape. But a comprehensive interpretational program, employing guided walking tours and carefully researched documentary films, can establish a more balanced view of the past.

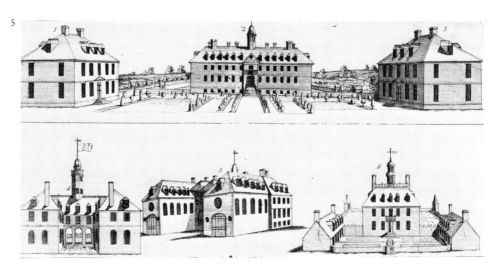

6.6 (Continued). *Like most Renaissance town plans, that of Williamsburg* deployed its monumental buildings in symbolic representation of the relationships among religious, political, military, and cultural institutions. Thus the main axes were Duke of Gloucester Street, leading from the College of William and Mary to the Capitol. This axis was intersected at midpoint by the Palace Green, with the Governor's Palace at the end and the church, courthouse, and armory clustered around the intersection. When planning for the restoration began in the late 1920s, two of these monumental structures were missing altogether (palace and Capitol); college, church, and courthouse survived, albeit in degraded state. The consensus at that time was that, without these key buildings restored to their original role in the cityscape, the town would not be intelligible to the visitor. Hence the decision was made to reconstruct and restore all of them to their pre-1776 state.

Archival material was voluminous on all of them. Archaeology soon exposed the location and shape of the long-vanished palace and Capitol: but visual information was missing until a researcher working at the Bodleian Library at Oxford University came across a key document—the so-called Bodleian Print (5). This depicted the exteriors of college, palace, and Capitol with fair accuracy. By correlating this information with other data, reconstruction of them became possible. Thus the townscape is again delimited by the focal points that were the raison d'être of the plan.

College of William and Mary *(left)*; Governor's Palace *(above)*; Provincial Capitol *(below)*.

9

10

6.6 *(Continued). The 1776 "cut-off" date applied to both the town* as a whole and its individual buildings. This led to the removal of all postrevolutionary additions, the repair of all mutilations, and the reconstruction of all vanished pre-1776 elements. In cases like that of the Brush-Everard house, c. 1717, this meant only the removal of a nineteenth-century porch and dormer and the replacement of the latter with an accurate replica *(above)*. Sometimes it led to the demolition of entire post-1776 buildings—e.g., center house in *(11)*. But the cumulative expertise of Williamsburg professionals is apparent in their handling of the Prentis store *(11)*. Initially it was restored to the condition shown in *(12)*. But increasing doubts about the accuracy of this restoration led to its being closed. More exhaustive research led to important revisions *(13)*. The shop floor was raised to the level of the brick water table; a new wood-framed roofless stoop replaced the earlier brick platform; and normal 12-over-12 wood sash replaced the bow-front shop windows. Such ongoing reexamination of earlier curatorial decisions, in the light of increasing knowledge and experience, is evident also in changing practices in landscape and garden design and maintenance. Today's policy aims at maximum authenticity and verisimilitude in both the artifact on display and its interpretation.

11

12

13

103

text of contemporary black consciousness, even black employees dressed in historic costumes of butler and cook are apt to be offensive. And yet, sooner or later, the problem must be faced. Perhaps here, as elsewhere in the American South (Mount Vernon, Monticello, Carter's Grove), the best way to interpret this important aspect of our history would be through the use of carefully researched documentary films and the sale of appropriate brochures and monographs.

THE RESTORATION OF INDEPENDENCE HALL

Quite appropriately, the historic monument which has been the most recent focus of American expertise in the field of restoration has been Independence Hall in Philadelphia. In a ten-year campaign ending in 1976, this little baroque palace was subjected to detailed historical, morphological, and physical examination. In the process, a wide range of serious structural weaknesses were revealed, many of them, ironically, due to earlier "restorations." These required such radical surgery that, in the end, the building was eviscerated. Only the roof and all major masonry walls were left intact. All interior surfaces—paneling, ornamental plaster and woodwork, mantelpieces and stairs—were carefully removed. Each element was photographed, measured, described, and stored. As in an archaeological excavation, this sort of analysis made it possible to reconstruct the complicated morphological evolution through which the structure had gone since its beginnings in 1732.

Only when this process had been completed was it possible to prepare comprehensive working drawings for the reconstruction of the fabric. To consolidate such seriously weakened elements as floors, roof, and bell tower—as well as to "beef up" resistance to the load of thousands of tourists who pass through the hall daily—a steel armature was inserted into the floors, walls, and roof. Only then was it possible to reinstall the decorative surfaces. The cosmetic consequences of this radical intervention are dramatic. Naturally, in an artifact with so long and complex a history as Independence Hall, it was impossible literally to return every single element to its pre-1776 condition. But the overall objective was to give the entire fabric as nearly as possible its appearance on July 4, 1776.

CONSERVATION OF BUILDINGS

Conservation, as we have seen, is a highly specialized aspect of the broader field of historic preservation. It has been defined as "physical intervention in the actual fabric of the building to ensure its continued structural integ-

6.7 *The Major Agents of Physical Deterioration.* Photochemical and electrochemical actions result from the collaboration of physical and chemical agents. Biological agents use physical-chemical means to ingest and digest matter. Natural aging (promoted by joint action of many, though not necessarily all, of the environmental agents) is a gradual alteration involving changes in the properties and chemical state of materials. It is characterized by color and volumetric changes, loss of cohesive and adhesive strength, and embrittlement.

Chemical	Physical	Biological
Oxygen	Radiant energy	Vegetation
Ozone	Sunlight	Algae
	Ultraviolet	Bacteria
Carbon dioxide	Infrared	Fungi
		Lichens
Sulfur dioxide	Heat (high)	Plant roots
Hydrogen sulfide	Cold (frost)	
Acids, alkalies, salts (airborne or in solution)	Cycles of heat and cold	Insects
		Ants
		Moths
Water	Abrasives	Silverfish
Ground water	Dirt, soil particles	Termites
Cleaning solutions	Airborne dust and smoke	Wood beetles
Organic solvents	Water	Rodents
	Liquid	
	Vapor	Man
	Cycles of relative humidity	
	Matter in motion	
	Mechanical stress	
	Impact shock	
	Wave or mechanical vibrations	

SOURCE: Sheldon Keck, "Life Expectancy of Materials and Problems of Increasing Visitor Use," *Preservation and Conservation,* The Preservation Press, Washington, D.C., 1976, p. 332.

rity." Modern science and technology offer the architectural conservationist an unprecedented range of diagnostic tools and therapeutic measures which would have been inconceivable only a few decades ago. These make it possible, in theory at least, to reclaim even seriously damaged building fabrics and extend their effective life for decades into the future.

All human artifacts, like all material objects generally, are subject to the continuous and ineluctible attrition of the terrestrial environment. These forces are bewilderingly complex, as is apparent from Keck's chart, above. Their action can never be halted; only the consequences can be minimized by continual care and maintenance. To date, most conservation expertise has developed under laboratory con-

1

6.8. *For all its pivotal role in our history, Independence Hall has had a precarious life.* Its aesthetic and physical integrity was repeatedly violated by extensive remodelings and "restorations"; and it narrowly missed sale and demolition before achieving its present sacrosanct status. Built in 1732–1735, the Pennsylvania State House was the scene of the deliberations that led to the Declaration of Independence. The "cut-off" date for any definitive restoration would therefore necessarily be July 4, 1776. The 1960 campaign of restoration-cum-consolidation was forced by the fragile state of the fabric. The brick shell was almost completely eviscerated, interior details, finishes, and surfacings being peeled away as in an archaeological excavation. Each stage was photographed and written up in a daily log.

A cardinal rule was that as much of the original fabric as possible had to be preserved. Thus a new steel armature was interwoven into the sagging wooden floors and roofs (*3*). Original wood paneling—supplemented where necessary by replicated elements—was then reinstalled (*4*). The current appearance of the Assembly Room corresponds as closely as possible to pictorial and written descriptions of its state on that fateful day. But none of the furniture is actually associated with the room and some of it is replicated (*2*).

2

ditions, carried on with small artifacts destined for the controlled climate of the museum. Under such circumstances, diagnosis can be precise and therapy can be exactly practiced. The sheer size of buildings, and the fact that they stand in the uncontrolled climate of the outdoors, precludes the mechanical application of art conservation to architecture. Nevertheless, it is to the art conservator that architectural conservators must turn for basic principles.[3]

Fortunately, architectural fabrics, unlike works of art, must have a minimum structural durability in order to resist the mechanical forces of gravity and wind; they are thus automatically resistant, in one degree or another, to all the other forces described in Keck's formulation. Nevertheless, they also age and display all the pathologies of aging: and these increase in both variety and severity with rising levels of environmental pollution. Thus the conservationist will be increasingly called upon to intervene in safeguarding the physical integrity of historically or artistically significant buildings.

Generally speaking, traditional American architectural fabrics are of two broad types: monolithic mass masonry and skeletal or composite structures. They were fabricated of varying amounts and combinations of the following materials:

1. Wood
2. Metals: cast iron, wrought iron, modern steels; copper and sheet metal
3. Masonry: stone, brick, ceramics, concrete
4. Earth: mud brick, adobe, *terra pisé*

For either decorative or protective reasons, most of these structural systems were sheathed internally and/or externally with applied membranes. Thus:

1. Floors: wood, tile, brick, stone
2. Walls: plaster (painted, papered), wood, glass, masonry
3. Roofs: shingles (wood, slate, tile), sheet metals (copper, lead, steel), built-up membranes (felt, asphalt, plastics)

Each of these materials has its own physical and chemical characteristics. Each has its own pathologies. Each has its own specialized routines of therapy and maintenance.[4]

CONSERVATION OF WOODEN FABRICS

The overwhelming majority of American buildings have always been (and still are) of wood. Even those historic buildings whose exterior walls are of brick or stone will usually have floors, interior partitions, and roofs framed of wood. Hence the conservationist will typically deal with a wide variety of wood structures in various states of physical deterioration. The agents of attrition are varied and complex, the more so because they interact with one another.[5] But exactly *how* one is to conserve a given wooden artifact—i.e., the profundity of intervention—will depend upon two quite different considerations, cosmetic and structural. The two are by no means identical: thus, continuous painting of a wooden beam might well conceal grave structural weaknesses due to fungi or insect attack; whereas many a shabby wooden wall is structurally sound, needing only a good coat of paint "to make it look like new."

When the failure is structural, radical intervention may be mandatory: the member must be either repaired or replaced. If the member is concealed, as by a parquet floor or paneled wall or plaster ceiling, it might actually be preferable to replace it with a new one. It might be necessary to reinforce or even to replace the wooden member with a steel one. In both cases, it must be branded or stamped to identify it securely for future curators. This was found necessary in the recent restoration of Independence Hall, where the greatly increased floor loads due to tourists required the insertion of a steel armature.

Where the failing member has great historical, associational, or artistic significance, consolidation of the original fabric may be mandatory, no matter how costly or complicated the intervention. This is a fairly common problem in art conservation, where valuable paintings or decorative polychromy exist on wooden backings which have been desiccated by insect or fungal attack. The most dramatic application of this process to large structures occurred in the early 1960s when the Swedish government decided to conserve the warship *Vasa,* a 1,400-ton vessel which had sunk in Stockholm harbor on its maiden voyage in 1628. After a long and delicate operation, the wreck was raised to the surface and towed to a specially built dry dock, where, in saturated atmospheres, it was injected from stem to stern with polyethylene glycol. Thus consolidated, the wooden structure and all its equipment now constitute a unique museum of naval history (Fig. 7.7).

Such a total consolidation is far too complex and costly for any but the most valuable artifacts. But the technique could be readily employed in the consolidation of isolated structural members, such as exposed beams and trusses which might have rotted from leaking roofs and gutters. Where such members are visible and patching or bracing therefore undesirable, there is the possibility of inserting plastic rods, in much the same way as steel is used to reinforce concrete, before the desiccated member is injected. The result is a reinforced, reconstituted member.

Effective chemical means now exist for treating wood against moisture, fire, insects, and fungi. Such chemotherapy is complex, sometimes costly, and sometimes hazardous.[6] It is naturally much simpler when the artifacts are small and can be treated under the controlled conditions of a laboratory.

But entire buildings can be treated in situ, as was recently demonstrated in the fumigation of the restored Royal Palace in Honolulu to rid this wooden structure of termites.

American buildings of monumental pretensions, during the eighteenth and nineteenth centuries, were often wooden facsimiles of masonry proto-types. Many of their decorative elements—balustrades, balconies, cornices, and entablatures—have many unprotected joints in which ice and water can accumulate. They thus present serious problems in conservation. Replacements in wood require skilled craftspersons and are short-lived out of doors, especially where flashing and caulking are difficult. Under such circumstances, molded fiberglass replicas from casts of the wood originals are being increasingly employed. Although the ultimate life-span of such replicas is not securely established, they have a number of advantages: they are dimensionally stable; they are rust- and rot-resistant; and they do not support combustion. Being impermeable, they are moistureproof, and they may be painted like wood.

The precise cosmetic condition to which old wooden fabrics are to be returned by conservation must be based upon careful sociocultural examination of their historical origins. This is especially important in architectural polychromy: laboratory analysis of paint samples is important. But it should be remembered that paint itself was a luxury which most vernacular architecture could not afford until after the Revolution. In the countryside, the appearance of painted buildings would be even later in time. Hence most wooden surfaces (clapboards, shingles, board-and-batten) would have lacked the protection of paint and would have become warped, weathered, and cracked quite early on. The aesthetic consequences of such a condition are discussed in Chapter 11.

CONSERVATION OF MASONRY FABRICS

Although masonry (brick, rubble, cut stone) is dominant visually in the American streetscape, it is stereometrically quite primitive when compared to the Gothic churches and Renaissance palaces of Europe. The typical nine-teenth-century American load-bearing wall will range from 12 inches to 16 inches in section (for brick); and from 24 inches to 36 inches in rubble-stone masonry. In such simple masonry forms, conservation problems will normally only be cosmetic; and structural failure, even when it occurs, will be immediately evident on the surface. Thus, the conservation of vernacular masonry will lie well within the competence of the skilled mason—provided he has the technical training outlined in the new courses described in Chapter 18. The conservation and maintenance of traditional brick and stone masonry has been the subject of an increasingly wide technical literature.[7]

6.9. *Antique wooden structural members can have such important associative or aesthetic values* that conservation of the actual integument is mandatory. Often they are seriously deteriorated as a consequence of insect or fungal attack, so that until recently their preservation has been either extremely difficult or even impossible. The development of a new family of synthetic resins, with remarkable cohesive and adhesive powers, now affords the possibility of reconstituting such members.

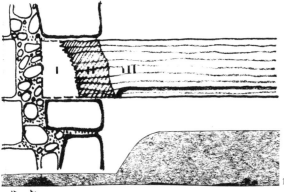

Epoxy resins—water-clear, inert, and dimensionally stable—can be injected into the desiccated wood, filling the interstices and creating in effect a new material.

A new variation of this technique can be used in cases where the bearing of a wooden beam has rotted in its masonry socket (*1*).

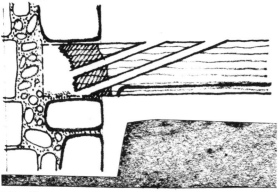

Holes are drilled through sound wood into rotted wood (*2*).

Plastic rods of smaller diameter are inserted in holes, extending into the socket (*3*).

Epoxy resin is injected into cavities, desiccated wood, and space around rods (*4*).

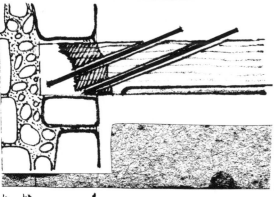

The resin, when cured, produces a reinforced wooden member as strong as or stronger than new. The intervention is invisible: the wood can be sanded, painted, or polished to match the rest of the member.

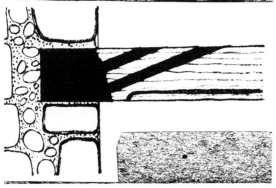

In Europe, the proportion of monumental structures built of solid stone masonry is vastly larger than in the United States; and obviously most of them are vastly older. Thus the European conservationist faces a much wider range of more serious problems than his American colleague—from the care of the pedimental sculptures in the Parthenon, to the conservation of such great cathedrals as those of Rouen and Chartres, down to the care of such comparatively modern structures as St. Paul's Cathedral in London. The physical integrity of these monuments is at risk. It is likewise apparent that the *rate* of attrition to which they are subjected is rising alarmingly all around the world. (The deterioration of the Parthenon has been as large, if not indeed larger, in the century and a half since Lord Elgin took the marbles to London, than in the entire preceding 2 millennia since they were carved!) As we have seen (Fig. 6.7), a bewildering array of factors is involved in the weathering process, and it is now obvious that many of these pathogenic forces are new, the consequence of environmental pollution by urbanization, industry, and transportation.

The attrition of stone is so widespread that the whole syndrome has been dubbed "stone disease," and scientists in many countries are trying to isolate the specific pathogens and develop the appropriate therapies. A vast literature is the result. Because of the relative newness and modest nature of most American brick and stone masonry buildings, conservation is often a matter of nothing more than cleaning and repointing for aesthetic rather than structural reasons. Cleaning methods have been summarized by Theodore H. M. Prudon, who gives the relative advantages and shortcomings of each method: dry grit blasting; wet grit blasting; water washing; steam cleaning; chemical cleaning with acid, alkaline, and organic cleaners.[8]

CONSERVATION OF TERRA-COTTA

One special form of ceramic material which enjoyed wide popularity in American architecture c. 1880–1920 was terra-cotta. Fabricated both as hollow tile for fireproofing steel skeletons and as an exterior surfacing material with a fired-on vitreous glaze, it was used extensively in such prestigious skyscrapers as the Wrigley Building in Chicago and the Woolworth Tower in New York. It was commonly assumed to be an "eternal" material, as long-lived as the famous faience Lion Gates at Persopolis. But unhappily, most American cities have much more difficult climates than Iran, with wide diurnal and seasonal temperature fluctuations, along with frosts, high winds, and heavy precipitation. The result is that terra-cotta surfacings on hundreds of great American buildings are now showing signs of serious failure, especially in the northern part of the country. The major cause of

6.10. Insect infestation is a real and present danger to wooden buildings in the tropics. During the restoration of Iolani Palace, the last nineteenth-century seat of the Hawaiian dynasty in Honolulu, it was discovered that the wood-framed floors and roof were actively infested with termites. To eliminate them from the structure, it was decided to fumigate the palace under pressure. Since the most effective gases were lethal, it was decided to encase the entire structure in a sealed plastic tent. With the insects eliminated, infested wooden members could be impregnated with chemical insecticides, damaged elements removed and replaced with new wood.

2

6.11. Tallest and most splendid of skyscrapers when it was opened in 1913, the Woolworth Tower is undergoing cosmetic surgery on its neo-Gothic façades. The polychromed terra-cotta blocks with which it was sheathed—once considered to be the most durable of building materials because of their impervious vitreous glazing—began to show serious signs of failure just half a century later. When ornamental crockets started falling off the pinnacles, they were wrapped in nylon mesh (*1*), and a long-range research program of the cause and the cure began. A foot-by-foot examination of the exterior revealed characteristic signs of distress: the vitreous glaze was spalled, blistered, crazed, and cracked. Under the vicious freeze-thaw cycles of wet New York winters, the bond between the glaze and its porous underbody had failed. This permitted moisture to migrate through the underbody to the metal cramps that held the block in place (*4*). A growing crust of rust on the metal led to internal pressures on the block, thus guaranteeing further deterioration.

Such processes, once begun, cannot be either halted or reversed. Across the years, ad hoc efforts to repair failing blocks with cementatious grouting or caulking had proved to be both temporary and unsightly (*5*). Replacement of all terra-cotta seemed therefore inevitable— though not necessarily all at one time. But replacement with what? Aside from the fact that the terra-cotta industry had all but disappeared, the failure of the original material hardly argued for a repeat. Synthetics such as fiberglass were rejected because of as yet unproven durability and life-span. Concrete seemed the logical alternative. By strict control of mixing formulae and fabrication methods, facsimile blocks can be made that excel the strength of the terra-cotta and closely match its color and texture. To minimize rust, the new blocks are attached by means of stainless-steel anchors. The actual restoration process will presumably be continuous until all terra-cotta has been replaced. But after the first campaign to correct dangerous conditions (mostly in the tower above the forty-eighth floor), replacement can be phased to meet ongoing rates of attrition.

3

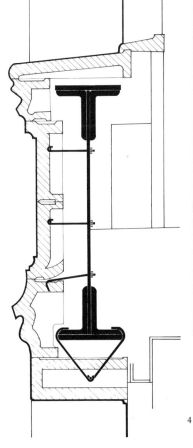

5

4

115

the problem seems to be a different coefficient of expansion between the vitreous glaze and the burned-clay body. This leads to cracking, chipping, and spawling, which in turn permit water to penetrate into the wall. Aside from expanding and contracting with the freeze-thaw cycle, this also leads to rusting of the metal cramps which hold the terra-cotta in place. The disastrous consequences of this process are to be seen on the Woolworth Tower, yet, because of the relative newness of the problem, there are no established methods of conservation. In a recent paper on the subject, John Dixon suggests several alternatives, including replacement of damaged terra-cotta units with fiberglass-reinforced plastic or fiberglass-reinforced concrete ones.[9]

CONSERVATION OF CONCRETE FABRICS

Reinforced concrete is a relatively new structural material (its invention is commonly attributed to the Frenchman Joseph Monier in 1867). Its use as an architectural medium, that is, employed for its own textural and color-istic values rather than concealed behind conventional sheathing, is even more recent. Because of these factors, we have little experience in conserv-ing it against either cosmetic or structural failure. Thus the recent conser-vation work on Unity Temple in Oak Park, Illinois, is of unusual interest. This famous building designed by Frank Lloyd Wright was one of the first to exploit the new material for its own inherent aesthetic properties: in Wright's own words, "to be cast complete, ornament and all, in forms— and to be 'let alone' as 'Architecture' after the forms were removed." It was a monolithic structure using a pea-gravel aggregate throughout the entire mass. After the formwork was removed, the surface had been washed and brushed to expose this aggregate, giving the building its distinctive texture.

Over the years, cracks developed in the structure, partly due to settle-ment and partly to temperature stresses. The concrete itself was porous, with many small voids between the particles of aggregate: because of this, steel reinforcing bars near the surface rusted and caused extensive spalling and cracking. In 1961, the first efforts were made to conserve the structure. At that time, according to Robert Bell, architect of the recent conservation, " . . . the walls were coated with a concrete mix and bonding agent which looked more like stucco and did not resemble the appearance of the original wall material. The entire structure, including decorative details, was coated with a portland cement paint containing an admixture used as a bonding agent. Further deterioration of the structure was arrested but the original color and texture of the concrete was lost. In addition old cracks continued to open up. A waterproofing solution was used in an attempt to seal them but it created permanent unsightly tape-like patterns on the walls."

Several techniques for restoration of the surface were explored. One involved

> . . . removing the cement coating from the buildings and then repairing the surface with a flash coat of sand-cement shotcrete after cracks and spalled areas were repaired. The flash coat would then be abrasive blasted to reveal the original aggregate. The sample using this technique was not satisfactory, primarily because of the great difficulty in usually blending repairs with the original wall surfaces.
>
> Other methods were also tried. It was found that hand-applied concrete mixes did not bond well to the original wall, even though they duplicated the original satisfactorily.
>
> Samples using epoxy bonding agents and hand-applied aggregate bonded extremely well to the original wall, but the long-term performance of the epoxy was questioned and the texture was not a satisfactory restoration of the appearance of the original wall.

The technique finally adopted was a two-stage process. First the 1961 cement coating was etched away to expose the original pea-gravel aggregate: this was accomplished by heavy abrasive blasting, using a slag grit. Then a new surface was pneumatically applied, using a liquid cement mix with a pea-gravel aggregate, to a depth not exceeding ¾ inch. This coating was troweled smooth, then blasted again with slag, to expose the pea-gravel aggregate. Although protective coatings of silicone and acrylic were tested, the material finally adopted was linseed oil in two coats, the first cut 50 percent with mineral spirits, the second undiluted. The resulting surface closely resembles the original.[10]

CONSERVATION OF METAL FABRICS

The conservation of metal structures, like that of reinforced concrete, is another comparatively recent phenomenon and for much the same reasons. Metal skeletons—first in cast iron, then in wrought iron, finally in steel—appeared only after the first quarter of the last century. They were usually employed in either commercial or industrial buildings, where they have only recently begun to be recognized as either historically or aesthetically significant. Besides this, after a series of disastrous fires, it became apparent that steel skeletons had to be encased in a shell of masonry fireproofing. Thus, though the steel frame made possible the visually dominant skyscraper, the frame itself played no direct role in its aesthetic impact. Only in such exoskeletal structures as the Brooklyn Bridge and the Eiffel Tower was the steel as important aesthetically as it was structurally. And here, radical conservation was never necessary because continuous, ongoing maintenance was taken for granted.

Cast-iron fabrics, on the other hand, were always designed to be seen:

6.12. *Frank Lloyd Wright's Unity Temple* is notable on several counts. It is a magnificent example of his mature Prairie Style applied to a nonresidential building. It is also one of the world's earliest examples of the use of reinforced concrete, naked and unadorned, in a monumental edifice. Because of its plasticity, concrete was an optimal medium for Wright's ambitions for a form of flawless monolithic geometry. But, over the years, Unity suffered the deterioration to be expected of a concrete structure in a climate like Chicago's. These failures were initially perceived as being merely cosmetic, but since they were never adequately treated, they began to threaten the integrity of the structure itself (*2,3*). By 1970 it was clear that a radical program of conservation was required.

Conservation was complicated by the way in which Wright had designed and constructed Unity. It was a poured-in-place reinforced-concrete shell (remarkably advanced in its engineering) with an exposed aggregate finish. How Wright achieved this finish has never been clear. There were no expansion joints or, judging from early photographs, traces of any form work. However, horizontal "pour lines" are visible in these pictures: it is not known if Wright either anticipated or approved of the stratified appearance they produced.

In any case, the decision was made to restore the building (*1*). To correct the structural failures (*2*) and eliminate the purely cosmetic defects (*3*), architect Robert Bell had to mount a long and complex conservation program. The original concrete had to be deeply etched by abrasive blasting to ensure a good mechanical bond between it and any new surfacing. To reconstruct the diamond-sharp geometry of the building and its ornamental details, wood forms of appropriate size and shape were nailed in place to act as screeds for hand-troweled reconstructions (*4*). After this, a new coating was uniformly sprayed on, using a mix of pea gravel, no. 1 Portland cement, and no. 2 torpedo sand; some small-grained glacial flint was added to produce the dense texture of the original. This new finish was troweled smooth by hand (*5*). As a final step, the entire fabric was given another light abrasive blasting to expose and clean the aggregate.

118

As one of the country's oldest reinforced-concrete buildings, and the first to be designated as an historic monument, Unity Temple epitomizes the problems connected with their conservation. The paradox is that, from a purely structural point of view, concrete is easily repaired. But cosmetically the problem is more difficult. The visible traces of patching and repairs are all but impossible to conceal. The only satisfactory solution is to refinish the entire surface, either by a continuous coat of stucco, as at Unity, or by conventional painting.

6.13. *Ease of disassembly and reconstitution* were among the advantages claimed by James Bogardus, nineteenth-century iron foundry master, for his patented system of cast-iron construction. But the claim was seldom put to the test: his buildings and hundreds like them were smashed by the wreckers' ball. As the only surviving Bogardus building, his Lang Stores (*1*) was a technological monument of first magnitude. When the Manhattan district in which it stood was to be cleared for redevelopment, the decision was made to disassemble it for reassembly elsewhere. There was no local precedent for an intervention of comparable delicacy. Nothing was known of how brittle the old cast iron might have become or whether bolts and screws, rusted in place for decades, could be removed without fracturing the iron members. The entire salvage operation was therefore seen as a prototypical demonstration of the feasibility of saving a few examples of an endangered architectural species.

3

4

The Bogardus structural system was a true curtain wall—non-load-bearing, modular, prefabricated, and bolted together. It consisted of columns, beams, and molded spandrels (the windows had originally been wood casements) (4). As anticipated, the disassembly was tricky. The nuts and bolts were so rusted in place that they could not be released mechanically. By cautious trial and error, the crew (all of them professional house wreckers) learned how to cut off recalcitrant bolt heads by hosing down the area around the acetylene torch (3, 5), thereby preventing warping and cracking from local overheating. By careful work, they took the building apart with no breakage at all.

5

6

6.13 (Continued). The Lang Stores disassembly was completely documented. Measured drawings had been completed in advance and were used as a basis for coding each part of the prefabricated facade (6). The entire process was monitored by professionals who kept a daily log and photographic record. The component parts were then taken to a nearby yard where they were cleaned of accumulated grime, paint, and rust and then given a rust-inhibiting prime coat. To minimize handling in the process of reuse, they were stacked in the order they would be required, i.e., first-floor members on top. (In a final tragicomic episode in the life of this historic building, the parts were stolen from the site and sold for scrap. The thieves were caught but the stolen parts were never recovered!)

7

8

consequently they always had aesthetic pretensions. Yet ironically cast iron was never intended to be "read" as metallic. It is a fascinating aspect of Victorian taste that it was always painted to look like some other material. Architectural members were modeled to simulate their lithic prototypes and were painted to simulate marble or stone. (Only in the 1851 Crystal Palace in London was the polychromy abstract; there compression members were painted in cerulean, tension members in scarlet, redundant members in lemon yellow.) The subject matter of cast-iron sculpture and garden ornaments was usually anecdotal—human figures, animals, flowers, foliage, or fruit—and it was colored accordingly. In short, cast iron, like modern synthetic plastics, was never conceived of as having its own independent aesthetic identity.

Interest in the conservation of our surviving cast-iron architectural fabrics, most of them prefabricated curtain walls applied to conventional structures, is sufficiently widespread to merit the appearance of a national society dedicated to the subject and a growing literature on the subject.[11] As a consequence of this new interest, the largest remaining body of cast-iron buildings in the nation, a 20-block area in lower Manhattan, has been declared a historic district and a number of individual cast-iron façades have been preserved and restored around the country. Three of these projects involved fairly radical intervention. The Lang Stores in New York were disassembled for proposed reconstitution on another site nearby. The cast-iron façade of the Z.C.M.I. store in Salt Lake City was disassembled to make way for a new building and then reassembled on the same spot as a freestanding screen along the street front. The cast-iron façade of the Wilmington Opera House was conserved in situ. Although modest in scale and limited in number, these projects at least suggest the broad outlines of conservation techniques for handling these increasingly valuable old metal fabrics.

CONSERVATION OF EARTHEN FABRICS

Structures made of earth—mud brick, rammed earth, mud and stone masonry—are products of one of the world's oldest building technologies. By the same token, the technology is one of the most primitive, dominating the desert and semiarid regions of the world. In the Southwestern United States it was the dominant way of building from the pre-Columbian native peoples, on through the Spanish and Mexican regimes, up to the opening of the twentieth century.[12] Under preindustrial conditions, the ongoing maintenance and repair of earth structures rendered them virtually ageless. Thus the pueblo of Taos, New Mexico, was already inhabited at the time of the Spanish conquest in 1610–1612. It remains inhabited and virtually intact today. Even in arid regions, such adobe structures were always vul-

6.14. *The cast-iron and sheet metal façade of a Victorian department store* in Salt Lake City has been successfully reintegrated into the fabric of its modern successor. Zion Commercial and Mercantile Institute, an enterprise of the Church of Jesus Christ of Latter-Day Saints, had become a landmark in the capital of Mormonism. It occupied a strategic block downtown, but when plans for a giant new store were first announced, there was no provision for preserving the original. However, a campaign to save it quickly revealed how much it was cherished and plans were revised to incorporate the façade in the new complex. It was disassembled; its components were cleaned and replicas for missing parts cast. As reconstituted, the façade acts as a free-standing screen standing 10 feet out from the new show windows. The result is a handsome, airy loggia 3 stories high whose coffered ceiling is a tin ceiling from the 1870s store (*4*). The detailing of the steel armature is both elegant and discreet: it follows the profile of the cast-iron colonnade but is formed and painted so that its subservient role is clear. A new polychromy in brown, beige, and gold leaf adds to the overall felicity of the development.

3

4

1

6.15. *Restoration of the cast-iron façade of the Wilmington, Delaware, Opera House* resembled that of the ZCMI in Salt Lake City and was supervised by the same architect, Stephen Baird (see Fig. 6.14). In this case, however, the façade remained intact and all work was carried on in the field. (Like many Victorian buildings, the opera had only one finished "front"—it being assumed that the party walls would be concealed by neighboring structures.) Three levels of intervention were employed: the restoration of the mutilated street-level shop fronts (*1*); conservation of the largely undamaged upper floors; and reconstruction of the vanished Second Empire attic story (*2*). Cast iron being one of the few materials on which sandblasting can be safely employed, it was used on the opera. It proved to be an optimal method for removing a century's accumulated paint from the intricately detailed architectural ornament. Except for the polychromed Masonic emblem on the central gable, the entire façade was painted in the original off-white. The auditorium of the opera has also been restored by other architects.

2

1

6.16. *Conservation of mud masonry.* A large percentage of the human race has lived in mud-built structures (sun-baked brick, adobe, *terra pisé*, wattle and mud daub, etc.) and they are admirably adapted to desert and arid climates. But little is known about scientific conservation methods. In preindustrial cultures in which it was a viable building technology, the solution was continuous, ongoing repair. Under such a maintenance program, buildings could last for centuries. Thus the Palace of the Governors in Santa Fe *(above)* is said to date from c. 1610, while a fortified village in the northern Sahara *(below)* is ageless. But how much of the actual integument of either is "original" is moot. Although there have been numerous American attempts to consolidate, preserve, or waterproof mud-built structures, the results have not been notably successful. The best conservation method seems to be the oldest—continuous repair, especially to protect walls from erosion of blowing rain and footings against capillary rise of groundwater.

2

6.17. *To make way for a street widening,* a baroque church in Warsaw is moved back. If the topography is level and the distance short, the moving of even a large and weighty structure like this is commonplace. (*a*) Foundations are prepared at the new site; (*b*) a steel cradle is slipped under the building; (*c*) church is rolled to site, lowered into place on its new base. Properly braced to prevent twisting and bending while in movement, this church reached its new destination with glass and plaster undamaged.

6.18. Often the only way to save an endangered building is to move it to a new site. How feasible this strategy will be will depend upon a number of logistical factors: the size and structural nature of the fabric; the distance it must be transported; and, most critical, the itinerary of the move itself. If the building is relatively small, compact, and lightweight, the logistics will be fairly simple, as in the case of this rare 1720 Dutch house. Donated to Old Bethpage Village, an outdoor architectural museum in Nassau County, Long Island, this building could be moved only after careful preparations. The timber-framed roof was disassembled and trucked separately to the new site. Later porches and additions to the fabric were removed and the structure internally braced and mothballed for transit (*1*). Although the airline distance of the move was short, it led through a densely built-up area. Arrangements had to be made to bypass low bridges; local utilities had to lift overhead wires and signal lights (*2*) and police escorts had to be arranged. Once placed on new foundations at the new site, the house was restored to its original 1720 condition. Restoration drawings, based upon archival research, had already been prepared; but as always in such cases, critical information on the morphological development of the house derived from a close study of the fabric itself. The end product is now on display (*3*).

1

House ready for transit, roof removed, internally braced, and mothballed.

House in transit: utility crew in cherry picker has raised signals for passage.

2

3

6.19. *Advanced technology to move a fifteenth-century church.* The old Czech town of Most found itself, a decade ago, sitting on top of one of the nation's richest coal deposits. But because it was the brown coal of the region, it had to be surface-mined; and because of its importance to the national economy, it was clear that Most had to move. It was decided to transfer the entire community to a new town some 2 kilometers back from the fields. Most of the town's old buildings were sacrificed in the move. But because the church was both a rare and a fine example of the hall-type vessel (i.e., with side aisles the same height as the nave), it was decided that preservation was mandated.

The simplest method would have been disassembly and reconstitution in the new town. But this was not possible because the church had important murals in the apse and late-gothic painted decorations on walls and vaulting. Hence the decision to move the church intact. Such a complex and delicate intervention required a number of phases. (*a*) The entire interior was firmly laced together with a steel armature. (*b*) Electronic stress gauges were installed to monitor movement in the masonry fabric; these were connected to a computer. (*c*) A new concrete slab was inserted under the church. (*d*) It was jacked up to permit construction of four parallel railroad tracks leading to the new site. (*e*) On each track were placed 13 specially built cars, each carrying an hydraulic jack controlled by the computer. This permitted any movement registered by the stress gauges to be automatically compensated for by the jacks. (*f*) Finally, the church was slowly moved up the tracks to its new site, where new foundations had been prepared. Undamaged in the move, the church has undergone complete conservation.

2

3

132

nerable to climatic attrition, especially rain and ground water. But since repair required a minimum of skills, tools, and material, their conservation by the native population was a simple matter.

Today, many old earth-built structures are achieving the status of historic landmarks, e.g., pre-Columbian ruins at Casa Grande, provincial missions and monasteries throughout the Southwest, the Palace of the Governors in Sante Fe, and the pueblo of Taos. Their conservation implies a new expertise which is just beginning to be systematically explored. In a recent paper, James R. Clifton summarizes some of the problems of conservation:

> Although adobe has had a long history of use, the technology for its preservation has had a much shorter period of development and a great deal of research still needs to be carried out. Basic guidelines, however, can be evolved by understanding the inherent nature of the materials and how its fundamental properties can have a bearing on structural problems and on climate- and environmentally-caused deterioration.[13]

PRESERVATION VIA MOVING

All too often in the modern world, the only way to save a valuable old building is to move it out of the path of some construction activity—a highway, dam, or airport—which is putatively more important than permitting the historic building to remain in situ. Ironically, some of our most successful outdoor architectural museums are the by-products of just such pressures. Technically, the moving of even large buildings is an old American tradition. It was commented upon by many European visitors, including Charles Dickens and Mrs. Trollope, and reflected the real economic value which inhered in any still-usable artifact in preindustrial America. The details of any such operation today—whether the building is to be moved intact, cut up into manageable parts and reassembled on the new site, or completely disassembled to be reconstituted elsewhere—depend upon a number of variables. Among them are the nature of construction (wood, masonry, metal); the bulk and weight of the artifact itself; the logistics of the move (street widths, power lines, tunnels, and underpasses). The transport of small, compact wood-framed buildings, such as those at Sturbridge or Bethpage Village, is a commonplace event. In contrast, the transportation of large monumental structures like the Baroque Church of St. Anne in Warsaw or the Church of the Virgin Mary in Most, Czechoslovakia, are much more complex operations.

Technically more conventional though more dramatic because of the distance involved was the transfer of the Church of St. Mary Alderbury from London to Westminster College in Fulton, Missouri. Indeed, the same powerful technologies which threaten the continued existence of historic

6.20. *Moving buildings over water is an old American tradition.* The logistics are simpler than land transport, though not without the hazards of high tides, tricky currents, and sudden storms. Thus there was a certain poetic logic in the decision by the National Park Service to move the Old Harbor Lifesaving Station by water, some thirty miles from Chatham to a new site on Cape Cod at Provincetown. The station, last surviving example of a once familiar building type, was built in 1897 for the old U.S. Lifesaving Service, predecessor of the Coast Guard Service. It was threatened by beach erosion in its old site, so the decision was made to transfer it to a more stable and accessible location. In preparation for its trip, the wood-framed, shingle-clad structure was sawn in two, braced and mothballed, and lashed to a steel cradle. A fifty-ton crane then lifted it onto a barge, which was towed to its new home (*2*). The restored station is operated as a museum of lifesaving by the Park Service.

2

structures in situ also make possible salvage operations which would have been inconceivable a few short decades ago. This new technical capacity has been demonstrated by the transportation of the stone-carved portals of the Temple of Abu Simbel to escape the rising waters of the constructed lake at Aswan, Egypt, and the current transfer of the temples on the island of Philae, also at Aswan, to a new man-made replica a few miles upstream.

Unfortunately, all too many historic buildings cannot be saved in toto, either on their original site or in new outdoor locations. In such instances, the preservationist must retreat to the position of saving as many significant elements as possible. Sometimes they can be preserved out of doors, displayed in the landscape, like sculpture: the Chicago Art Institute has done this with the portal of Louis Sullivan's Board of Trade Building. Sometimes entire façades can be incorporated in new structures on the same site: this has occurred with the marble fronts of two Egyptian revival town houses in Philadelphia and the cast-iron façade of the old ZCMI department store in Salt Lake City, Utah.

Sometimes architectural fragments can be preserved only by installation in a museum. This has recently been accomplished with the reconstitution of Sullivan's great board room in the new wing of the Chicago Art Institute, and recently the Metropolitan Museum of Art installed the living room of Wright's house for Francis W. Little in its new American Wing. Many great American art museums—the Boston Museum of Fine Arts, the Metropolitan and the Brooklyn in New York, the William Rockhill Nelson Gallery in Kansas City—are the repository of many historic interiors which might otherwise have been lost altogether. The practice of preserving entire rooms, complete with their furnishings, by installing them in museums had its initial vogue in the 1920s. The practice was subsequently somewhat discredited, however, when museums were discovered to be stripping great rooms from houses which were in no danger of being demolished. Today no reputable museum would accept a room under such conditions. Thus both the Chicago Art Institute and the Metropolitan agreed to accept the fragments of the Board of Trade and the Little house only after long and bitter battles to save them in situ had failed.

7

Reconstitution of Damaged Fabrics

The process of artifactual aging—whether due to natural agents (insects, fungi, freeze and thaw) or man-made forces (atmospheric pollution, vehicular vibration)—is ineluctable. Left to itself, aging threatens the physical integrity of all material objects, artificial or natural. Until fairly recently, our capacity to slow down this process or to reverse its consequences was limited. The tools and technology simply did not exist to permit us to intervene on any but the most limited basis. A decayed wooden member or crumbling masonry element could have been removed and replaced with new, sound materials. But there were no means of consolidating or reconstituting the old integument, no matter how valuable it might be.

Today, modern technology has greatly extended our capacity to rescue old artifacts. But how much money, how much expertise, are to be expended upon the reconstitution of a seriously damaged artifact will depend upon the artistic or cultural value assigned to it by society. For example, the Giotto frescoes in the Florentine church of Santa Croce, severely damaged in the great flood of November 4, 1966, are of supreme artistic value; but they are comparatively insignificant historically. On the other hand, the original copy of the Declaration of Independence, elaborately protected in the Library of Congress, has little artistic value but is of supreme historical significance to the United States. In both cases, great technical expertise has been expended upon them—on restoration of the damaged frescoes and on conservation of the relatively undamaged manuscript. One might properly say that the decision to preserve them for posterity was a matter of supreme cultural importance, justified at no matter what cost.

Modern scientific and technical developments have extended our capacity to intervene in the life history of damaged artifacts to an extent undreamed of even a few decades ago. Much of this new expertise has been developed by art conservators working in museums and laboratories around the world. Although, by definition, the artifacts are small in size and exist in the controlled environment of the museum, this work establishes new parameters for the conservation of the larger architectural fabrics which must survive in the natural environment.[1] The newer advances indicate that, short of complete incineration or atomization, almost any building can be restored to full-scale three-dimensional integrity if adequate funding is available.

Currently, reconstitution is taking place at two quite different technological levels. The first employs traditional skills and tools. Here we find old buildings being taken apart in very much the same way as they were originally constructed, i.e., by hand, member by member. They are then reconstituted: in situ, as in the ZCMI Building in Salt Lake City or the Old Capitol in Springfield, Illinois, or in new locations, as in the transfer of St. Mary Alderbury from London to Fulton, Missouri. In all such cases, the task involves skilled craftspersons using conventional hand tools. Even here, of course, great sophistication is often required. Thus conservators working with the Italian Soprintendenze dei Belle Arte have faced major problems in the conservation of old mosaics in the region of Venice and Ravenna. Because of structural failures in the walls and ceilings to which they are attached, it has often been necessary to detach the mosaics and mount them on new, inert, and dimensionally stable backings. Since it is their irregular faceted surfaces which give these mosaics their famous life and sparkle, it was necessary to develop techniques for making a cast or mold of each panel so that each individual tessera maintains its precise, three-dimensional relationship with its neighbors. This has been successfully accomplished.

A second level of reconstitution, however, employs revolutionary new methods and tools and permits much more radical interventions. These all revolve around the possibility of *consolidation* of damaged architectural fabrics by means of injection and impregnation. This is being employed in both masonry and wood fabrics with spectacular results. In the case of masonry, the impregnating agent is a portland cement grout; in the case of wood, one of the new synthetic polymers or epoxies. In both cases, impregnation alters the actual granular or fibrous composition of the fabric: in being consolidated, it often becomes much stronger than it was when new. In the case of masonry—where the material is composed of discrete and impervious particles—the cement grout is used to bond them into a new, monolithic unity. In the case of wood, however, the injected epoxy actually penetrates the fibrous mass, converting the desiccated wood into a material with quite different properties from those of natural wood.

The basic equipment which makes this possible is the power drill and motorized pump. The drills are high-speed and vibrationless, tipped with carbon steel or diamond. The masonry drills are water-cooled: they can safely penetrate conglomerate materials and fragile old rubble masonry which might collapse from the vibration of the old fashioned drill.

Impregnation may be employed at two different levels: it can be used to consolidate the mass of the fabric into a monolithic whole, as in the case of the rubble masonry of York Minster or the wooden hull of the warship *Vasa*, or it can be employed to insert wholly new skeletal members into extant structures. This is accomplished by consolidating the old fabric, drilling holes at the points where reinforced beams or columns are to be created, inserting the reinforcing rods, and then consolidating them in place by grouting under pressure. This technique has been successfully employed in the campanile of the cathedral at Burano, Italy: an old brick tower has thereby been converted into a reinforced brick masonry monolith. But the same technique can be employed in reinforcing old wooden members: here the impregnating agent is epoxy and the reinforcing rods of molded fiberglass and epoxy.

Another important application of the "drill and fill" method is its use in inserting new foundations under unstable old buildings. Here a three-dimensional latticework of new concrete piles is created to stitch the superstructure to the soil beneath it. This technique is similar to above-grade interventions. Holes are drilled through the existing foundations and deep into the soil beneath them. Although the exact location of piles will vary with the job, they create a three-dimensional latticework (hence the Italian term *radici*—"roots") which literally tie the old structure securely to deep subsurface levels. The advantages over conventional methods are obvious. This technique avoids costly, time-consuming hand excavation. More important, it involves the absolute minimum of risk to the old structure—especially when, as at York and Burano, the superstructure has been previously consolidated.

In the White House and Independence Hall, two of America's most historically significant monuments, we find fabrics which have been subjected to centuries of interventions of different types. Sometimes they were strictly functional (the insertion of heating, lighting, or plumbing systems); sometimes they were candidly aesthetic ("to make it look better," "to make it look like Mr. Lincoln's day"). But whether well advised or merely well intentioned, the cumulative impact of all these interventions had been to compromise hopelessly the physical integrity of both buildings. The White House reached a crisis stage in 1948, when President Truman and his family were hurriedly moved to Blair House across the street. Independence Hall was closed for complete restoration in the mid-sixties.

In both cases, the experts agreed that radical surgery was mandatory: the masonry shells and wood-framed roofs would be conserved; but the interiors would be eviscerated and a new, fireproof armature of floors, walls, and ceilings would be inserted inside them. The evisceration itself was extremely careful, especially in Independence Hall, where as much as possible of the original timber framing was preserved. As the disassembly proceeded, all significant decorative elements (paneling, stair rails, mantels,

7.1. *Thanks to recent developments in the technology of concrete construction,* many old masonry structures are being saved which, only a few decades ago, would have been doomed. Both new tools and new techniques are involved. The tools include improved hydraulic pumps and high-speed, vibration-free drilling rigs. The new techniques include the pressurized injection of cement grouting into friable old masonry to convert it into stable-mass concrete. Italian engineers, currently leaders in this highly specialized field, are responsible for saving two historic structures which would otherwise have been lost: the bell tower of the Cathedral of Burano, on the island of that name in the lagoon of Venice (*1*); and the sixteenth-century Cathedral of Pienza (*3*). The Burano tower is an eighteenth-century brick shaft modeled after the famous prototype in Piazza San Marco. Like all buildings in this region, this campanile was built on timber cribbing carried by wooden piling driven into the muddy bottom of the lagoon. The failure of these traditional foundations was threatening the imminent collapse of the tower. But before new concrete foundations and new concrete piling could be inserted under it, the tower itself had to be consolidated. This was accomplished by a series of delicate operations: a webbing of reinforced concrete members was created within the brick walls by drilling holes in them, inserting steel reinforcing rods, and then injecting cement grout into the cavities around the rods. The result is an invisible concrete armature inside the wall, which ties the tower together like a corset (*2*). Then broad concrete footings were poured under the tower, beneath which were clusters of concrete piles. Here again, holes were drilled into the soil, spiral reinforcing inserted in the holes, and cement grout pumped into the cavities to form reinforced concrete piling. Identical techniques were employed to save the sinking church (*3*). Here, new concrete footings under the walls and columns of the nave were carried by new concrete piling fabricated in situ (*4*).

140

3

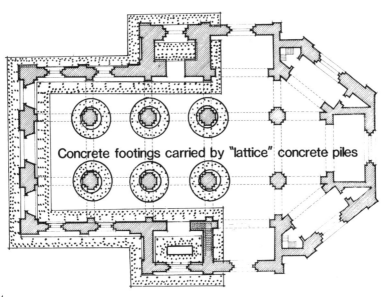

Concrete footings carried by "lattice" concrete piles

4

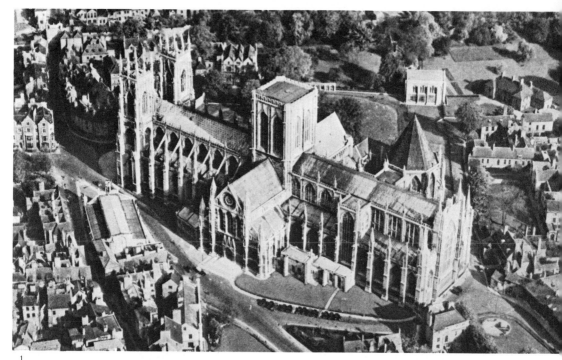

1

7.2. New and active fissures in the masonry of the great tower of the Minister at York, England, were an obvious sign of distress in its fabric (3). Radical intervention was indicated if the building was to be saved. Analysis by the architects suggested two sources of trouble: failure of the ancient foundations, and failure of the rubble core of the gothic masonry due to desiccation of the ancient lime mortar. This, in turn, suggested two urgent therapeutic measures: insertion of new, greatly enlarged foundations of reinforced concrete under the tower piers, and consolidation of the entire mass of the tower into a solid monolithic concrete mass. Actually, consolidation had to precede foundation work lest the entire tower crumble into dust. Employing the injection method used in the Venetian churches, holes were bored on 3-foot centers from the outside face of the wall; grout was then pumped in (under low pressure to avoid blowouts), beginning at ground level and working upward, after which the masonry was repointed and washed down. The intervention is thus literally invisible. After the tower, the east and west walls of the 800-year-old fabric have been similarly conserved.

The architects' analysis of the stresses inside the tower (5) revealed urgent need for insertion

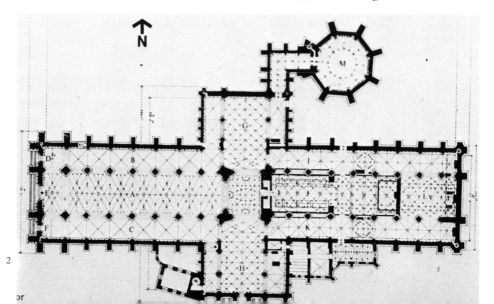

2

or

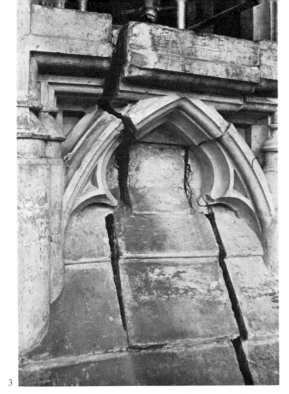

3

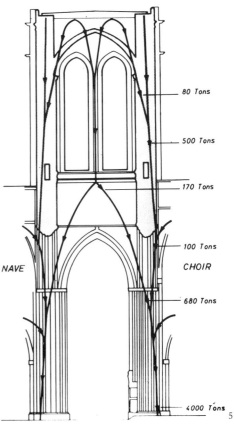

NAVE   CHOIR

80 Tons

500 Tons

170 Tons

100 Tons

680 Tons

4000 Tons

5

of a reinforced-concrete collar beam below the lantern (6). After the tower had been consolidated, high-speed, vibrationless drills could be used to cut channels for insertion of stainless-steel reinforcing bars. These were securely embedded by more pressure grouting, creating a monolithic collar beam inside the Gothic masonry. New foundations under piers were created by a 50-foot collar around Norman footings ("C" in 4). In holes drilled diagonally through the entire mass, stainless-steel reinforcing rods were inserted and grouted into place. Hydraulic flat jacks were installed ("B," 4) to maintain the tower's equilibrium during construction.

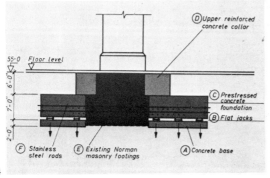

D Upper reinforced concrete collar

55·0 Floor level

C Prestressed concrete foundation

B Flat jacks

F Stainless steel rods   E Existing Norman masonry footings   A Concrete base

4

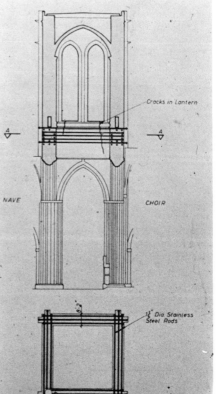

Cracks in Lantern

NAVE   CHOIR

Dia Stainless Steel Rods

6

7.2. *(Continued)*. Since excavations for new foundations under the tower would require extensive excavations in any case, the architects had proposed to use the space for a small museum of cathedral muniments. But discovery of important Norman, Saxon, and Roman ruins soon converted a normal construction site into an archaeological dig *(7, 8)*. Thus plans for the museum were enlarged and elaborated *(9, 10)*. After new foundations had been completed *(10)*, a reinforced concrete lid was placed over them and the Minster's original marble flooring replaced. Excavations under the west end of the nave also added greatly to an understanding of the morphological development of the Minster; they will be accessible to study by qualified scholars. The church was kept open to the public during the entire 8-year campaign of restoration without structural mishap or personal injury. The decision to keep the church open proved sagacious; large crowds and contributions showed that the public is as interested in the *process* of restoration as in the restored artifact itself. The entire Minster has been cleaned, and offers a glowing image of the aesthetic intentions of Gothic architects.

7

8

144

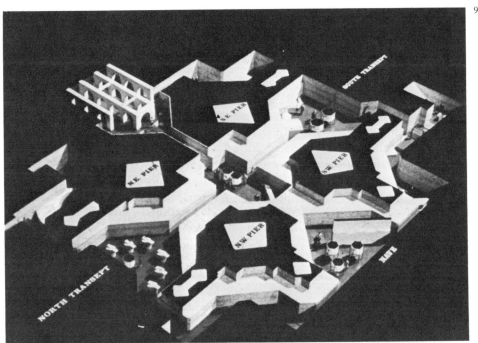

plasterwork, and so on) were removed, photographed, and measured and then sent to workshops and laboratories for conservation. This work, coincidentally, offered the trained observer important evidence of the morphological evolution of the building itself: together with documentary research, it permitted the preparation of comprehensive histories on both structures. When the new armature was completed, the process was reversed: floors, walls, and ceilings were sheathed with the original-decor woodwork and plaster or facsimiles where originals were missing.

Because of the building's ongoing use as the residence of the President, the restoration of the White House was obviously subject to many nonhistoric and extra-aesthetic restraints. There was, moreover, no single fixed point in time to which it should be restored. Independence Hall was a different matter altogether. Its unique historical significance centered on the events which culminated there on July 4, 1776. Hence every resource was employed to return the monument to exactly that physical condition in which it would have been on that historic day.

Independence Hall, Philadelphia, Pennsylvania: Of all the historical monuments in the United States, this little provincial example of the English baroque is the most important, as the scene of the signing of the Declaration of Independence. Hence its complete restoration, timed for the Bicentennial celebrations, was recognized as a project of national importance. The building had, of course, been many times "restored," remodeled, and modernized in the two centuries since that famous event. Indeed, one of the very reasons for its shockingly precarious state when work began in 1962 was precisely all those interventions. As the investigation of the structure proceeded, the miracle seemed to be that it had not collapsed long before. So serious was its condition and so complex the causes that it was decided to eviscerate the old brick shell completely. But unlike the case in most demolition projects, it was decided that every item removed—nail, brick, scrap of plaster or wood—was to be photographed, cataloged, and preserved. This procedure was essential if a definitive history of the physical evolution of the building was to be reconstructed. Work therefore proceeded as in a standard archaeological dig.

The fundamental objective of the restoration was obviously to return the building's appearance as nearly as possible to its state on the day of the signing. To this end, extraordinarily complete documentary research went hand in hand with a physical examination of every square inch of the structure as its "innards" were progressively exposed. Generally speaking, the interior surfaces—floors, paneled walls, plaster ceilings, decorative door frames—were intact when work began. These were all removed for study and conservation. But behind these surfaces, termites, rot, fire, and, above all, ignorant or reckless carpentry had made a shambles of the structure itself. Therefore, the masonry shell and the wooden skeletons of floors, partitions, and roof had to be reworked, strengthened, and knitted back together very much as in a case of orthopedic surgery. Steel reinforcing had to be laced throughout it in order to take the live load of thousands of tourists; and since all such reinforcing had to be invisible when restoration was complete, great ingenuity was demanded of architects and engineers. Simultaneously with such structural consolidation, conduits, pipes, and ductwork to carry lighting and air conditioning, as well as security systems against fire and vandalism, had to be threaded through floors, walls, and ceilings. Only then could the surfaces original to July 4, 1776, be reinstalled.

Old State House, Springfield, Illinois: This Greek revival structure was designed by the architect John F. Rague and finished in 1837. It served as the State Capitol until 1876, when a new Capitol was erected; it served as the Sangamon County Courthouse until 1965. Both before and after its abandonment, it had been through many alterations, having even been jacked up some 18 feet into the air to permit the insertion of a new ground floor in the 1870s. Although the exterior had preserved most of its features, all the interior features—monumental halls, stairs, and legislative chambers—had disappeared.

The salvation of so damaged a structure is thus as unusual as was the way in which it came about. Viewing the Capitol as being of little artistic or historic significance, the local urban redevelopment agency proposed in 1963 to demolish it to make way for a three-story parking garage under Capitol Square. This proposal generated an authentic storm among local historians and preservationists because of a largely forgotten historical event: the body of Abraham Lincoln had lain there in state, in the Old Senate Chamber, before interment in a local cemetery. These people quite properly took the position that this was a historical incident of truly national significance; and that, far from the building being demolished, it should be restored to its condition on that sad April day in 1865. After months of controversy, during which all the standard arguments for and against demolition were advanced, a compromise was finally reached. The subterranean garage would be inserted beneath the Capitol Plaza and the historic building restored on top of it to its 1865 condition.

The precise way in which this compromise was effected was ingenious. The old masonry building would be dismantled and its significant elements preserved for reuse. Since the only elements remaining from the 1865 period were external (walls, columns, cornices, pediments, and cupola), only these were saved. The individual cut-stone blocks were numbered, photographed, and "mapped." As demolition proceeded, they were stored in the sequence in which they would be needed in the reconstitution of the structure. Also as demolition proceeded, all interior surfaces were examined as they were exposed, for information on vanished stairs, doorways, vaulted ceilings, and the like. (This was crucial information because, with

1

7.3. This 130-year-old building has been disassembled and then reconstituted in situ. The reasons for such a radical intervention were historical, not artistic: for the old Illinois State Capitol in Springfield had been the site of the rise and fall of Abraham Lincoln as a national figure. Here, in 1858, he had made the famous "house divided" speech which catapulted him into the presidency. And it was here that his body lay in state after his assassination in April 1865 (*1*). Originally constructed in 1837, the Greek revival structure was abandoned by the state in 1876 and sold to Sangamon County for use as a courthouse. Subsequently it had undergone many vicissitudes, having been continuously mutilated across time (it was raised 11 feet in 1898 to provide a new floor!) before being repurchased by the state in 1965. By that time, nothing of the splendid Greek revival interiors remained (*10, 12*). Some people in Springfield, regarding it as an obstacle to progress, proposed its demolition to make way for an underground parking garage. Instead, a successful campaign to restore it to its 1858 condition was launched.

It was decided to disassemble the old building, stone by stone, and—after construction of the garage—to reconstitute it, inside and out, in its original 1838 condition. Technically notable in many respects, the project is also interesting because the architects had little pictorial or graphic material on which to base design decisions. The 1865 lithograph of Lincoln's catafalque in the House of Representatives, with its critically important information, was the only picture ever found. Therefore the reconstruction of the interior volumes—monumental chamber, hallways, stairs, etc.—was derived largely from a day-by-day, on-site analysis of the fabric as it was taken apart (*2, 3*). Such artifactual evidence, when paired with archival information, enabled the architects to prepare working drawings for the eventual rebuilding. Except for the visual evidence in the lithograph (coffered dome, Corinthian colonnade, semicircular plan), design of the interiors had to extrapolated from contemporaneous buildings of the region and pattern books known to have been available to the original architect, John F. Rague. The furnishings are a mix of originals, appropriate to the time and place, and custom-built replicas.

The lid of the garage consists of series of inverted concrete cones, each carried by a concrete column (*4*), hollow to provide drainage for the lawns and trees of the reconstructed landscape of the square.

148

4

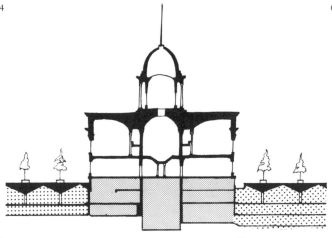

6

5

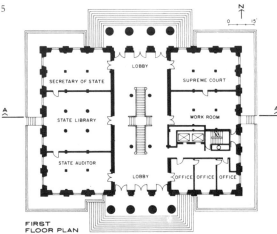

N

0   15'

LOBBY

SECRETARY OF STATE

SUPREME COURT

STATE LIBRARY

WORK ROOM

STATE AUDITOR

LOBBY

OFFICE OFFICE OFFICE

FIRST
FLOOR PLAN

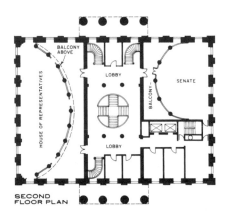

BALCONY
ABOVE

LOBBY

HOUSE OF REPRESENTATIVES

BALCONY

SENATE

LOBBY

SECOND
FLOOR PLAN

7.3. *(Continued).* The concrete armature on which the stones of the old walls were to be hung were constructed first (7). It provided three subterranean floors of fireproof storage vaults for the State Historical Commission. Above this, at grade, the 2-story skeleton was constructed for the capitol proper (4). After this, the subterranean garage was constructed, whose roof would carry the restored landscape of the old capitol square (6). The external walls consisted of the golden dolomite limestone blocks, all 3,300 of which had been numbered, cataloged and stored, pending return to their original location (8). They had been trimmed down to 9 inches from their original 2-foot thickness. In the reconstituted walls, they were laid up against a concrete block backing (9). The roof and dome, framed in steel to replicate the original profiles, were sheathed in the same terne metal with which the original building had been covered. Note that the entire building, in its new state, has been returned to its original relationship to the square.

9

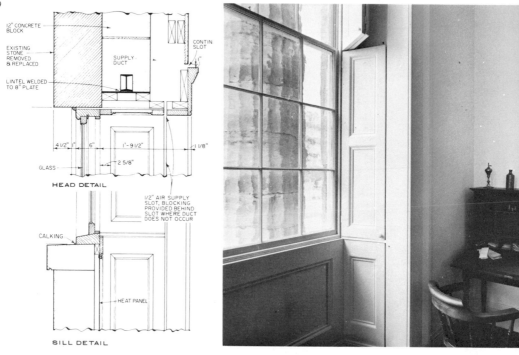

12" CONCRETE BLOCK

EXISTING STONE REMOVED & REPLACED

SUPPLY DUCT

CONTIN SLOT

1"

LINTEL WELDED TO 8" PLATE

4 1/2"   1"   6"   1'-9 1/2"   1 1/8"

2 5/8"

GLASS

HEAD DETAIL

1/2" AIR SUPPLY SLOT, BLOCKING PROVIDED BEHIND SLOT WHERE DUCT DOES NOT OCCUR

CALKING

HEAT PANEL

SILL DETAIL

7.3. (Continued). The interiors of the capitol are all conjectural reconstructions, the only original material in the fabric being the dolomite blocks in the outside walls. As can be seen in the section (9), these are backed with concrete block. Finish walls of plaster on metal lath are placed 9 inches out from the masonry to allow for ductwork. Double-hung sash and shutters are accurate replicas of wooden originals, but the molded spandrel below is actually a thin metal panel for radiant heating. Air-conditioning vents and light sources are similarly concealed in cornices and paneled soffits (10).

10

153

the exception of one lithograph showing the Lincoln catafalque in the Senate chamber, no graphic or pictorial evidence on the interiors was ever discovered.

When the building had been completely disassembled, excavation for the garage was completed and the three-story subterranean structure erected. On top of this, a reinforced concrete armature for the Capitol itself was built. It enclosed the original 1865 volume and provided for the insertion of the original stairs, halls, and chambers. The three-story basement under the Capitol proper was developed as a fireproof archive. The salvaged marble blocks were then hung on the concrete frame, columns reerected, and roof and cupola constructed to correspond to the original profile. Interior architectural treatment and furnishings approximate those known, from literary evidence, to have been in use at the time. Today, the reconstituted Capitol Building serves as a moving memorial to the martyred President, in addition to offering offices, libraries, and archives for the State Historical Commission.

York Minster, York, England: The saving of this great Norman-Gothic structure can be more properly described as consolidation than as reconstitution, since the entire structure remained intact throughout a long, complex, and costly campaign in the years 1966–1975. Although, in the end, the entire structure has been conserved and cleaned—with dazzling cosmetic consequences—the aspect of the operation which is of interest here was consolidation of the failing masonry of the great tower over the crossing and of the east and west fronts. This astonishing feat was accomplished through the perfection of two new processes:

1. The injection under pressure of liquid cement grout into old masonry fabrics with decayed mortars and resultant cavities.

2. The use of new water-cooled, vibration-free drills which permit the drilling of even weak and friable masonry masses.

3. The combined use of the two methods to permit the insertion of reinforced-concrete skeletons and diaphragms into the rubble masonry without disturbing it by cutting channels and chases.

By the adroit use of such means, the architect, Bernard Feilden, and the consultant engineers, Ove Arupt Partners, first converted the huge 232-foot rubble tower into a solid monolithic column. Then, supporting it by means of hydraulic jacks, they replaced the failing Saxon foundations with massive modern concrete blocks. A fantastically delicate engineering feat, accomplished without a single death or serious accident, this task was enormously complicated by an unexpected archaeological find. Directly under the crossing, but running on a typically Vitruvian diagonal, were the remains of the Roman *principia*, the administrative building of the legion quartered in York (Eboracum). As a result of this immensely important find, the original plans for a small muniments museum under the crossing were radically revised. Since archaeology led to much more extensive excavations than planned, it was decided to use the void for a large and handsome subterranean museum of Roman York.

As it stands today, the whole vessel, with its conserved monuments and glorious stained glass, re-creates the long-forgotten luminous splendor of Gothic architecture—the state so eloquently described by Le Corbusier in his prescient phrase *"when the cathedrals were white."* But long before its completion, the project was attracting thousands of visitors who contributed substantially toward its financing. And today, as with the somewhat comparable project at the Cathedral of Coventry, the Minster has become one of the most important tourist meccas in England. This suggests that, in the current climate of public opinion, the very *act* of preservation generates as much interest as the beauty of the monument itself.

The conservation methods employed at York give us the means of saving many

7.4. *All that remains of one of Louis Sullivan's grandest Chicago skyscrapers* are two reconstituted fragments: the entrance portal (below) and the Trading Room (*10.1*). These two fragments, now installed in the Art Institute of Chicago are all that was salvaged in the long and bitter battle to preserve the entire building in situ. Nevertheless, in the longer view, the struggle must be ranked as worthwhile. Many Chicagoans were sensitized by the battle itself to the importance of historic preservation. And the fragments remain as poignant reminders of Chicago's splendid heritage.

7.5. *Moved on its 300th anniversary to a new site,* 4,500 miles from home: the London church of St. Mary Aldermanbury was disassembled and shipped to Fulton, Missouri, where it was reconstituted in 1966. Originally built c. 1181, and rebuilt by Christopher Wren after the fire of 1666, St. Mary's had once again been gutted by the Nazi air raids of 1940. It stood in ruined condition until given to Westminster College to commemorate the speech that Winston Churchill had delivered there. The disassembly process was orthodox: each marble façade was photographed and measured drawings prepared, showing size, shape, and location of each stone (*1*). Actual stones were stenciled with corresponding numbers, packed in sequence of disassembly, and shipped to the new site. In the reconstituted church, these stones are actually only the exterior veneer for a modern brick masonry shell. The metal-framed roof replicates the silhouette of the original wood-framed fabric lost in the raids. Similarly, the lead-covered clock is a facsimile atop the reconstituted marble tower. The interiors of the building, which serves as the college chapel, all replicate the wood and plaster detailing of the Wrenian original.

1

7.6. *Reconstituted Philadelphia facade:* when Penn Mutual Insurance Company decided to double its office space on Independence Square, it faced a delicate problem in urban aesthetics. A handsome old building in the "Egyptian" style of the 1840s occupied part of the site. Already owned by Penn Mutual, it was the birthplace of its corporate ancestor, the Pennsylvania Fire Insurance Company (*1*). It was also an important surviving remnant of the old 3-story town houses that had once enframed the Square. Thus both company and town had reasons for maintaining its presence: the question was, how? The architects' solution was to disassemble the old marble façade, clear the land behind it, erect the new tower, and then reconstitute the façade as a free-standing screen in its original position (*2*). In its new role as surrogate for the lost building, the marble façade was mounted on a reinforced concrete armature (*4*) and creates a loggia for the new tower (*5*).

It might have been even more effective had the façade of the adjacent town house (now demolished to expose the entrance to the tower) been similarly preserved. Nevertheless, the spatial integrity of the Square—especially from the point of view of the passerby—is helped by the reappearance of the familiar Egyptian façade.

old masonry structures which hitherto would have been hopelessly doomed. The grout-injection method permits the conversion of all types of desiccated rubble masonry into solid monolithic structures. It has been used with signal success in some of the great vaulted brick-built palazzi of Italy, and some variation of it will doubtless be finally adopted in saving the ailing Tower of Pisa. In Italy, as we have seen, a related technique has been applied to the foundations, e.g., the creation of a network of interlaced concrete pilings. In both the Campanile at the Cathedral of Burano and the Duomo at Pienza, the resulting lattice acts literally like tree roots to anchor the structure to the soil.

Warship **Vasa,** *Stockholm, Sweden:* The raising of this great wooden warship, submerged since it sank on its maiden voyage in 1621, and its reconstitution into an artifact which can be exhibited indefinitely, is another dramatic example of the great potentials of the new technology.[2] An artifact of great significance for the history of technology, the vessel could have been retrieved from the Stockholm harbor only as a consequence of advances in naval engineering. But equally important, the fragile fabric of the vessel could have been conserved only by spectacular advances in chemistry. For it was only by injecting every cubic centimeter of the waterlogged wood with epoxy polymers that it could have been prevented from turning into dust when brought to the surface and exposed to normal atmospheres. As it was, the vessel, supported by pontoons, was towed underwater to a specially constructed floating dock. Here an atmospheric environment of fixed temperature and 98 percent humidity has been continuously maintained. Under these controlled conditions, not only the vessel but all the artifacts aboard (for it sank fully fitted out with the latest in naval equipment) are being conserved. When the process is complete, the pulpy wood will have been reconstituted into a new composition which looks like wood but has all the physical characteristics of Lucite. An artifact of great historical importance will have been saved, if not for all time, then at least for the forseeable future.

The techniques employed on the *Vasa,* which can obviously be applied to any desiccated wooden fabric, are already in wide use in the conservation of wooden works of art. But the process is expensive, time-consuming, and workable only under strictly controlled environmental conditions. Hence it would perhaps be employed only on artifacts of extraordinary historical or artistic value. Its application to orthodox architectural problems is thus limited. However, a variant has recently been ingeniously employed in the desiccated roof trusses of a number of English churches, where the bearing ends of some of the trusses were found to have rotted away as the result of moisture in the walls. Since the trusses were otherwise sound, the ends were reconstructed in solid epoxy, with reinforcing rods of the same material cemented into deep holes bored into the sound portions of the truss. Such a limited application would be especially useful where the conserved member is exposed to view and therefore plays an important cosmetic role in the aesthetic ensemble. If the surfaces of the member were carved or painted, as in a coffered ceiling, the technique would be the only way in which the original could be preserved in situ.

Temple of Aten, Thebes, Egypt: One hitherto almost insuperable task has been the reconstitution of fabrics whose constituent parts exist, but exist in a completely dismembered state. Their reassembly is comparable to the piecing together of a large, three-dimensional jigsaw puzzle. The computer offers an obvious solution to such problems, and it is now proposed to employ it in the reconstitution of the Temple of Aten. This Eighteenth Dynasty structure, built by Amenhotep IV (Ikhnaton), dates from the fourteenth century B.C. and was deliberately razed by Ikhnaton's successors. It was long known only from its shattered polychromed bas-reliefs and architectural ornament, and its actual site has only recently been established. The broken fragments had been used as rubble in-fill in the walls and columns of a new temple to Amun nearby in the reign of King Harmhab (1345–1314 B. C.).[3] This temple, in its turn, had long ago been reduced to ruins, thus exposing the hidden fragments of its predecessor. Because of the unusual interest attached to the innovative pharaoh, the reconstitution of the temple (and especially of its great bas-reliefs) has long intrigued archaeologists and historians. But the task of sorting out thousands of fragments and fitting them back together into their original visual relationships seemed insuperable, since, done by hand, it would have required hundreds of thousands of man-hours.

But now, with the computer, the task is soluble.[4] Using new techniques developed by Ray Winfield Smith of the University Museum of the University of Pennsylvania, the fragments are being photographed. Each picture is scanned by the computer, which stores this information and then, bit by bit, puts the jigsaw puzzle back together. By use of the printouts of these data, the individual fragments can be numbered and cataloged and, when the time comes for the actual physical reconstruction of the temple, set into their proper position. Since the temple itself was structurally simple—a trabeated masonry shell—its rebuilding poses no problems. Perhaps, for reasons of economy, it might be feasible to construct a reinforced concrete skeleton which replicates the volume of the temple and hang the bas-reliefs upon it, as was done with the Illinois State House.

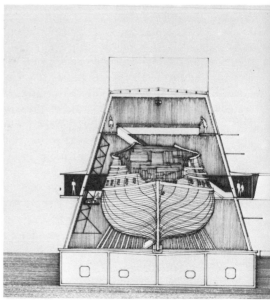

7.7. Reconstitution of the warship Vasa: sometimes an artifact is so pregnant with historical significance that its restoration is culturally justified, no matter what the cost or trouble. In such cases, no surrogate, facsimile, or replica will suffice: the actual integument of the original is required for study and analysis. Such was the sentiment in Sweden in connection with the warship *Vasa,* a paradigm of Swedish naval might when it sank on its maiden voyage in Stockholm's harbor on a calm day in 1621. It went down with a full complement of men and material: if retrieved and conserved, it would constitute an encyclopedia of information on advanced seventeenth–century naval technology.

3

4

5

7.7 (Continued). Location of the wreck had always been known; but the technical problems of raising it—not to mention subsequently conserving it—had been insuperable. Finally, in 1961, salvage work was begun, investigation by divers suggesting that the hulk and its cargo had been surprisingly well preserved by the cold salt waters. The decision was to raise it (*1*) and quickly transport it in a special cradle (*2*) to a special harborside museum which would have been built to receive her (*3, 6*)

Actually, the technology involved in raising an old hulk like the *Vasa* is more familiar than those needed to conserve it once exposed to open air, since organic materials which have survived infestation by anaerobic bacteria while submerged will quickly turn to powder if allowed to dry out. Consolidation of such waterlogged materials has become possible with the perfection of a new group of synthetic resins, the epoxies. Under controlled conditions, these substances can be injected into desiccated materials, where they fill all cavities and set up into a strong binding agent. When cured, they are very strong, chemically inert, dimensionally stable, and colorless. The impregnated tissue emerges as strong as, if not stronger than, the original. The intervention is invisible (if the epoxy was transparent); otherwise it can be painted and polished to match the original. Since the whole process requires controlled environmental conditions, the new museum was equipped to provide them (*3, 6*).

6

Extended and Adaptive Use

As we have seen (Chapter 4), the reworking of extant structures to adapt them to new uses is as old as civilization itself. Indeed, it was the characteristic mode of energy conservation until about a century or so ago, when the concept of technological (as opposed to physical) obsolescence began to gain ascendancy in the Western world. Even so, the remodeling of old buildings continued to be a common practice until after World War II when, due to a number of changed circumstances, it began to fall into disrepute. The first was that the reworking of any old fabric is labor-intensive, and the cost of labor—always high in America vis-à-vis materials—was high and rising. To this economic deterrent was added a series of federal income tax provisions which permitted a capital tax loss on demolished buildings and important tax incentives on the cost of new construction. Together with the prestige of the new and up-to-date, these circumstances gave irresistible support to the theory that it is always cheaper "to tear it down and start over."

The remodeling of old buildings had characteristically involved "improving" or "modernizing" them—i.e., *concealing* the fact that they were old by manipulating their surfaces to "make them look like new." In other words, no value attached to either the historical or aesthetic attributes of the old buildings; the only justification for conserving them at all was strictly utilitarian. From this point of view, ornamental features were regarded as counterproductive since they tended to date the building. Thus they were stripped off, concealed behind veneers of various sorts, or simply painted over. Clearly this handling of old buildings reflected the American attitude toward used artifacts in general. Unless the artifact was a "genuine antique" (in which case it was subject to an entirely different evaluation), it was "used," "secondhand," "old-fashioned"; hence all traces of the aging process were to be concealed.

It is a measure of how profoundly our attitude toward the built environment is changing that this type of remodeling is now generally discred-

165

8.1. *Remodeling vs. restoration at Corning, New York:* an early and prototypical example of the role played by historic district designation in the economic revitalization of small-town main streets. Many basic shifts in patterns of urban development (including, most recently, shortages in energy sources and soaring energy costs) are leading to a turn-around in the decades-long attrition of small towns like Corning. One aspect of this renewed vitality has been the growing recognition of the historic and aesthetic value of old commercial buildings—structures that had previously been considered as mere obstacles to progress. Earlier efforts to extend the useful life of these buildings usually took the form of "remodeling" them. Conceptually, this involved altering their appearance: concealing the fact that they were old by trying to make them look new. This policy of cosmetic masking has proved to be neither physically nor aesthetically durable. Remodeling did not halt the drift to suburbia: it often seemed to accelerate it.

In Corning, a grass-roots movement of local history buffs and local merchants led to the formation of the Market Street Restoration Agency. The Agency, in turn, has been responsible for the architectural restoration and economic revitalization of the entire downtown business district. The goals, though nominally quite modest, are actually profound: they recognize that any attempt to modernize an entire street by cosmetic means—that is, to try to make it conform to some preconceived state of visual unity—is ultimately doomed. Most nineteenth-century buildings in most American towns have a basic typological uniformity: 3-bay row houses with a shop at street level and 1 or 2 residential floors above. But they were designed with a wide variety of eclectic façades, executed in a range of materials. It is this variety within a wider unity that is being rediscovered in Corning. Generally, interventions are modest: old veneers and applied surfaces are removed (*9*); original colors and textures conserved; shop fronts and sash restored where necessary to original configurations; signage reduced in size and stridency (*1, 2*). Street furniture—paving, streetlamps, benches, paving, and trees—is handled by the Agency itself.

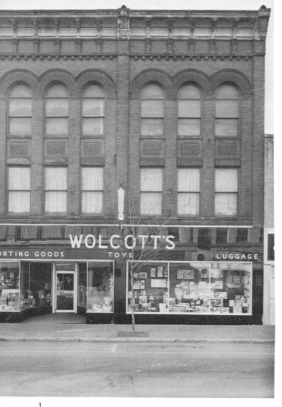

1

2

3

4

5

6

8.1 *(Continued).* ***Fortunately for preservationists,*** most commercial façade remodelings have been cheap and lightweight affairs, as easy to remove as they were to install. Fortunately also, they usually left ornamental details such as cornices and entablatures intact. Thus restoration of this Corning shop front (*9*) revealed the original handsome sheet-metal cornice intact beneath a slovenly screen of aluminum siding nailed to an improvised wood frame.

ited. This changed attitude reflects our growing realization that *all* old buildings have a certain value—economically, scenographically, sentimentally—and not merely those whose historicity or artistic value is already established. It also reflects a radical revision of our value system for classifying buildings according to style. Thus, until very recently, the Greek revival of the 1830s—or, at the very most, the Gothic revival of the 1840s—was considered the last idiom worthy of preservation. The eclectic "Victorian" styles of the last half of the nineteenth century and the eclectic revivals before World War I were considered valueless. Even the moderne and art deco modes of the twenties were beyond the pale.

All old buildings have a structural and artistic integrity which, in the light of our changed attitudes, must be respected. At the same time, it must be remembered that the vast majority of buildings in American cities will not, when individually considered, have any great historic or artistic significance. This will hold especially for commercial and industrial structures and for mass urban housing. And whatever monumental pretensions these buildings might have had externally, few of them will have interiors of any special merit. Hence, interventions for adaptive use will ordinarily be more conservative externally than internally since the building's role in the streetscape will be more urbanistic than narrowly architectural. The interior volumes, on the other hand, are susceptible to much more radical manipulation.

Only within the past two decades have the economic scales begun to tip again in favor of retrieval and recycling as opposed to demolition and/or new construction. Here again fundamental economic forces are at work. For now it is apparent that adaptive reuse of old buildings is more economic not only in general terms (e.g., the conservation of energy represented by the built environment), but absolutely (i.e., relative costs of old and new built space).

This phenomenon has been perceptively analyzed in a special study by the Advisory Council on Historic Preservation, *Adaptive Use: A Survey of Construction Costs.*[1] The Report points out that, with the growing concern for the natural environment in the late 1960s and early 1970s, the idea of recycling buildings took on new significance, applying the conservationist attitude to the man-made environment as well. But perhaps the single most important factor to further the cause was the change in the state of the economy in the mid-1970s. As fuel and material costs skyrocketed faster than labor costs, new construction, being oriented to intensive use of new materials, and heavy machinery, became prohibitively expensive for many.

Building permits were difficult to obtain in areas previously ripe for intensive development. When construction was undertaken, building materials were not only very costly, but often slow to arrive. Rising costs of demolition also discouraged land clearance activities. Environmental con-

1

8.2. *An added century of useful life* was won for the 100-year-old Baltimore City Hall by a program of restoration and retrofitting—but only after a long and sometimes acrid battle by local preservationists to prevent its demolition. The 1875 structure by George A. Fredericks (*1*) stood in the center of Baltimore's vast urban renewal district, and the conventional wisdom of the sixties dictated its replacement by a new (and putatively better) building. But, as things turned out, it was saved and recycled—and at 32 percent less than the estimated price of a new replacement. The restoration architects faced a two-pronged task: preserving the Second Empire exteriors and monumental interiors and providing safer, more convenient accommodations for all the activities connected with the municipal government.

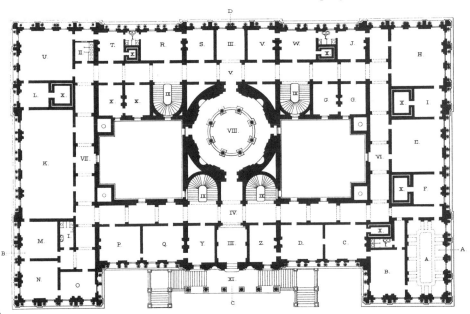

2

By an imaginative manipulation of the interior volumes of the old load-bearing masonry shell, the architects increased usable floor space from 53,000 to 98,000 square feet. The reorganized floor layouts accomplish this by new interior circulation systems, including new stairs and 4 new elevators; enclosure of old courtyards; creation of new mezzanine floors inside lofty old office spaces; and the complete rehabilitation of the underused basement floor (9). Circulation of the public is reorganized along a new central spine that cuts across the rotunda and connects new stairs and elevators (4), while interdepartmental circulation is handled by new smaller corridors under mezzanines. The entire building has new heating and ventilating systems, new illumination, and new sanitary facilities.

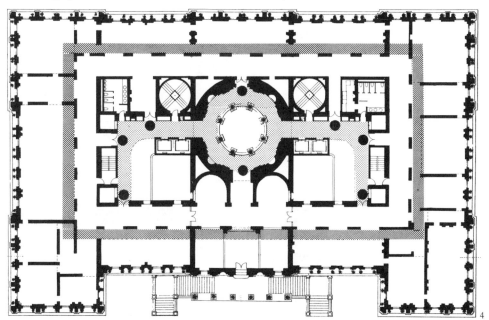

4

5

6

172

8.2 *(Continued). A civilized equilibrium between old and new* has been achieved in the Baltimore City Hall. Significant monumental volumes, such as the Mayor's reception room (*5*) and the great rotunda (*6*), have been scrupulously restored to their original Victorian splendor. Other, more utilitarian spaces with no historical interest or aesthetic pretensions have been handled in a straightforward contemporary manner. Thus the two courtyards have been freed of a century of accumulated clutter and converted into handsome, top-lighted circulation cores for public circulation (*8*). Similarly, the old basement has been raised to a new level of amenity by exposing its great masonry foundations. The circular vault under the rotunda has been converted into a handsome exposition space (*9*).

8.3. *In Prague, an old Gothic nunnery* becomes a new museum of art. Until a few years ago, the fourteenth-century Convent of St. Agnes was a derelict old slum, the result of a century of use and abuse as rental housing. Now, under a comprehensive program of demolition, restoration, and consolidation, the medieval complex is being returned to something approaching its original condition. Functionally, it is being adapted to house the National Museum's great collection of Gothic and medieval painting and sculpture (*1, 2*). It has not been easy for, like most very old buildings, St. Agnes had been subjected to ceaseless alterations and modifications and—in its last phase as a slum—mutilations. There was also scanty archival material on many of these evolutionary developments. Hence, initially, plans for its

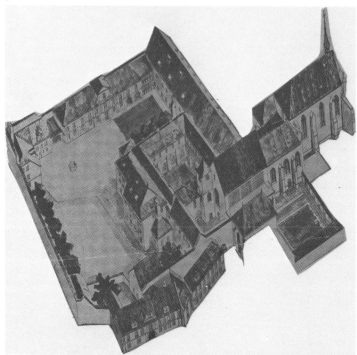

rehabilitation could be only provisional: the moment work began, the project became an archaeological "dig" and plans had to be revised in the light of new findings. Thus, removal of the stucco from the walls of one of the courtyards revealed traces of a lost cloister at ground level and an open loggia under the roof (3). Designs were revised to restore both (4).

Because of this continuing flood of new data on the morphological development of the complex, it was both unwise and impracticable to attempt to restore it to any single point in time. There is no reconstruction of totally vanished elements, but in one instance a lost chapel will be replaced with a contemporary reinforced concrete hall which roughly repeats the plan and profile of its predecessor (center of model, 2).

8.4. *Faneuil Hall Market: restoration of the fabric.* When this Boston project was initiated, the complex was still fundamentally intact but its visual integrity had been seriously compromised by added floors, altered roof lines, changed fenestration, etc. (*3*). The decision to restore the market to the form created by the architect Alexander Parris in 1825 (*1*) was rationalized on both historical and aesthetic grounds. It was the second-oldest commercial complex to have been conceived of as a monumental entity (New York's Fulton Market was a little earlier). And its artistic impact derived largely from its unitary design, the standardized warehouse blocks offering a strong visual frame to the domed and porticoed market hall (*2*).

2

176

Preservation of the function: Faneuil Market had been an innovative building type to begin with—an integrated food and produce center with a retail market flanked by offices and warehouses for wholesale dealers in such commodities as tea, coffee, rice, sugar, etc. (3). And it had preserved that function throughout its history, though with diminishing effectiveness owing to shifting patterns of transportation and harbor facilities. This basic function has been preserved by the current developers, though the market is now exclusively retail, the renovated office blocks rented by a wide range of tenants. The shift from wholesale to retail and the elimination of all trucking and private cars has radically altered the street life, making it one of Boston's most active retail areas.

8.4 (Continued). Two photographs of Faneuil Hall Market, taken a century apart, illustrate the vast environmental changes that have followed the shift from a wholesale produce market (5) to its current status as a chic food and restaurant center (6). The rehabilitated market, which can attract 250,000 customers on a summer weekend, has transformed the economic life of the harbor district of Boston. The change is viewed by some critics as another example of the "gentrification" that often follows historic district preservation. However, this complex has never had a residential population; hence the process of rehabilitation and restoration involved no displacement of one sector of the population to make way for a wealthier one.

cerns and "no-growth" attitudes led to other obstacles such as suburban sewer moratoria.

About the same time, planners and city officials began to acknowledge the failure of many of the grandiose schemes of urban renewal and slum clearance programs of the 1950s and 1960s. It was recognized that rehabilitating instead of demolishing sound but decayed structures offered a more economically and socially less disruptive means of renewing cities. Planners and city officials were coming full circle and joining with the environmentalists and the inhabitants of the neighborhoods that were originally slated for destruction to come up with new ideas such as neighborhood conservation and urban homesteading. By the mid-seventies, it became evident that conservation of the built environment had become a basic tenet of many community development programs.

Compared with new construction, adaptive use offers many advantages. Not only do recycled projects generally require less capital to start and take less time to complete, meaning less money tied up for a shorter period before rents start coming in, but they are by nature labor-intensive projects, relying less on expensive heavy machinery and costly structural materials. Beyond the benefit to the developer, these factors produce social benefits by conserving resources and employing proportionately greater numbers of workers.★

There are obvious benefits to reusing existent buildings. Older buildings are frequently better built, with craftsmanship and materials which cannot be duplicated in today's market. Late nineteenth and early twentieth century buildings were constructed with care and lavish decoration seldom possible in contemporary buildings. These structures have thick walls, windows which open, high ceilings, and other amenities not found in new buildings. Also, these buildings were designed to use natural light and ventilation, often being natural energy savers. In sum, old buildings provide more interesting and varied environments for people to live, work, shop, and eat.

Despite the obvious economies of retrieving and recycling older structures, actual cost comparisons with new construction have been hard to come by. Thus, the Advisory Council's report includes a survey of 35 recently completed adaptive-use projects, giving actual costs per square foot and relating them to actual costs of comparable new construction in the same region at the same time. Five building types were studied: (1) apartments; (2) museums; (3) office buildings; (4) retail establishments; (5) theaters.

★This has been duly noted by the General Services Administration in endorsing proposed legislation that would establish a preference for using recycled buildings of historical or architectural significance for federal office space. In doing so, they noted that adaptive-use projects employ more laborers per structure than comparable new construction projects.

1

8.5. *Redundant railroad stations* are one of the nation's largest categories of orphan building types. The Terminal Station in Chattanooga, Tennessee, abandoned in 1970, was rescued by an imaginative group of local business men who saw its possibilities as a tourist attraction. Choosing the flamboyant name "Chattanooga Choo-Choo" (from a famous popular song of the forties), they have adapted it for a series of restaurants and a motel into a highly successful middle-brow tourist enterprise. The exteriors and the monumental old Waiting Room have been rather carefully restored (*1, 4*), while the former Concourse has been exuberantly redecorated in eclectic fashion (*5*). Train sheds have been partially restored and partially removed to take a collection of old locomotives, Pullman cars, and trolleys which accurately reflect that portion of popular culture known as "railroad buffs"; 28 of the antique Pullman cars have been adapted for use as luxury motel suites.

2

3

180

4

5

6

8.5 *(Continued). **The Terminal's train sheds,*** though reduced in number, still shelter a collection of old railroad cars which, interesting in themselves as antiques, have been converted into some 50 air-conditioned suites operated by a new 300-room motel in the former marshaling yards at the rear. Old electric trolleys make the run from station to motel and back for a 10-cent fare. With its unabashed vulgarity, Chatanooga Choo-Choo's immense success shows the pervasive power of American popular culture.

7

The Advisory Council report makes a number of general observations. The data confirm that, although adaptive use is not always cheaper than new construction, the cost of adaptive use falls within the range of new construction costs. It would seem, then, that adaptive use stands as an equally feasible alternative to new construction. Actual cost differences for any given project will, of course, vary with the amount of work needed to adapt a particular building to the desired use.

The survey indicates that demolition costs inside the buildings being recycled are minimal, normally only 1 to 4 percent of the total project cost. Structural costs are also low, normally varying from about 5 to 12 percent of the total project cost, which is less than half the average expenditure for new construction. This reflects the fact that little structural work is normally required when reusing an old building. Architectural costs vary above and below the average for new construction. Generally, in projects where the maximum effort was made to reuse the existing interior and exterior materials, the costs are substantially below those for new construction. Conversely, where decisions were made to alter the existing fabric substantially, the costs rose.

Mechanical costs, like those for architecture, were both above and below those for new construction. Again, where the costs were low, normally complex climate control equipment and fire protection systems were not installed. Where the costs were high, extensive fire protection equipment was necessary due to the nonfireproof nature of certain old buildings. In addition, because many old buildings do not easily lend themselves to the installation of the tremendous quantity of ductwork and chases normally required with sophisticated mechanical equipment, mechanical equipment will likely remain an expensive item in adaptive use construction.

The survey shows that demolition and structural costs are minimal in adaptive-use projects. These represent areas where considerable savings can be made. It appears that the determining factors of the overall cost of adaptive-use construction will be in the architectural and mechanical work. Through the architect's ingenuity and inventiveness, the costs may be kept down.

1

8.6. *A historic block of an old English village has been preserved* by recycling these modest seventeenth-century houses into a deluxe hostelry. The Swan Hotel at Lavenham, some 50 miles out of London, is a new institution in a county in which new construction is all but impossible. Exploiting the local color of the old wattle and daub houses, it has restored and retrofitted them with all modern conveniences. They contain most of the guest rooms and successfully screen the new and necessary facilities (dining room, lounge, kitchen, and services), which are inserted in the reorganized back gardens of the houses. Parking is provided in a walled and landscaped area at the rear (2). The old houses have been discreetly conserved, inside and out, and the interiors furnished with a pleasant mix of period furniture.

2

The
SWAN HOTEL
LAVENHAM

8.7. *Derelict fishing village into a romantic seaside resort:* the village of Sveti Stefan, on the Adriatic coast of Yugoslavia was dying, along with the dwindling fishing industry which had once supported it. Treating the entire, densely built-up fabric of the village as a megastructure, the national tourist agency has converted it into a delightful resort hotel. Because of the genial climate, village lanes can serve as corridors, piazzas as outdoor cafés; the church serves as the hotel lounge. The indigenous character of the old houses, uniformly constructed of a local honey-colored limestone and roofed in local tiles, has been carefully conserved; furnishings employ local handicrafts and indigenous folk art. The entire complex is traffic-free, guest parking being restricted to the mainland.

9

Reconstruction, Reproduction, and Replica: Use and Abuse

The act of replication,* so fundamental to the industrial production of utilitarian goods, is singularly hazardous when applied to works of art and architecture. By its sheer presence in quantity, the replica can coarsen and corrupt public appreciation of the prototype. The cultural consequences of replication are most apparent in small and mobile artifacts—paintings, sculpture, objets d'art. Fortunately, the sheer cost and difficulty of replicating a building in full-scale, three-dimensional reality is very high: as a consequence, it is not so common a phenomenon.

Replicas and reproductions have always been troublesome for archaeologists, curators, and collectors; and for obvious reasons, since even the well-intentioned replica, i.e., one not intended to be sold as an original, has a disconcerting tendency of turning up, sooner or later, on the antiquities market. Deliberate fakes such as the "Etruscan" warrior, bedeviled the curators of the Metropolitan Museum of Art for decades before it was finally exposed as fraudulent, can cause no end of worry and expense. Hence most museums and galleries do their best to weed out copies and replicas (unless, of course, the replica is itself an antique, as in the case of Roman copies of Greek sculptures). Thanks to the growth of international expertise and scholarship in works of art, the circulation of fakes is increasingly restricted.

There are broad cultural reasons why museums do not want to exhibit copies and replicas alongside of originals. One of the museums' functions is

---

*We use the term in its strict meaning—i.e., "to duplicate, copy, or repeat"—in contradistinction to the term "reconstruction," with which it is often confused. In the first instance, we mean to describe the erection of an exact copy of a still-extant original, usually on a site or in a context far removed from the prototype. In the case of "reconstruction," we describe the re-creation of a vanished building, erected on the same site as the original and designed to act as its surrogate in the original context.

didactic, i.e., to teach us how to discriminate between the real and the fake, how to appreciate the unique and ultimately irreproducible qualities of the original. This education takes place at two levels, reflecting the way in which our value judgments are developed. One level is subjective, the sheer sensual stimulation we get from seeing and feeling the artifact; the other is more objective, cognitive, reflecting our knowledge of how our culture evaluates the beauty, uniqueness, and monetary value of that artifact. The two are umbilically connected and interact to determine our final aesthetic estimate of the object. (Thus if we *know* that the painting is a

9.1. *The "Etruscan" warrior,* once a centerpiece of the classics department of New York's Metropolitan Museum, has long been relegated to the cellar. But while it remained on display, it was the center of controversy among Etruscologists, who were disturbed by its stylistic anachchronisms. This astonishingly clever forgery was finally exposed, and the forgers themselves tracked down, by a team of art historians, chemists, and ceramicists, using a whole range of analytical techniques. But while the forgery remained unexposed, it constituted a threat to a whole system of values carefully constructed by decades of scholarly, hard work

Rembrandt, our judgment will be high; if we are told by an authority that it is a fake, our judgment drops precipitiously.)

The same value-making process applies to larger artifacts like towns and buildings. The past century has taught us that reconstructions and reproductions of vanished buildings are culturally hazardous. There is a growing recognition of the fact that, in the last analysis, it is all but impossible to produce permanently convincing fakes. Time has its own merciless way of exposing them. Viollet-le-Duc was the best-educated and most talented restorationist of the nineteenth century. The architectural infill he inserted into the semiruined fabrics of Carcassonne and the Château of Pierrefonds must have seemed to him and his contemporaries thoroughly convincing. Yet today they appear almost comically Victorian. Each epoch leaves its own imprint upon everything it makes, including its version of its own past. Nevertheless, there *are* today situations in which the reproduction or replica can be used as a surrogate for the missing original. These situations can be described as lying along a sort of scale of descending urgency.

A reconstruction of a vanished building may be justified for urbanistic or ambiental reasons, as in situations where it played a vital role in some monumental composition. This was the justification for the reconstruction of the long-vanished Governor's Palace and Capitol in Williamsburg (see Fig. 6.6). These two monumental structures had been conceived as termini for two of the three main axes of the town; the surviving building for William and Mary College being the third. In formulating policies for the restoration of Colonial Williamsburg, i.e., the way it was in 1776, it was felt that the *raison d'être* of the town plan would be unintelligible to the visitor unless these two buildings were reconstructed.

A similar case can be made for the recently completed reconstruction of the Royal Palace at Warsaw. Forming one entire side of an important square in the Stare Miasto, the palace had been completely leveled by the Nazis in World War II. Whether or not to reconstruct it had been debated for years, largely on ideological grounds. (This despite the fact that dozens of other palaces elsewhere had been completely restored.) Finally, it was decided that reconstruction was desirable. Unlike the case of Williamsburg, the Poles dealt with a monument which most Varsovians over 40 would have known and one for which elaborate documentation—literary, photographs, and measured drawings—existed. The reconstruction thus required a minimum of conjectural restoration.

There are historical personages and events which might be so important to their nation as to justify the reconstruction of buildings in which they lived and acted, even though the building itself might long ago have disappeared. Two characteristic examples would be the Church of John Huss in Prague and the Benjamin Franklin Homesite in Philadelphia. In the case of

1

3

2

4

5

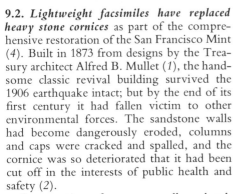

6

7

9.2. Lightweight facsimiles have replaced heavy stone cornices as part of the comprehensive restoration of the San Francisco Mint (*4*). Built in 1873 from designs by the Treasury architect Alfred B. Mullet (*1*), the handsome classic revival building survived the 1906 earthquake intact; but by the end of its first century it had fallen victim to other environmental forces. The sandstone walls had become dangerously eroded, columns and caps were cracked and spalled, and the cornice was so deteriorated that it had been cut off in the interests of public health and safety (*2*).

Conservation of masonry walls and columns followed orthodox practice. Replacement of the original stone cornice was impracticable, however, because of earthquake hazards. Instead, facsimiles of fiberglass-reinforced polyurethane were substituted; these were prefabricated in modular panels which replicated the original exactly. They were hoisted into place (*4*) and bolted onto brackets embedded in the walls (*5*). The brackets were adjustable, to permit accurate alignment of the prefabricated units. Finally, the joints were caulked with a sealant to approximate original masonry joints (*6*). The restored Mint now houses a museum, a computing center, and a variety of federal offices.

191

1

2

3

4

9.3. *The 1876 Centennial Exposition in Philadelphia* was so enormously popular that a movement arose to perpetuate it. (*1*). Congress responded by approving construction of a new building in Washington to house a portion of the Philadelphia exhibit materials. The new museum, located adjacent to Renwick's romanesque castle for the Smithsonian Institution, was designed as a red-brick and limestone echo of its parent institution (*2*). Opened with great fanfare in 1881, the Arts and Industries Building housed for many years a dwindling array of 1876 memorabilia. But by the mid-sixties, it was empty and seemed doomed to disappear, when the Smithsonian decided on a novel scheme for its regeneration. To mark the 1976 anniversary, it would restore the building to its original condition and reinstall its original collection. Restoration of the fabric, inside and out, has been scrupulously accomplished (*2, 3, 4*). The exhibition itself, named "1876," is not an exact replica, since less that 15 percent of the original objects could be recovered. But the objects are authentic to the period and the display is designed to re-create the atmosphere of bouyant confidence of the post–Civil War period. The visitor is thus confronted with a novel experience: a museum building and a museum exhibition, both generated by the same historical event. Even more novel is the fact that both were "brand-new" then and have been conserved to appear as brand-new today.

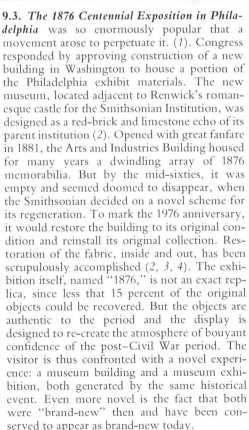

5

9.3 *(Continued)*. The 1876 Exhibition displayed a staggeringly diverse array of artifacts—ranging from seashells and stuffed bears to locomotives and drill presses. Ordinarily, the Smithsonian would display them in an "as found" condition, wear and tear being interpreted as a part of their history. But because of the special circumstances surrounding both the 1876 and the 1976 events, it was decided to restore all the artifacts to the state in which they would have been shown a century ago: bright and shining, polished and ready to go. The colors, varnishes, and burnished metals so dear to late-Victorian machinery designers and cabinet-makers have been carefully restored. Where original finishes and decorations had been lost, they were reconstructed on the basis of known analogs.

the Prague church, in which Huss had preached some of his most important sermons, it was decided to reconstruct completely the two-aisled Gothic chapel in which those sermons occurred. Extensive historical and pictorial documentation existed. The site was cleared of later buildings, archaeology completed, and the reconstruction drawings prepared. The reconstructed church now serves as a museum.

Initially, the same process had been contemplated for the Franklin homesite (Fig. 14.6). Fortunately, this approach was abandoned, largely because the most extensive research had failed to turn up any visual materials showing how the building might have looked in Franklin's day. It was decided, after a complete archaeological investigation of the site, that the subsurface cellars would be consolidated and roofed over to serve as a subterranean exhibit space. Above grade, and based on the foundations, would be erected a three-dimensional metal skeleton which would trace out the conjectural outlines of the roof, chimney, and walls of the original building.

This same technique had been employed by the Italians some years previously at an archaeological site at Piazza Armerina in Sicily (Fig. 14.4). Here the superstructure, an aluminum skeleton sheathed with transparent plastic, replicated the conjectural masses of a great Roman villa. The main purpose of the shelter was to protect a series of extremely important mosaic floors. Unfortunately, two unexpected problems have somewhat reduced its effectiveness: the soft plastic, easily abraded by blowing sand, is becoming increasingly opaque; and the greenhouse effect of the translucent roofs produces uncomfortably high temperatures inside the enclosure, especially in summer.

At a smaller scale, it may often be necessary to reproduce missing elements *within* a given building which has been mutilated by fire, neglect, or remodeling. This is especially the case in buildings with formal pretensions whose serial patterns (windows, dormers, chimneys, colonnades) are so disrupted as to make comprehension difficult or impossible. This type of replication of parts has been employed in a recent American project: the restoration of the Greek revival commercial blocks on either side of Boston's Quincy Market. The Quincy is a rare example of nineteenth-century large-scale developments, and its uniqueness as historical example of this period outweighs the aesthetic value of subsequent alterations. The decision to restore its original visual unity must be accepted as correct.

At a still smaller scale, there is the problem of missing elements in a decorative feature (a column missing from a portico; a bracket or coffer lost from a cornice). Such voids must be infilled with replicas. For future curators, such replicas ought to be marked in a permanent way, e.g., by punched or branded dates or even by being executed in a new material, such as molded fiberglass.

There are an increasing number of situations in modern life in which

1

9.4. *Quite appropriately, in view of its key role* in the theocratic system of the Church of Jesus Christ of Latter-Day Saints, the Mormon Temple had been placed at the center of its capital, Salt Lake City. But its symbolic importance as the seat of one of the world's fastest-growing religious organizations had not been fully expressed in the cityscape *(1)*. Recently, this has been changed by some rather radical urban surgery. Mormon headquarters was in need of expanded office facilities, and it was decided to build these along a newly created monumental plaza on the axis of the Temple *(8, 9)*. The construction of the new plaza required razing a number of minor buildings. Their disappearance led, in turn, to another aesthetic problem: the rear façades of the beaux arts Hotel Utah, never designed for public exposure, were rudely revealed *(3)*. To correct what was fundamentally a problem of urban aesthetics, an architectural strategy was devised. The hotel would be enlarged to bring its north wall up to the edge of the new plaza; the addition would be designed to match the old building in mass and scale and faced in white terra-cotta blocks which exactly replicated the original. The decision was not without risks: terra-cotta blocks from this period (c. 1910)

have recently revealed startling deterioration (see Fig. 6.11), and the commercial production of terra cotta has all but ceased. Terra-cotta failures seem, however, to be confined to the northeast quadrant of the nation, with its high precipitation and freeze-thaw cycles; such anomalies are absent from the semidesert climate of Utah. And a leading manufacturer of ceramic products, once a terra-cotta producer, was persuaded to fabricate the replicas for the hotel addition *(4)*. The result of this intervention is eminently successful. The old hotel, always important in the downtown skyline, now plays a new, heightened role in the surrounding streetscapes, its visual integrity consolidated from all directions.

196

2

3

4

5

9.4 *(Continued). The new plaza in Salt Lake City* is a good demonstration of an urban complex whose whole is greater than the sum of its architectural parts. Except for the Temple, with its idiosyncratic gothic profiles, none of the buildings which face on it has any great architectural distinction; and the landscape design of the plaza itself seems unnecessarily severe and coarse. Nevertheless, the urbanity of this section of downtown Salt Lake has been measurably increased by the intervention, and the Temple itself given an enhanced presence in the cityscape *(7)*. Much of this change is due to the restored hotel. One oddity of beaux arts architects was that, for all the flamboyant detail which they lavished on their main façades, they were penurious when it came to rear and party walls. Their egregious error in the old Hotel Utah has been neatly corrected by the architects of the additions.

1

9.5. *New status in the cityscape:* although it dates only from 1908, the Bank of California in downtown San Francisco is the oldest structure in the area—a distinction due to the fact that its predecessor had been demolished, and plans for the present structure prepared, before the great earthquake of 1906. Because of its landmark status, bank officials decided to preserve it and construct their new office tower next door. This decision led to a reexamination of the visual role of the old building in its new context. Two key questions in urban aesthetics were involved: (a) how to handle the connection between the Corinthian temple form and a curtain-walled skyscraper, and (b) how to handle the visual slum on its roof. The first problem was satisfactorily solved by setting the façade of the new tower back some 20 feet from the older one. This permitted the colonnade and entablature to be returned and securely received by the sheer granite plane of the fire tower (*1*). The second problem was neatly resolved by replacing the cluttered old roofscape (*2*) with a handsome landscaped terrace serving the employees' lounge on the fourth floor of the new tower (*3*). Both of these design strategies, simple in themselves, reinforce the presence of the old building in its new urban context. For pedestrians at street level, the old banking room is seen to much better advantage than before; while the new terrace, overlooked by hundreds of windows in its taller neighbors, is converted into a handsome little piazza in the sky.

200

2

3

the replica of the still-extant artifact—acting as a more durable surrogate for an aging, failing, and/or uniquely valuable original—may be either desirable or even necessary. Generally speaking, the use of replicas in architectural or urbanistic settings involves the removal of small, discrete, and fragile decorative elements from the raw exposure of the natural environment of the site to the controlled environment of the museum or art gallery. The increasing need for such substitutions is recognized around the world. It is a result of the increasing impact of environmental pollution upon the masonry, ceramics, metals, and woods of which historic structures have been built. Thus the marble portrait busts from the Baptistry of Pisa Cathedral and the heroic sculpture of *David* by Michelangelo, have been moved indoors into museums, their place outdoors being taken by exact replicas. The buildings of the Athenian Acropolis, especially the Parthenon and the Erechtheion, are among the more spectacular victims of environmental attrition. A comparison of sculpture in the British Museum in London (taken there by Lord Elgin in 1803–1812, in one of history's more spectacular examples of artistic piracy) with those left in situ show that the *rate* of decay has been proceeding on a logarithmic, not an arithmetic, curve.[1] Thus, the decision was made to remove the priceless old sculptures into the nearby Museum of the Acropolis. Their place on the Erechtheion has been taken by facsimiles in reinforced concrete.

There is yet another area in which replicas of historic artifacts are playing an increasingly important role; namely, in those historic sites and monuments in which the educational interpretation of processes is functionally important. Here the facsimile has several advantages. For example, in the interpretation of commercial activities (grocery stores, apothecaries, customhouses) or of technological processes (historic laboratories, foundries, sawmills), a wide range of tools, machines, and furniture is required for demonstration purposes. Such items are nowadays often valuable "antiques" in their own right and hence subject to theft and vandalism. They are too valuable and too fragile to be handled by casual visitors. Moreover, for maximum verisimilitude, the demonstrations themselves require new tools and instruments—not new in design (they should be archaeologically accurate) but physically sound, sharp, bright, and rust-free. Until recently, most open-air museums have furnished their stores, shops, and workplaces with "authentic antiques": apothecary at Shelburne (Fig. 17.1), grocery at Richmondtown Restoration. While handsome in their own right, such artifacts do not make for a vividly realistic demonstration. (No general store in 1875 would have offered for sale a century-old box of table salt or patent medicine; certainly no customer would have bought it!)

More recently, however, American institutions are turning to bright, new-looking facsimiles of historic wares and tools. The general store at Sturbridge is stocked with bright new merchandise. The customshouses at

Salem, Massachusetts, and Monterey, California, are similarly stocked with the sort of new artifacts which one would have seen on the clipper ships when they were still crossing the seas. Among other unexpected advantages of such a policy are greatly simplified security and housekeeping problems. Plimoth Plantation has found very low rates of theft of replicas, whereas traditional exhibits report high and rising thefts of antiques. Moreover, the use of replicas permits visitors to touch and handle them. At the plantation, for example, the visitor who has never had the experience can lie down on rope-strung beds with their corn-husk mattresses and homespun sheets "to feel what it was like."

Plimoth Plantation, the museum village in Massachusetts, is wholly a replica, a conjectural reconstruction of a long-vanished community which is not even located on its original site, which, of course, is occupied by the modern city of Plymouth. Replicas are also exclusively employed *inside* the Plimoth buildings. Like the houses themselves, these are all as close an approximation of the originals as modern research and scholarship can make them. They are all new: what is more important, they *look* new, as they would have five years or so after the establishment of the settlement. This is an important aspect of the central interpretive philosophy at Plimoth. Since the entire complex is a replica, every effort is made to shift the visitor's attention from the artifact to the life-styles and processes it made possible. In this sense, Plimoth's antiantiquarian, anticonnoisseurship emphasis is the reverse of that found at Deerfield or Williamsburg, where everything in the field of view is authentic in its provenience even if it is displaced in space. Traditionally, these museum houses have been equipped with authenticated antiques. The wide range of artifacts so displayed has been collected at great effort and expense. They are interesting historically; they are often handsome; in today's inflationary market they are also extremely valuable and hence vulnerable to theft. In short, authentically museum-quality artifacts have developed an independent status, irrespective of the context in which they are shown.

But there are an increasing number of commercial and industrial sites which, even more than the groceries and apothecary shops already mentioned, suggest the need for a different type of verisimilitude in display and interpretation. Two examples will suffice: The Edison Laboratories in East Orange, New Jersey, and the recently installed 1876 Centennial collection in the Arts and Industries Building in Washington, D.C. In both cases, one is dealing with authentically antique artifacts; but they are being displayed to illustrate scientific or technological processes and activities. They should thus be displayed in working condition. Unfortunately, this has not been achieved in Edison's own office and laboratory. Nominally, it has been preserved in exactly the condition he left it shortly before his death in 1932.

But in actuality, all the equipment and apparatus with which he was working is now in sad cosmetic state. Glass beakers which would have been sparkling, scales which would have been polished, test tubes and tubing which would necessarily have been immaculate—all these now show the cumulative attrition of nearly half a century of nonuse. If the intention of this exhibition is to dramatize Edison's activities as a scientist and inventor, whose work was patient, methodical, and precise, then it would have to be maintained in an appropriately immaculate condition. Admittedly, this criterion poses difficult, perhaps even insuperable, curatorial problems. But if displays of this sort are to be installed at all, suitable maintenance across time must be considered an integral part of the decision.★

At the 1876 Centennial installation, quite a different set of parameters are to be observed. To begin with, of course, all the equipment and machinery on display is "brand-new," none of it having been used in the intervening century—a paradox due largely to its having been either in a museum or in dead storage for the last century. Before being reinstalled in the new exhibit, all of these artifacts have been carefully cleaned and polished, with paint and varnish renewed, signage and trademarks restored, original cabinets and showcases refinished. The result is a dazzlingly successful re-creation of a small portion of that great Victorian fair. For it to remain effective, however, totally new standards of housecleaning and maintenance will have to be continuously followed.

There are other occasions on which replication of extant architectural tissue may be the preferred treatment. Many old buildings, especially in urban locations, were never cosmetically complete because they were designed for interior or corner lots. Only the façades, i.e., the elevations designed for exposure to public view, were fully developed, being assumed that neighboring buildings would mask the unfinished party walls. Such neighboring buildings were often never built or have been subsequently demolished. Party walls are thus exposed to view—scar tissue which was never supposed to be seen. Ordinarily, this new nakedness is handled in cavalier fashion. The exposed wall is left untouched or stuccoed or the entire building is given a new skin, such as porcelain enamel or aluminum siding, to make it "read" as a unit. But increasingly, one deals with old buildings seen in new contexts whose importance in the streetscape is too vital visually to be handled in such a fashion. Here, to give the newly exposed buildings the cosmetic integrity to which it is entitled, it is appropriate that the surface treatment of the original monumental façades be replicated on the newly exposed ones. Thus the building is given a new four-dimensional importance to the pedestrians who walk around it.

★The entire Edison project is being reorganized by the National Park Service to effectuate precisely this new museological objective.

204

This technique has been successfully employed in recent modifications in the old Hotel Utah in Salt Lake City. A beaux arts building surfaced in white terra-cotta and white brick, the Utah occupied a strategically important corner diagonally opposite the Mormon Temple. A recent urban improvement created a new monumental plaza on axis with the Temple. In the process, several smaller buildings were demolished and the rear of the Hotel Utah was exposed, becoming in effect the south face of the new plaza. Instead of wrecking the old hotel or resurfacing it with a "modern" skin, the decision was made to enlarge the hotel, extending it to the boundary of the new plaza, and to surface it with a terra-cotta skin which exactly replicates the original. It was an inspired decision, since it consolidates, both sentimentally and visually, an urbanistic element which has been a favorite landmark and meeting place for almost three-quarters of a century.

Considerations of much the same sort dictated the handling of the old Bank of California building in San Francisco. It had been built in 1908 as a typical Corinthian banking room (of the sort Louis Sullivan so detested) on a busy street corner of the financial district. But it became necessary to expand the bank's accommodations in the late 1950s. Initially, the plan had been to demolish the little Beaux Arts palazzo and erect a 24-story tower in its place. However, because of its historic importance (it is the oldest building in that part of the city, since plans for its construction were already finished before the great earthquake of 1906), it was decided to erect the office tower next door and restore the original banking room. This decision posed subtle problems in the integration of old and new tissue. To guarantee the old banking room a new visual prominence in the cityscape, it was decided to set the new tower back from the building line. But this would expose a portion of the old party wall never designed for exposure. Hence the original granite façade (stylobate, columns, and entablature) had to be returned along the newly visible side wall. Furthermore, the new tower had to offer a "solid" wall to receive it; this was functionally accomplished by locating one of the two fire towers at this point. The result is a thoroughly satisfactory "hinge" between old and new construction.

Another interesting aspect of this same project is the way in which the old banking room was given a new, cosmetically acceptable roof. Originally, the bank had been the tallest structure in the area. What transpired on the roof behind the parapet, in the way of water towers, elevator shafts, and so on, was supposed to be visible to none but God. But over the years, the old palazzo became surrounded by high-rise buildings: its roof became a visual slum upon which thousands of office workers looked down. Therefore, in the rehabilitation of the old banking room, all this obsolete rooftop apparatus was swept away and a new formal terrace was created in its place. This new "piazza in the sky" also serves as recreation area for the bank's employees, whose dining rooms open onto it.

9.6. *Most urban buildings* are designed on the assumption that side and rear walls will never be exposed to public view. Thus the scar tissue left on one building when its neighbor is demolished causes a severe visual disturbance of the streetscape. Structural correction of this condition is neither simple nor cheap. A trompe l'oeil replica of the street façade, like this one by the painter Richard Haas, offers a beguiling alternative. The cast-iron street front is carried around onto the party wall with astonishing verisimilitude on this New York City loft building.

One of the most winning (even if perhaps transient) uses of replication is the treatment of a cast-iron-fronted loft building in lower Manhattan. The brick wall was stuccoed and then painted in a grisaille trompe l'oeil facsimile of the cast-iron street façade. The effect is astonishingly effective. It was an economical wall and—unlike many interventions of this sort—has the virtue of being easily reversible.

The special uses of replication cited above are more significant than the average modern architect—trained to believe in the absolute superiority of contemporary ahistorical design—is apt to realize. But the architect who intervenes in established urban tissue deals with conglomerations of buildings which (as often by accident as

9.7. *Two options in cosmetic surgery for architectural scar tissue* left by the demolition of adjacent buildings. In one case, the demolition of an adjacent townhouse left rudely exposed the party wall of Columbia University's Casa Italiana (*1*). A monumental new plaza, faced on three sides by monumental new buildings, left this traumatic evidence unattended. The façade should have been completed in the fashion clearly intended by the original architects, McKim, Meade & White (*2*). Instead, the architects of the plaza plastered over the raw brick and walked away, arguing that there were "no funds" for cosmetic repairs to the fourth wall of what in effect is a grand outdoor room: an odd ethical response to a serious aesthetic question.

by intent) have achieved unique morphological configurations. Such situations impose a new sort of responsibility upon the architect, call for new modes of behavior. If the situation compels an architect to deal with a building which he or she finds aesthetically offensive and cannot handle it sympathetically, then he has a simple alternative: to refuse to accept the commission altogether.

The importance of this new attitude becomes very clear when we deal with what used to be called remodelling. Characteristically, remodeling connoted not only changes in the fabric of the building (new plumbing, heating, cooling, and lighting systems) which would raise the level of amenities. It also implied purely cosmetic changes (usually the stripping off of ornament and the application of light glass or metal skins) which would make the building "look new." This assumption that improved livability had to be matched by parallel changes in appearance comes directly out of Detroit and its annual model. The venality of such style changes in automobile design is too well established to merit extended discussion here. What is not so often remarked upon is the correlation between short aesthetic life and reduced trade-in values. Such styling is even more reprehensible in buildings with their incomparably longer life-spans. Every Main Street in America is a sad and expensive junkyard of attempts to mask the fact that all Main Streets are the cumulative result of decades of growth. We should respect that growth, not attempt to paint it out.

Situations in which the use of replicas seems least justified are those in which they are not really essential to the aesthetic enjoyment or intellectual comprehension of the architectural complex to which they belong. Four projects of this type—all of them American—can be cited as examples of this type of misdirected expertise. The reconstructed Stoa of Attalus in Athens; the full-scale replica of the Parthenon in Nashville, Tennessee; the Eclectra Havemeyer Webb Memorial Building at Shelburne Village, Vermont; the J. Paul Getty Museum of Art in Malibu, California.

The Stoa, for all its immaculate research and execution in white marble, makes the excavated ruins of the Athenian Agora look shabby, neglected, and secondhand. The magnificent collection of archaeological materials housed in the new Stoa could have been better displayed in a more discreet and frankly contemporary museum building. Such a new building should not be visually obstrusive in the Agora. It should be farther back from the site; or screened with heavy planting; or, even better, located underground.

The "world's only full-scale, full-colored replica of the Parthenon" was built in Nashville as part of the 1895 Centennial Exposition. Originally fabricated of plaster and lath on a light metal armature, it was completely reconstituted as a reinforced-concrete structure in the early 1930s. The initial motivation for the replication was literary and associative, not historical:

with its many colleges and universities, Nashville called itself the "Athens of the South." Today, this preposterous fake has acquired a certain historicity of its own, but it is hard to imagine a situation in which such a transplanted replica would be built again.

The Webb Memorial Building is a yet more exotic concoction. Externally, it is designed as a facsimile of a handsome Greek revival country house of which Mrs. Webb had been very fond but which she had never been able to acquire for her museum. The facsimile "looks like" its wooden prototype; but it is built of reinforced concrete for fireproofness. But, in plan, it bears no relation to the original house, being instead compartmentalized into rooms sized and proportioned to accept a series of fine French boiserie from the Webbs' New York town house. (The paneling had, in turn, been earlier stripped from eighteenth-century houses in France.) In these rooms is displayed a fine group of French paintings collected by

9.8. *The archaeological museum at the Agora in Athens* may indeed be a very accurate reconstruction of the Stoa of Attalus whose site it occupies. It may also be a satisfactory gallery for the exhibition of Agoran artifacts. But in its pluperfect condition it caricatures the field of ruins in which it has been erected. If a museum were needed here, it would have been much wiser to have designed it as a neutral modern building or, better still, to have buried it belowground. As it is, the new building, instead of helping one understand the old Athenian marketplace, makes the rest of the site unintelligible.

9.9. *This chaste Greek revival farmhouse* is not precisely what it seems. The original stands miles away in the Vermont countryside: this replica has recently been built in the architectural museum of Shelburne Village. The original is of wood; this copy, in reinforced concrete. The prototype has rooms furnished in Victoriana; the copy has galleries paneled in French boiserie and hung with impressionist paintings. It is hard to see what didactic function is served by such a misapplication of money and expertise in a museum noted for its American antiques.

9.10. *This replica,* "the world's only full-scale, full-color copy of the Parthenon in Athens," stands in a Nashville park where it houses a collection of plaster casts of the Elgin Marbles in the British Museum. A relic of the Tennessee Centennial Exposition of 1896, this genial hoax has a certain historicity in its own right; such replications today belong to Disneyland.

Mrs. Webb during her long and remarkable life as a collector and connoisseur. Although such a collection certainly merits its own museum, it is impossible to conceive of a gallery less suited stylistically or a context less appropriate than Shelburne Village itself, which houses one of the country's greatest collections of American folk art, handcrafts, and vernacular architecture. If the function of a museum is to raise the level of taste and comprehension of its visitors, the Webb Memorial must be rated as a failed tour de force.

The most recent addition to the American list of replicas is in many ways the most disturbing: the J. Paul Getty Museum at Malibu, California. The design of this new museum is said to be "based upon" the so-called Villa dei Papyri at Herculaneum. But in fact, in addition to using the (only partially excavated) ground plan of this buried villa, the new museum buildings includes elements from several other Roman villas in Pompeii. There is a bewildering mixture of authentic antique architectural elements alongside facsimiles and replicas of others. The lavish polychromy of painted walls and highly polished marble floors and dadoes is highly speculative, only a small portion being original and none of it from the Herculaneum villa. In addition of this, the whole complex stands on top of a large, partially submerged garage and has a superimposed second-floor range of galleries holding an unexceptionable collection of European art. The total effect is authentically hallucinatory. Whatever the value of the artifacts exhibited, the museum building itself cannot enlighten but will almost certainly confuse the average layperson who is eager to learn more about classic antiquity. Both the Nashville and Malibu projects are hazardous culturally. The prototypes of both are still extant, even if in mutilated form, and can be experienced at first hand by the average tourist. The two facsimiles, in all their sharp-edged geometry and dubious polychromy, serve mainly to blur the impact of the originals.

There is yet another category of facsimiles with which it is possible to deal a bit more gently, if only because of the fact that they never made any scholarly or aesthetic pretense of being an accurate copy of any single monument from antiquity. One is San Simeon, the southern California home of the late William Randolph Hearst; a second is Villa Vizcaya, the Miami home of the late James Deering; the third is Beauport, the house which Henry Davis Sleeper built for himself in Gloucester, Massachusetts. All three of these extraordinary houses were the creations of wealthy collectors with highly idiosyncratic tastes. Perhaps the most interesting of the three is Villa Vizcaya, since it was designed by a talented and highly knowledgeable connoisseur, Paul Chalfin, for a client with taste and knowledge. Chalfin actually wrote a kind of historical scenario for its architecture and decora-

9.11. *A remarkable tour de force of historicizing eclecticism*—unmatched for its size, elegance and connoisseurship—Villa Vizcaya is now the Dade County Art Museum in Miami. The 1916 house and gardens are the joint creation of a client who was himself a knowledgeable collector and his architect, who was an unusually well trained connoisseur. The results of this collaboration between James Deering and Paul Chalfin is qualitatively different from most of the great eclectic houses of the pre–World War I period. These tended to be commissioned by *nouveau riche* patrons who, without any real knowledge of or interest in antiquity, used antique architectural settings to reinforce their own social ambitions. If Vizcaya seems aesthetically superior today, it is largely due to the program around which it was designed and built: a scenario of architecture, decoration, and landscape design aimed at simulating an Italian villa which would have been continuously occupied by the same family between 1550 and 1810. This theme gives the entire complex a beguiling verisimilitude. Time itself has converted this fairy-tale assemblage for a rich eccentric into an authentically significant social document.

Externally, the architecture of Vizcaya is unabashedly eclectic, a composite of replications, more or less literal, of Italian prototypes. The interiors, on the other hand, are almost entirely surfaced with antique elements—tesselated floors, wood-paneled walls, polychromed wooden ceilings, stone chimney breasts—removed from old Italian palazzi. Insofar as the Vizcaya gardens represent any specific Italian landscape, it is probably the semitropical shores of Lake Como. The villa itself anticipates the style later made famous by Addison Mizener at Palm Beach—stuccoed walls trimmed out in coquina, a local limestone that resembles Italian travertine. Garden houses, terraces, walls, and sculpture are surfaced in the same material, as is the famous stone boat landing stage (*1*). Here oceangoing yachts, approaching through a channel dredged in the shallow waters of the bay (and marked by lantern-topped wooden piles in the Venetian manner) could embark and disembark James Deering's guests.

4

5

6

9.11 (Continued). A building like Vizcaya confronts its curators with special problems in interpretation. Unlike the orthodox museum of decorative arts, the Vizcaya interiors were designed and furnished according to a chronological scenario: a sixteenth-century Florentine salon (5); a seventeenth-century Palladian loggia (6); an eighteenth-century French–Venetian drawing room (7); a smaller Empire parlor (8). These make very convincing ensembles. But their provenance is not always secure. Like many American collectors of the period, Deering and Chalfin kept skimpy records of what they bought and from whom. They relied upon their own expertise in deciding whether or not the artifact in question was a "genuine antique." This mode of behavior, unexceptionable in the case of a private collector— becomes a problem only when the collection is institutionalized as a museum. Then the curatorial staff has the task of cataloging the collection, establishing as far as possible the exact provenance of each item, and interpreting it accurately to the visitor. It is a long and tedious process.

7

8

9.12. San Simeon, one of the homes of William Randolph Hearst, is now operated by the California Department of Parks and Recreation as a museum house. Like Villa Vizcaya (*9.11*), it is a significant social document, but in Hearst it documents a personality far different from that of the discriminating and reclusive James E. Deering. It was commissioned by Hearst when he was the press and movie mogul documented by Orson Welles in *Citizen Kane*. At that period, Hearst was an omnivorous collector who kept several agents busy with indiscriminate buying all around Europe. (Eventually he had several warehouses packed with purchases ranging from baroque jewelry to a crated stone castle.) But this huge collection did not reflect any centroid of personal taste or any real interest in antiquities, as is obvious in San Simeon's main library (*3*) or morning room (*4*). The house itself was designed by Julia Morgan, one of the country's first woman architects, in the so-called Spanish colonial style made popular by the San Diego Exposition of 1916 (*2*). San Simeon is closely related to Hollywood set designs in both its vulgarity and its technical virtuosity. A responsible analysis of such cultural phenomena should constitute an integral part of the interpretation to the public of this historic complex.

tion, the plot being that the house would have been built, altered, and enlarged across some two and a half centuries, ending with the Napoleonic conquest.

None of these houses, as artifacts with ambiguous proveniences, meets the criteria of the *National Register of Historic Buildings*. And yet all of them, in their own idiosyncratic fashion, have historic and aesthetic merit. Moreover, we must remember that history itself has its own paradoxical power of validating historical fakes. Thus, though they are anomalous artifacts which fail to meet the strict standards of art historicans and museologists, they are an integral part of our cultural heritage. Ways must be found for properly classifying, preserving, and especially interpreting them. (This latter is critically important: the official brochures of Beauport and the Villa dei Papyri are suffocatingly coy and evasive when they are not actually inaccurate.)

10

The Architectural Museum, Indoors and Out

Museums began as repositories for homeless artifacts of all sorts which, for an endless variety of reasons, could no longer survive in their original habitat. At first, they tended to be mere collections reflecting the tastes and idiosyncrasies of their owners. In the modern world, of course, the museum has been transformed into a qualitatively different order of magnitude: it has become a cultural institution of prime importance. But its task remains fundamentally the same: to provide optimal environmental conditions for the study and enjoyment of rare and/or valuable artifacts, small enough to be easily moved around the world.

Until fairly recently, however, the curatorial problems connected with the preservation of very large objects such as complete buildings has been handled on an ad hoc, pragmatic basis. A range of museological institutions has been invented: the historical village (Williamsburg); the historic district (Vieux Carré); the historic house museum (Mount Vernon); the outdoor architectural museum (Skansen).

Simultaneously, however, the standard art museum was gradually extending its collections to include archaeological fragments (the Elgin Marbles at the British Museum; the Altar of Pergamon in Berlin). Gradually, also, recognition of the need to preserve the so-called decorative arts spread. In some European centers, this took the form of creating entire museums devoted to furniture, furnishings, and interior architecture—e.g., the Kunstgewerbe in Vienna and the Victoria and Albert in London. No comparable specialized museums have developed in the United States. Instead, the function was assumed by existing museums of fine arts: the "historic room" appeared. It was a museological response to the need, not only to preserve decorative arts materials, but also to display them in an authentic or at least appropriate context. Sometimes, also, an isolated room was all that could be saved in the demolition of an historic building.

219

1

10.1. *The "historic museum room"* (i.e., the room which has been removed from an old building and reconstituted in the controlled environment of the museum) is usually a last-ditch strategy to preserve at least some elements of an important building which would otherwise vanish without leaving a trace. It is not an optimal solution; from the curatorial point of view, the best is usually to preserve the artifact in its original context. But often it is the only course open, and a number of American museums have saved such rooms (usually on an ad hoc basis). These today constitute an immensely valuable cultural and artistic resource.

The preservation of the Chicago Stock Exchange's Trading Room is a recent example of this strategy. When it became obvious that, despite a long battle to save it, Louis Sullivan's historic skyscraper would be demolished, the Chicago Art Institute volunteered to house it in a new wing then being planned (1975–1977). As reconstituted, the room exactly re-creates Sullivan's great polychromed vessel, but only parts of its visible surfaces are actually original: the wainscoating, sash, and doors in the walls; the marble sheathing and bronze capitals of the columns. Some of the light fixtures are original, as is much of the stenciled wall decoration. Fundamentally, however, only the visually accessible, two-dimensional surfaces of the room are original. The dazzling impact of the room derives now, as it always had, from the barbaric richness of Sullivan's painted polychromy: coral, lemon yellow, sapphire, and gold leaf. The conservation of these surfaces is a masterpiece of expertise. Originally done in oil on canvas, much of the stenciling was damaged, faded, or soiled. It had to be cleaned in order to reconstruct the original color scheme and replicate sections damaged beyond repair. The final result affords a rare opportunity to confront a lost aspect of Sullivan's genius.

220

10.2. *Skansen, the prototype of all "open-air museums"* (*1*), was opened in a Stockholm suburb in 1891 and has become the model for similar architectural museums around the world, including many in America. It was created by an ethnographer, Artur Hazelius, who had begun in 1872 the great Nordic Museum of material culture. Dissatisfied with the limitations which standard museum practice placed upon the display and interpretation of vernacular material culture, he became convinced that such artifacts could be understood only when seen in their architectural and horticultural contexts. Moreover, he conceived the even more radical idea that such open-air exhibits should be active demonstrations of the activities, processes, and life-styles of popular culture. Hazelius, a pioneer in folk life studies, wished to preserve and interpret the material culture of rural Sweden's farms and villages. Although Skansen began on an ad hoc basis, it has developed into a definitive national collection of folkloristic architecture and furniture, costumes, tools, plants, and animals. Its 150 buildings, from every province in Sweden, range in date from 1574 to the mid-1800s and in type from alpine herdsmen's huts to prosperous peasant houses. There are churches, including one with trompe l'oeil baroque interiors, and one stuccoed villa with interiors decorated in a provincial version of Louis Seize (*5*). Except for a few masonry buildings in the reconstructed village, all the Skansen architecture is wooden, much of it of log construction from before the days of the steam sawmill. All in all, the museum today is very much what Hazelius aspired to—a living demonstration of the skill and virtuosity of anonymous Swedish craftspeople, working in a difficult climate with a limited range of resources at their disposal.

SKANSEN

44 WOLVES
THE BEAR-PITS
BIRDS OF PREY
Fallow deer
Badgers Wild boars
Red deer
Bellmansro Entrance
European Bisons
Polar Bears
Reindeer
Cows Goats
The Birds-Pond
Solliden Entrance
Dancing Floors
Hazelius Entrance
The Monkey House
Hasselbacken Entrance
Sol Liden
Escalator
Main-Entrance

P Parking
T Lavatory

0   50   100   150   200 Meters

2

10.2 (Continued). Skansen is laid out on a rocky peninsula (2) to afford realistic settings for the individual exhibits (3, 4), which cover the whole spectrum of rural and village life. Every effort is made to achieve verisimilitude in the landscape: domesticated plants and animals are

3

222

appropriate for time and place, as are levels of maintenance and housekeeping. Only the villa from Skogaholm, country seat of a rich urban family, reflects the high-style urbane taste of the city (5). All else is in the astylar idiom of farm and village.

A number of American museums now display historic rooms in their galleries (Boston, Brooklyn, Cleveland, and Kansas City, inter alia). Perhaps the largest and most varied collection is that of the Metropolitan Museum of Art in New York: its rooms range from a first-century Pompeian bedchamber, through Venetian, French, and English interiors, to the American Wing, currently (1980) undergoing a complete reorganization in a greatly expanded building. Although the historic room no longer enjoys the prestige it once had—partly because of the once widespread custom of buying rooms from old houses which were not threatened with demolition—it still is a useful technique for saving architectural fragments which would otherwise be doomed. Two recent demonstrations of this utility are the Sullivan Board Room of the Chicago Board of Trade, recently installed in the Chicago Art Institute, and the Living Room of Wright's Frank Little Residence that was recently installed in the American Wing of the Metropolitan.

THE OUTDOOR ARCHITECTURAL MUSEUM

The outdoor architectural museum (*plein air* in French, *Freiluftmuseum* in German) is a much more recent institutional invention than the standard art or historical museum. As a type, it is ordinarily dated from 1891, the year in which a famous Swedish folklorist established Skansen on what was then the outskirts of Stockholm. Arthur Hazelius's decision to establish this new kind of museum sprang from his dissatisfaction with existing anthropological and ethnographic museums. Not only did they necessarily confine their exhibits to small artifacts which could easily be housed in a conventional museum: costumes, tools, household fabrics, and so forth; even more seriously, they exhibited these artifacts in isolation from the physical contexts and life-styles which had produced them. Hazelius's ambition was to establish a national museum of folk architecture and handicrafts of the same order of comprehensiveness as the great art museums dedicated to the presentation of high-style, urbane art. In the century since Skansen was first opened, it has undergone great changes and expansions. Even more significantly, it has become the prototype for museums of folk life in many countries around the world. In many smaller countries, such as Romania, Denmark, Norway, and Finland, these new museums are conceived of as being authentically national collections, representing all the regional variations of village and vernacular buildings of every sort, from beehives to churches.

Initially, as at Skansen, the architectural museum tended to be a more or less ad hoc collection of artifacts of different proveniences, casually dispersed in the landscape. But this sort of installation tended to be visually disconcerting and didactically counterproductive, since it presented in one field of vision artifacts which in real life would never be experienced together. Consequently, in the newer museums, as for example Frilands-museet outside Copenhagan and Old World Wisconsin, large tracts of empty farmland have been developed as the setting for collection of farm and village structures from every principal district of Denmark and Wisconsin. Each group is laid out and landscaped as a visual unit, the houses, barns, and surrounding fields separated and screened from adjacent displays by heavy plantings of trees. Here, the effort at maximum verisimilitude goes so far as to import the indigenous flora of each region. The Copenhagen museum has other interesting features. Although the day-to-day house-keeping of the entire plant is immaculate, it is all accomplished by traditional means. There are no mown lawns: all grass is cropped by domestic animals (cattle, sheep, goats, and geese)—usually neutered males to guarantee docility and eliminate problems connected with caring for young animals, milking cows, and so on.

As a concomitant to maximum verisimilitude in re-creating the physical ambience of folkloristic and vernacular settlements, increasing attention is being paid to active, ongoing demonstrations of the crafts which supported them in the first place. Thus there are vegetable gardens, cultivated fields, herds of sheep and cattle. Wood carving, broom making, blacksmithing, and pottery making are carried on. In the houses, flax is spun, wool carded, quilts made. Baking and butter and cheese making are demonstrated. The enormous popularity of such activities is a measure of the hunger of modern industrialized people to see at first hand how things are made. Such activities are sometimes criticized by self-styled realists as being "artificial." In a sense, of course, they are—but no more than any museum function where, by definition, artifacts and processes must be removed from their real-life context in order to be exhibited at all. In fact, all formal academic training is also, by this narrow definition, "artificial." In all preliterate human societies, *learning* was always the opposite face of *doing*. As we have pointed out elsewhere (Chapter 1), human beings have paid a high price for the separation of theory and practice which is the mark of modern industrial society. In very large and diverse countries such as China, the U.S.S.R., Canada, and the U.S.A., the concept of a single comprehensive national museum of architecture is probably unworkable. A system of regional museums seems much more appropriate; and that, in fact, is the direction which affairs have taken in America. Old Sturbridge Village, Shelburne, Cooperstown, Old Bethpage Village and Old World Wisconsin are examples of regionally oriented institutions.

In the United States, the preservation of vernacular architecture and folkloristic artifacts actually preceded the emergence of folk-life studies as an academic subdivision of ethnography. In fact, many of our most important institutions began as the private hobbies of rich collectors. The Winterthur du Pont Museum in Delaware, today one of the world's greatest col-

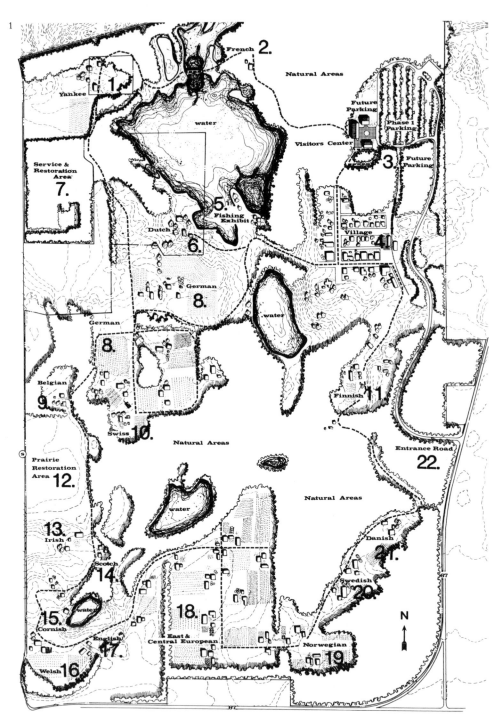

Map of Old World Wisconsin. 1. Yankee farm. 2. French farm. 3. Visitors' Center. 4. Village. 5. Fishing exhibit. 6. Dutch farm. 7. Service and restoration area. 8. German farm. 9. Belgian farm. 10. Swiss farm. 11. Finnish farm. 12. Prairie restoration. 13. Irish farm. 14. Scottish farm. 15. Cornish farm. 16. Welsh farm. 17. English farm. 18. East and Central European farms. 19. Norwegian farm. 20. Swedish farm. 21. Danish farm. 22. Entrance.

10.3. *An innovative outdoor museum* designed to celebrate the multinational ethnicity of Wisconsin was opened by the State Historical Society in 1976. On a large undeveloped tract, typical farmsteads representing all of the ethnic groups who settled the state are being re-created. All artifacts used are of authentic provenance: houses, barns, outbuildings; furniture and household goods; tools and farm machinery. When the farms are put into operation, historically appropriate crops and livestock are employed. The homesteads are dispersed naturalistically in the landscape, so that each is visually complete and self-contained (*1*). To ensure that the collection of farms would be both comprehensive and accurate, two types of research were carried out. Archives and libraries were scanned for visual and verbal documentation (*2, 3*); and a physical survey was made of the state to locate and photograph potential exhibits (*4–7*). On such a basis, appropriate buildings are acquired, either by gift or purchase. Depending upon their location and construction, they are prepared for transport and reconstitution on the museum site. Ultimately, all the farmsteads will be operated as working establishments, such as the German truck gardens shown in (*2*) or the Norwegian homestead in (*3*). Ultimately, there may be as many as 25 or 30 homesteads on display, in addition to the Wisconsin village which will be re-created near the Visitors' Center (4 on map).

2

3

227

4

5

6

7

228

10.3 *(Continued). Each of the farmsteads in Old World Wisconsin* has been designed for maximum verisimilitude by the Department of Landscape Architecture of the University of Wisconsin. Plot plans replicate with fidelity typical layouts of each ethnic group, reflecting the special building techniques and planning concepts that the pioneers brought with them to the new world. For example, the Scandinavians in Wisconsin employed several variations of the log cabin (*4, 8*). Some Pomeranian Germans continued to use late-medieval half-timbering until the present century (*6*). The whole process of disassembly, transportation, and reconstitution of selected houses is under the supervision of a staff of restoration architects, landscape architects, historians, and archaeologists. Traditional tools and methods are employed, as in the reassembly of a Finnish log cabin (*8*). Although not all buildings in any given group necessarily come from the same original farm, they will all have a common provenance. Farmhouses, barns, fields, and gardens will interpret the life-styles of the ethnic group represented. Thus, the Finnish farmstead (*9*) has a sauna (lower left) and a hay barn built out in the hay field (upper right).

8

9

1

2

10.4. *Some outdoor architectural museums,* like this one at Kihzi Island in Soviet Karelia, are highly specialized. Here the intent is not so much to replicate the total environment (see Skansen, 10.2) as to exhibit a collection of typologically related artifacts. The wooden churches of Kihzi date from the eighteenth century, when this part of northern Russia was being opened up for settlement by Peter the Great. They demonstrate the remarkable visual memory of the settlers, able to replicate on the frontier the great masonry churches they had left behind in centers like Novgorod and Zagorsk. And they demonstrate the astonishing virtuosity of the craftspeople who could translate into shingled wooden shells the lead-sheathed cupolas of the cosmopolitan Byzantine style. The 22-domed Church of the Transfiguration of 1714, with its carved and polychromed iconostasis, is original to Khizi (*1, 2*). Others, like the Lelikozero Chapel (*3*), come from neighboring villages in the lake Onega archipelago. The Kihzi collection also includes secular buildings—farmhouses, barns, windmills—from the same peasant culture as the churches.

10.5. *Mystic Seaport museum* is one of several American institutions dedicated to maritime, rather than dry-land, activities. Although a simulated settlement, it is located on the Connecticut coast, a locus of nineteenth-century shipbuilding and whaling industries.

10.6. *Old Sturbridge Village Museum,* a collection of buildings of the 1700s and 1800s, simulates a typical Massachusetts town. The buildings, all authentic for the area, are organized around the church and village green.

10.7. *A reconstruction of the vanished settlement* of Abraham Lincoln's youth, New Salem, Ill., has one authentic building from the period: the restored Onstott Cooperage shop (*above*). In this complex the museological aim has been to re-create the rough and ready life-styles of the first wave of immigrants into the primeval lower Illinois woodlands.

10.8. *Old Bethpage Village* is a notably successful project, begun in the early 1960s, to receive some of the old buildings being displaced by the rapid postwar suburbanization of western Long Island. Initiated by the Nassau County Museum, Bethpage was established on one of the few farms to have survived the subdivisions. The only buildings original to the site are the Powell Farm complex. They have been restored to serve as a demonstration center for early-nineteenth-century farm life (*bottom, right*).

lections of American decorative arts and a center of graduate studies in the field, began as the private home of Henry Francis du Pont. Much the same thing may be said of Shelburne, near Burlington, Vermont, the museum of Americana established by Mr. and Mrs. J. Watson Webb; Greenfield Village, the museum of Americana established by Henry Ford as part of his museum at Dearborn, Michigan; and Old Sturbridge Village in Massachusetts, the creation of two brothers, Albert B. and J. Cheney Wells.

The Winterthur collection is wholly housed in the great mansion of the du Pont family. But all the others are typical outdoor museums—in other words, the old buildings in which the artifacts are displayed are themselves part of the collection. Another characteristic of these institutions is that, as collections, they are highly idiosyncratic, reflecting the prejudices and preferences of strong-willed and immensely wealthy amateurs. Thus Mrs. Webb's museum boasts enormous collections of decoys, quilts, and wooden Indians (as well as the family railroad train, the last of the Lake Champlain steamers, and a lighthouse—the latter two on dry land!). The Ford Museum has the country's largest collection of heating and cooking stoves, while one of du Pont's specialities was Chinese export ware. Finally, they share another characteristic: the collections were largely undocumented and uncataloged as to provenience. Now that they have become institutionalized, one of the great tasks facing the curatorial staff is to complete this important work.

Some architectural museums have been created in response to the sheer pressure of the urbanization of their regions. Thus, Upper Canada Village, on the north shore of the St. Lawrence River above Montreal, was established as a "home" for some of the hundreds of old buildings which were doomed by a series of dams and locks along that international waterway. The displaced buildings were moved to the new site and organized into a farm and village complex which simulates a mid-nineteenth-century riverine settlement. The same formula has been followed at Old Bethpage Village on Long Island, where a range of buildings (a church, houses, a mill, and an inn), doomed by the urbanization of the area, have been moved to a new location. The village, designed and operated as a part of the Nassau County Historical Museum, is structured to resemble a typical farming village at about the time of the Civil War. The almost instant touristic success of such new institutions (250,000 per year at Upper Canada Village, 200,000 at Old Bethpage) is another index to how important a cultural vacuum they fill. The newest and most comprehensive museum of this type is Old World Wisconsin.

Although the typical outdoor architectural museum in the Skansen tradition attempts to replicate (or at least simulate) an actual landscape or scenographic situation, other more specialized institutions are sometimes very useful. For example, on an island in Lake Onega, north of Leningrad, the

234

Soviets are creating a museum of wooden architecture of the far north, moving in log-built houses, churches, and monasteries from a wide radius around the lake. The museum makes no pretense of re-creating any single village and has living accommodations only for the staff and a small number of overnight visitors.

At Grabovno, in Bulgaria, there is an interesting museum installation of a different type. Here, along a little river with a very rapid fall, the museum has installed a range of old water-powered mills and workshops to demonstrate all the early pre-steam-engine industrial operations necessary to support a provincial town around 1800. The processes demonstrated include sawing, milling, felt- and papermaking, forging, leather tanning, and pottery making. Each workshop is staffed by a master craftsman and apprentices; and the artifacts they produce, all of them of traditional design, are sold in the museum stores. We do not have any exact equivalent of Grabovno as yet in the United States; the closest approximation would be Mystic Seaport in Connecticut. Here is to be found a specialized collection of buildings, all of which were associated with maritime activities in New England before the advent of steam.

While the museum village at Cooperstown is scenographically a typical New York State settlement, it actually is a highly specialized collection of buildings and artifacts. All of them are of local origin (none from more than 30 miles away), and all of them date from the period between 1783, when the territory was first opened for settlement, and 1845, when factory-made metal tools and equipment began to replace local artifacts, mostly of wood. These restrictions give the collection an extraordinary interest.

As we have seen, many actual villages and towns are nowadays functioning as outdoor architectural museums, even though philogenetically they are of quite different origins from such artificially constructed projects as Skansen or Sturbridge. Generally speaking, these are settlements which, through some accident of history, have survived down into present times with little or no disturbance to their physical fabric. Williamsburg is, of course, the most famous and the least typical because of all the work which has been done on it. But there are many other examples of groups of original buildings, standing on their original sites, with little or no contemporary infill. Among such sites are Harrisburg, Vermont; Deerfield, Massachusetts; two Shaker villages at Hancock, Massachusetts; and Lexington, Kentucky; Marshall, Michigan; Madison, Indiana; and Columbia, California. Some of these towns (Marshall and Madison) are living American communities which happily have neither grown nor withered. Others, such as Deerfield and the Shaker settlements, have little or no permanent population and function as museums. For all of them, tourism is a substantial and growing economic factor.

Another handling of small towns of unusual architectural interest is exemplified in Sveti Stefan, a small fishing village on the Adriatic coast of

1

2

10.9. Plimoth Plantation is one of the most innovative of all American architectural museums. It celebrates one of the great events in American history: the landing of the Pilgrims at Plymouth Rock in 1620. Yet, unlike other historic-site museums which place emphasis upon antiquity and authenticity, Plimoth Plantation consists exclusively of reproductions and replicas. Not even its site is authentic, since contemporary Plymouth, Mass., some 7 miles away, covers the landing site at Plymouth Rock. The museological posture of Plimoth is thus the reverse of museum villages like Deerfield or Williamsburg, where great effort and expertise have been expended to establish the provenience of every artifact on display. Lacking such a collection (old houses, old furniture, old tools), Plimoth has nevertheless turned what might seem a liability into an asset. Every replica on display is as accurate as modern archaeological, anthropological, and historical research can make it. But the interpretational programs concentrate not upon it but upon the functional processes which it supported, e.g., adz = shingle-making; cornhusk mattresses = sleeping; churns = butter-making; goats = milking; wheat-straw = thatching. This policy of active demonstration instead of inert display has proved to be extremely successful. Its cultural impact is strengthened by Plimoth's association with Brown University, with whose graduate departments in anthropology and archaeology it carries on cooperative research and apprenticeship programs.

The original colonists at Plymouth were not only literate Britishers: as militant dissenters, they were also vocal and litigious. Thus the records they have left are extraordinarily complete and constitute a rich historical resource for staff and students—making possible, for example, a computerized minibiography for practically every colonist.

When completed, Plimoth Plantation will approximate the settlement c. 1630 (*1*). But its completion is indefinite: in fact, construction of new buildings is more or less continuous (*9*) and the process has been made an integral part of the interpretive program. Every effort is made to maintain historical verisimilitude. Housekeeping, indoors (*6, 7*) and out (*4*), is aimed at re-creating the life-styles of what was effectively a late-medieval English village.

236

3

4

5

237

6

10.9 *(Continued). The policy of using replicas* instead of their antique prototypes has several unanticipated consequences. It means that docents and visitors alike can handle pewter plates, sit on rush–bottomed chairs, lie on cornhusk mattresses, with greater freedom than if these artifacts were valuable antiques. It thus reduces cost of breakage and incidence of theft, as well as reducing costs of fire and theft insurance. The effectiveness of such a policy depends upon the training and motivation of the curatorial staff: at Plimoth Plantation, they provide an interpretive program that is both informative and entertaining.

7

There are no guided tours at Plimoth. Instead the docents are engaged in a range of day-to-day tasks which, if asked, they are happy to explain. The result is that the museum visitor moves through activities indoors and out which replicate those which would have occupied the townspeople 350 years ago. Since the social history of the town is richly documented and the focus of ongoing research, these activities have maximum verisimilitude. Whether it is sheepherding (*8*) or housebuilding (*9*) methods, materials, tools, even dress and toileting, all activities have been carefully researched.

9

Yugoslavia, which has been converted into a resort hotel (Fig. 8.7). The Soviets are handling some of their old walled monastery towns in the same manner, converting the entire complex into a museum cum motel. Something of the same sort is to be found in historic towns such as Rotenburg-am-Tauber in Bohemia and Telč in Czechoslovakia (Fig. 19.1). Both towns have been designated as national historic monuments. They are to develop as tourist attractions, but all modifications are under strict design controls, to maintain their artistic character.

All the outdoor architectural museums described here are, in effect, collections of "authenticated antiques": that is, they consist of artifacts (buildings, furnishings, artworks, and tools) whose provenance has been firmly established by scholars in the field. One argument often advanced against such institutions (and especially the historic house) is that they are "dead," "inert," "lifeless." Another is that they too often celebrate the upper-class, urbane life as opposed to that of the urban poor or the small farmer or pioneer. There is some substance to such charges: in any case, by focusing attention on artifacts which have become valuable antiques, they too often do seem to be aimed at the wealthy connoisseur or collector. In reaction against such tendencies, there is a growing feeling that the architectural museum should interpret the artifact "actively," in conjunction with documentary materials, in order to teach history in a more dynamic fashion. Emphasis should be more upon the processes which the artifacts supported than upon the artifacts themselves.

This feeling has led to the increasing use of demonstration activities aimed at showing the spectator how a given historical process actually worked: how corn was milled or flax spun; how pewter was cast or butter churned; how hams were smoked, lard rendered, or bread baked. There is no doubt that the active re-creation of such processes is immensely popular with the modern public, divorced as it has become from firsthand knowledge of how *anything* is made. When the activity is structured to permit participation instead of passive demonstration, it becomes even more attractive, especially to young people.

There are, however, negative aspects to such participatory programs. The process itself may be hazardous for the unskilled (e.g., splitting wood shingles or cooking on an open fire). In addition, the antique tools and equipment used in such demonstrations may be either too rare or too fragile to be used by any but experts.

It is in such a context that two unusual institutions—Plimoth Plantation in Massachusetts and the Historical Archaeological Institute at Lejre, Denmark—merit special attention. Both take as given the principle that active teaching is the paramount function of the outdoor architectural museum. Both are based upon human settlements which no longer exist. The Plimoth Plantation of 1621 is buried under the modern town of Plymouth, Massachusetts; prehistoric Lejre vanished millennia ago in the Danish bogs

(Fig. 17.2). Thus neither museum had authentically old artifacts (buildings, tools, furnishings) at its disposal. Both have converted this liability into an asset. Both projects use replicas and facsimiles exclusively. These are as accurate as modern archaeological, anthropological, and historical research can make them; but there is not an "authentic antique" in the lot. This policy permits the free use of the artifact, by either demonstrator or participator, without extravagant concern about breakage, wear and tear, or theft.

Both Plimoth and Lejre aim at the vivid re-creation of the life-styles with maximum verisimilitude; but they differ in one important respect: archival and documentary resources. Plimoth Plantation not only dates from a historical period. It was also richly documented by a population which was both literate and litigious. It left a written record of sermons, lawsuits, land titles, wills, deeds and inventories so voluminous that it is possible to create biographies of practically all the first generations of Pilgrim settlers. At Lejre, on the other hand, there is no written record at all. The only resource is artifactual: the remains of people, animals, tools, and houses which the acid peat bogs happen to have conserved astonishingly well. Even so, there are enormous gaps in the record. Hence any re-creation of the life-style of this prehistoric settlement must be based upon constructing new facsimiles of everything and then testing each by actually doing the task it is assumed to have supported.

11

Cosmetic Consequences
of Intervention

Although it may indeed be only skin-deep, the cosmetic condition of a building has a profound effect upon our reaction to and judgment of it. The visual information conveyed by its appearance forms an important part of our experience as a whole. (Sound, odors, temperature, and touch are also important sensory inputs, but many of them are subsumed by vision; and in any case, visual perception is overwhelmingly the most powerful. A blind person might be moved by the incense and sound of a high mass in Chartres but, lacking sight, his or her experience of it will be tragically reduced.) Thus it is vision which enables us to say of a building that it is dark and gloomy or bright and airy; to decide whether it is new or old, loved or neglected; ultimately, whether it is beautiful or ugly. But from information derived from visual scanning, we also fabricate another set of judgments as to its physical condition or structural stability. Such judgments are not necessarily valid. The stained, cracked, and spalling discolored stucco of seventeenth-century buildings in Mexico might lead to a totally unwarranted conclusion of structural weakness; whereas a new coat of white paint on a New England farmhouse might conceal evidence of imminent collapse. In short, the cosmetic appearance of architectural surfaces forms the basis for two quite different levels of response: associative and diagnostic.

Under such circumstances, the visual appearance of many old buildings in Central Europe might suggest structures weakened by decades of decay and neglect; yet those very buildings might have been carefully restored only a few years before. This is typically the case in Central European cities like Prague or Krakow, where the burning of brown coal for heating produces smoke that quickly discolors stuccoed surfaces. For all its unhappy visual consequences, such processes might continue for decades without serious damage to the stucco. On the other hand, the same combination of gases would set into motion a complex chemicophysical process in marble and limestone which would lead to serious decay which would be concealed by a surface coat of grime. This is typically the case in many Gothic structures in northern Europe. While surface cleaning might be the first stage in therapy in both cases, for aesthetic reasons in the first case and diagnostic in the latter, the removal of the surface crust on fine-scale limestone or marble sculpture might result in the loss forever of irreplaceable detail.

On the other hand, serious structural defects may display very few cosmetic consequences. Wooden beams may be riddled with termites or dry rot without any external evidence. The White House, whose outdoor and indoor surfaces had always been carefully maintained, turned out to be on the verge of actual collapse when its structure was carefully examined in 1948. Similarly, cracks in the walls of the cathedrals at Norwich and York were alarming only to specialists who, by their location and direction, could interpret them as warnings of grave structural weaknesses requiring immediate attention. (Subsequent work revealed that the rubble interiors of the masonry were riddled by voids caused by desiccation and migration of the Norman mortar: thousands of gallons of cement grout had to be injected into them to consolidate them.)

Entirely aside from the physical condition of the exposed surface (or of the structural member behind it), the philosophical aspects of its preservation are thorny and complex. These deserve far more attention than they have received to date. One pivotal question takes this form: when our intervention (whether preservation, restoration, consolidation, or reconstitution) is complete, should the building "look old" or "look new"? Should replaced elements be left to "weather naturally" or should they be "antiqued" to meld into the older tissue around them? There are competent experts on both sides of this argument. (Karol Estreicher has restored the Collegium Maius in Krakow so that all new material is antiqued to match the original. The curators of the Folk-museet in Copenhagen, when they must repair one of their old wooden farmhouses, use new unpainted wood just as the peasant would have done.)

The same problem is raised to even more critical levels in such activities as the cleaning of entire historic districts, such as the Marais district of Paris, or the restoration of the polychromy in many English churches. The visual consequences of such interventions are often startling, compelling many people radically to readjust their ideas of how Paris "ought" to look (bluegray, the way the impressionists saw it) or of Westminster "the way it always was" (i.e., before it was cleansed of centuries of soot, smoke, and dust).

While the individual, layperson or expert, is entitled to preferences in such matters, the preservationist must develop broader, more objective and more comprehensive criteria for evaluating such decisions. Certain parameters can be established. For example, the preservationist should address the following factors:

1. The aesthetic ambitions of the original designers or owners of the artifact must be taken into account. Most monumental architecture is urbane and upper-class in origin, the expression of life-styles which had developed very precise standards of display, etiquette, and propriety. These were implemented by very definite regimes of maintenance, housekeeping, and repair. In the Western world, at least, a cosmetic effect of wealth, affluence, good repair, if not shiny newness, would have been the criterion of the owners. And however fond one may have been of the Louvre when it was still a sooty blue-gray in color, one can rest assured that neither Francis I nor his architect, Pierre Lescot, visualized the Pavillon de l'Horloge as looking that way. Not only was the Louvre largely built of a tawny pink stone: much of its sculptural ornamentation was conceived of in that value and chroma, as is apparent today, now that the stone has been cleaned. Thus, we might say that when monumental, upper-class architecture must be restored, the cosmetic criteria should be those of the creators, i.e., newness, brightness (of polychromy and gilt), and good housekeeping.

2. The reverse probably applies to most vernacular, peasant, or primitive construction. Although all buildings were at one time new and bright, and the builders probably proud of them in that state, it is doubtful that there were any conscious standards of keeping them that way. (Painted houses or barns, for example, would have been an unheard-of luxury for even prosperous American farmers until the last century or so.) Weathered shingles, mossy stones, patched fences, and sagging gates would have been standard cosmetic conditions; only the village church might have been periodically painted or whitewashed, its cross or weather vane gilded. In the landscape, there would have been no concept of the barbered lawns, clipped hedges, and pleached allées of urbane upper-class architecture and townscapes. The aesthetic criteria of the restoration of folk and vernacular buildings should reflect this condition.

3. For ruins (e.g., abandoned forts, castles, prehistoric sites) entirely different aesthetic criteria would apply. The stabilization of above-grade remnants and their maintenance across time would determine basic policy. In cold or wet climates, protective measures against moisture and freeze-thaw cycles would be mandatory (e.g., Fountains Abbey in England). In hot, humid climates, radical control of vegetation would be mandatory, irrespective of what the original landscape designs might have been (e.g., Mayan ruins in Yucatán and Guatemala).

All buildings, like all material objects, have color. But the term *architectural polychromy* applies to that cosmetic aspect of the building in which colors are manipulated according to preconceived systems, for specific aesthetic ends. Such polychromy is achieved by two means: (1) by exposing the physical structure and integral pigmentation of the building materials themselves, e.g., the grain and color of wood, the veining of marble, the monochrome of slate or cast iron; (2) by applying the colors, patterns, and textures of nonstructural membranes, e.g., wallpapers, frescoes, paints, and stuccos. Polychromies based on integral pigmentation are usually thought of as being more durable than applied membranes such as paints. In a sense, this is true, since the characteristic cellular structure of wood or crystalline structure of marble is three-dimensionally continuous. But from a cosmetic point of view, the exposed surface of an integrally colored material is quite as vulnerable to attrition as any applied membrane. Thus coal smoke with a high sulfur content is quite as hostile to marble or limestone as to painted metal or stucco. The principle difference is that the process of attrition is more easily reversed in three-dimensional pigmentation than in two-dimensional membranes. Tarnished metal can be burnished, marble polished, wood sanded to restore its original appearance: applied membranes ordinarily have to be replaced.

In any case, all surfaces everywhere are subject to attack from the same environmental forces, physical, chemical, and mechanical. Heat and cold; moisture and dryness; sunlight and darkness; gravity, wind pressure, and vibration—all are constantly at work. These forces, in turn, determine the nature and scope of biological attrition from animals, insects, plants, and fungi. Thus the ammoniac feces of Venetian pigeons combine with salts and gases of the Venetian atmosphere to produce acute degradation of Venetian marbles. Thus, too, it has been found that the deterioration of old stained glass in English churches is a function of the microclimate generated by its orientation. Glass in north-facing windows will have mosses, lichens, and fungi which cannot survive on the south; but southern and western glass will be subjected to much greater thermal and photochemical stress than that in the shade. Thus the condition of different windows of the same age in the same church may be radically different, demanding radically different therapies.

In architectural terms, this environmental attrition is expressed in terms of soiling, fading, rusting, and discoloration; cracking, flaking and erosion; efflorescence and incrustation from precipitated salts. These forces interact to cause a bewildering array of pathologies which cannot be diagnosed, much less treated, without a fundamental knowledge of the processes involved. This is a field in historic preservation which is just beginning to be placed on a scientific basis. Ironically, the conservation of works of art, i.e., of movable artifacts displayed in the controlled climate of the museum, is much more advanced than architectural conservation. Preservation architects have much to learn from this allied field of activity, as is clear in the published proceedings of the Williamsburg Conference of 1972.

There are philosophical as well as methodological problems to be faced in the restoration of old polychromatic systems. As we have seen earlier in this chapter, the very concept is much more highly structured in upper-class, urbane, and monumental architecture than in folk or vernacular buildings. Either extrinsically (as in Gothic wall paintings and stained glass) or intrinsically (as in Renaissance use of exotic veneers in marble and wood), color plays a decisive role in the iconographic and symbolic function of the building. Across time, these polychromatic systems have become dimmed, soiled, or faded, acquiring patinas from burning incense, candles, and fireplaces. Thus, by slow and imperceptible degrees, the Gothic church was converted from a glowing, light-filled vessel of pinkish-beige Caen stone or pearly white limestone, ablaze with gilt and color, into the dark cavernous voids we know today. By the same token, taste accommodated itself to these altered chromatic values so that today the average tourist assumes that these churches were "always that way." One needs only to see the recently cleaned interiors of York Minster or Westminster Abbey to realize how dazzlingly different were the aesthetic ambitions of the original architects and prelates who built them.

In the light of current archaeological and laboratory research, it is now apparent that we have consistently underestimated the brilliance, not to say stridency, of the coloration of the architecture and decoration of the past. The Renaissance assumed that Greek architecture and sculpture had always been a pure chaste white. Even as late as the 1850s, sculptors such as Hiram Powers were astonished at the growing evidence that, on the contrary, they had been consistently polychromed. Recent archaeology has unearthed evidence that Periclean taste in color was actually garish. There are sculptures in the Acropolis Museum in Athens whose painted surfaces are very close to the painted figures on a circus carrousel: chlamyses in emerald, mammary glands tinted pink, mustaches and pubic hair painted jet black.

We now know that eighteenth and nineteenth-centure polychromy, especially of interiors, was much more brilliant than had been universally assumed. The first basic research into American paint colors was carried on at Colonial Williamsburg. This led to the formulation c. 1940 of a palette of colors which were accepted for decades as objectively valid for eighteenth-century architecture. Subsequent research, employing much more sophisticated methods of chemical and optical analysis, has shown this palette to be inaccurate. The original colors were brighter, harsher, more intense; the decorative color schemes much less bland and muted than had been assumed. (The recently restored polychromy of the great Adams rooms at Syon House near London and the reception rooms of the Otis House in Boston are both based on these new research techniques. The results are startlingly different from what would have been assumed only a decade ago to have been an accurate restoration.)

VISUAL CONSEQUENCES OF
STRUCTURAL INTERVENTION

It can well be argued that in polychromy, as in other areas of preservation, the wisest policy is the most conservative—i.e., the least done, the better. The intervention which is most easily reversed is one of not intervening at all in the first place. This has been the experience of art conservators, especially in the past few decades, because of the rapid evolution of scientific methods of research, analysis, and treatment. Unfortunately, however, it is often not possible to leave the polychromed architectural surface undisturbed. Any of a number of situations might compel therapeutic intervention. If the subject is a wall painting or fresco, it might be threatened either by processes at work in the structural fabric behind it or by destructive environmental factors attacking from the outside or, most commonly, a mix of both. This is the case with many of the frescoes in Italy, where the only way to save the work of art is to detach it from its base and remount it on a new, free-standing backing which is chemically inert and dimensionally stable. In such bases, cleaning the fresco will be an essential prelude to diagnosis and treatment.

If orthodox restoration to some fixed historical date is called for, then later decorative surfaces will certainly be disturbed. Very often, as in archaeology, one layer will have to be peeled away to discover what lies beneath it. In old buildings, this can lead to very important discoveries. Thus, in the process of restoration of the royal palace of Wilanów near Warsaw, some of the state rooms were found to have as many as seven complete sets of wall paintings superimposed on one another. Again, in what seemed to be a routine investigation of floor and ceiling construction in the Hradčany Palace complex in Prague, some exploratory probes were made in the baroque plaster ceilings. (These ceilings had been installed in the eighteenth century as a fire deterrent in accordance with the decree of Maria Theresa.) Behind these plaster surfaces were discovered some 20 handsome Renaissance ceilings consisting of stenciled beams which in turn carried some 2,100 painted wooden panels, no two of them alike. The plaster had, ironically, kept them in perfect condition. Thus, what had begun as a routine structural probe led to a discovery of such magnitude that plans for the adaptive use of the palace had to be radically revised. A similar discovery, though of smaller scale, occurred in the eighteenth-century Vernon House in Newport, Rhode Island. There, in the process of cleaning the wood-paneled walls of the dining room, an extraordinary painting in the Chinese style was discovered on the plaster walls behind the panels. Since both paneling and painting were original and excellent examples of their kind, it was decided to hinge the panels, accordion-fashion, so that both surfaces are accessible for inspection and display.

Finally, in old and complex buildings, the very first step in preparing a long-range program of preservation will be a detailed visual examination of the entire fabric, indoors and out. Such an examination will require the removal of soot, efflorescence, and rust as well as clinging vines and mosses. This will require the erection of scaffolding, in itself an expensive operation, and dictates that corollary operations such as cleaning should take place at the same time. Thus, even if no signs of structural failure are uncovered, there will be a perceptible alteration of the cosmetic aspect. If, on the contrary, serious structural weaknesses are discovered, then the visual traces of intervention will be correspondingly severe. Examination of the huge tower over the crossing at York Minster revealed that the entire masonry mass had to be consolidated. This meant the drilling of hundreds of holes on 3-foot centers and the injection of thousands of cubic yards of grout. Decayed stones had to be replaced, traces of drilling and injection had to be removed, all mortar joints had to be repointed. Under circumstances such as these, the architect had no choice but to leave the entire massive tower as clean as the day it was finished. The results are astonishing: never have the original intentions of the Gothic architect been more spendidly displayed.

There are specialized cases of preservation in the fields of science and technology where immaculate cleanliness and/or perfect maintenance would be a sina qua non of the curatorial function. Under such a heading would fall scientific exhibits such as the observatory at Greenwich in London, recently reconstructed and reequipped with great care to re-create the seventeenth-century conditions of its founding. To replicate such an atmosphere, the old equipment is carefully maintained: lenses are polished, metal parts kept rust-free and shining, all moving parts oiled. As we have seen, such curatorial standards are not always observed: *vide* the Edison Laboratories in East Orange, New Jersey.

THE RESTORATION OF LOST POLYCHROMIES

All of this suggests the complexity, philosophical as well as methodological, of intervention in polychromatic systems. It also suggests the hazards of subjective aesthetically based decisions before all the facts are in.

Problems in this highly complex and still-evolving field can be grouped under three different headings:

1. How is the polychromatic system to be recorded and described?
2. How is the information to be stored for easy retrieval?
3. How is the data to be used for optically accurate reconstructions?

Descriptions of architectural polychromy may be (1) verbal, (2) pictorial, or (3) chemical. All three methods have their virtues: all have their limitations. For example, it is helpful for the preservationists, working on an eighteenth-century house, to learn from a contemporaneous document that its paneled wall was painted "Spanish brown"; or of a Gothic revival porch that its ceiling was painted "cerulean" or "sky blue." Such information about an antique color scheme is valuable in telling us chiefly what *it was not*. It is not an adequate guide as to precisely what *it was*.

Most literary evidence suffers from this inherent limitation, i.e., it is verbal, not pictorial. Before the perfection of photography, lithography, and color printing, literary information of paint colors and polychromatic systems is overwhelmingly verbal and therefore (except for formulae and recipes) unreliable. When colored plates appeared at all, they were expensive, hand-painted, and usually reserved for botanical or zoological subjects (e.g., Audubon's paintings of American birds or the flower prints published by Joseph Paxton). Even color swatches were rare: Downing's use of them in *Cottage Residences* (1842) is unique for the period. According to Dornsife, chromolithographs of exterior color schemes first appear in books after 1860; paint manufacturers are furnishing color cards of their ready-mixed colors in the 1870s; and full-colored chromos of suggested color schemes are common by 1885.[1]

Full-color photographic recording of architectural polychromy, while often beguiling, is also often unreliable. A bewildering number of variables obtrude at every stage of the process: the variable quality of color films; the luminous conditions under which the exposure is made (especially the conflict between artificial and natural light sources); the developing of the film; the production of the color-separation plates; the paper and inks used in printing; finally, the skill and care of the printers. All of these factors negatively influence the accuracy of four-color printed information on architectural polychromy. (As for storage, the pigmental instability of color film is notorious.)

Chemical and spectroscopic analysis of any material affords objectively verifiable information as to its physical composition. Thus, literary sources give chemical formulas and recipes for paints and mortars which, despite archaic terminology and mensuration, make replication possible. Modern chemical and spectroscopic analysis of actual samples gives very precise information on their composition. Even these latter techniques, however, are not apt to reveal the actual formula for any given sample. They are not certain to pick up trace elements which are often of key importance in the final color of the material; nor will they explain color changes due to aging (as in old varnishes and glazes).

Obviously, direct visual examination of the actual artifact is indispensable in any effort to collect and describe information on a polychromatic system, not to mention the repair or reconstitution of that system in situ.

In the process of color matching, paint chips or small swatches of the artifact are examined microscopically under lamps of a known color temperature. They can then be optically matched with color cards from a recognized system such as Munsell. If the information thus acquired is to be stored in verbal form, the identity is written: "Munsell color No. ——." This process, too, has its limitations, including the infinite number of possible gradations between one color chip and its neighbors in even the most fine-grained color matching system. If the information is to be stored in pictorial form, a microscopic slide is made. Skilled personnel are, of course, required in any case.

All these techniques should be employed in tandem, since it is only by checking all possible data from all possible sources that a reasonably accurate description of an extant polychromatic system can be achieved. But of course, even when we have succeeded in accurately documenting it, we will have described only its present state, not its original condition. We have already seen the prime importance of cleaning as a first step in architectural conservation. This becomes critically important in problems of color identification, since accumulated soil is the first obstacle to apprehending the original system. But many anomalies, such as fading and color shifts, are due to obscure chemical and physical processes which are little understood and hence difficult to reconstruct. What one needs in such circumstances is some sort of optical bench mark against which to measure mutations in the polychromatic system under investigation.

PICTORIAL SOURCES FOR HISTORIC POLYCHROMIES

Paintings are a prime source of information, not only on the architectural polychromies of their respective periods, but also on interior decorative schemes in general. Almost all portraits carry, in their backgrounds, some information on the dwelling places of their subjects. Indeed, many European paintings, from Gothic times down to the present day, are as much portraits of interior spaces as of the people who inhabit them.[2] The information on color which they give us is doubly significant: first, because it was as accurate originally as the artist could render it; and second, well preserved by the protected environments of palaces and museums.

Reference to such pictorial sources would help in resolving many difficult problems in restoration, e.g., current controversy in England around the restoration of the polychromy in the funerary art of English churches. No one challenges the fact that these tombs and catafalques were colored, especially during Gothic and early Renaissance times: enough traces of original pigment remain to establish that point beyond doubt. The real question is how bright, how intense, how varied were the colors. The hand-colored illustrations in the books of the period—executed in durable enamels and protected against environmental attrition by the books themselves—afford us vivid analogs of the color preferences of the period.

Eighteenth- and nineteenth-century American paintings offer comparably significant information on the forms and colors of the architecture of the period. We can assume that these paintings are "documentary," i.e., the artists recorded optical reality as well as their talent and training permitted. Even in studio landscapes, where the subject matter was idealized, the artists strove for maximum verisimilitude. And even when the painter is a folkloristic autodidact, the information given us is apt to be fundamentally reliable; e.g., the house *would* have had five windows across the front even if they are drawn out of scale; the sleigh in front of the country villa *was* part of the family life-style, even if the painter had difficulty with horses.

Surviving paintings have, by definition, been more or less well preserved. And when they have been cleaned and conserved by modern specialists, they give us important information on the color preference of the period. (Generally, it seems to have been brighter, more vivid, or more garish than the antiquarians had assumed!)

Naturally, not all restoration projects will require or support all the kinds of research discussed in this chapter. But where the restoration or reconstruction of a historic polychromatic system is decisively important, these research methodologies will prove useful.

CONSERVATION OF WALL PAINTINGS, PAPERS, AND FRESCOES

Modern art conservators have perfected the techniques whereby it is now possible to conserve any type of decorative membrane: canvas, paper, or paint film—or, for that matter, three-dimensional plaster ornaments. It is likewise possible to remove such artworks from the walls of buildings in which the integrity of the work is threatened by changes in the wall behind it. Italian conservators have been the leaders in this new field and have developed it to an astonishing extent. They can detach the fresco or painting from the supporting wall and remount it permanently upon a new dimensionally stable and chemically inert backing. The mural can then be "rehung" like an easel painting, either in its original position or elsewhere. The Italians have perfected techniques for removing murals from curved or irregular surfaces. More recently, they have perfected the means for removing the cartoons underneath the fresco on the undercoat of plaster where the artist sketched out his designs before beginning to execute the finished fresco. The same specialists have even perfected techniques for the removal of entire mosaics from floors, walls, and ceilings for remounting like painted murals. In such work, the tilt of each individual tessera is maintained, thereby preserving the texture which gives the mosaics their life and sparkle. American preservationists will seldom be confronted with buildings in which large wall paintings play any important role; and, fortunately for them, expert assistance is readily available when they need it.

12

Insertion of New
Systems in Old Fabrics

CONTROL OF THE THERMAL AND
LUMINOUS ENVIRONMENTS

Few old buildings were ever heated in winter to what would today be considered acceptable comfort levels. None of them was ever cooled with refrigerated air—though many old buildings in areas of long, intense summers were designed for maximum shading and effective ventilation: vide Charleston, Mobile, and New Orleans. Thus almost any old building which is being recycled today, for whatever use, will almost certainly require the insertion of mechanical systems aimed at increased comfort, amenity, and safety. The degree of this intervention will, however, clearly be modified by the new type of tenancy envisaged. If it is a case of the adaptive use of an old warehouse into modern apartments, then radical internal modifications are clearly mandatory: new heating and cooling systems; new electrical and illumination systems; new plumbing and sanitary equipment; new elevators and stair towers; and so forth.

But if a historic building is to be restored to its original condition (even if operated only at a museum level), then quite different types of intervention are called for. They might on occasion be fairly radical (e.g., the insertion of steel members in Mount Vernon and Independence Hall to carry the heavy tourist loads), but *such interventions must by definition be invisible.*

It has been argued that, for maximum verisimilitude in the experience, a museum house should be no better heated, cooled, ventilated, or illuminated than it would have been originally. There are persuasive arguments for such a position. From a purely sensuous point of view, a cool room heated only by a fragrant wood fire and lighted by only a whale-oil lamp or a couple of candles might well give us a more vivid sense of the life-styles of the eighteenth century. Because of the added sensuous dimension that they offer, many historic house museums feature cooking (fireplace cookery at Cooperstown and Sturbridge; stove cookery at Hancock Shaker Village). All these activities are under the continuous control of trained personnel, and they are wholly demonstrational, not participatory. Under such conditions, the danger of fire can be held to a minimum. It could also be argued that old furniture, built of solid wood and using animal glues, would be better protected against shrinking, warping, and cracking. But the unhappy fact is that the open flame of fireplace, lamp, and candle offer great risks to any old building, especially one open to the public.* The heating problem in museum houses in cold climates can be sidestepped, simply by not opening the house to the public in cold weather. And in areas where winter tourism is light, the practice is fairly common; e.g., Shelburne Village, near Burlington, Vermont. The other side of the argument—that the museum house should have no more summer comfort than that afforded by natural ventilation—is often unacceptable for another reason. Most middle-class American tourists travel in the summertime; and just as they would refuse to eat in a non-air-conditioned restaurant or stay at a non-air-conditioned hotel, so would they be reluctant to spend much time in a non-air-conditioned historic house museum.†

Once the decision is made to introduce such systems into old buildings, a number of questions must be faced: aesthetic, structural, economic. In the normal old commercial or industrial building, there were seldom any interiors of any monumental pretensions—with the possible exception of street-floor lobbies. Hence fairly radical alterations to the interiors are possible. Depending upon the taste and discretion of the architect, wholly new arrangements can often be very satisfactory. It used to be argued that the insertion of large elements into old fabrics (e.g., centralized air conditioning, elevators, stair towers) made such conversions economically prohibitive. But the enormous inflation in new construction costs has reversed this, as we have seen (Chapter 3).

In old monumental buildings, where maintenance of the aesthetic integrity of the interiors is as important as that of the exterior, matters are much more complicated. It will often be difficult to conceal electrical conduit and heating pipes: bulky ductwork from centralized air-conditioning systems is usually out of the question, although chimney flues can sometimes be used either for supply or for return air. From the purely cosmetic point of view, panel radiant heating is a most desirable method of heat transfer (as opposed to radiators, grilles, and diffusers). Here, either copper

*Any combustion is a potential hazard in an old house. Thus, in the restoration of Olana, the Frederick Church House near Hudson, New York, the old steam radiators were rehabilitated but a new heating plant was installed in a new underground chamber some 250 feet from the house.

†Obviously, different criteria apply to art and archaeological museums, where rare and/or fragile artifacts will require their own special environments: precise control of temperature and humidity, atmospheric filtration, strict control of natural and artificial illumination, and so on.

coils for hot water or electrical resistance wires are embedded in a new plaster ceiling. Unfortunately, however, these systems, too, have their drawbacks: copper coils have been known to leak; faulty controls on the electrical system can lead to fires; both systems are expensive to install, and the high cost of electricity in many parts of the nation is another deterrent.

An extremely interesting system of heating and air conditioning has been included in the reconstituted Old State House at Springfield, Illinois. Here, radiation under all the windows is in cast-iron panels which replicate the wooden panels under the original windows. Supply and return outlets for the air-conditioning system are incorporated into the panneled soffits of beams, arches, and embrasures. It must, however, be remembered that this building was completely dismantled and reassembled on a concrete armature. This permitted the architects great freedom in the positioning of ductwork, vents, lighting, and the like.

With the escalating costs of energy, the problem of making old buildings more efficient thermal containers achieves new urgency. Here again, the ultimate use of the recycled building will be the critical factor. In most cases of adaptive use, modifications of interiors will in any case be called for. Hence the installation of thermal insulation and vapor barriers can be readily accomplished by furring out exterior walls to receive them. New insulating glass and even new sash with weatherstripping can be installed. In buildings of historical or aesthetic significance, such new sash and glass should replicate the appearance of the old, as is currently being done in the restoration of the Woolworth Building in New York City.

But in orthodox restorations of old houses, the problem of weatherproofing and insulation becomes much more complicated. Normally, the interior surfaces of such structures—painted or papered plaster, paneling, marbelizing, and so on—are valuable historically (because they are original to the house) and aesthetically (because they have irreproducible patterns, patinas, or profiles). Of course, it is possible to remove even these and then reinstall them on insulated walls—the Italians do it all the time with frescoes—but it requires skill, time, and more money than is ordinarily available. As we have seen, it has been done in such nationally important buildings as the White House and Independence Hall.

If the house is of frame construction, there are a number of insulation materials which can be applied in sheet form or blown into the interstices between exterior siding and interior plaster. Most of them are chemically inert and fire- and fungus-retardant. Some blown insulation tends to compact across time, and some tends to pick up and hold condensed moisture (always a danger when there is no vapor barrier on the inner face of the insulation). Some of the newer insulations are so-called foaming agents: they are pumped in as effervescent foam and congeal into a spongelike substance, but their permanence and safety are now being questioned.

Since an important source of heat loss is by infiltration, calking and weather stripping of all doors and windows are important; they are also invisible if carefully installed. In areas of extreme cold, it may even be necessary to install storm sash. If so, it should be clear sheets of undivided glass and installed *inside* existing sash to minimize intrusive appearance.

ILLUMINATION OF THE HISTORIC STRUCTURE

In devising the illumination system for any building dating from before the common use of illuminating gas but especially before the use of the incandescent electric bulb, we face both conceptual and technical problems. Before the use of gas and electricity for lighting, all buildings would have had very low levels of illumination, both artificial and natural. For the modern tourist who comes to "see," such illumination would be unsatisfactory. When we use the equivalent of hundreds of candles to illuminate an ordinary living room, it is hard to adjust to a luminous environment in which a family room might have been lighted by only one or two candles or, more probably, only by an open fire. There is another paradoxical aspect to all preelectrical lighting fixtures. Without exception, torchères, candelabra, chandeliers, lamps, and lanterns made much of the fixture; that is, the designers lavished so much attention on the fixture that it became more important than the flame itself.[1] This emphasis has, of course, been completely reversed in modern illumination: with diffused, indirect, and reflected lighting, the actual light source disappears altogether; only a wash of light remains.

This offers no special problem for adaptive-use projects. But for buildings in which historical accuracy is important, the problem is acute. Since the open flame of lamp and candle is too dangerous, the commonest tendency is to use antique fixtures wired for electricity, with small bulbs which in shape, size, and luminosity approach those of the original candle or lamp wick. But this technique leaves other problems unsolved. For example, some monumental buildings have architectural features which cry aloud for a wash of indirect lighting: the dome of the U.S. Capitol is one; the barrel vault of Old Touro Synagogue in Newport, Rhode Island, another. Until the perfection of modern light bulbs, neither could have been seen under the actual luminous conditions to which the designers clearly aspired. Even the ring of open gas jets which was used early on in the Capitol, however festive in appearance, must have more obscured than illuminated the dome above it. In such monumental interiors it seems entirely appropriate to use indirect lighting to model the surfaces even when the original chandeliers and candelabra are also employed.

There are other situations, however, in which modern light sources are distracting. For example, museum houses often display paintings and sculptures which have an independent value above and beyond their decorative role in furnishing the room. Since the light levels are ordinarily too low to appreciate the finer points of the work of art, recessed fixtures with pinpoint fixtures are trained on them. Aside from being anachronistic, such special light effects disturb the luminous balance of the room as a whole. If the art is of museum quality, it would probably be preferable to display it under standard gallery conditions.

EXTERIOR ILLUMINATION OF HISTORIC STRUCTURES

The exterior illumination of buildings is an almost wholly new field with little or no historic precedent upon which to draw. Monumental urbane buildings might have had a few bronze or wrought-iron lanterns with which to light up their main entrances on special occasions. On feast days, an old church or palace might have its façade picked out in rows of candles or lamps. American streets were never adequately lighted, either for reasons of aesthetics or for safety, until the appearance of the arc lamp around the turn of the century. Thus, the gas-fired iron streetlamps which are now being replicated across the country add a romantic note of verisimilitude to the street scene and are probably adequate for residential areas. But the floodlighting of monumental buildings, especially those which play an important role in the cityscape (e.g., the Wrigley Tower in Chicago, the Invalides in Paris, the Washington Monument in Washington)—all these seem eminently appropriate. The fact of being artificially lighted from below, as opposed to being naturally illuminated by the sun from above, does indeed reverse the modeling of the artifact in a fashion which the original designers could not possibly have foreseen. It does not follow, however, that they would not be displeased. One thinks of Horatio Greenough's unsuccessful attempts in 1842 to illuminate his heroic figure of Washington when it still stood in the center of the Capitol Rotunda for which it was designed. Moving torches and flambeaux around the sculpture, he tried to evolve an illumination scheme which would modify the daylight which fell down from the cupola. He did not succeed with open flames; it is doubtful if he could have done it with gas; only modern lamps and reflectors could have accomplished his purpose.

In any case, one could argue that, historically, it has always been a human ambition to live in a "city of light." The great fireworks displays along the Seine during the days of Louis XVI and the lighted tableaux which Leonardo staged in the Ducal Gardens in Milano are vivid proof of this ambition. A society which can place a camera on Mars should have no problem in lighting its cities.

13

Restoration and Maintenance of Historic Landscapes

Of all the immense variety of American landforms, natural or man-made, we normally regard only a limited number of types as meriting curatorial attention for scenographic, scientific, or historical reasons. We might classify these as follows:

1. Natural undisturbed landscapes: Niagara Falls; the Grand Canyon; Yosemite National Park

2. Public botanical gardens: New York Botanical Garden; Arnold Arboretum, Boston; Fairchild Arboretum, Coral Gables, Florida

3. Ornamental urban landscapes: Central Park, New York; Sunset Park, San Francisco; Boston Fenway

4. Private "pleasure" gardens: Mount Vernon; Longwood Gardens, Delaware; Magnolia Gardens, Charleston; Governors' Palace, Williamsburg

5. Working historical farms: Sturbridge Village, Massachusetts; Old Bethpage Village, Nassau County, New York; Carters Grove, Williamsburg

6. Historic industrial sites: Erie Canal, New York; Saugus Iron Works, Salem, Massachusetts; Paterson–Great Falls industrial complex, New Jersey

7. Archaeological sites: Franklin Homesite, Philadelphia; Jamestown, Virginia; Canyon de Chelly National Monument, Arizona; Fort Ticonderoga, New York

Agricultural, forest, or mineral lands are managed according to strictly utilitarian norms. Any aesthetic or historic significance in such activities is incidental: no farm or factory is apt to be handled museologically until it has ceased to be productive. Even the concept of protecting "natural wonders" against fortuitous destructive human agents is a very recent development—especially with Americans, who for centuries could regard the primeval landscape as simply an inexhaustible resource, suitable only for exploitation. Even now, protection is inadequate: where they are protected in national parks, such natural phenomena as mountain peaks, geysers, waterfalls, and primeval forests are not thought of as falling under the jurisdiction of the landscape architect. Since the forms themselves are "God-made," conscious designing is not thought of as appropriate.

Of course, even here our attitudes are changing in such areas as the seashores, where human action along the interface between nature and people has reached critical proportions. Here the federal government has been compelled to intervene by creating a new system of National Seashore Parks with unprecedented controls of development and activity. But these must be described as *preservative* measures. The only serious proposal for the *restoration* of a natural form for purely aesthetic reasons was the 1971 study for the aesthetic enhancement of the American Falls at Niagara. Prepared for the International Joint Commission by the U.S. Corps of Engineers, this extraordinary project included the building of scaled working models of the American Falls to explore the visual consequences of such massive interventions as the removal of the accumulated talus at the foot of the falls or the raising of the level of the Maid-of-the-Mist Pool to conceal the talus.[1] Fortunately, after a study of several years, the entire project was abandoned as an ultimately futile attempt to halt geological processes (Fig. 13.2).

The very idea of "restoring" a natural geological phenomenon such as Niagara Falls to some putatively "better" state may have its comic aspects. (The geological forces are not only ineluctible but, in the case of Niagara, extremely active: the entire gorge is reckoned at being only some 12,000 years old!) Nevertheless, the proposal dramatizes the fact that modern technology makes quite possible interventions in the landscape which would have been inconceivable only a few short decades ago. Thus we have seen the transplantation of the monumental temple of Abu Simbel to a new site above the lake created by the Aswan Dam in Egypt. And in that same artificial lake we see the creation of a new facsimile of the island of Philae. On this new island will be reconstituted the Temple of Isis, which is currently being dismantled and moved to the new site.

The preservation and/or restoration of an artifact such as a botanical garden or a historical farm confronts us with problems quite different, philosophically and practically, from those of architecture per se. For though, like all human constructs, gardens are anthropocentric, each will have an important component of living tissue, obeying its own organic laws of growth and decay. Thus, in our landscape designs, we use nature—may even on occasion want them to "look natural"—but we are by no means prepared to "let nature have its own way." This paradoxical duality is at

13.1. *Fifty years ago, such great natural features* as Yosemite *(1)* or the Grand Canyon *(2)* seemed eternally secure under the curatorship of the National Park Service. But today the remorseless pressure of motorized tourism and the commercialized sports which it makes possible exert unanticipated threats to the physical and visual integrity of these putatively "primeval" ecologies. They compel us to formulate radically broader and more comprehensive standards for the preservation of such natural landscapes, which are, in effect, extremely fragile artifacts.

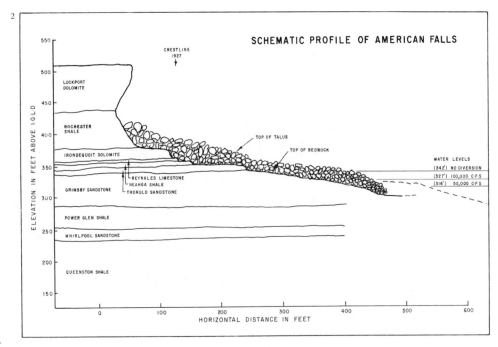

13.2 *The capacity of modern technology to manipulate* the natural world is in daily evidence. Usually the evidence is dismaying: carcinogenic wastes in the Hudson; strip mining in West Virginia; soil erosion in the Great Plains. These same technologies could, of course, be employed to restore and preserve these damaged landscapes on the same grand scale: unhappily, they seldom are. This lends special poignancy to the 1971 proposal of the U.S. Corps of Engineers to reshape Niagara Falls for aesthetic improvement. The scheme is at once heroic and farcical: heroic in the sense that it demonstrates our capacity to intervene in natural geological processes for cultural ends; farcical because it is based upon a series of subjective value judgments—that the perpetual mist at the base of the American Falls makes it less attractive to tourists than the Canadian Falls (*1*); that the mist should be eliminated by removal of the

264

scree at the base (*4*); and that once this cosmetic intervention has been completed, it should be made permanent by stabilizing the Falls with a reinforced-concrete armature concealed behind the base. The Corps employed advanced engineering research to validate its proposals. After a geological analysis (*2*), it built a scale model of the Falls. This permitted a scale reproduction of the river's flow on a seasonal basis. It also included a scale replica of the scree at the Falls' base (*3*). The fallen stones are movable, permitting a photographic record of the clearing of the mist as they are gradually removed (*5–8*). Finally the study included the design of a huge concrete armature to preserve the Falls in their "improved" condition. The cultural absurdity of this particular proposal should not obscure the fact that such technological expertise can be fruitfully applied to valid projects like the replication of the isle of Philae at Aswan.

13.2 *(Continued).* The scale model of Niagara Falls showed that the mist was indeed caused by the scree at its base (*5*) and could be progressively reduced by its phased removal (*6, 7*). The removal of all the scree would eliminate all the mist and yield the Corps' concept of how the "natural wonder" would look in its unnaturally tidied-up state.

5

6

7

8

13.3 *The capacity of modern technology to re-create* whole landscapes has been brilliantly demonstrated at Lake Nasser on the Nile. First the rock-cut temple of Abu-Simbel was sawn into pieces and then reconstituted on a new site above the rising waters. Now an entire temple complex is being disassembled and moved to another and higher island in the lake. The complex is the Temple of Isis, a seventh-century B.C. precinct on the island of Philae. The entire fabric of some 50,000 huge blocks will be reconstituted on the island of Agilkia; this island is itself being reshaped into a facsimile of Philae so that, when completed, the entire complex of buildings and landscape will replicate the original lost beneath the waters of the new man-made lake.

the heart of all landscape design but it is obviously most critical in landscape preservation. Up to date, we have had little experience here and have a totally inadequate theoretical apparatus for dealing with it.

PHYLOGENETIC ORIGINS OF AMERICAN LANDSCAPE DESIGN

The immediate sources of American landscape concepts are largely English in the sense that, in the eighteenth and nineteenth centuries, English experience was a sort of lens through which the visual stimuli of the great world were made available to Americans. (Thus, A. J. Downing [1815–1852], whose books made him our first

267

influential theoretician in the field, was a shameless plagiarist of English landscape and gardening literature.) But the English landscape forms were, in turn, derived from two great foreign centers: the Renaissance and baroque gardens of Italy and France; and the gardens of China and Japan. (Thus one of the most characteristic elements of the English garden, the rockery, was a brilliant adaptation of Oriental design concepts and botanical material.) A common denominator of both these design sources was a strict control of the varieties, size, and scale of the plant materials employed. This control might be most obvious in the French parterre, with its knife-edged geometry and color; but it was equally dominant, even if invisible to Western eyes, in the classic gardens of China and Japan.

For all its air of naturalism, the Japanese garden was designed and planted at full scale and held that way across centuries by continuous pruning. Loraine Kuck cites a grove of fully grown cherry trees, transplanted in full flower, to meet the whim of a thirteenth-century princess; and pine trees famous for their shape pruned, needle by needle, with tweezers![2] But the great formal gardens of the West, although conceived of as planted at full scale, seldom were in fact: even Lenôtre would have had to wait a few years for his full effect to be achieved. And few of these formal gardens have been maintained across time at the precise scale called for in the original designs.

The allées and parterres of Versailles have been held in substantially the same form as visualized by the architect Lenôtre, as is clear from a comparison of seventeenth-century prints with contemporary photographs. But most Renaissance-inspired gardens have long since lost their original appearance. Thus it is difficult for the contemporary visitor to Villa d'Este at Tivoli to visualize how different are the gardens today from their finished form as conceived by the architect Pietro Ligurio. Contemporaneous prints show us a patterned *tappeto* (literally, a patterned carpet) designed to be seen comprehensively from the elevated terrace of the villa. Today—with the uncontrolled growth of centuries—it has become a sequence of disconnected shaded vistas: lovely in its own way but in no sense corresponding to its original raison d'être.

The same metamorphosis is to be found in all the older formal gardens in the United States, especially those in Virginia, South Carolina, and the Deep South generally. To *preserve* them in their present state would be a complicated task in itself: but to *restore* them to the state visualized by their original designers would be incomparably more difficult. Where original plant material survives, restoration might dictate impossibly severe pruning. Moreover, if strict botanical accuracy were a criterion of the restoration, it would imply the replacement of modern plant types by antique varieties which might be difficult or impossible to locate today.

Landscape architects who are seriously interested in the management of historic landscapes will have to abandon these antitemporal and antienvironmental postures. They will have to face the fact that, unlike their architectural peers, they will be working with living tissue. This confronts them with change in their medium at two different time scales: changes in size, scale, and form of individual plants; and changes in the very species and varieties in use at any given historical period. This means that very few historic landscapes, at least in the Western world, have a physiognomy corresponding to the ambitions of the original designers.

The parameters of today's landscape architectural profession, like those of architecture itself, are all conceptually organized around abstract, internationalized norms. That is to say, landscape theory and practice pay little or no attention to the regional dimensions of botany, climate, or history. As in architecture, this leads to the impoverishment of both theory and practice in the entire profession. For landscape forms are even more the prisoners of specific environmental parameters than are architectural ones. The raw materials of architecture—steel, glass, air conditioning—*can* be used in any part of the world. (Whether they *ought to be* is altogether another matter.) But the raw materials of landscape design can be used only in appropriate climatic regimes. The forms of both architecture and landscape can, however, be exported anywhere. The glass-walled skyscraper is used in Leningrad and Lima while the roofless plaza, evolved for the Mediterranean, is mechanically repeated in Boston and Winnipeg. In similar fashion, town planning patterns perfected in the genial climate of southern England are mindlessly repeated in Warsaw and Mexico. It is not only that these immigrant forms become wasteful exotica in their new locale. What is much more serious is that their importation effectively prevents the invention, development, and refinement of new architectural and landscape forms which would be experientially viable for that locale.

All the world's great landscape forms are umbilically tied to both their geographical and historical contexts. For example, it is impossible to study the courtyard in all its permutations (atrium, loggia, patio, plaza, cortile) without recognizing it as a wonderfully elegant response to a specific set of environmental forces—forces which have not changed and are not apt to change within historic time. Where the courtyard has been successfully transplanted, it has invariably been into habitats similar to its point of origin. Thus, in Los Angeles, the plaza may be paved in reinforced concrete rather than the Parian marble of Delos; the fountain may have been designed by Calder rather than Praxiteles; the plants may be modernized hybrids of those once used in Córdoba centuries before. The Los Angeles patio may not at all resemble its Mediterranean progenitor. But its beauty and viability derive from the same responses to the same stimuli within the same environmental restraints. It becomes grotesque only when transplanted to Chicago or Helsinki.

Modern horticultural technology may have somewhat extended the distance across which plant materials and landscape forms can be trans-

1

13.4. *The soaring interest of Victorians in botany, horticulture, and landscape design* led to the development of new landscape forms both public and private: urban parks and monumental cemeteries, botanical gardens, arboretums and conservatories. Of these, the conservatory was the most spectacular as it was the most innovative. Since it was dedicated to the cultivation of tender exotic plants, it required much more precise control of environmental forces than conventional open-air gardening. This led to the perfection of both daring new structures in glass and metal and revolutionary new heating systems. Beginning as a luxury item for the very rich, e.g., Joseph Paxton's glasshouses of the 1830s for the Duke of Devonshire, the conservatory went public: in Paris in 1834 with the Jardin des Plantes *(3)*; in London in 1845 with Decimus Burton's splendid Palm House for Kew Gardens *(1)*. In Amer-

2

3

ica the process was somewhat delayed. Jay Gould had built a conservatory of truly monumental proportions by Lyndhurst on the Hudson in 1881. By the end of the century a public conservatory had become de rigueur in most American cities. Most of these are still extant, and many, recognized as historically significant, are being restored. Among them are the Phipps Conservatory in Baltimore's Druid Park (4) and the elegant little dome structure in San Francisco's Sunset Park (5). One of the largest—the Enid A. Haupt Conservatory of the New York Botanical Garden (2)—was restored in 1980. The steel and glass fabric has been scrupulously returned to its 1901 configuration. The interior plant communities have, however, been reorganized to bring them into line with contemporary standards of teaching and interpretation to the lay public.

4

5

271

ported. Thanks to new chemicals for the control of rotting, growth, and flowering, and to new technologies for the control of light and temperature, the great lily grower Jan de Graaff was able to hybridize lilies from the ends of the earth, producing plants with wholly new characteristics which could never have developed under "natural" circumstances. Thus, too, it is now possible to replicate the golf courses of cool and misty Scotland in the desert climate of Palm Springs. But the transplant can be accomplished only at the cost of great expenditures in irrigation, fertilization, and chemical therapy for the exotic grasses, and it cannot survive even a short-term failure of the life-support system. Generally speaking, the environmental restraints on plant life are fixed and immutable. Perhaps this is the explanation for another paradox of contemporary landscape design: the way in which it has given up plant materials almost entirely. The internationalized form can be freely moved around even if the flora associated with it cannot. Ergo, forget the plants—as in most monumental landscape projects in American cities today: City Hall Plaza in Boston, National Gateway Park in St. Louis, City Hall Plaza in Chicago.

NEW PERSPECTIVES ON LANDSCAPE RESTORATION

The accurate reconstruction of a vanished garden requires the same mix of archival and archaeological documentation as would be needed in the restoration of historic buildings. Archival materials on old gardens and landscapes are, however, apt to be even more fragmentary and inconclusive than on old buildings; and landscape archaeology is, as we shall see, in its infancy. This paucity of archival material is due to several factors. In the first place, until fairly recently, there was no literary tradition for recording or describing any but the most palatial or urbane of landscape features. Most horticultural and agricultural activities would have been in the hands of gardeners and peasants who, if not actually illiterate, would have transmitted their expertise by apprenticeship, Thus, as in many other areas of human activity, e.g., cookery and diet, such conventional wisdom would have lain in submerged strata, completely below the reach of literature. And this paradox does not begin much to change, at least in Europe, until the opening of the sixteenth century. One does not find a real body of garden and landscape literature until the first years of the eighteenth. (It should be remembered that the first systematic efforts at a scientific typology and nomenclature for plants began only with the great Swedish botanist Carolus Linnaeus [1707–1778].) And even in such literature, the landscape restorationist will find very little graphic or pictorial evidence of the plants or gardens being discussed. Thus, for example, it has not been possible for scholars to agree upon a satisfactory hypothetical reconstruction of the gardens in the villas of Pliny the Younger, despite his very full verbal descriptions of them.

One of the rare cases of reliable pictorial evidence of historical gardens and landscapes has been the paintings of the Venetian artist Bernardo Belotto (called Canaletto). This eighteenth-century artist toured Europe, painting portraits of palaces and gardens on commission, in much the same way that artists painted portraits of the owners. His work has proved to be so accurate that his Polish paintings have been used as basic documents in the restoration of many buildings in Warsaw, including Wilanow Palace (Fig. 13.10). Unfortunately, not many such art sources exist for the rest of the world. One surprising source has proved to be the series of "water lily" paintings by the French impressionist painter Claude Monet. Despite their dematerialized ethereal beauty, these canvases are fairly accurate recordings of Monet's own gardens at his summer house in the town of Giverny, near Paris. These gardens (along with the studio and greenhouses of the painter) have been restored under the supervision of Gerald van der Kemp, director of the Louvre. The paintings are being used as guides to the reconstruction of the pools, bridges, and treillage which had fallen into disarray after the death of Monet in 1926.

Beginning with the middle of the nineteenth century, gardens and landscapes have of course been recorded photographically. Such photographs offer objective recordings of unique value, enabling the specialist not only to identify the plant materials employed in the subject garden but also their size, shape, and spatial disposition. How such photographic data can be employed for the accurate restoration of a Victorian estate has recently been demonstrated by Prof. Robert Harvey, in his work on the grounds of Terrace Hill, the mansion in Des Moines now being restored as the official residence for the governor of Iowa. Especially interesting has been Harvey's technique for locating the point in space from which each photograph was taken as a means of accurately reconstructing the plan and contours of the grounds.

LANDSCAPE ARCHAEOLOGY—A NEW RESOURCE

The other indispensable resource for landscape restoration is, of course, archaeology. Landscape archaeology differs from the orthodox kind only in the sort of evidence which it seeks. However, since much of this evidence is of organic nature, it has survived far less well, leaving much more evanescent traces than the marble, brick, and stucco of architecture. Thus, until comparatively recently, the landscape record was overlooked and destroyed by conventional archaeologists. This state of affairs has begun to change in recent years, especially in the classic sites of Greece and Rome. Thus we

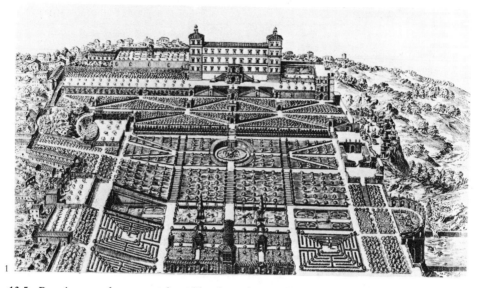

1

13.5. Renaissance pleasure gardens, like those designed by Pietro Ligurio for Villa d'Este in Tivoli, Italy, were conceived of in essentially architectonic terms as roofless extensions of the palaces they served. Their aesthetic effect depended upon continuous, rigorous pruning and immaculate housekeeping, with little or no interest in botany per se. Thus the cool and bosky aisles of Villa d'Este today *(2)* bear little resemblance to the sun-flooded parterres of a 1573 engraving *(1)*. Restoration of such gardens to their original appearance, even if desirable, would be all but impossible, since the overgrown plant materials would not survive the required heavy pruning; besides, many of the original varieties have disappeared.

2

have the extensive landscape restorations of the approach to the Athenian Acropolis as well as the planting in the Agora.[3] More recent work in downtown Pompeii by the American archaeologist Wilhelmina Jashemski has had remarkably suggestive results. Her investigations have been able to locate and identify several individual botanical specimens—trees, vines, shrubs—as well as garden forms. Even more significantly, she has reinterpreted urban history in Pompeii by proving that there were successful truck gardens, vineyards, and orchards even in downtown Pompeii on land for which orthodox archaeology—finding no trace of architecture—could suggest no plausible uses.

Landscape archaeology is now, even if somewhat belatedly, proving its importance in the United States. Pioneering work in scientific garden archaeology has been a feature of Colonial Williamsburg since its founding fifty years ago. It has been systematically employed in the reconstruction of the gardens and conservatory of Mount Vernon as well as in the reconstruction of the gardens laid out by Thomas Jefferson at the University of Virginia in Charlottesville, Virginia.

Perhaps the most ambitious recent reconstruction of a vanished American garden has been that of the Paca House in Annapolis, Maryland. Although the house and grounds of this famous eighteenth-century mansion were amply documented in the letters and journals of its time, the garden itself had long since vanished beneath a sprawling addition to the house itself, plus a bus station and a parking lot. When the decision was made in 1965 to demolish the addition, restore the mansion, and reconstruct its garden, no graphic or pictorial evidence of what it looked like had been uncovered, and despite subsequent research, little more was found—a sketch of the house from the garden dating from the 1820s, and the background of a portrait of Colonel William Paca himself, painted by Charles Willson Peale in 1772. The reconstruction, therefore, was based largely on archaeological investigations. These succeeded in establishing the original boundaries and contours as well as locating some of the garden's major features, including a gazebo, walls, pools, drains, and paved paths. On the basis of such physical evidence, plus extensive literary data on the plant materials popular at that time, the garden has been completely reconstructed to an assumed date of 1976.

In view of the potentials of contemporary scholarship, it is indeed quite possible to construct prototypical gardens and landscapes on the basis of archival evidence alone. This is especially true for America after 1800, since it was following this period that a body of horticultural and agricultural theory and practice began to form and, with it, its own literary corpus. Such a hypothetical reconstruction has been made for Boscobel, a historic house museum near Garrison, New York. This federal house was reconstituted on its present site in 1959, after having been disassembled on its original site, 20 miles down the Hudson, to make way for a Veterans Administration Hospital. The original landscape layout was not documented at the time of the move, and a totally new layout was designed by the landscape architects for the new site. In retrospect, it is clear that this new layout is historically inappropriate, reflecting the aesthetic criteria of a wealthy Westchester suburb of the 1950s rather than a gentleman's farm of 1810. In an effort to create a more appropriate environment context for the mansion, extensive research into the life-styles and physical configurations of comparable Hudson River farms has been carried out. Horticultural and agricultural literature of the period 1800–1810 was examined. Aesthetic theories of landscape and garden design were studied. All available plans and illustrations of such farms were collected. This research has formed the basis for a new development scheme aimed at re-creating not only the forms but also the animal and plant life and agricultural activities of such a farming enterprise.

Nevertheless, even with all the resources of modern research and archaeology, misconceptions about old gardens are all too easily developed and uncritically accepted. Thus, largely on the basis of remaining wall paintings in Pompeii, it had been until recently assumed that all the courtyards of Pompeiian houses had been sun-flooded, formally patterned parterres, accented with small clipped and potted shrubs. But, in the light of

13.6. *Two aristocratic garden traditions—European and Japanese*—have combined to form the principal genetic sources of American landscape and garden design. For all their radically differing physiognomies, the two traditions share similar attitudes toward the natural world. Both are based on the concept of stasis—i.e., that the garden is to be designed and built as a full-scale finished artifact, like any other constructed object, and that it is to be kept that way across time. Since this ambition runs counter to living processes of growth and decay, it subsumes careful and continuous maintenance, an expensive and hence aristocratic enterprise. Yet, in aesthetic terms, the two traditions differ radically, especially toward the plants them-

1

selves. Baroque designers had little interest in them (at Versailles, Le Nôtre might well have preferred color-fast plastic foliage and AstroTurf lawns to real boxwood and grasses (*1*) and Louis XIV might well have not noticed the difference. Japanese aristocracy, on the other hand, had a great interest in botany and horticulture. Thus, though the housekeeping of the gardens of the Sanzenin Temple (*2*) or Shugakuin Palace (*3*) in Kyoto was no less rigorous than Versailles (valuable old pine trees were barbered with tweezers, needle by needle!), the objective was to conceal the traces of human intervention, not to dramatize it as at Versailles. In any case, the curatorial task is simpler in both instances because of their history of long and scrupulous maintenance.

1

13.7. *New light on old Pompeii:* although architects have dug in the earth for centuries, they too often regarded the earth itself as merely an obstacle to the artifacts they were seeking. As a result, critically important evidence on land forms and plant life was lost forever. Wilhelmina Jashemski, digging in the often dug soil of Pompeii, has examined it carefully for evidence of horticultural (rather than architectural) activities. As a result she is proving that areas hitherto thought of as inexplicably "vacant" were actually thriving market gardens, orchards,

278

2

3

4

and vineyards. She has found fossilized remains of fava beans, hazel nuts, grape seeds, and figs (*5*). With such clues, large vineyards were discovered near the ampitheater (*1,2*). Filling with plaster the root cavities left by trees and shrubs smothered in the A.D. 79 eruption, she has established the size and varieties of small vines (*4*) and large trees (*3*). By such methods, she has redefined the urban morphology of downtown Pompeii.

5

MARTEL'S NEW YORK CENTRAL PARK.

1

13.8. *Proposed restoration of the Ramble in Central Park, New York:* though the park today retains much of the scenographic splendor of Frederick Law Olmsted's splendid original (*1*), a closer scrutiny reveals the disastrous consequences of decades of neglect and abuse (*3*). None of the original planting, in all its visual richness and botanical variety, is left: weed plants have largely taken over; erosion from rainfall and frost creep has removed the topsoil, altered Olmsted's carefully contrived topography, and silted up his water bodies. Since there has never been a coherent maintenance and preservation program, the park has been subjected to a century of ad hoc interventions. Weed plants have closed out important vistas and new ones have been created without reference to Olmsted's intentions. Significant old structures have vanished and trivial new ones appeared. These disasters have been compounded in recent times by rising vandalism and diminishing gardening and police staffs.

Fortunately, this state of laissez-faire neglect is ending. For the first time in its history, the park has an office of Curator, with its own staff and budget, and is initiating a series of programs and projects aimed at reversing the disastrous past. One of these projects is for the restoration of the section known as the Ramble *(center left, 1)*. One of Olmsted's favorites, the Ramble is a naturalistic garden laid out in a rough outcropping of glaciated granite. This romantic, irregular terrain created many microclimates which Olmsted cannily used for a variety of plant communities. Obviously many factors make impossible the literal return of this landscape to its 1859 condition—contours, for example, have been irreversibly altered. But the restoration plan calls for the reestablishment of many features such as the Rill (*2*), which will be rescued from its present plight (*3*); the streambed will be restored, the wood-railed footpath reconstructed, and the original planting replicated (*4*). One of the Ramble's important attractions is bird-watching (it is a stopover on an important flyway for migratory birds). Therefore trees and shrubs offering food and shelter for avian visitors will figure prominently in the planting plans.

280

The Cave in the Rambles, c. 1868.

The Cave in its 1979 condition.

The Cave: proposed reconstruction.

281

13.9. *Perhaps as famous as any garden in the world* is that of the French painter Claude Monet at Giverny, well known for the dozens of ravishing paintings he made in the years before his death in 1926. The centerpiece was usually the pond, beflowered with the lily *nivea,* spanned by a wisteria-draped footbridge, and brooded over by weeping willows (*1*). For all its naturalism, the pond was a construct of Monet himself, formed by damming the swampy little river Epte; and despite its rustic air, the garden was carefully manicured by Monet and his gardener. But since Monet's death the pond had become silted up, its lilies dead and margins weakened by muskrats, the bridge decrepit, and most of the original plant materials dead from neglect. But now the whole garden (with Monet's house across the road) has been carefully restored to its original configuration, thanks to the generosity of an American garden aficionada, Lila Acheson Wallace. The pond has been dredged (*4*), the banks stabilized by steel bulkheads (*5*), and the little blue bridge reconstructed (*2*). All of the original plant materials have been replaced so that in a few years' time visitors will see again the enchanting landscapes of the great painter.

1

13.10. *Restoration of the eighteenth-century parterres at Wilanow Palace, Warsaw,* was based upon archaeology and a remarkable set of paintings by the Venetian painter Bernardo Bellotto (1720–1780) which he executed for King Augustus III in 1762 (*1*). Landscape paintings are often valuable sources of information on old gardens, even when not especially well drawn. But Bellotto, who painted these "portraits" on commission, was famous for his accuracy. Indeed, Bellotto's paintings of a number of Polish sites, including Warsaw itself, were vitally important in the postwar reconstruction of such monuments as Wilanow Palace (*2*), now a museum of the decorative arts.

2

Jashemski's researches, it now appears more probable that the whole city was shaded with a continuous canopy of great trees, willows, sycamores, and olives. In just such a context, the reconstructed gardens of Williamsburg are now being reexamined and reinterpreted by a second generation of restorationists. The original archaeology of many of the gardens there had revealed typical geometric patterns of paved paths and edged beds. In the initial reconstructions of the 1930s and 1940s, these were all assumed to have been ornamental flower gardens (or "pleasure gardens," as they were called in the eighteenth century). But recent reexamination of the social and economic history of the original householders indicated that many of them could not have afforded the gardeners required to maintain them. Thus, it seems much safer to assume that, where such bedding existed at all, it was used for vegetables and herbs.

In the restoration of landscapes and gardens associated with historic personages (e.g., the gardens of the great plant explorer Dr. William Bartram, in Philadelphia), botanical and horticultural accuracy is quite as important as topographic or aesthetic veracity. Such accuracy is all the more important in the gardens of men like Washington and Jefferson, since both men were passionate gardeners and left unusually complete records and diaries of their gardening activities.

Botanical and horticultural accuracy is also essential in another type of landscape preservation: the working historical farm. Here, curatorial emphasis is not upon formal design, since the original intention would have been exclusively utilitarian. Instead, the didactic purpose of the restoration would be to demonstrate the processes of agriculture and husbandry: the actual types of animals and produce grown; the tools and methods used in planting, cultivation, and harvesting; and/or the buildings required by the processes—barns, corncribs, root cellars, icehouses, and the like. The design and management of the working historic farm obviously requires new levels of expertise for which few American landscape architects are prepared.

The curators of most historic sites and monuments, like the curators of museums and galleries, have an understandable ambition to see their artifacts displayed in the most favorable fashion. Such an ambition does not, unfortunately, always correspond to historical fact. Most urbane, ruling-class landscapes were designed on the assumption that, like the architecture they surrounded, they would always be maintained in optimal condition. We know from rich documentation that Louis XIV had very high standards for the day-to-day care of his palaces and gardens. We can therefore safely assume that Versailles and the Louvre glowed with the luster of faultless housekeeping when he and his court were in residence. To maintain these levels of housekeeping today is therefore fully consistent with the historic record. However, as we have seen, when this same maintenance is applied to a country town like Williamsburg, the maintenance question takes on another significance.

285

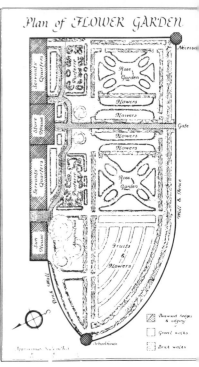

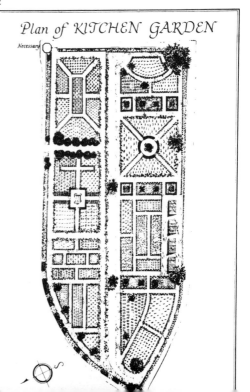

13.11. Mount Vernon's flower (1) and vegetable gardens (2) are probably the nation's oldest landscape restoration, just as they are almost certainly the longest in continuous cultivation under a single curatorial policy. Since Washington was a devoted horticulturalist and an impeccable record keeper, the gardens today probably come as close as possible to re-creating the originals. The relatively mild climate permits the year-round program of propagating, planting, and harvesting which would have been in effect in Washington's day. The result is a range of activities which adds interest and verisimilitude to the tourists' experience with Mount Vernon.

Fortunately, the curators of such institutions are increasingly aware of the dangers of "prettifying" the past and are evolving new methods for avoiding it in the future. We have seen a good example of this new approach illustrated in the Danish Frilandsmuseet near Copenhagen (Fig. 10.3). A comparatively new installation, built from scratch on open farmland, the project is landscaped to contain a series of farm groups, each typical of a different district of Denmark. The result of this carefully calculated policy is a sequence of rural landscapes which probably come as close as possible to the realistic replication of the actual nitty-gritty texture of preindustrial farm life.

A number of American outdoor museums are now moving to put not only their ornamental landscaping but also their gardening and agricultural exhibits and activities on a sounder historical basis: Sturbridge Village and Cooperstown Farmers' Museum are two examples. Perhaps the most radical reversal of a tendency toward prettification of historical landscapes is to be found at Plimoth Plantation. In this remarkable institution, in an effort to re-create nineteenth-century life-styles, all the outdoor areas of the village—gardens, dooryards, and streetscapes generally—are maintained in as realistic a state as possible, including the presence of free-running goats, geese, and swine.

At Shaker Village near Pittsfield, Massachusetts, the restoration of a nineteenth-century settlement of this remarkable sect is well along the way. Here, buildings are being restored in orthodox fashion; even more interesting are plans to revive an industry in which the Shakers pioneered: the commercial production and distribution of flower and vegetable seeds. This involves the reestablishment of the plots in which the seeds were sorted and packed.

Another development in this same area of landscape restoration is the so-called living historical farm (Fig. 13.13). Here, actual farms are put back into full-scale operation, giving visitors the increasingly rare experience of walking through agricultural activities which are not simply being staged for their benefit. The National Trust of Great Britain has long had a policy of operating the farms of many of its historic great country houses in this manner, thus adding to both the interest and the income of these places.

In the United States, the most recent addition to outdoor museums is one of working historical farms called Old World Wisconsin. Located near the center of the state at Eagle, it is significant because, unlike most other institutions of this type, it is the result of carefully researched, long-range planning by the State Historical Society. When finally completed (it is already in operation), it will constitute a definitive collection of farmsteads, each representing one of the 20-odd ethnic groups that were the first settlers of the state. Each ethnic unit is designed to interpret the life-style of a group. Buildings, furnishings, tools, and equipment are authenticated for time and place, and all activities—housekeeping, gardening, farming, dairying, and so on—are carefully documented for historical accuracy.

If the purposes of the peasant farm were purely utilitarian, those of formal palace gardens were purely aesthetic. Hence the restoration of these latter forms presents another set of problems. Since the visual integrity of the clipped boxwood maze or pleached allée is its very reason for being, any gap in its geometric patterns is just as counterproductive as when the planting has been allowed to grow out of scale. Both problems have been encountered in a number of the imperial gardens around Leningrad. At the former czarist palaces of Peterhof, Pushkin, and Pavlovsk, the formal allées and parterres had been allowed to grow completely out of scale by World War II. Then, during the 900-day Nazi siege of Leningrad during the war, all three palaces were occupied by German troops. In addition to looting and burning the palaces, these men cut down most of the trees for fuel, tank traps, bomb shelters, and the like. The consequences were ravaged landscapes in which both formal gardens and naturalistic English-style parks were hopelessly compromised. Their restoration was as urgent as that of the palaces proper.

Soviet landscape architects, faced with this task, confronted some very difficult choices. For example: should simple infill or replacement of missing trees and plants be attempted? This would be aesthetically unsatisfactory, since years, if not decades, would elapse before the restoration would be complete. Should the status quo ante 1941 be the object of restoration? But this would be technically very difficult, since the transplantation of very many large trees would be called for. Or should the most radical solution be adopted, namely, removal of all surviving plant material and reconstruction from the ground up, using historically accurate and properly scaled plants? After much careful discussion of the alternatives, the last policy has been adopted. Thus, in a comparatively short period, the aesthetic unity of architecture and landscape will have been restored.

It is apparent that the preservation of historic landscapes, like the preservation of historic buildings, confronts the profession with new and exciting challenges. At the same time, however, it demands conceptual changes in the professions themselves: subtle but critically important shifts in perspectives, from emphasis on the art of creating to that of caretaking. It involves intervening in the life of extant organisms, each with its own prehistory, as a medical doctor works with a patient; and not creation de novo, like that of the sculptor or painter. In such a shift, understanding of the landscape's past and concern for its future will demand new levels of modesty, tact, and discretion on the part of the designer.

13.12. *One of the nation's boldest landscape reconstructions* came about almost fortuitously, as a spin-off of a larger urbanistic battle against a proposal to build a large, multistory office and residential complex in the heart of historic Annapolis. It would have necessitated the demolition of the 1756 mansion of William Paca, a signer of the Declaration of Independence. Fortunately the Maryland General Assembly acquired it in 1965 and turned it over to Historic Annapolis, Inc. for restoration. The house itself was largely obscured by a 1906 hotel which had been wrapped around it; a big, shabby parking lot covered the site of the garden (*2*). Orthodox restoration of the mansion had been planned from the beginning, but the idea of reconstructing the garden emerged only by degrees. Although it had been famous in Paca's day, little was ĸnown of its appearance—the only sketch ever discovered was an early-eighteenth-century sketch of the terrace façade of the house (*1*). Thus reconstruction was a largely ad hoc process. The old hotel was demolished (*3*) and the rubble carefully removed. Careful bulldozing exposed the earlier contours, and then orthodox archaeology took over. When 1765 grades were fairly clearly established, excavations established buried features (*5*).

2

289

3

4

5

6

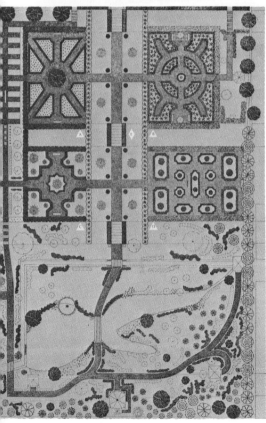

7

13.12 *(Continued)*. Final plans of the Paca Gardens became possible only by degrees (7) as demolition and clearing of the hotel began to expose hitherto unknown features of the topography. For example, the profile of the mansion and its relation to the garden showed the early sketch (*1*) to be correct. Original contours had been lost under a century of manipulation, so that delicate bulldozer "skimming" was needed to establish 1765 levels. Then orthodox archaeological investigations were made over the entire site. These established type and location of brick walls; size and location of canal and pond (their existence known from records); levels and locations of terraces and paths (*3, 4*). Two long-lost features were known from early paintings: the chinoiserie bridge and the octagonal pavilion with its Mercury-topped cupola (*6*); the foundations of both were discovered by archaeology. Designs of the parterres are conjectural, though they are based on analogous "knot gardens" of the period. The plant materials—many described in contemporaneous papers—are appropriate for the time and place. The completely restored and furnished mansion is often used by the U.S. Department of State as a guesthouse for distinguished visitors.

291

13.13. *Winter (1) and summer (2) on the Pliny Freeman farm* at Sturbridge Village, Mass. The success of the working historical farm with the American public stems from a basic pedagogical principle: demonstrations of process—even when they do not permit participation—are a most effective means of imprinting them on the minds of the spectators. This is especially true when the spectator has no firsthand experience with the process. Thus, for the city dweller, nothing can explain the meaning of the tool *plow* as meaningfully and unforgettably as seeing the process of *plowing*. The fact that the end product is food further strengthens the imprint.

14

Protection and Interpretation of Sites and Ruins

The great burst of archaeological activity of the past century, especially since Schliemann's sensational discoveries at Troy in 1871, was admirably aimed at the exploration and interpretation of the past. The impact of such activities has been immeasurable: it has altered our whole conceptual picture of human history. Together with parallel activity in anthropology, it has given us totally new perceptions of cultural evolution. But it cannot be denied that, in the process, such radical interventions into the life of hitherto buried sites and monuments has had undreamed-of consequences for these artifacts themselves. The consequences have been of several related but separate orders of magnitude. The first is the most familiar: in their eagerness to expose and retrieve the buried remains of one epoch, archaeologists have had necessarily to remove all later strata of deposits, destroying them forever. Recent advances in photography and other techniques of documentation have somewhat mitigated this negative aspect of archaeological investigations: at least the lost material is now being recorded.

The disturbance of the historical record by no means ends here, however. Small artifacts and even larger movable fragments discovered in the process of excavation are removed from the site to a museum. And usually the museum is far removed from the site, so that the artifacts will never again be seen in their proper contextual setting. The logic of this procedure is, so far as it goes, impeccable: most of the artifacts discovered in any dig could not long survive naked exposure to the climate of the site—let alone to the attentions of honest tourists and dishonest grave robbers. So the security of the museum, with its artificial climate, is the logical repository for such artifacts (if the museum is close to, or even on, the site, so much the better).

But this leaves unanswered the problem of the site itself. All too often, once the archaeologists' curiosity has been satisfied or their funding

14.1. Gutted by Nazi fire bombs in World War II, the Cathedral of Coventry, England, was the subject of a long postwar debate over how the old gothic ruin was to be handled. Should it be restored? Completely reconstructed? Replaced by a new building of contemporary design? Or should the ruined nave be preserved as a memorial to those who had died in the air raids, and a new church built alongside it? The latter option was selected. The roofless shell of red sandstone would be consolidated (*1*) and the lightly damaged bell tower would be restored (*2*). A new sanctuary of contemporary design would be erected along the axis of the north transept. The new church, designed by Sir Basil Spence, winner of a national competition, is concrete framed and sheathed in the same red sandstone as its predecessor (*2*). The project has proved to be enormously successful, attracting so many pilgrims that the floor of the old nave, restored with a beautiful English lawn, has had to be repaved.

14.2. *Ruins like those of Fountains Abbey* in Yorkshire have long been popular features in English and European landscapes—so much so that fake ones were often built where real ones did not exist. But ruins are fragile artifacts even more vulnerable to environmental attrition than enclosed and inhabited buildings. Thus, despite Ruskin's demand that they not be tampered with, ruins require continuing maintenance if they are not to disappear altogether. Only masonry fabrics can be left roofless in the open air, and even they will require structural consolidation to guarantee physical stability. Such interventions must obviously be discreet, if not indeed invisible. Thus the topless walls and roofless vaults have been grouted with cement mortar to minimize moisture penetration and prevent the growth of vines and saplings. This work is continuously inspected by the abbey staff.

If the ruin is too fragile or the climate too severe to guarantee survival, then the only alternative will be to "move it indoors," either by constructing a shelter around it *in situ,* as at Piazza Armerina (14.4), or by transferring it to a specially built museum, as with Lincoln's birthplace (14.3). But this type of intervention in the life of the artifact raises problems of another sort. The protection not only alters its physical environment: it also radically alters the visual context in which it is experienced. This, in turn, suggests that the architectural design of the shelter be as neutral and visually recessive as possible, as at the Franklin Home-site in Philadelphia (14.6).

14.3. *A bizarre confrontation between container and contained:* a limestone mausoleum in Hodgenville, Kentucky (*1*), shelters the little log cabin (*2*) in which Abraham Lincoln is said to have been born. Instead of this portentous temple, looming at the top of a monumental stairway, a more appropriate solution might have been a modest pavilion—abstract, smaller, and transparent—located in a Kentucky woodlot of the trees Lincoln knew and loved, cedar, white oak, black walnut, hickory, and dogwood.

exhausted, the site is abandoned to the vicissitudes of weather, vegetation, and vandals. There are, of course, some praiseworthy exceptions. In Great Britain, for example, many medieval sites, such as Fountains Abbey and Bury St. Albans, have been meticulously excavated and recorded. The below-grade remains have then been reburied, the submerged walls being traced out with modern topping at grade level, so that the plan of these great monastic complexes can be seen and comprehended by the tourist. The above-grade remnants have also been carefully consolidated to preserve their structural integrity. The results are highly satisfactory from both an aesthetic and didactic point of view. But few of the world's great sites have been similarly protected. An isolated monument like the great prehistoric mud-built city of Çatalhüyük has been excavated and then left to dissolve in the savage rains of Anatolia. Urban sites fare little better, though the forces of attrition may be the feet of tourists instead of the hooves of sheep, goats, and camels.

It is not a problem susceptible to easy solutions. For example, on those sites where an elaborate architectural structure has been erected to protect the monument from weathering, the shelters may be satisfactory function-ally but are often aesthetically obtrusive. For example, the structure erected over the excavated portion of the Roman villa at Fishbourne in England is effective climatically but disturbing visually, making it difficult to imagine what the villa might have looked like in three-dimensional reality. The mar-ble temple which has been erected over and around the log cabin in which Abe Lincoln was born is simply grotesque. On the other hand, the Italian authorities have exercised great care in the design of the structure erected to protect the mosaic floors of the Roman villa at Piazza Armerina in Sicily. An elegant fabric of light aluminum framing members and clear plastic sheathing has been designed to trace out, in almost phantom form, the room shapes and roof lines of the original structure. The problem here is that the soft plastic is easily abraded by blowing sand and is now translucent rather than transparent. The contemporary structure erected to protect the fossils in Dinosaur National Monument, is architecturally pleasing but, in that desert climate, hellishly hot!

Perhaps the solution arrived at for the Franklin Homesite in downtown Philadelphia is, from an aesthetic point of view, the most satisfactory of all. The entire complex of houses which Benjamin Franklin erected for himself during the 1780s had long ago been demolished to make way for other structures. After its purchase by the federal government in the 1940s, the entire site was cleared and archaeologically investigated down to undis-turbed soil. Originally, it had been planned to reconstruct all of the van-ished buildings, but it was decided, in the case of Franklin's own house, that visual evidence was simply inadequate to justify a reconstruction. Therefore, it was decided to cover the excavations with a concrete slab

14.4. *One of the greatest sets of Roman mosaics* ever discovered adorns the main rooms of a fourth century A.D. imperial villa at Piazza Armerina in southern Sicily. When excavated in the 1950s, the mosaics were found to be in excellent condition, undamaged by war, fire, or earthquake. Their importance was immediately recognized, as was the urgent necessity of protecting them from the weather and the tourists they would inevitably attract. There was no possibility of restoring the villa in any conventional sense. No walls higher than 6½ feet remained in place (most were no higher than 1½ feet) and the roofs had long ago collapsed into the rubble which had protected the mosaics themselves. The problem therefore was: what sort of structure could be devised to meet the contradictory requirements of protection from the elements and exposure to tourists who would come to see the ruins? Excavations made a conjectural reconstruction of the plan fairly easy (4). Surviving columns around the

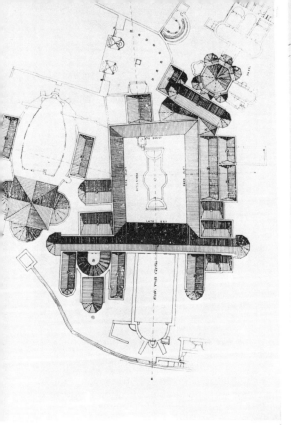

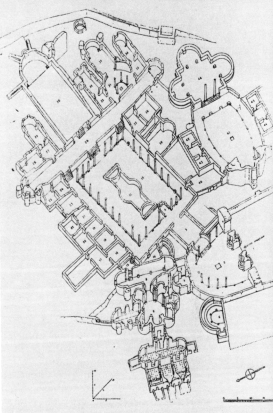

3 4

5

central courtyard established the vertical height of the eaves (*2*): and, traditional Roman roof profiles being well known, it was possible to reconstruct a roof plan (*3*). Such data could be used to establish the overall geometry of the great mansion. But if a literal replica of plastered masonry walls and timber-framed tiled roofs was undesirable, what was the alternative? Such considerations led the authorities to a highly innovative decision: the entire villa would be enclosed in a transparent cage whose form would be a phantom of the masonry original. Fundamentally, the structure is a lightweight aluminum skeleton sheathed with translucent plastic panels. Externally, the effect is extraordinary: the villa looks like a photographic negative of the original (*1,2,5*). Internally, the translucent surfaces re-create the geometry of the rooms the mosaics once adorned while at the same time flooding them with diffused light (*7,8*).

6

7

14.4 *(Continued).* ***The luminous superstructure that encloses the imperial villa*** also includes a system of metal walkways that make it possible to view the mosaics without walking on them *(7,8)*. For ventilation, most of the walls are panels of fixed louvers *(1,9)*. The roofs are double, to reduce transmission of heat and glare and create a ventilated attic space *(9)*. The entire installation meets the primary requirements for such a radical intervention in a historic artifact: it is clearly modern and cannot be confused with the original fabric; its installation has done little damage (note how the new skeleton straddles old walls and pavements); the new shelter is prefabricated and bolted together and could be disassembled at any time.

8

9

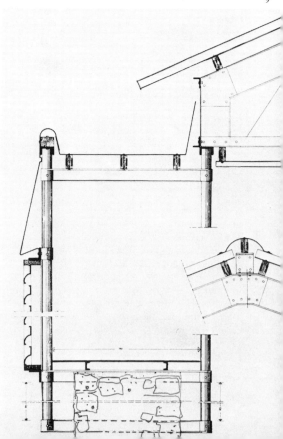

14.5. *Interpretation Center, Dinosaur National Monument, Utah.* A clear example of functionally derived form, this structure protects a paleontological, rather than an archaeological, excavation. Therefore, no questions of historical accuracy or stylistic appropriateness were involved in its design. The main function of the great glass-walled gallery was to protect ongoing work on an important set of fossils and to provide viewing facilities for park visitors *(1)*. The bold form derives directly from the rock face it shelters; it also sits well in the arid landforms around it. For all the boldness of the design, its idiom is neutral and astylar and might well serve as a prototype for aesthetically satisfactory shelters for important pre-Columbian ruins in adobe and terra pisé *(2)*.

1

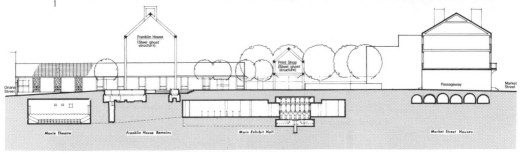

Venturi and Rauch, Architects and Planners
John Milner, Architect
de Martin - Marona & Associates, Exhibit Design

Franklin Court · I. N. H. P. · Philadelphia
National Park Service

SECTION

GARDEN AND MAIN EXHIBIT

28 August 1973

2

302

3

14.6. *The museological handling of Franklin Court,* Benjamin Franklin's home in Philadelphia, marks a new level of maturity in American preservation activities. In preparation for the 1976 celebrations, the National Park Service had completed an exhaustive program of archaeological and archival research on the development of the site. The original assumption was that the house and grounds would be reconstructed and furnished as an orthodox museum house. But research uncovered little pictorial or graphic evidence of what the house had actually looked like. Beyond this, the reconstruction of vanished buildings had come to be viewed with increasing misgivings by the NPS. So it was decided *not* to reconstruct the house itself (although the façades of the Market Street rental houses would be reconstructed). Since the entire site had been excavated down to undisturbed soil (all evidence of gardens, wells and cesspools, cellars, and foundations having been securely recorded), it became possible to locate the new museum and movie theater below grade in the former courtyard (*2*). The roof, or lid, of this subterranean complex was then developed as a landscaped diagram of its plan during Franklin's day (*1,5*). The only vertical dimension to this diagram is afforded by the metal frames of the homestead and coach house, with astonishing effectiveness. Although there is some planting, most of the surfacing is masonry. Especially successful is the manner in which the ground-floor plan of the house is traced out in paving: walls in granite, floors in bluestone. The display is made even more moving by inscriptions carved in the floor—excerpts from letters between Franklin and his wife during his absence in Europe. The few remains of the cellars have been conserved in below-grade illuminated cases. These may be viewed through concrete "periscopes" (*3*).

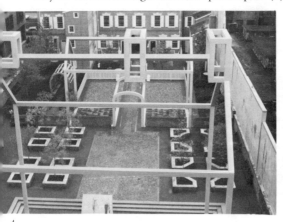

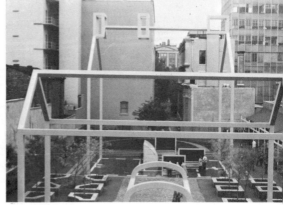

4

303

5

6

14.6 (Continued). *Because they were well documented visually* (especially by the traces of floors, walls, stairs, and roofs on party walls of adjacent houses) it was decided to reconstruct the façades of the rental houses along Market Street (*6,7*). But these replicated façades are merely the outer skins of a steel-framed museum of the archaeology of the site (*8,9*). By a system of stairs, balconies, and catwalks, the visitor is encouraged to examine at close hand the actual integument of the houses. These architectural remains are supplemented by a display of artifacts discovered on the site and accompanied by explanatory diagrams and legends. This combination of cognitive and sensuously perceptible information makes for a brilliant interpretation of the morphological development of the site—a more stimulating re-creation of the vanished houses than any actual reconstruction.

8

9

305

14.7 *The happiest future for the archaeological monument* occurs when it can continue to fulfill its original function, as in the case of the fourth-century B.C. theater at Epidaurus in Greece. Carefully excavated and restored by the Greek Archaeological Service, it is the scene each summer of the reenactment of the same tragedies and comedies for which theaters of this type were originally conceived and built.

(converting that space into a subterranean air-conditioned museum): the outlines of the house, garden, and outbuildings are marked in various stones on the upper surface of the slab. The volume of the house itself is traced out in a simple metal skeleton so that it reads as a sort of outline or diagram. Considering the abstract nature of the design, it yields a surprisingly moving experience.

Documentation
of the Heritage:
Quantification, Analysis,
and Classification

Before any country can develop a comprehensive policy for the care of its artistic and historic heritage, it must be able to quantify, identify, and classify the artifacts in question. Although this might seem a perfectly obvious precondition, it is a remarkable fact that the process has not been completed in any country on earth. In fact, it is far from complete even in those countries (Britain, France, Italy) where national responsibility for preservation has been recognized for decades—in France, for over a century. In the United States, the edition of *The National Register of Historic Places* lists only 12,000 monuments when in fact there are hundreds of thousands, if not indeed millions, of individual structures that merit inclusion. This will be particularly true if we broaden our definition to take into account significant new categories of cultural goods: aboriginal or pre-Columbian sites; rural and vernacular buildings; and industrial structures of all sorts (factories, bridges, mills, canals, and railroads).

The issue of our completing such national inventories as rapidly as possible is not merely a question of preserving these monuments in four-dimensional reality. It is also a problem of mapping our own cultural topography. For, with the rapid urbanization of the entire world, our dilemma is becoming that of preserving the knowledge that *these artifacts even existed*. From this latest urgency comes a new type of specialized activity, "salvage archaeology"[1]: the process of keeping one jump ahead of the bulldozer to at least record what it is in the process of destroying forever.

This urbanization employs regional systems of highways, airports, hydroelectric dams, and nuclear plants. Typically, these radical interventions are made with only a cursory understanding of their impact upon the natural environment (vide the Alaska Pipeline or the Teton Dam, whose collapse was a regional disaster). Engineers and technicians pay even less attention to the cultural topography of cities such as Boston or San Francisco, where they often behave as though they were operating in the unexplored and/or uninhabited terrain of the Upper Amazon. Many of the consequent outrages to the built environment, it is true, are due more to ignorance than to malice. But if the terrain had been previously surveyed and mapped for buildings and sites of historic or artistic significance, then it would obviously be easier for the engineer to make allowances for them in plotting trajectories. By the same token, it would be easier for the indigenous inhabitants to defend their native habitat from needless ravishment and degradation.

The survey or inventory is thus the sine qua non of preservation planning. The methodology of such work is more or less standardized around the world. Survey teams in the field employ a printed form for each individual building. These forms provide for the salient facts: name, owner, location, date of construction, architect. They normally call for a photograph of the principal façade and a plot plan showing the building's location (including compass points, latitude, and longitude). There is usually space for some written description of the stylistic features of the building and whatever historical information is readily available.

The more complete the information included on this form, the more valuable the inventory becomes. But the preparation of even a single-page report requires a sizable investment in time and labor. Also, even the simplest forms imply a certain degree of expertise on the part of the surveyor. Since such trained personnel is both expensive and in short supply, several measures have been developed to maximize its effectiveness. One is to regard the first survey as a kind of coarse-grained scan or sweep of the entire district. (This is often done by one or two people equipped with auto and cameras.) These forms can then be analyzed by experts and the more significant buildings selected for examination and research in greater depth.

But any evaluation by definition involves subjective judgment—a difficult enough task even for trained professionals. Moreover, such evaluations, being verbal, cannot be either stored or retrieved in a computer bank. Therefore, a graphic rather than a verbal system of indentification is desirable. This is the principle involved in the inventory form developed by Meredith Sykes for Parks Canada. The form includes small-scale line drawings of all the characteristic elements of Canadian buildings, including stylistic variants—roof forms, dormers, chimneys, cornices; door and window embrasures; wood, brick, and masonry wall textures, and so on. The surveyor needs only to match these elements visually with the appropriate dia-

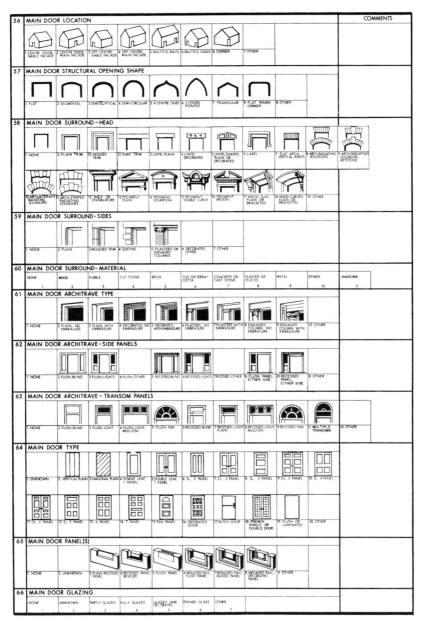

15.1. *Historic building inventories* furnish the basic data on which all preservation activities are based. But the standard survey forms have several inherent limitations. Data are all recorded in verbal, not pictorial, form—a necessarily imprecise means for communicating the visual characteristics of the building. In addition, questionnaires compel value judgments ("What style is the door: Federal? Greek revival? Queen Anne?"), which can vary widely even among experts. But the most severe limitation of such verbal descriptions is that they cannot be quantified for computerized storage and retrieval. This paradox is overcome by the inventory system developed by Meridith Sykes for the Canadian Inventory of Historic Buildings. Forms provide graphic descriptions of every variant of each architectural component. The suveyor checks off that diagram which most closely resembles the building being surveyed. Since each item and subitem is coded, information can be readily put on punch cards for computerized storage and retrieval.

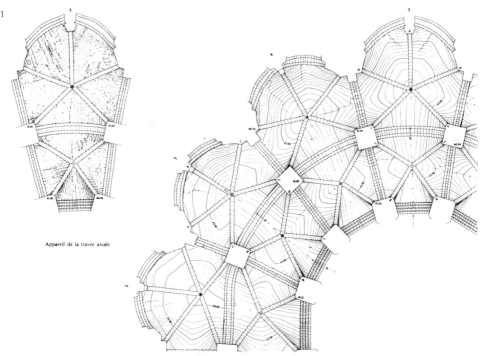

Appareil de la travée axiale

15.2. *Stereophotogrammetry is the quickest,* most accurate and often the only practical method of making accurate measurements of an object. Moreover, the object can be of any size, shape, or degree of complexity. Thanks to aerial stereophotography, entire landscapes can be accurately and rapidly plotted, e.g., the Acropolis at Athens (*4*). Short of making a cast, photogrammetry is also the only way in which the contours of artifacts such as sculpture can be accurately reproduced (*2*). Conventionally, photogrammetry has been used to produce two-dimensional line drawings of architecture, as in this cross section of the Jesuitenkirche in Innsbruck (*3*). But increasingly, photogrammetric studies are being employed for analytical, rather than merely documentary, purposes. Since the stereo plotter can be used to plot contours, it can be used to scan and record architectural surfaces which have never before been accessible for close scrutiny. Thus photogrammetry in the apse vaulting of Saint-Denis near Paris reveals plastic deformations in nominally uniform vaults (*1*). It also permits study of these abnormalities in order to determine if they are the traces of structural failures and whether or not the failures are old and stable or new and active. Only in the latter case would scaffolding be required. Such new sources of information will play an important role in the maintenance of historic structures.

Photogrammetry is still relatively expensive, largely due to the high cost of plotting equipment and the shortage of skilled operators. But its superiority over manual recording of buildings is absolute.

310

Jesuitenkirche, Innsbruck (BDA) 3

4

311

gram. Such a recording technique guarantees that a minimum of subjectivity enters into the description; more important, these data can readily be computerized. And the significance of such a data bank is clear. As we have seen, it makes possible the immediate retrieval and identification of all historic sites or buildings which might lie in the trajectory of any proposed construction project.

Finally, for those buildings rated as of prime importance, a *historic structures report* is prepared. This will cover the social history of the building and its occupants; its morphological development across time, described in both verbal and graphic form; a complete set of measured drawings (drawings of record); and a complete photographic coverage. The historic structures report becomes, in turn, the basis for contract working drawings and specifications if the building is to be preserved, restored, or adaptively reused.

MEASURING THE ARTIFACT

The first stage in the preparation of drawings of record is obviously to make accurate measurements of the building in question. At this stage of study, the task of the investigator is to record only the palpably evident characteristics of the structure—not "what it might have been" or "what it ought again to be": these are questions to be asked and answered later in the process of preservation. On small and simple structures, a team of two or three can quickly do the job with simple equipment: measuring tapes, ruler, perhaps a theodolite. Photography should always be an integral part of the operation, because even hand-held casual snapshots record data which will be very important back in the drafting room. Color photography at this stage is unnecessary unless the polychromy of the building is an important part of its cosmetic corpus.

But many buildings being surveyed today are neither small nor simple, so traditional teamwork will not suffice. Until recently, making field measurements of large buildings (e.g., skyscrapers, church steeples) was either hazardous or expensive because of the scaffolding required. Now, thanks to the perfection of stereophotogrammetry and rectified photography, buildings of any size and complexity can be accurately recorded and subsequently transcribed into standard graphic form. Photogrammetry, a highly accurate recording method, is an optically simple procedure but requires both highly skilled operators and complex and expensive machinery. It is based on the use of paired photos viewed in stereo, which makes it possible to take measurements in either two or three dimensions. In recent years, in addition to its great value in simple recording, it has been found very useful as an analytical tool in investigating deformations in architectural elements (e.g., Gothic vaulting) which have not previously been visible, much less analyzable. A monograph on the subject prepared by the Comité International de Photogrammetrie Architecturale and published by UNESCO (Paris, 1972) summarizes the advantages as follows:

> Only photogrammetry allows the separation of the survey work on the site from the drawing up of the plans. (The on-site work is also achieved far more quickly and with less effort.) The photogrammetric record makes a true technical record of building and sites, an archive which can be used for differing purposes and one which it is always possible to refer back. These records—the establishment of which is of prime importance—completely fulfill the requirements of the Hague Convention on the protection of cultural objects. They are one of the essential requirements on which to base inventories and research.
>
> It is easily adapted to all sorts of recording work, from simple outlines to the most accurate and detailed survey. The methods of making a photogrammetric archive will depend to some extent on the type of final survey drawings aimed at, but from the archive drawings of various types can be produced.
>
> It records the true shape of a monument at the time of photography, with complete objectivity, with no preconceptions as to design or orientation, whatever the complexity of the architecture or the decoration. This actual shape forms the basis for all work of conservation and restoration. It gives the possibility of measuring both deformation in a building and the corrections of perspective intended by the architect to make the apparent form more harmonious. Indeed the objective survey of the actual shape has the legal value of an exact statement of the state of the monument.
>
> It ensures a rigid uniformity of the survey, each element, each detail being recorded with the same accuracy. The scientific study of the monument or site can then be based on firm data.
>
> It gives the means of undertaking extensive survey works in a time which can be very short at a cost which, for equal quality (except in certain cases), is much lower than for any other survey method. Rationalization of survey methods made possible by photogrammetry contributes greatly to the efficiency of preservation.
>
> The complexity of the equipment of photography and plotting and the qualifications of the technicians who carry out the work increase with the complexity and above all with the size of architectural or archaeological elements to be surveyed. But the acquisition of the necessary equipment and the formation of teams of specialists can proceed gradually and at different levels.[2]

A simpler and less costly method of photographic recording is so-called rectified photography. Since this is produced from a single photographic image, it produces only a two-dimensional representation, but at a specified scale. The process can be made graphically, optically (with camera lucida), or photographically (with a rectifier made especially for the purpose).

15.3. *Rectified photography is a quick and easy method* for graphic documentation of small buildings. Here such a photograph is being used as basis for a graph that plots the shape, size, and location of each stone in an old masonry house. This is in preparation for the disassembly and subsequent reconstitution of the stone-built structure on a new site. Each stone will be stenciled with its appropriate abscissa coordinates on the photographic grid, which can be used by the mason for an accurate reconstruction of the original fabric. The mortar used will be chemically and cosmetically appropriate.

PHYSICAL EXAMINATION OF THE ARTIFACT

Historic buildings for which interventions of one sort or another are envisaged require an examination in much greater depth, literally as well as figuratively, than those which are merely being recorded. Here, indeed, questions of "what it might have been" and "what it ought to be again" become matters of pressing importance. To set a sound base for such interventions, archival research and physical probing ought to be carried on simultaneously, since the artifact often fills voids in the historical record just as the document supplements the incomplete evidence of the artifact itself. Physical probing involves two forms of on-site examination: archaeology and nondestructive examination of above-grade structures.

By definition, archaeology destroys or, at the very least, irrevocably disturbs the spatial sequence of the objects it is investigating.[3] In order to reach earlier strata, later and less deep ones must be removed. Regardless of how carefully the upper strata are documented (measured, examined, photographed, described), they are gone forever. Realizing this, archaeologists are themselves increasingly conservative. Reversing their traditional attitudes, when hunger for new discoveries drove them on, they now dig only where there are overwhelming reasons; it is now generally understood that the best place for preserving the material remains of the past is underground.

Of course, under the conditions of modern life, many sites cannot remain undisturbed. Archaeologists find that they *must* dig to preserve for posterity material remains which would otherwise be lost forever before the advances of highways, subways, airfields, hydroelectric installations, and the like. Salvage archaeology, as it is called, becomes an essential cultural activity under such circumstances. And some of the most significant archaeological finds of recent times have resulted from subway construction in ancient cities such as Rome and Mexico City. In the latter case, many important pre-Columbian monuments are being discovered. Some of the new stations have become archaeological museums themselves. Also in Mexico City, slum clearance activities in preparation for a new complex of office and apartment blocks accidentally uncovered the lost ceremonial center of Montezuma's capital. As a result, the whole complex was redesigned to incorporate the archaeological remains as a permanent feature of the complex. Much the same thing happened in London, when, in the process of clearing bomb-damaged districts for redevelopment, a portion of the medieval wall of the city was uncovered. This fragment, together with its excavated moat, became the centerpiece for the Barbican district.

But archaeology, including especially landscape archaeology, is an integral part of the documentation process for the preservation of extant structures. It can reveal important changes in the size, shape, and location of elements in the structure—changes which might not have been recorded in documentary form. Such information can often force the radical revision of previously held concepts. Thus, site archaeology led to the complete reformulation of the restoration program for Phillipse Manor at Tarrytown, New York.

EXAMINATION OF ABOVE-GRADE STRUCTURES

Unlike archaeology, with its well-established techniques for the examination of below-grade ruins, the examination of extant structures as a prelude to restoration and preservation is often handled in a careless, slapdash manner. All too often everyone is anxious to "clean out the place," "tidy up," "throw out the junk." In the process, material may easily be discarded which in fact contains important evidence of changes or previous states of being. This is especially true of American houses and domestic architecture in general. These tend to be largely or wholly built of wood; and carpenters, loath to throw good lumber away, would typically reuse sound scraps in remodeling or alterations. In the hands of skilled preservationists, such "cannabalized" scraps will often carry priceless evidence of previous conditions—paint marks, nail holes, worn areas, and so on. And demolition must proceed with similar care. Workers should be carefully trained to be on the lookout for any significant scraps in much the same way as excava-

315

tors at the archaeological site are trained to throw nothing away before it is examined by experts.

The examination of any extant building often involves the peeling away of one membrane (paint, wallpaper, wood paneling) in order to reveal the structure beneath it. As in archaeology, this means the destruction of the outermost strata or membranes. Hence the preservationist and crew must be constantly on the alert for potentially important evidence. Daily field notes ought to be maintained, along with photographs of each stage. In the demolition of masonry structures which are scheduled for reconstitution, the wall should be photographed after each stone has been sequentially numbered with an indelible paint to facilitate its reerection. Again, as in archaeology, "test borings" or "trial trenches" are often advisable. The latter are especially valuable in masonry structures which have been covered with many coats of plaster or stucco. Very often, a trench cut diagonally across each bay of a plastered wall and no deeper than the plaster itself will reveal important evidence of shifted openings, blocked-up windows, previous color schemes, and the like. Such measures are especially important in monumental architecture where elaborate decorative finishes such as frescoes, murals, or wallpapers might be expected to exist.

Of course, the preservationist must often examine the building to determine its structural stability as opposed to merely cosmetic condition. Such examination also implies great discretion, since many old buildings apparently in sound structural condition show an alarming tendency to collapse, like the old one-horse shay, at the slightest intervention. As David M. Hart has pointed out in a recent monograph:

> Until recent times it has been very difficult if not impossible to determine components, structural condition, physical condition and alterations in a building's fabric without removal of plaster or woodwork, or in some way causing damage to the historic finishes or structure. Investigation of historical buildings has been particularly frustrating to persons associated with preservation and conservation, as the need to unearth construction details is thwarted by the fear of destroying valuable architectural evidence. Flashlights, small mirrors, metal probing devices such as shim stock and wires, rules, and sometimes a small drill have all been part of the traditional tool kit of the architectural scholar in the hunt for clues as to the origin or later changes in a structure.
>
> In the past one has had to take apart the building in order to discern how various elements appeared, and to inspect these elements for structural analysis and dating purposes. This necessitated adding nail pullers, pinch bars, hammers and other implements to the tool kit. These investigative tools are all limited in their application to probing of buildings, and for obvious reasons a method of non-destructive probing is preferable as no damage is done to the historic fabric.
>
> The ideal non-destructive system for probing historic structures would incorporate the following characteristics:

1. Low cost of equipment, low cost of operation

2. Portability

3. Easy operation

4. Safety

5. Easily interpreted results

6. Ability to quickly determine the architectural configuration of large areas

7. High resolution and contrast of readout

8. Results easily stored, and retrievable

9. Ability to penetrate all types of material encountered in buildings, and to display results with adequate contrast

It can be seen that a system incorporating all of the above characteristics—namely, a three-dimensional, television-type readout, battery-operated camera that weighs 12 pounds, which can penetrate brick, stone, wood, metal, earth and plaster, and display this information on a color screen, is further capable of instant adjustment from wide angle to micro-operation—is unfortunately unavailable at present.

We now use many of the traditional-type non-destructive tools such as rapping the wall with one's knuckles or a small tool, magnetic stud finders, and ultra-violet light sources. However, none of these methods gives precise results. The portable X-ray system seems to be the most effective and practical non-destructive process available that gives a well-defined picture of building elements that are not able to be viewed with the naked eye.[4]

The whole process of the nondestructive examination of extant structures, as a preliminary to any type of intervention, has been so brilliantly summarized by Henry Judd, formerly senior restoration architect of the National Park Service, that it is here quoted at length:

> Accurate restoration of these structures is, at best, difficult and specialized work, requiring a knowledge of architecture, building technology, craftsmanship, and history. The restorationist must be able to recognize and evaluate the various parts of the building fabric and piece together numerous small and seemingly insignificant bits of documentary and physical evidence, like a giant jigsaw puzzle. As with any puzzle, missing pieces complicate the assembly and if too many are missing the job becomes impossible. We must, therefore, avoid destruction or loss of these pieces of evidence if we want an accurate restoration.
>
> Many times a serious loss of this evidence occurs during the initial clean-up when there is an urge for a quick show of progress. Even the application of normal housekeeping measures properly applicable to a modern structure nearly always result in a loss of evidence which may make an accurate restoration virtually impossible. Quite often the structure is acquired after years of neglect by former owners. Strange as it may

seem, poverty and neglect, although detrimental to the physical condition of the fabric, may have prevented a loss of critical evidence which, with prosperous owners, might have been "cleaned up" and thrown away.

In cleaning up the grounds, we need to remove the underbrush, weeds, and ever-present bottles and cans, always remaining alert to identify and save derelict materials which may have been part of the historic building fabric. Care must be taken to watch for and preserve historic walks, foundation remains, garden plots, and even plant materials. The location of debris may also indicate the location of now-missing features. A concentration of broken glass or hardware fragments near an old foundation may indicate a former window or door location. No broken hardware, old shutters, window sash, doors, or other abandoned materials should be discarded until we understand what they are and if they are significant to our restoration.

Small pieces which seem insignificant at first sight may prove to be of great value. Between a joist and a wall in the Assembly Room of Independence Hall in Philadelphia, the restoration crew found a dentil from the original cornice of the room that had been removed in a massive remodelling in 1815. Once identified, this little fragment gave, by proportion, the size of the complete cornice and all paint layers from the original construction until 1815. This tiny piece, about half the size of a pack of cigarettes, could easily have been overlooked.

A building must be made and kept water tight if it is to survive. All too often, when the building is acquired the roof leaks, window sash and doors are missing or doors and shutters hanging on broken hardware are flapping in the breeze. After securely attaching proper identification, doors and shutters might be removed and carefully stored. Care in storage is important as improper stacking may warp them, excessive humidity might rot them, or the storage areas might be subject to vandalism or fire. The better approach would be to repair them and leave them in place. There will be less chance for loss or damage.

At this juncture, make only those repairs necessary to prevent further damage. In securing window and door openings avoid damaging original fabric when installing plywood panels over the openings; remember, the building must breathe to prevent condensation on the interior.

If the roof leaks, cover it temporarily with tar-paper, leaving all below intact. If it is so far gone that it must be replaced, determine if you have all the information to restore it correctly. Here many problems can arise. Do you know the correct roofing material? Do you know its exposure to the weather? The nailing patterns on the roof boards may indicate exposure; however, there may be nailing patterns for several successive roof coverings. Identifying the correct one for your period requires some knowledge of the history and technology of nail manufacture as well as roofing.

The technology of flashing and sealing of joints and angles has changed over the years. While reproducing early flashing mechanically may not prove practical, you must understand it to reproduce the visual effect. Consider also the cornice, missing or surplus dormers and chimneys. The ridge, hips and valleys were probably installed far differently that what is common practice today.

Water intrusion in masonry walls is usually the result of disintegrating mortar joints and seldom to the failure of stone or brick itself. The use of improper techniques and materials in consolidating masonry not only destroys the visual effect but often does permanent damage to the fabric and may accelerate deterioration in the future. It is a common error to assume that hardness or high strength, such as found in modern cement mortars, are desirable for permanence in repointing: in fact, quite the opposite is true. Because cement mortars are usually harder than the wall material, normal movement of the building due to expansion, contraction, settlement and other normal stresses will cause it to abrade the softer original material causing spalling and cracks. Cement mortars also shrink causing hairline cracks which can absorb water. Mortars with a high lime content are generally better suited for repointing a building of any age but in particular an important historic structure. There is very little shrinkage in either lime or aggregate and it has a low volume change due to atmospheric conditions. It is relatively soft and does not abrade original fabric. If small cracks do appear, small amounts of lime dissolve in the rain and are precipitated into the void. A small amount of white portland cement may be desirable to improve handling characteristics. New mortars should match original in color, texture and tooling. If possible obtain color from the sand or other aggregate used. Do not match a weathered or dirty surface; new pointing will get dirty soon enough. If the pointing is correctly done, waterproofing agents should be unnecessary. Some surface porocity may be desirable. If a silicone or similar material is used, make sure water cannot get behind it from leaking roofs or osmosis. If water does enter, it could build up salts behind the penetration and spall off the surface. Freezing of that water will have the same results.

Ground water must also be drained away from foundations. Proper grading should be considered first, but avoid destroying original grades or the evidence of them. Roof or ground gutters can be installed, if only temporarily. The installation of permanent gutters will require a knowledge of materials and design used in earlier periods. Early stone foundations were often laid with a rough exterior face below grade. Water seepage through this face may have leached out the mortar leaving the equivalent of a dry wall. These walls can be grouted, but only by disturbing the adjacent soil. If you must excavate to grout the walls, remember that the filled-in builders trench is usually rich in artifacts.

Insect damage and rot must be halted. First find and evaluate the cause. Chemicals used in treating these problems may create others. Some gases used in fumigation may damage the building's contents, such as books, furniture, draperies, or wallpaper.

Deteriorated fabric such as structural framing may contain evidence of a former window or door or the location of vanished porch or wall. If a deteriorated part must be replaced before the restoration, record it in position by photography and carefully prepared measured drawings. If possible remove the piece intact, label it carefully, and store it for future reference by the restorationist. Proper identification is essential. If the removed part cannot be identified in future years, it will serve no purpose.

Altered buildings almost always contain reused material—many times used out of the context of their original use. It is important to recognize such fragments and save them. In an 18th-century house in Nashville, Tennessee, which had been enlarged and altered in later years, the original stairway of the earliest portion of the house had been removed. Evidence on both floors showed the confines of the stairway but little else. When removing a doorway which had been installed at the time the stairway was removed, a reused piece serving as a stud was found. It proved to be a post which reached from floor to ceiling where the stair had turned in a series of winders. Evidence on this single piece gave the restorationist the following data:

1. The height of the stair risers

2. Nosing detail of the stair tread

3. The number of winders and the height above the floor that they commenced

4. Design of the boxed stringer

5. Height and profile of the stair rail

6. Detail of the hallway baseboard

7. Size and swing of the door to a closet under the stair

8. Type of hinges used on the door

9. The original two-color paint scheme of buff and prussian blue of the entry hall

Reused materials from alterations made after the period of historic importance can also prove to be important as it may help explain other evidence not clearly understood. Independence Hall is a case in point. In 1815, when it ceased to be the Pennsylvania State House and became Philadelphia City Hall, the decorative features of the room in which our Declaration of Independence was signed in 1776 and our Constitution in 1789 were removed and a new interior installed of the style then in vogue. Because of the public indignation over the destruction of this very historic room, the 1815–16 woodwork was removed in 1831 and the room converted back to a style of the historic period, but unfortunately not of the correct order and design of the original. The craftsmen in 1831 used salvaged 1816 woodwork as back-up material and the material thus saved indicated the design of the 1816 room.

From the multiplicity of detailed evidence still on the walls, we could differentiate the evidence pertaining to the 1816 room, the 1831 room and later changes from the "historic" room of 1776.

Even buildings on the site which postdated the structure you are primarily concerned with require examination. At the home of General Phillip Schuyler, whose property was involved in the Battle of Saratoga in the

American War for Independence, there was a tenant house built many years after the period of historic interest. We noted that this house was framed with materials from an earlier structure reused with no regard to their original relative positions. In dismantling the tenant house, we set aside the reused pieces and by matching cuts and the incised Roman numeral code, we found we had a large part of the framing for General Schuyler's 18th-century barn.

The buildings that we acquire are often in serious need of paint. Many times the finish is so deteriorated that it must be removed before repainting. Areas may also be found that have never been painted or were painted only in recent years. Before proceeding, you should record the colors of all layers and match them against a standard that can be referred to in future years such as the Munsell Color System. Where possible save areas with all paint layers intact for the restorationist to study in future years.

From a study of 1864 photographs of "Arlington House," the pre-Civil War home of General Robert E. Lee, it was obvious that the shutters were not the dark green that had been used for about a hundred years. The shutters now on the house had recently had all early paint removed so no evidence of the early color appeared to be available. A maintenance man recalled that one shutter, which had been badly deteriorated and replaced with a new one, had been discarded on the trash heap. Fortunately it was still there. A study of this shutter revealed the early color to be a light brown. If that shutter had not survived we would have had no way to determine the early color and the evolution of the color scheme on the house.

Paint can also serve as a dating tool. The number of layers on pieces installed at different periods will vary. By comparing the layering on fabric of known date you can usually date questionable members in a relative way. As an example, we found that the stairway of the home of President Andrew Johnson in Greeneville, Tennessee, was not the original. Was it installed during a remodelling which occurred just before his return home from the presidency in 1869 or in a major alteration made by his daughter some 10 years after his death? By comparison of paint from pieces that could be securely assigned to both dates, we were able to determine that the stairway was erected in 1869 and was indeed known to and used by Andrew Johnson.

Recording what you found and all that you have done is of upmost importance. This may be done by both photography or accurately measured drawings as appropriate. The restorationist must know what has been done and, from experience, we find memory is not infallible. In recording remember that all may not be level, plumb or square. Distortion that is a part of the structure should be recorded so that new or replacement parts can be designed to fit and derelict or loose members can be reinstalled in their original locations. Many intricate details may better be recorded by rectified photography and in extreme cases by photogrammetry. The standard black and white photograph is to record detail; pretty transparenices to show your friends should be done separately.

In summary, before rushing into a restoration project, hesitate a bit. Be sure "evidence" so essential for an accurate restoration is not destroyed in the initial work and clean-up. At the earliest possible moment have your structure recorded. Keep a record of what you have done. Label loose fabric as to use and provenience and store where its preservation is assured.[5]

DRAWINGS OF RECORD

Any structure slated for preservation, restoration, or adaptive use will, of course, require detailed documentation. In addition to the historic structures report already described, the preparation of a definitive set of drawings and photographs precisely recording the state of the building at the time of the survey is mandatory. Standards for such drawings vary somewhat from country to country.* These drawings will include plot and floor plans, elevations, sections, and large-scale details of significant architectural details. Since it is almost impossible to record by any graphic means the cosmetic condition of any surface (cracks in a masonry wall, flaking paint, efflorescence or moss on a stucco surface), detailed photographs are increasingly used to supplement the information of the drawings themselves. Where polychromy is an important aspect of the element being recorded, color photography may be desirable even though there are notorious variations in film, printing, paper, and the like. Especially rare or valuable murals or frescoes may justify careful recording by an artist in watercolor or oils, like the remarkable documentation in the WPA Survey of American Folk Art.

However, drawings of record are not to be confused with standard working drawings. Under existing conditions, they may include such information as dates for different parts of the fabric where firm evidence exists—e.g., "These windows date from 1909 remodeling," "Plaster ceiling replaced after 1927 fire." But drawings of record should not include any speculative or hypothetical reconstructions of changed or vanished elements. Such reconstructions might well be useful at a later stage in preparing designs for restorations as a means of summarizing *all* the information—documentary, visual, and archaeological—which would have been amassed in the research process.

Working drawings are just that: actual guides prepared by the architect to direct the work of intervention in the old fabric. They should show three conditions: (1) "as is"; (2) existing elements to be removed; (3) new ele-

*In the United States, graphic standards developed by the Historic American Buildings Survey of the National Parks Service are generally followed.

ments to be inserted or constructed. For clarity's sake, it is often advisable to print the two later conditions as transparent overlays to facilitate direct and immediate comparison in the field without the need to refer to any other documents. In the preparation of working drawings, it must be remembered that, in old buildings, many conditions will be discovered which could not have been anticipated before the building was, so to say, opened up. Such discoveries can often force radical revisions in the proposed work, either for structural or for artistic reasons.

16

The Fourth Dimension
of Preservation

The very act of exhibiting an artifact to public view—be it a painting, an old house, or an archaeological site—creates an unnatural interface between the viewer and the viewed. This is a totally different relationship from that which normally exists between user and used or owner and owned. And it leads to an unprecedented process of attrition of the artifact itself. This process of exposure, of access to the treasures of one's culture, is a phenomenon of the contemporary world. It responds to the need for alienated peoples to reestablish some experiential contact with the material evidence of their own past. There can thus be no question as to the validity of the process itself.

Nevertheless, it must be recognized that the very act of exhibition, exposure, or display subjects the artifact to wholly new levels of risk. One of the crucial problems of preservation today is thus the development of policies, technologies, and tools for reducing this abrasive wear along the interface to acceptable minimal levels and holding it there across time. In short, it is not enough that the artifact be *restored* to an agreed-upon state of being: steps must simultaneously be undertaken to *preserve* it in that condition. A recent manual from the National Park Service summarizes the problem succinctly:[1]

> Maintenance. The very word conjures up images of scrubbing, polishing and dusting. Gone is the glory of architectural investigation and skilled craftsmanship. Here to stay, however, is the *real* preservation responsibility for the historic property. The fact that maintenance suffers from a low priority image to both the public and the building management does not diminish the true importance of this vital portion of any preservation program.
>
> The skilled person removing dirt from buildings, making routine repairs or adjustments, and in other ways retarding a building's deterioration is performing work which requires skill and sound judgement. Both managerial and financial support are essential if these skilled maintenance

workers are to carry out their work adequately, and this support must continue until that day far in the future when methods are developed to give absolute protection from the attacks of climate, chemical and biological agents, normal use, and intentional abuse.

The attrition to which artifacts are exposed takes five distinct, even if related, forms:

1. Environmental exposure ("weathering")
2. Abrasion: wear- and-tear of fabric
3. Vandalism
4. Theft
5. Fire

The first of these forms is the result of the play of natural forces upon the artifact: heat, cold, water, wind, vibration and gravity, and so forth. Of course, all such forces operate upon all objects, all of the time; only in the controlled environment of the modern laboratory could they be absolutely held in abeyance. But the modern museum can radically alter the *rates* of such attrition, as in the already mentioned case of the Elgin Marbles in the British Museum. Again, the Park Service maintenance manual formulates the problem quite clearly:

> All objects are in process of change whether living creatures, inanimate plants, or inorganic matter. Organic materials such as wood, paint and asphalt deteriorate, returning to the earth to nourish the currently growing crop of organic materials. Many inorganic building materials try to change from the refined state back to the original oxide, such as rust; other materials, such as stone, which are already oxides, wear away as the result of abrasion, freezing and thawing, etc. A major part of the dust and dirt encountered in maintenance is just small pieces of rock in the process of becoming smaller and smaller. The purpose of preservation maintenance is to slow down the process of change. The techniques of slowing down change are many: cleaning, shielding from sunlight, applying protective coatings, maintaining uniform temperatures, and controlling water both in a liquid and vapor form.
>
> Preservation maintenance holds back deterioration, but cannot eliminate it. The deterioration process can be greatly restrained by maintaining a nearly inert and controlled environment, as with the original Declaration of Independence. With buildings, however, these conditions are not possible without excluding the public from the premises. Cessation of deterioration is impossible but high quality maintenance will retard it, so that the public can see, feel, pass through and experience our historic heritage.[2]

The most active form of attrition is the consequence of merely exposing the artifact to public access. Characteristically, modern cultural tourism creates a situation in which large crowds walk around, into, through, and over monuments and sites which were never designed to support such traffic.★ The stream of friends, visitors, and simple curiosity seekers who visited Monticello in Jefferson's day—eating his food, sitting in his chairs, sleeping in his beds—was great enough to bankrupt that hospitable man. But in the year of 1976, several hundred thousand people trooped through his house and gardens; they neither dined nor slept there—they were not even supposed to touch anything except the floor on which they walked. But the abrasion of their shoe leather, the sheer weight of their bodies, took a measurable toll of the fragile old fabric. In Washington's Mount Vernon, the load was spectacularly more severe. Some 2 million people passed through the mansion in 1976. Protective covering on the floors must itself be replaced every three months.

In Mount Vernon, as in most historic structures subject to heavy visitor traffic, measures were long ago adopted to strengthen the old wooden structure. New steel members were threaded through the fabric between floors, in basements, and in attics to create a kind of hidden metal armature. But in many historic monuments, the overloading is spatial as well as gravitational. In Mount Vernon, again, on a busy summer day, crowds file through the mansion in a constant chain, almost in lockstep like a chain gang!

Much of the damage to the physical fabric of the artifact as a consequence of overcrowding at the height of the tourist season cannot be properly called vandalism at all. The oily trace of fingerprints on Mount Vernon's stairways, the beaten-down verges of the gravel paths in the Roman Forum, the overflowing trash baskets in Central Park are not due to malice but to saturation. Of course, such abuse of the artifact sets in motion a sort of descending spiral of attrition which, unless constantly corrected, does lead to vandalism. For there is a paradoxical way in which a neglected or abused landscape seems to encourage further abuse and neglect. The behavior of the public in a public space is definitely affected by the level of housekeeping in that space. (The Tivoli Gardens in Copenhagen and Disneyland in California are vivid demonstrations of this behavioral phenomenon. Both of them are intensely used, but they are at the same time the tidiest and the most continuously "housekept" public spaces anywhere.)

The much-discussed decline of public manners has perhaps some objective basis. Certainly the abuse of parks and landscapes is more visible than

★Some monuments are too fragile to permit any public exposure at all. In the so-called Tomb of the Thracian Horsemen—a fifth-century B.C. tumulus tomb discovered a decade ago at Kanzaluk, in southern Bulgaria, the unique frescoes have been preserved by being sealed for 2000 years in a completely unchanged environment. Human visitors—bringing increased temperatures, increased humidity and CO_2, not to mention dust, germs, and spores on their clothing—are barred from this special microenvironment. Even specialists, wearing masks and gowns like surgeons, are admitted for only limited periods, their presence monitored by delicate instruments. Meanwhile, a full-scale hand-painted replica has been installed in the National Museum in Sofia.

heretofore, and some of this may indeed be due to a basic shift in public attitudes toward the public domain. It is not easy to prove, however, that tourists were tidier in the past than they are today. What is much more probable is that the very nature of debris has changed: a picnic which only a century ago left only a few chicken bones and some crusts of bread today produces a bewildering waste of plastic containers and wrappings, aluminum cans, used photo flashbulbs, nonreturnable glass bottles, and the rest. All of this indestructible waste is ironically called "disposable" when, in fact, because of its inorganic nature, is is not biodegradable. The best way to reduce this kind of litter is to make it too expensive to throw away. As Oregon and New Hampshire have recently shown, the compulsory use of reusable containers with a compulsory deposit on each one has resulted in a spectacular reduction in litter in parks and along highways.

Vandalism—which can be described as the deliberate or malicious abuse of the artifact—is no new phenomenon, as the carved initials and graffiti along the streets of Pompeii bear ample evidence. There is no doubt, however, that today it constitutes a real and rising threat to the existence of all artifacts exposed to the public, from monumental sculpture to subway cars. Here again, neglect plays a role in the rising curve of vandalism; that is, the first graffito seems to encourage newer and more outrageous levels. But it would appear that "setting a good example" is not enough to discourage the true vandal: the application of police power is needed. The sheer presence of a uniformed guard, even if unarmed, is a powerful restraint on vandalism.

One of the most obvious ways in which to reduce these sorts of attrition on historic artifacts is to lighten the load by better distribution across time and space. Neither is easy. In the case of Mount Vernon, for example, the load could be greatly reduced by increasing the price of admission, but that would be a very unpopular move. It would ease the load on the mansion if the crowds could be more evenly spread across the year; but many of the visitors are out-of-state children and a visit to Mount Vernon is for them largely confined to the summer. Colonial Williamsburg is, from this point of view, more fortunate. Something over a hundred buildings have been restored or reconstructed there but, until recently, only a few of them were open for guided tours; the balance were used as housing for the staff, i.e., seen by the tourists only from the outside. To correct the resulting overcrowding, the management has recently trebled the number of buildings open to tours. In addition, it has restored and opened up Carters Grove, a nearby James River plantation. It has recently constructed a completely new museum of decorative arts where it can display its enormously valuable collection of Anglo-American antiquities. All these additional attractions will act to lighten the load on the various components of the complex as a whole.

Ironically, the very vehicles which make cultural tourism possible for most of us (giant planes, international buses, private automobiles) play a decisive role in the degradation of the historic environments which they make accessible. Their negative impact is registered at several different levels. To begin with, since they all depend upon the faulty combustion of fossil fuels, they contribute importantly to atmospheric pollution, which, as we have seen, is a principle factor in stone diseases. In addition, the sheer physical presence of these vehicles in the neighborhood of historic buildings degrades that environment visually. Many world-famous sites—the courtyards of the Louvre, the piazzas of Florence and Sienna, even the parvis of the cathedral at Chartres—are literally no longer visible because of parked and moving vehicles occupying spaces which were designed for the pedestrian. To stop or even reduce this form of attrition on the historic center brings the preservationist into head-on conflict with powerful commercial pressures. It will take strong laws and effective enforcement at both local and national levels to eliminate this particular form of attrition.

From a national point of view, a most obvious way of reducing the tourist load on existing sites of artistic, historic, or scenic interest would be to increase the number, accessibility, and public awareness of additional sites of similar value. Most countries—including those which have been heavily traversed by tourists for centuries—have many sites of real interest which are lightly visited. This is true not only of Italy and Greece, with the accumulated monuments of millennia. It is also true of much newer countries like the U.S.A. and Canada. Indeed, it was with the idea of exploiting these underused touristic and recreational resources that the state of Michigan commissioned a definitive survey of every site and monument in the state. This survey formed the basis of a system of brochures, maps, and signs and markers to imprint upon the minds of the Michiganders the rich variety of points of artistic, historic, or scenic interest within their own state.

A somewhat comparable though more ambitious project has been proposed in Canada. It proposes to link together into a national system a series of natural wonders (Niagara Falls, Lake Louise) and historic sites and monuments (old roads, canals, ports, villages, forts, and frontier settlements)—many of them unknown and/or presently inaccessible. This network would be served by a parallel system of modern roads, inns, and campsites, close enough for easy access to any site in the system but far enough away to protect it from the noise, smell, and visual confusion of motorized traffic.

Clearly, another severe form of attrition to which the historic artifact is exposed is that of simple theft. Theft is a qualitatively different phenomenon from vandalism, which represents a venting of hostility against society upon an "innocent" artifact. The motivation for theft is pecuniary gain: normally, it is to the thief's interest to *protect* the artifact which he is stealing. The rise in thefts of historically and artistically valuable artifacts has been spectacular in recent decades, and the curve is still rising. This phenomenon is undoubtedly a reflection of inflationary pressures on the antiques markets of the world. As a consequence, thefts from museums, galleries, and historic houses have become fully professionalized. From the very care exercised in the choice of artifacts, it is clear that the selection is done by experts, irrespective of who does the actual stealing.

The experts cannot claim to be even one step ahead of the thieves: each day produces new horror stories, many of them fascinating in their ingenuity. One of the latest variations is the kidnapping and holding for ransom of a work of art which is so well known in the art world as to be in effect unsalable. While the settlement made by the insurance company is always lower than the market value, the ransom moneys can nevertheless be very large. In fact, museological insurance itself is on the verge of becoming obsolete. With the soaring appraisals of works of art, on the one hand, and the parallel rise in insurance rates, on the other, many museums are finding it necessary to abandon insurance altogether. In addition to being very valuable, the stolen object is often also irreplaceable even if replacement funds were made available. Thus the reasoning has developed that money spent on insurance might be more wisely spent on improved guard service and better intrusion alarm systems.

Nothing needs saying about custodians except that they are irreplaceable, and the more plentiful and more honest the better. In many countries, e.g., Italy, Greece, and Turkey, they are wretchedly underpaid and overworked. (Thus one can understand, even if one cannot condone, the story of the guards at the great Pinacoteca di Brera in Milan who slept through a recent spectacular break-in. Their explanation was that they turned off the alarm system because, when tripped, it disturbed their sleep!) In most museums and historic houses, most of the artifacts are too large and bulky to be carried away in broad daylight. Smaller artifacts are displayed in locked cases. Hence the practice in most institutions is to position custodians at strategic points in the galleries so that their fields of surveillance overlap. But in some historic house museums, to introduce a maximum verisimilitude, small movable objects are displayed in their normal positions on tabletops, mantlepieces, cupboards, and so on. They are highly vulnerable to theft. In such cases, the standard practice is for specially trained docents to lead small groups (four to six persons) on a fixed circuit from one room to another, locking the entrance door immediately after entering, unlocking the door to the next room only upon leaving. This system, which permits close supervision by the docent, has proved effective at such institutions as the Du Pont Museum at Winterthur.

But most thefts occur at night or during holidays, when the buildings are empty of visitors and at best lightly staffed. To assist the custodians, a wide range of anti-intrusion alarm systems have been devised. The devices are almost always electronic. They are activated by sensors designed to respond to the sight, sound, weight, and even body heat of the would-be thief. Having detected evidence of intrusion, these systems can silently transmit the information either to a central control board in the institution or to the local police. This maximizes the chance of the burglar being caught in flagrante delicto. Other systems are designed for the opposite effect, i.e., to raise such a racket that the intruder is frightened away. (One manufacturer of such equipment offers a wide range of transcribed sound effects, including one of a roaring lion!) Whether used separately or in tandem, all of these systems ultimately depend upon an adequate and well-trained custodial staff.

FIRE: THE ULTIMATE ATTRITION

Most artifacts exposed to view in any museological installation, including the buildings themselves, are highly vulnerable to fire—not to mention the water damage and violence which accompany the fire-fighting process itself. Even buildings which are literally fireproof have contents which support combustion. Often the gases generated by such fires cause more damage to occupants and artifacts alike than actual flame. (Thus, it was the smoke of a small and quickly controlled fire in the New York Museum of Modern Art which, picked up and distributed by the air-conditioning system, caused hundreds of thousands of dollars' worth of damage to canvases hung elsewhere in the building.)

The Four Stages of Fire

The typical fire develops in four distinct stages:

1. *Incipient Stage:* In the incipient stage, although no visible smoke, flame or significant heat is being developed, a condition exists which generates a significant amount of combustion particles. These particles are created by chemical decomposition. Too small to be visible to the human eye, they behave like gas, rising to the ceiling. This first stage of fire usually develops over a long period of time: minutes, hours, even days. If the incipient fire can be detected at this stage, extinguishing it is a fairly simple matter, and damage is minimal.

2. *Smoldering State:* If the fire condition continues to develop, the quantity of combustion particles increases to the point where their collective mass becomes visible: this is commonly called smoke. There is still no flame or much heat; still little irreparable damage. (Often, though, there is enough damage to a painting or delicate object so that restoration work could be required.)

3. *Flame Stage:* As the fire condition develops further, the point of ignition occurs. Flames appear, heat increases.

4. *Heat Stage:* At this point, large amounts of heat, flame, smoke, and toxic gases are produced, and a full-scale fire rages. This stage usually develops very quickly from the third, often in seconds.[3]

331

Fires can be generated from a bewildering range of causes, from a faulty electrical connection to a bolt of lightning. Normally, they begin in a small way and in the first phase develop slowly. (See "The Four Stages of Fire," on p. 331.) For this reason, early detection is critically important. In recent years, a number of early warning detection devices have been perfected. They have been summarized by Fischer as follows:

Ionization Detectors

The ionization type of smoke detector, defined as a "device which detects the visible or invisible particles of combustion" generated by incipient fire conditions, is widely regarded as the best all-purpose early-warning device. This sensitive detector internally generates a stream of electrically charged particles which, in turn, produces an electrical current of very small magnitude. Changes in the electrical conductivity are caused by impinging particulate combustion products and incipient fires are thereby sensed. Since the ionization detectors react to both visible smoke and aerosols too small to be seen with the naked eye, and since these aerosols are released throughout all stages of fire development, the ionization detector is always viable. For added reliability, automatic compensation for variations in air flow, temperature and other parameters that can affect conductivity often is incorporated in the ionization detector.

Photoelectric Detectors

Another common type of smoke detection device is the photoelectric detector. These are optical devices that respond to visible smoke, but do not detect the "invisible" particles. When smoke obscures or blocks the passage of light to the detector's sensing cell, an alarm is triggered. Dust or similar objects can cause false alarming, but these usually can be prevented by time delays or beam guards.

Thermal Detectors

Thermal devices also are valuable for applications such as furnace rooms, garages, cafeterias, and other areas where particles of combustion from normal activities would set off smoke detectors unnecessarily. These detectors usually fall into two classifications. The first category would be the fixed temperature devices, such as bimetallic thermal elements or eutectic fuses, which alarm when a certain prechosen temperature is reached. The other type are electric or pneumatic devices that activate an alarm when the temperature sensed rises at a faster than normal rate.[1]

Early-warning detection systems are designed to trigger fire alarms, both for the custodial staff and the nearest fire department. The simplest human response is with the portable fire extinguisher: dry chemical extinguishers leave little residue, which can be easily cleaned up. For most museum houses, the old fashioned sprinkler system is almost the worst solution. All such installations are unsightly, but much more serious is the damage which the water itself will do to the artifacts it is designed to protect. Because of this, other chemical suppressants are being increasingly employed.

Halon is a halogenated gaseous compound, much denser than air, which can be liquefied by compression and stored for use. Released into a fire area, halon interferes with the chemical chain reaction existing during combustion. Stopping the reaction, halts the fire.

While occasionally used in hand extinguishers for local application, the prime value of halon is in total flooding of an area. For this use, the museum must be divided into zones with doors that automatically close and ventilation that stops on receiving a fire alarm signal. Within a few seconds of detection, the halon is released and floods the area, effectively quenching the fire.

Colorless, odorless, and electrically nonconductive, halon can be breathed and is considered safe at concentrations of up to 75%, but prolonged inhalation is not recommended. Provisions must be made to evacuate all occupants of a halon-flooded area as quickly as possible. For this reason, and because it is a relatively expensive fire extinguishing agent, halon protection is best suited for use in vaults, conservation/restoration laboratories, and computer rooms of the museum.

Carbon dioxide extinguishing is a common method of smothering a fire. It is not suitable for occupied areas, except after a personnel evacuation. Dry chemicals, high expansion foam, and other extinguishing agents also are available for areas such as vaults and storerooms, housing valuables where water could cause damage.[5]

17

Two Levels of
Interpretation

The interpretations of the historic site or monument occur at two distinctly different levels: professional and popular. In the first instance, the professional staff (architect, archaeologist, art historian, social historian) examines all the available evidence (excavations, buildings, artifacts, and documents) in order to reconstruct the monument either hypothetically (in models and drawings) or in full-scale, three-dimensional actuality. Then, and only then, does it become possible to interpret the monument for the education or edification of the general public. Interpretation at this secondary level is becoming a subspecialty in itself.

Orthodox archaeology has always based its interpretation of a given site or monument upon a parallel examination of the artifact itself and the literature related to it, moving back and forth from artifact to document to ensure as accurate an interpretation as possible. Necessary as it is, such a methodology has its shortcomings. Even on well-documented ruins or buildings, there are bound to be gaps in the information. On prehistoric sites, there will, of course, be no documentation at all. And even where there is ample documentation, it will often be verbal rather than graphic, with all the uncertainties and ambiguities which that implies. It was in response to this situation that one of the pioneers in historic preservation, Helen Bullock, as research historian with Colonial Williamsburg in its early days, made an important contribution to interpretive methodology. Ms. Bullock was given the challenging task of establishing cultural and technological parameters for restoration of the Williamsburg kitchens to their prerevolutionary state. She had many resources to begin with: dozens of kitchens in varying states of decay, repair, and alteration; a fine and growing collection of culinary tools, utensils, and fireplace equipment; and a unique collection of cookbooks of the era. She soon discovered, however, that even these resources did not afford sufficiently precise guides to the restoration and furnishing of specific kitchens.

Her own experience as a homemaker who had done a moderate amount of cooking soon convinced her of the incorrectness of the then-common prototype of the colonial kitchen, with its huge fireplace filled with a roaring fire of 6-foot logs surrounded by a vast array of pots, pans, spiders, ladles, and the rest. So, for a clearer understanding of what was cooked and how, Ms. Bullock turned to her cookbooks. But here, too, she faced problems. Quantities and cooking instructions were all given in colloquial terms: "a pat of butter the size of a walnut"; oven temperatures measured by holding one's hand in to a count of 10 or 20. Even more disconcerting was the fact that most of the recipes dealt with exotic dishes. (Obviously, standard everyday dishes were too much a part of the homemaker's conventional wisdom to need writing down: any girl child would have known how to make biscuits by the age of eight.) So, to check out the variables and eliminate the impossible, Ms. Bullock decided on an unprecedented step: using the artifacts and the literary sources, she would attempt to *replicate the actual processes* of frying, baking, boiling, and grilling.

The results of this sort of research were immediate and dramatic. It became at once apparent that the roaring Yule log fire was as much a part of colonial mythology as the first Thanksgiving turkey. No one could have cooked anything on such a fire. Instead, by trial and error, Ms. Bullock found that the cook would have had a number of small fires going at the same time on the same large hearth, each of a different size and hence a different temperature. She found that common-sense considerations of comfort dictated the locus of different cooking operations across the hearth, as well as convenient storage positions for various tools and utensils. Safety was another consideration in the housewife's motions. The process of cooking over an open fire was inherently dangerous under any circumstances—open flames, boiling water, frying fats, sparks from falling logs were all constant hazards to the colonial cook and her children—especially since the work was all done from a stooping or squatting position. Ms. Bullock recreated these postures, including means of extinguishing accidental fires.

As a direct outgrowth of such modest and empirical beginnings, a whole new dimension for historical research and interpretation is beginning to appear in widely scattered institutions. Here the centroid of studies has been literally transferred from the classroom to the actual monument and the dominant disciplines are archaeology, anthropology, and folklore. (The students are graduates in these and related subjects.) This new methodology has been developed in response to special situations where orthodox methods are inadequate. Such cases occur with prehistoric monuments and sites, where there is no written record; and in those where the physical remains are too scanty or disturbed and the written record too fragmentary to furnish a safe basis for preservation, restoration, or reconstruction. In an effort to span more safely the voids left by such missing archival or archaeological data, as well as to check out the assumptions of previous scholars who have worked on the same or similar problems, these new specialists are developing new routines for themselves and their students. They are "living out" the daily lives of the people who built and inhabited the structures under study. That is, using the same tools, wearing the same garments, eating the same foods, they are trying to *replicate the life-style* which the buildings would have supported, enclosed, and protected.

THE DANISH EXPERIMENT

The results of this new methodology are proving to be both startling (because they often compel radical revisions of accepted concepts of what life there was "really" like) and fruitful (because whole new perspectives for exploring both the recorded and the prehistoric past are opened up). One of the pioneers in this type of work has been the Danish prehistorian Hans-Ole Hansen of the Archaeological Research Center at Lejre, Denmark. To summarize his work briefly, his task for the past decade has been the investigation of the Iron Age culture of Denmark. Working with selected village sites dating from about 200 B.C., he and his students conducted experiments of two kinds. The first consisted in new methods of interpreting the results of orthodox archaeological investigations, the second in trying to determine prehistoric ways of life from these archaeofacts.

In the first case, the questions are of this sort: Can the so-called flint scraper really scrape skins? Do the clay structures normally interpreted as meat-smoking ovens really smoke meat? or the so-called pottery kilns really fire pottery? By erecting posts in the pattern of postholes, do you get an accurate three-dimensional replica of the Iron Age house? And if so, can you live in it? In the second case, the questions were of a somewhat different order: given the known type of corn grown in the neolithic period, and the known implements of tillage, harvesting, and milling, what would the yield per acre be? Or, given the looms attested by archaeology, how many worker-hours would be needed to produce the Iron Age garments actually found in Danish peat bogs? How would they be worn? How warm would they be?

Professor Hansen and his students erected six "Iron Age" huts, following the ground plans of excavated huts, putting adz-hewn timbers in postholes, erecting wattle-and-daub walls and thatched roofs of varying pitches. The students then tried to live in these huts for periods in summer and winter. Immediately, old preconceptions began to be shaken. The smoke hole over the centered fire pit did not draw out the smoke as anticipated; moreover, when rain fell, it extinguished the fire. When the smoke vent was shifted to the downwind gable end, it worked. In winter, things were incomparably worse. They found the huts literally uninhabitable and had to modify the design repeatedly before things got any better.

The same sorts of experiment were carried on with replicas of tools and clothing excavated on the site and with processes like the tanning of leather and the dyeing and weaving of fabrics. Experimental patches of primitive grain and flax were sown, in fields plowed with replicas of plows found in the peat bogs. Pot making was carried on to test assumptions about clays, kiln design, firing temperatures. (Ultimately, the students reconstructed the prehistoric techniques so well that flourescent dyes had to be added to the replicas to avoid confusion with the prototypes!)

The fundamental purpose of the Danish experiments was academic, i.e., to raise the level of prehistory and further the education of young historians in the process. The reconstructed settlements were not designed to be exhibited to the general public—in fact, a number of them were burned down to see how closely the pattern of ashes matched those of prehistoric conflagrations. Nevertheless, the experiments have attracted such widespread popular interest that some of these early settlements have been restored and are being operated as open-air museums.

THE PLIMOTH PLANTATION EXPERIMENT

Another project employing much the same investigatory and experimental techniques is the reconstructed Puritan village of Plimoth Plantation near Plymouth, Massachusetts. In this case, however, the purpose of the project is fundamentally didactic, i.e., to communicate an understanding of the way of life in the colony's first ten years after 1627. In a sense, it resembles Colonial Williamsburg, but with very important differences in both structure and operation. According to a former director, the anthropologist-archaeologist James Deetz, "the village is presented as a living community, where people perform the routine tasks involved in the life of the time." But unlike Williamsburg, the village is not "prettied-up" and bowdlerized. Every effort is made to replicate *exactly* the domestic life-style of what was essentially a late-medieval community. Slops are thrown out kitchen doors to feed wandering geese and pigs. There are no ornamental gardens: the houses (all replicas, naturally, since modern Plymouth occupies the original site) are as accurate as modern research can make them. There is a minimum of printed information or programmed guiding. The young student-docents actually live in the replicated cabins, carrying on their daily chores; members of the public are free to "visit" them, asking whatever questions occur to them. Every effort is made to focus attention of the processes rather than the artifacts. To this end, the visitor is told that there is not a single authentically antique object in the entire village. Like the houses themselves, the objects are all replicas. Among other advantages, this enormously reduces the security problem which most museums nowadays confront.

Most of the docent staff are advanced students in anthropology, archaeology, and history whose living out of the life-styles of 1627 is itself a form of research. (For example, they spend a certain number of days in the village in midwinter with no more amenities than those enjoyed by the Pilgrims.) At the same time, they carry on regular programs of archival research and archaeological investigations in the town of Plymouth, as well as in isolated sites known to be contemporaneous. Thus they are operating at two levels: laying the basis for the complete documentation of the social and cultural history of the colony; and communicating this new knowledge to the public in the most accurate and informative possible fashion.

From a didactic point of view, the functions of these two institutions (Lejre and Plimoth) are somewhat different. Lejre is fundamentally a research facility aimed at enriching the training of archaeologists and anthropologists. It is only incidentally a site aimed at educating the general public (although it has proved so popular that parts of it are now open to the public). Plimoth Plantation, on the other hand, is primarily aimed at educating the general public; only incidentally is it proving to be a valuable experience for young archaeologists and anthropologists who may very well have little or no contact with historic preservation sites once they complete their academic work. Nevertheless, both institutions suggest new training patterns for young professionals: a mix of orthodox academic instruction combined with fieldwork and laboratory exercises which no university could offer or afford by itself. They also suggest a national program of support for the thousands of historic sites and monuments which are in need of their type of expertise, often cannot afford it, and cannot find the experts even when they can.

SITE INTERPRETATION FOR THE PUBLIC

The didactic potential of the historic site is very great. It might be argued, in fact, that the most effective way to teach history to the general public is by interpreting historical incidents in terms of the actual scenes in which they occurred. Such an interpretation serves both to enrich the visitor's understanding of the monument and as an effective way of imprinting historical information on the visitor's memory. This interpretation can be accomplished in any number of ways:

1. Guided tours led by trained docents (as at Winterthur or Williamsburg).

2. Equipping the visitor with individual headphone sets and taped lectures covering a predetermined route through the monument (as at the Metropolitan Museum, New York).

3. *Son-et-lumière* performances for a massed audience (as at Versailles).

4. Documentary films on the monument (as at Sunnyside or Philipse Manor, New York).

5. Live demonstrations of relevant activities (blacksmithing and weaving at Cooperstown; gardening at Old Sturbridge; cabinetmaking at Williamsburg).

6. Guidebooks which visitors can consult as they move in and around the site.

Obviously, the effectiveness of the interpretation will be a function of the process itself. In most American historic house museums, the level of interpretation ranges from mediocre down to very poor. Professional operations such as Williamsburg

17.1 *The apothecary shop at Shelburne Museum* is an artifact of unusual interest: an 1800s drugstore, completely intact, including an adjoining workshop with the kilns and retorts in which the druggist distilled many of his portions. Equally notable is the display of nineteenth-century bottles, jars, and boxes in which the pharmacopoeia of the times was packaged. Like the shop itself, all these are valuable antiques, of interest to collectors and connoisseurs. But their display in this context represents a more conservative policy than that of other museums, e.g., the general store at Sturbridge Village, which exhibits only brand-new facsimiles of the merchandise once sold there (Fig. 17.3).

17.2. *Re-creating the Danish past:* normally archaeologists rely upon two main sources of information for their investigation of past cultures: artifacts and archives. In "normal" digs, these two sources interface quite well: what the document does not reveal, the excavation may, and vice versa. But in prehistoric societies, such as this Iron Age settlement at Lejre, Denmark, there is no written record. To fill this gap, archaeologists have to borrow from the anthropologist: they analyze the artifact (weapon, hoe, plow, or pot) and try to reenact the process which it might have once supported. It is a pragmatic, trial-and-error method: for the investigator, it is hard and often uncomfortable work. At Lejre, the staff spent many winter days dressed in facsimiles of the leather clothing they had uncovered in the peat bogs. Among other things, they were trying to find the proper location for the smoke holes in the recon-structed thatch huts. They built such huts and then burned them in order to compare the ash traces found in the excavations. By such methods, they were able to reconstruct the Iron Age settlement (*1*) as well reenact their use of such tools as the plow (*2*).

17.2 (Continued). At Lejre, all the processes necessary to maintain the life of a prehistoric settlement have been reenacted (often reinvented) by the staff: cattle raising (2); woodworking (4); childcare (5); saddlery and harnesses for horses (3). Many of these processes have been accurately reproduced by such empirical methods. (In fact, the potters were so successful that their facsimile productions had to be stamped with a metal die in order to prevent their being mistaken for authentic Iron Age antiques!)

As a working museum, Lejre is an integral part of the three-level national museum system of Denmark: standard, big-city archaeological and anthropological institutions; open-air museums to display the environments of the country in historic times; and projects like Lejre where the public can not only see how artifacts from vanished cultures were made and used but actually use them if desired. Because of the success of Lejre with the general public, much of its future research will probably be carried on at other sites, open only to scholars. Hans-Ole Hansen, the director of Lejre, founded it in 1963.

and Old Sturbridge Village tend to reach higher levels of technical polish in docents, films, and literature but even there the content of the interpretive material is often shallow, snobbish or parochial. In an effort to raise the entire level of the interpretive process, the National Park Service has recently established a national center at Harpers Ferry, West Virginia.

In Europe, very little emphasis is placed upon on-site interpretation. In great monuments like Versailles or Hampton Court, the visiting public sees only guards or custodians, never docents. Licensed professional guides are often available but must be hired by the individual tourist and can vary widely in both training and competence. On the other hand, in the United States, interpretation is much more active, the most usual form being that of docents leading small groups on guided tours through the monument. The docent is almost essential because American historic houses are typically furnished, decorated, and equipped for maximum verisimilitude, to give "that lived-in look." Since many of the artifacts are valuable, small, and easily hidden in a purse or pocket, theft is a very serious problem. Under such circumstances, the small, docent-led group becomes imperative.*

At its best, the docent system is probably the optimal way in which to interpret the historic monument, but its effectiveness is dependent upon several factors: (1) the educational program of the institution itself; (2) the training of the docent in the historical background and architectural significance of the building; (3) the personality of the docent. All too often, the institution will not have clearly formulated its educational goals. The docents will often be inadequately or improperly trained. All too often, they are volunteers who are unsuitable psychologically, being unable to strike that precise balance between commitment and detachment which the job requires.

There are several technological substitutes for the docent. One is the individual portable tape recorder with the taped interpretation of the material on view. This has several advantages. It allows for interpretive comments by distinguished scholars who would not be otherwise available. It gives absolute control of the material, guaranteeing high-level and consistent content. And it permits viewers to set their own pace for the viewing experience, something never possible with the group tour.

Another, more dramatic, application of technology to the interpretation of the historic monument is the *son-et-lumière* technique, first perfected by the French but now used around the world. The technique borrows from both stage and screen. A script is written, dealing with the historical

---

*The size of the group will vary with the situation. In many house museums they may be as large as 12 to 15. At Winterthur, which is richly furnished in the same style as when the Du Ponts were in residence there, visitors are led through in groups of four. For reasons of security, only one group occupies any room at one time, doors being locked and unlocked as it passes into and out of the room.

1

17.3. As displayed and interpreted at Old Sturbridge Village, the Asa Knight general store represents an innovative museological enterprise. The building itself, which is an original dating from before 1837, has been restored to the condition of that date. But operating on a newly formulated assumption—i.e., that the customers would have been shopping for brand-new merchandise, not century-and-a-half-old antiques—the Sturbridge curators decided to stock this store with bright and shiny facsimiles. The types of merchandise that such a store would have sold were carefully researched. It would have carried a line ranging from hardware and housewares (hoes and axes, churns, pails, and baskets) to foodstuffs (dried fruits, pickles, salted fish, spices, salt, and sugar) to notions (yard goods, threads, needles, thimbles).

2

3

Some of the decorated ceramics are originals (*1*), but the packaged hardware items are packed in carefully researched little boxes. The store would have sold sperm oil for lamps; this is stored in new barrels such as local coopers would have made (*3*). Other items might have been made by local craftsmen (brooms, wooden hay forks), but a surprising amount of the wares were already factory made (glassware, Castile soap, milk crocks, metal pails). The object of such efforts at verisimilitude is to make as vivid as possible to all visitors, but especially to schoolchildren, what vast changes have taken place in American life in the period between the crossroads general store and the giant regional shopping centers of today. Compare this policy with the more typical one illustrated by the Shelburne apothecary (Fig. 17.1).

17.4. The Puritans were literate, holding reading, writing, and arithmetic in high regard. They were also litigious, jealous of their rights, and indefatigable record keepers. Hence the curators of Plimoth Plantation, unlike those at Lejre, have an abundance of archival materials upon which to base their interpretations of New England life of the early 1600s. (Unlike the case of Lejre, however, they have no archaeological materials, since the entire project is a hypothetical reconstruction of the real Plymouth, 7 miles away: (Fig. 10.9). The Plimouth interpretations are very active. They involve reenactments of such street scenes as roof thatchers being watched by a group of "Indians" (2) and street dances staged by staff members, dressed in historically accurate clothing, playing seventeenth-century tunes on seventeenth-century instruments (1). This commitment to interpret the domestic life of the 1630s is also evident inside the houses. Great emphasis is placed on verisimilitude in housekeeping activities: floors covered with straw, chickens dressed and cooked in the main room (3); medieval table manners (4).

personalities who inhabited the building. It is then performed by professional actors and recorded. The tape is cued in with lighting effects and speakers in various locations on the site. The *son-et-lumière* performance is always performed at night, before paid audiences who view it from fixed seating which affords the necessary panoramic view of the monument. Although it can easily be vulgarized, *son-et-lumière* can be a surprisingly effective way to teach the history of a given site and period to audiences which might not otherwise be taught at all. The crowds, however, create serious problems of wear and tear on the landscape.

Perhaps the most powerful technological teaching aid is the documentary film. Although it has not been very widely used in America in connection with historic sites (and is often quite venal or vulgar when it has been employed), the documentary obviously affords the opportunity to re-create historical events in a fashion otherwise unattainable. Such unpretty aspects of the American experience as slavery—the submerged reality of such handsome monuments as Monticello and Mount Vernon—could be best handled in the documentary film. Here again, the critical factor would be that of editorial control, since the film can as well be used to bowdlerize historic fact as to explicate it.

Beyond question, one of the best of all ways to interpret the historic building is to re-create the activities and processes which it was originally designed to facilitate or expedite. Nothing explains an old kitchen better than cooking in it or an old grist mill better than milling wheat in it. The great popularity of such live demonstrations with tourists of all ages is sufficient proof of their effectiveness. But wholly new dimensions are being added to this type of activity at such institutions as Plimoth Plantation in Massachusetts. Here the entire life-style of the community is acted out by the docents. Instead of leading groups through the village, the visitors "visit" the docents in their "homes," seeing them at work in all domestic chores which made up the day. The docents perform all these tasks in as accurate and realistic manner as possible, using the same tools and instruments in the same manner as their early-seventeenth-century forebears.

18

Training for Professional Preservation: Preservationist, Conservationist, Craftsperson

The artistic and historic heritage is as immense and as complex as the whole physical environment itself. At once God-made and man-made, this environment is not merely the locus of the heritage: very often, it *is* the heritage itself. This may be self-evident in such natural wonders as the Grand Canyon or Niagara Falls. It is equally true of such "artificial" constructs as Mount Vernon or Monticello. For these must be seen as consisting not merely of the manison with its furnishings and outbuildings; they include not only the terraces, gardens, and lawns which surround it but also the larger landscape which encompasses and surrounds them. The whole 360° field of view—river, farmlands, forests, and hills—is an integral part of the artifact. It is therefore quite as important to preserve the essential integrity of this circumambient environmental frame as it is to preserve the mansion and its content. Experientially, they are one continuous seamless fabric, extending from the hearthrug right out to the horizon.

Such a comprehensive view of the heritage would not have been possible even a few short years ago. In the 50-odd years which have elapsed since the establishment of Colonial Williamsburg Restoration (the first fully professional project in the nation), the field of activity known as *historic preservation* has undergone enormous changes.

As we have seen (Chapter 4), it has changed in size. The field has changed in scope: our definition of what is artistically significant has been greatly broadened. Likewise, our definition of what is historically significant has been radically extended.

Our understanding of the importance of the contextual or environmental frame of the individual monument has steadily broadened. Where once the Vieux Carré in New Orleans was the only protected historic district in the country, there are now hundreds of such districts and they are increasing all the time. Finally, our approach to the artistic and historic heritage is conceptually less elitist than it was 50 years ago. The antiquarian connoisseurship so dominant in the early years of the movement is disappearing. Instead of assuming that upper-class, urbane, and monumental structures were the only ones worthy of preservation, we now recognize the importance of vernacular architecture and folkloristic artifacts as being equally important. Anonymous buildings, both urban and rural, are understood to be equally significant components of the patrimony: millworkers' housing, slave quarters, small farmsteads, and Rocky Mountain ghost towns are being designated as a matter of course.

It goes without saying that, defined in such terms, this great heritage cannot be embalmed, frozen, held in a state of museological stasis. Change is ineluctable in both artifact and context. But the rate and nature of this change can and must be controlled. We must recognize, as many countries already do, that a monument of prime importance must "own its view of the environment and the environment's view of it." This means that we must formulate and apply policies of environmental management which will guarantee that growth and change are congruent with the main historic and artistic requirements of the monument itself.

It is obvious that many different types of professional and vocational expertise will be required for this special aspect of environmental preservation. It is also clear that, to work effectively, these specialists will have to share a common philosophy, a common language, and a common methodology. How they achieve this cross-disciplinary training and experience will depend upon the country in which they live. If they are citizens of France or Czechoslovakia, for example, they will study, apprentice, and practice under the umbrella of a comprehensive national program. Whatever the shortcomings, real or putative, of such national bureaucracies as the Soprintendenze dei Monumenti or the Service des Monuments Historiques, they have the unquestioned merit of establishing nationally high average standards of training and workmanship.

Most national programs in Europe and Latin America are modeled after the French and Italian prototypes. Since we have no national agency in the United States comparable to these European institutions, responsiblity for formal professional training is being assumed by an increasing number of universities.* These academic programs all operate at the graduate level, on

---

*In 1975, some 26 American universities offered programs in historic preservation; approximately 45 more offered one or more courses in the same field (*Preservation News,* Washington, October 1975).

the assumption that students must have acquired a first degree in their own disciplines, whether architecture, art history, American studies, or law. Already one can detect a certain specialization developing within these academic programs. Some schools accept only students with undergraduate degrees within their own professional discipline; others offer programs which accept students with a much wider range of undergraduate experience. There are readily apparent justifications for both approaches.

In the architectural schools, the curriculum is aimed primarily at training students with an undergraduate degree in architecture to become specialists in preservation architecture. This implies training in those areas which, technically and legally, require the participation of a licensed architect or engineer. The other type of curriculum prepares students with a wider range of undergraduate degrees (including that of architecture) for a broader, more generalized role in all aspects of historic preservation, that is, the management of the entire artistic and historic heritage. Programs of this type tend to be synoptic, cross-disciplinary, with major emphasis on giving the student a broad conceptual overview of the entire field. In this sense, with their emphasis on generalization rather than specialization, they reverse the usual thrust of graduate education, i.e., "of knowing more and more about less and less."

The need for specialized training in the so-called design professions (architecture, landscape architecture, interior design) is especially acute. In these areas, American undergraduate training has tended to be ahistorical, if not, indeed, antihistorical. The curricula place great emphasis upon creativity, self-expression, artistic freedom: admirable criteria in themselves. Unhappily, they have led students conceptually to picture themselves as being perpetually in the avant-garde, of working always on a clean slate, of designing de novo: of creating isolated, freestanding monuments without any context, temporal or environmental. Such a bias in architectural education has led to important deficiencies in the attitudes of architects toward the built environment. On the one hand, it encourages them to impose their own subjective tastes upon a building to be restored instead of accepting its own aesthetic parameters. On the other, an ahistorical training leads them consistently to underestimate the physical and economic viability of any old structure.

Since legally a licensed architect or engineer must prepare the working drawings and specifications for any building involving public health and safety, architects will be pivotal figures in most projects for restoration or adaptive use of old buildings. Unfortunately, they are often ill prepared for such interventions. For example: it will be comparatively easy for them to design and build conventional balloon-framed wooden houses, of new materials and sited on new land. But to restore an old wood-frame house which has been subjected to two centuries of use and abuse requires a quite different order of professional knowledge and competence. The differences are at once narrowly practical and broadly theoretical. An old house might have old brick chimneys or stone foundations which require consolidation, either by the injection of cement grouting or by the insertion of new structural elements. Such interventions must take into account the dangers of disturbing delicate statical relationships, the hazards of new loads on old footings, the difference in strengths between old lime mortar and new portland cement, and so forth. Moreover, the cosmetic integrity of the old structure will require the concealment of all new work and the cleaning and restoration of original systems of polychromy.

But the very act of conservation of old buildings (as of old paintings or sculptures) raises important theoretical questions as well. If, for example, this old frame house happens also to have some important historical association (Washington slept on this bed, Jefferson drafted the Declaration of Independence on this desk, John Brown and his raiders staged their last stand behind this door) then the bed, the desk, the bullet-ridden door achieve a symbolic importance quite without parallel in conventional design. No matter how fragile, faded or termite-ridden, their actual physical integument must be conserved at all costs, demanding prophylactic and prosthetic measures never to be found in the construction of new artifacts. Such problems as these confront architects who aspire to work in historic preservation with the need for a new kind of theoretical apparatus. They must develop the capacity to work in modes of stylistic expression which are not their own; to learn to respect the aesthetic criteria of long-dead designers and craftspersons—criteria which might not be at all congruent with their own taste. They must have a willingness to investigate and then respect the historical development of the artifact in hand; an ability to subordinate their own preferences and prejudices to that record; and a readiness to collaborate with other specialists who will often have a more detailed understanding of the phylogenetic origins of the artifact in question.

None of this implies that the field does not require designers of taste and creative ability. On the contrary, a very high degree of talent and imagination is called for: nevertheless, stricter and more objective restraints upon personal expression are called for than in "normal" architectural practice. It is the task of those architectural schools which now offer courses in architectural conservation to inculcate these conceptual postures in their students.

Important as they may be, architects are only one kind of a number of professionals required in any comprehensive program for the preservation of the national patrimony: archaeologists, art historians, art conservators; landscape architects, botanists, and geographers; chemists, engineers, photographers and photogrammetrists, etc., etc. In order to collaborate with maximum effectiveness, such specialists also require formal training in historic preservation; and the training should be of the synoptic, cross-disciplinary nature already described. To illustrate the problem: students interested in focusing on some specialized aspect of conservation such as the diseases of stone or stained glass will obviously need a first degree in chemistry. But no undergraduate curriculum in chemistry is apt to offer them the opportunity to study the special pathologies involved in the attrition of stone or glass by environmental forces. Nor, paradoxically, is the standard graduate course in chemistry apt to encourage them to work with architects or art historians to master the aesthetic and cosmetic aspects of old masonry or old glass. An exactly comparable problem confronts structural or mechanical engineers who are interested in conserving old fabrics rather than constructing new ones. Neither undergraduate nor graduate curricula are apt to offer either incentive or opportunity to explore all the complex technical and cultural nuances of the problems thus raised. Only a new curriculum, specially designed to meet these new requirements, can fill the bill.

The broad outlines of this type of curriculum can be seen in the pioneering program of Restoration and Preservation of Historic Architecture now in being at the Graduate School of Architecture, Planning and Restoration at Columbia University.

One serious limitation of all American academic programs is that, by their very nature, they can offer little or no "hands-on" or "on-site" experience to students. Nor is there as yet anything approaching a coordinated national program of apprenticeship or internship.★ Thus students are required to fend for themselves—an unhappy situation in the best of circumstances. This problem, already serious, will grow steadily more pressing as the volume of work increases. Given the lack of any centralized program by the federal government, some alternative internship system will have to be evolved. One solution, proposed by the author, is for the creation of a nationwide consortium of schools which have programs in historic preservation. The consortium would, among other things, administer a national program of subsidized internships for graduates of the member schools. Each intern would be assigned to appropriate nonprofit projects in archaeology, museology, restoration, and so forth, for a stated period.

If European and American experience to date is any index, the vast majority of restoration or preservation projects will be of governmental or institutional nature. This suggests that most graduates of historic preservation programs will work as civil servants or institutional employees rather than as free-lance professionals. It is easy to visualize some architects devel-

★The only program approaching a national scope is the excellent summer survey teams of the Historic American Buildings Survey and the Historic American Engineering Record, both departments of the National Park Service. These surveys employ small teams of architects and historians for 10-week periods to measure and document a wide range of projects all across the nation. They constitute an excellent introduction to this aspect of the field and deserve to be enormously expanded.

oping a private practice in the area of architectural conservation:* but most architects, like most historians or archaeologists, are likely to function in curatorial or administrative capacities in specialized institutions. Precisely what functions they will discharge—administration, research, legislation, curatorial, or educational—will depend upon both training and temperament. At the present time, the entire American field is still fluid, in the process of becoming institutionalized: thus it offers an unusual range of opportunities for the imaginative and energetic newcomer.

Another limitation in American academic programs is that none of them deals in depth with the conservation of the actual fabric in the same way that art conservators deal with the artifacts entrusted to their care. This need for a new kind of specialist, the architectural conservator, has been the subject of a recent study.[1] The recognition of this new need, the study points out,

> . . . reflects an important change in philosophy in the historic preservation movement. During the early years of the movement, "restoration" tended to be stressed, and various standards of aesthetic connoisseurship often guided restoration work. In recent years, however, an increasing professionalization of the field has led to the recognition of a wider variety of approaches toward historic structures and the consideration of a greater spectrum of types of objects and artifacts as being worthy of preservation. Increasing emphasis is being placed on conservation rather than replacement of existing fabric. The pholosophical approach is shifting from the sentimental-aesthetic to the scientific in an effort to retain the integrity of a historic structure or site. . . ."

The architectural conservator who has emerged in this philosophical change is a preservation technologist who attempts to combine the perspective of an architectural historian with the overall approach of an architect and the scientific focus of a conservator. It is he who directs the intervention. The architectural conservator understands and is able to employ the following methodologies to a greater degree than others involved in the preservation of historic building fabric: (1) the chemistry of building materals; (2) the causes and processes of deterioration; (3) the interaction of environmental factors; (4) scientific tests (e.g. he is able to conduct scientific tests to determine the cause, effect, and solution to problems); and (5) direct intervention in the building fabric. . . .[2]

The architectural conservator must go further still [than the architect] in his knowledge of the history of building materials and contruction methods and their preservation needs. He must have training in the new technology and in scientific laboratory methods now being applied to the conservation of artifacts in other fields. The architectural conservator needs to be trained in, or know how to tap resources in, such sub-specialties of

---

*The French Service des Monuments Historiques has resolved this somewhat anomalous situation by employing architects both as full-time civil servants and as free-lance consultants working on special government projects for an individually negotiated fee.

chemistry as spectrographic analysis, radiocarbon dating, and resistivity analysis. He will need to know how to use new archaeological techniques for analyzing site evidence, computer technology for retrieval of recorded information, and photogrammetry for solving difficult problems of recording and producing accurately dimensioned visual records."[3]

In addition to formal academic training in architectural conservation, at both classroom and laboratory levels, there is a need for basic research in the aging process of building materials, both traditional (e.g., wood shingles) and modern (e.g., reinforced concrete). Problem-oriented research, the study says,

> . . . is also an immediate need; for instance, studies and test programs for evaluating the risks of condensation in insulating historic buildings; for developing efficient, safe paint removal methods; and for structural reinforcement methods for decayed wood and masonry. Lacking such problem-oriented test programs, hasty investigations are being done for specific building conservation projects with little documentation, follow-up, or communication to other conservators. Applications research is handicapped because it is usually not funded adequately. The pressure of time restrictions hinders good research, and professional liability risks inhibit innovation. Innovative test programs are an urgent need, perhaps utilizing old buildings of lesser importance as case studies.[4]

The study does not attempt to formulate a detailed curriculum for the training of architectural conservators. They need not necessarily be licensed architects; i.e., their basic training might be in chemistry or structural engineering. It does attempt to identify the specific skills and competences which would be required of them.

TRAINING OF CRAFTSPERSONS AND TECHNICIANS

It is obvious that any broad national program of preservation and restoration will require the training of a large force of workers in the traditional building crafts as well as technicians in modern building technology. In the first category would be carpenters, cabinetmakers, and wood-carvers; plasterers and masons; painters, paperhangers, seamstresses, and upholsterers; and others. In the second category would be plumbers, steam fitters and electricians; heating, cooling and ventilating craftspersons; and so forth. It is also apparent that, to work effectively together, these people, too, must share a common understanding of the special problems of preservation both among themselves and with the professionals in the field. Yet, today, there is no consensus on what relationships, if any, should exist between academic programs for training professional preservationists and vocational programs for training craftspersons in traditional building trades. Obviously, the professional will profit greatly from hands-on experience in workshops and construction sites. So, too, would craftspersons benefit from academic course work in architectural history and the decorative arts. Both would profit from laboratory experience and lectures in such subjects as stone disease or the pathologies of timber construction.

It is difficult, however, to see how a carpenter or brickmason with no more formal education than a high school diploma could participate in graduate-level science courses. The obverse is not necessarily true: a college graduate with sufficient aptitude and motivation should have no special problems in apprenticeship in the traditional crafts. Perhaps we should visualize an overall educational program with parallel academic and vocational tracks in which crossovers would be permitted to any student who is able and willing to operate at both levels.*

In the Western world, the training of craftspersons in traditional, preindustrial crafts is even more neglected than is the professional training of preservationists and conservationists. Indeed, at the end of 1977, there were only two centers offering a structured training program in the traditional building crafts.† Such young workers as are entering this very important area are doing so on a personal, ad hoc basis, picking up what training may be assimilated by observation and apprenticeship in small, scattered restoration projects. Their search for training is not made any easier by the attitudes of building trades unions, which tend to restrict apprenticeship and employment severely in their respective fields.

This is, of course, a reflection of the attitude of the entire construction industry toward the problems of retrieval and recycling of the built world, In an industry in which unemployment has recently been chronic and high, the potential economic importance of preservation is obvious because preservation and conservation projects, unlike conventional new construction with its emphasis on laborsaving technologies, are by definition labor-intensive rather than energy-intensive. Even now, few architectural firms have begun to specialize in this type of work: thus it is not surprising that few contractors with any expertise are to be found.

Ironically, most of the young people who are becoming traditional craftspersons seem to come from middle-class families. Most of them tend to be college graduates who see the crafts as one channel of escape from the

---

*Cervat Erder, head of the Restoration Department of Middle Eastern Technical University in Ankara, Turkey, suggests that, in countries like Turkey where highly skilled craftspersons may be semiliterate, training in both classroom and workshop should form an integral whole.

†Two such programs have recently been initiated. One is sponsored jointly by the Municipal Arts Society and Local 66, International Union of Bricklayers, both of New York City. The other has been initiated by the Durham Technical Institute of Durham, North Carolina.

routinized tracks of business and the professions. This is actually a significant cultural phenomenon. Working-class youth is notable for its absence, showing a class prejudice against any sort of hand labor (with its connotation of sweaty armpits and dirty hands) and its bias in favor of the clean quasi-white-collar activities of the service industries. Such attitudes on the part of young people from working-class backgrounds is probably an integral part of a larger attitude of the working population, namely, a prejudice against the handmade, the old-fashioned, the out-of-style in all its forms. Indeed, historic preservation today is unfortunately still an urbane, upper-class interest around the world. The world's poor and underprivileged have had too intimate an experience with living in neglected old buildings and neighborhoods to have any interest in their rehabilitation.

In America, at least, the trade unions seem completely to share this prejudice against the old, the used, the handmade. Even craft unions such as those of carpenters, masons, and plasterers (which might be expected to see in historic preservation new areas of employment for their members) have so far displayed no interest in it. On the contrary, in most communities in which there have been sharp battles for the preservation of historic buildings or districts (Boston, Providence, Savannah), the building trade unions have usually been solidly on the side of those activities which threatened them (new highways, airports, and industrial construction). It is apparent that the environmental crisis will have to be much more mature before a wide recognition of its implications will be shared by the working people of the world who currently see the massive application of technology as the unique road to material well-being, who regard aluminum, air conditioning, and glass as the iconography of this state of being.

FORMAL TRAINING NEEDED FOR
THE CRAFTS

None of this alters the fact that we must have training centers for the traditional building crafts. As long as preservation was limited to work on a few isolated great houses or monumental buildings, it was possible to find the necessary craftsmen, usually older and retired workmen who had had such apprenticeship training in their youth, before their crafts had been transformed by the massive application of mechanization to every branch of the field. Exactly what form such a training program will take is a matter of conjecture. It will almost certainly have to be governmentally initiated or foundation-financed, at least initially. And here, European experience could stand us in good stead. In France and Italy, where massive, long-range programs of restoration are in effect, it is possible for government agencies like the Monuments Historiques and the Soprintendenza dei Monumenti to recruit and train cadres of young craftsmen in their own national *chantiers*. In socialist countries of Eastern Europe, where the amount of wartime damage was vast and and postwar reconstruction has been correspondingly enormous, the need for skilled craftspersons was immense. Countries like the German Democratic Republic, Poland, and the U.S.S.R. have attacked the problem with energy and imagination. Its sheer size necessitated the creation of specialized construction companies with their own onsite apprenticeship training programs. Now, after some 30 years of continuous activity, the sad depletion of traditional craftspersons—aggravated by wartime mortalities—has been reversed. Not only have wartime damages been obliterated completely but whole centers of such cities as Leningrad, Warsaw, and Dresden have been restored to an unprecedented state of physical well-being. And in the process, the supply of trained craftspersons sizably increased.

The Czechs have carried this process further than most of their neighbors by establishing a nationwide network of government-funded ateliers in all the major areas of preindustrial handicrafts: stone and wood carving; ornamental plaster; iron forging and bronze casting; stained glass; polychromy and decorative painting; even tapestry weaving. Operating as cooperatives, these ateliers were guaranteed a firm economic base by work for the national restoration program. Especially interesting is the manner in which they have been staffed. In a (perhaps unwitting) echo of the Bauhaus, the ateliers are directed by older master craftsmen and staffed by young apprentices recruited from both the universities and vocational training schools. Although the economic base of these workshops was the nationwide program in historic preservation, they were also encouraged to accept commissions for the fabrication of contemporary designs in their own métier. This opportunity to execute designs for contemporary architects alongside repair and replication of historic artifacts has had a felicitous effect. It worked against a narrow and stultifying antiquarianism in the ateliers themselves. Since the Czech program aimed at the revitalization of entire crafts, some of which were all but extinct (e.g., tapestry weaving, stained glass, mosaics and tesserae), the atelier program had a long-range cultural value quite above and beyond its support function for preservation proper. The benign consequences of this policy are today everywhere apparent in Czech and Slovak handicrafts. Both aesthetically and technically, the expertise is noticeable, especially in such fields of design as furniture, lighting fixtures, glass, and metalwork.

Despite the obvious disparities between the economic systems of the U.S.A. and the socialist countries, there is no reason why Americans cannot profit from their experience. There are, in fact, a number of design schools in the nation which, if they desired, could broaden their curricula in two dimensions: (1) by beefing up the laboratory, workshop, and fieldwork incorporated in their programs so that students have greater hands-on contact with their work; (2) by the deliberate reintroduction of traditional vernacular and handicraft components into programs which have become ostentatiously "modern," "contemporary," or high-tech in their design emphasis.

It is entirely conceivable that the National Parks Service—already the owner of hundreds of historic monuments and sites—could organize its construction and maintenance work in such a fashion as to offer long-range, structured apprenticeship training programs to young would-be craftspersons. A prototypical example of such a program is to be found in the Conservation Workshops run by the Park Service at its Training Center in Harpers Ferry, West Virginia.

19

Preservation in
Two Socialist Countries

CZECHOSLOVAKIA

A broad program of preservation of the artistic and historic heritage, interesting in its quality and impressive in its scope, has been under way in the
Czechoslovak Republic since its founding in 1948. In the past several decades, thousands of buildings of all types and sizes have been restored by the
national government at a cost of hundreds of millions of Czech crowns.
These projects range from the preservation of entire towns, like those of
Telč, Tábor, and Slavonice, through great complexes like the historic core
of Prague, to individual buildings—large, like the Wallenstein Palace in
Prague's Malá Strana, and small, like some of the renovated inns in provincial centers.

Stylistically, these projects cover the whole spectrum of Czechoslovak
history (not prehistory: archaeological sites fall under the jurisdiction of
other national institutions). This spectrum is both wide and rich, since
Czechoslovakia, lying at the crossroads of the continent, has been strongly
influenced by every major artistic current of the last thousand years. Thus
one can see restorations of eleventh-century romanesque churches like that
of St. George in Prague; the dazzling baroque trompe l'oeil frescoes of
Český Krumlov Castle; or the late-nineteenth-century gothic revival of
Castle Lednice.

All of these artifacts have been restored with great skill and sympathy
for the styles involved. But throughout the country one can also see careful
restorations of buildings of more modest pretensions—like the burghers'
houses of Telč and Slavonice—as well as of more recent vintage. Thus the
National Theater in Prague (1868–1883), destroyed once by fire, rebuilt,
and now most recently restored, is a piece of Victoriana in which either Abe
Lincoln or the Prince Consort would have felt entirely at home.* A popular

---

*The National Theater, financed entirely by public subscriptions, was begun in 1868 and
gutted by fire in 1881, just before it was scheduled to open. It was completely rebuilt, after
another fund-raising campaign, and finally dedicated in 1883. It was understood by all to be a
nationalist protest against the Austro-Hungarian monarchy's policy toward ethnic minorities.

19.1. *Czechoslovakian towns—like the Czech countryside* in general—have an extraordinarily rich mix of architecture which goes back to romanesque, even Roman, times. And these towns are astonishingly intact, owing to two happy historical anomalies: the relatively low level of industrialization in nineteenth-century Central Europe; and the country's having come through two world wars with little destruction. As a result, there are very many towns and villages that merit special curatorial attention, the most significant of which have been designated as national historic monuments. Among such towns are Tábor, site of the great Utopian republic of Jan Hus (*1, 2*), and the market town of Telč, whose surrounding ponds are famous for their carp (*3*). In these towns, individual houses remain in private ownership though the surrounding farm and forest lands have been collectivized. Their traditional market function has thereby been radically altered and new economic activities have been developed to keep them viable. The national government visualizes tourism, with historic preservation and local handicrafts, as economically advantageous. Thus it has adopted a comprehensive program of grants-in-aid, interest-free loans, and technical assistance to individual homeowners who, in return, grant permanent scenic façade easements to the government. Under such programs, the town squares of Telč (*3*) and Slavonice (*4*) have been completely restored to their preindustrial appearance.

2

3

4

1

2

364

3   4

19.2. *Restoration of historic architecture* in Czechoslovakia covers a variety of cases. Sometimes the building is classified as of prime importance, as in the case of Prague's Strahov Monastery: it has been adapted to house the national museum of literature (*1, 2*). In other instances, the buildings are restored for their ambiental importance to the street scape, as in these houses in Prague (*3, 4*) and Litoměřice (*5, 6*). Working with such old buildings, restoration architects must often accommodate unforeseen (and unforeseeable) site problems, such as the discovery of important romanesque remains (*1*), and change designs accordingly (*2*).

5

6

secessionist coffee house in Prague has been carefully restored to its fin-de-siècle state. In Brno, Mies van der Rohe's famous house for the Tugendhat family has been reconditioned and given to the local architects' union for their regional headquarters: they plan to refurnish it as Mies left it. Two houses by Adolf Loos, one in Brno from 1909, one in Prague from 1929, have been completely documented and are scheduled for complete restoration—at, incidentally, no cost to the owners.★

According to a completed survey of the entire country, some 350,000 individual structures have been classified as historically and/or artistically significant enough to have been registered and "frozen" for conservation. It will require years, even under optimum conditions, for such a program to be completed. But all the buildings on this registry are now permanently protected. Any alterations, whether by public or private owners, must meet the standards set up by the State Institute for the Preservation of Historic Monuments and the Protection of Nature. All buildings of national significance are actually restored by this agency.

This program, so large for a country so small, would be totally impracticable if the restored or renovated buildings could not be put to some socially viable use. Indeed, cost aside, no country would want a landscape full of so many empty monuments. Hence the restoration program has been closely geared to the building requirements of the nation as a whole. The new social system of Czechoslovakia has created a wide range of new institutions, each with its own specialized building requirements. Housing, as in most countries, is the most acutely needed. So many of the old town and village dwellings which are restored are, in the process, converted into modern apartments. In fact, many historic towns and villages are being simultaneously restored and revised to conform to modern town-planning standards as regards fire protection, sanitation, traffic, and so on. Since these towns must be continuously inhabited, work must proceed in carefully phased stages. The renovation of the old walled market town of Jičín affords a good example of how the Czechs go about it. Here, valuable old buildings are being restored, substandard buildings of little historic or aesthetic value are being demolished, and new buildings are being planned, both as replacements in the old center and as supplements in the periphery beyond the ancient walls. Besides housing, there is also a great need for health and education facilities, for museums and assembly halls, for town and county offices, and so on. Many of these are being installed, and with

★Like the Soprintendenza dei Monumenti in Italy, or the Commission des Monuments Historiques in France, Státní Ústav Památkové Péče a Ochrany Prírody (State Institute for the Preservation of Historic Monuments and Protection of Nature) controls the fate of all buildings so classified. Unlike the former, the state office has greater powers and larger funds to finance the restoration of even privately owned structures, such as churches and private dwellings. Title to the property remains with owners.

surprising grace, in the palaces, castles, villas, and monastic establishments with which the country is so richly endowed.

The question of social utility is one of several yardsticks used for establishing a system of priorities in the conservation program. Another, for obvious reasons, is the physical condition of the building and the urgency of the needed repairs. Unlike many of the countries of Europe, Czechoslovakia suffered comparatively little damage in World War II. Nevertheless, the new communist state in 1948 took over a physical plant, many of whose sectors had suffered from long neglect. Between the two wars, during the first republic, the construction of new housing and factories such as that at Bata was well publicized internationally. But this modern architecture represented only a minute part of the country's total plant. Although

19.3. *New uses for old buildings* are often quite simple. The huge town house of the Wallenstein family, in the Malá Strana district of Prague, has been adapted to a variety of new functions. The main block (left) has been modified to house the Ministry of Culture. The former riding academy (top, center) has been adapted for use as an art gallery. The parterres of the formal gardens have been somewhat modified to serve as an outdoor concert hall for summer evenings. A vaulted loggia, out of sight at bottom of photograph, serves as a stage for musicians.

1

2

3

19.4. *The virtuosity of Czech artists and crafts-men* is dazzlingly apparent in hundreds of monumental interiors which have been conserved and are now open to the public. They include many churches, ranging from the heavily restored Romanesque church of St. George in Prague (*1*) to the almost perfectly preserved Gothic hall-church of Holy Trinity in Kutná Hora (*2*). In secular architecture, the range in the decorative arts is even wider, reflecting every nuance of changing European taste across the centuries. The magnificent polychromed plaster of the Renaissance parlor (*4*) and the witty trompe l'oeil murals in the ballroom (*3*) in the castle of Český Krumlov have been restored by specially trained conservators. Nineteenth-century interiors have been handled with equal skill and respect. The National Theater in Prague has restored interiors in which Lincoln would have felt thoroughly at home (*6*). A great country house, built by a nobleman who was a great admirer of Walter Scott, is a late gothic revival mansion which Pugin might have designed. It now houses a national research institute (*5*). Conservation work of this type is normally executed by special companies established by the State Office for Restoration of Historic Towns and Buildings. Conservators and special craftsmen are trained in national ateliers specializing in plaster work, cabinetry, metal-working, painting, etc.

4

5

6

Prague and the bigger cities had witnessed some of the nineteenth-century urban improvements which so radically altered the face of cities like Milan, Paris, and Brussels, the historic central cores were largely undisturbed.* For this reason, Prague has a larger body of undisturbed late-mediaeval, Renaissance, and baroque building than any other European capital today.

The Hapsburgs, after crushing the Bohemian autonomists in the battle of the White Mountain (1620), adopted a policy of economic attrition as one means of combating Czech nationalism. Even the royal castle, Hradčany, was locked up, untenanted, and neglected for decades on end. This neglect explains the recent (1963) sensational discovery of sixteenth- and seventeenth-century masterpieces in the castle. These 67 paintings, including 3 by Veronese and 2 by Tintoretto, have been cleaned and hung in the old riding academy of the castle, itself a beautifully restored rococo building.† This deliberate neglect, while fortunate from an art-historical point of view, nevertheless poses great problems for the agencies entrusted with the conservation of the national artistic heritage.

The current program is made possible by a series of acts of the national Parliament which are consolidated in the new constitution of 1960: this calls for the "conservation of nature and the preservation of the beauties of the country."[1] The wording is significant, for it links the preservation of the individual building to the landscape as a whole and gives Czech preservationists wider powers than most of their colleagues in the West. The work as a whole is under the jurisdiction of the Ministry of Culture. Here the State Institute for Preservation supervises the program nationally. To this institute was entrusted the task of formulating the criteria for evaluating monuments and works of art; for making a national survey of such monuments; and for working out priorities and schedules of conservation. Actual preservation of historic architecture is handled by another agency, the State Office for Restoration of Historic Towns and Buildings.

This agency performs all the tasks normally assigned to the architect's office: research, design, contract letting, supervision of work. The Prague office (there is a similar one in Bratislava) has a staff of some 250 architects,

---

*The Prague ghetto, adjacent to Staré Město (Old Town), was razed only at the end of the nineteenth century and rebuilt along beaux arts lines. The synagogue and cemetery, among the oldest in Europe, escaped destruction in World War II because the Nazis planned to make them into an anti-Jewish Museum, storing there religious art from ruined synagogues all over Europe. The synagogue and its ancillary buildings have been restored by the Czechoslovak government as a memorial to the Jewish victims of Hitler.

†After transferring 46 choice works from Prague Castle to Vienna, the imperial household staged a great sale in Prague in 1782, when the rest of the collection was dispersed to Dresden, Vienna, Munich, and London. But recently, Czech scholars, comparing the last catalog of the collection before its dispersal with current catalogs for these foreign collections, found many paintings unaccounted for. Hence a systematic examination of all paintings in the huge Hradčany complex was initiated. The new collection in the riding academy is the result.

370

civil and mechanical engineers, town planners, and art historians. This staff is organized into six ateliers: one for Prague Castle, seat of the government, including the presidential palace; two for the design of individual projects; one for town planning; one for public services and utilities; and a sixth for theory and art historical research. After some 16 years' experience, this is now a staff of specialists in conservation, restoration, and renovation.*

Working in teams, this staff makes a physical examination and historical analysis of each building or project; prepares all necessary drawings and documents, including all mechanical specialities required by new sorts of tenancy; and supervises the building process itself. The Czechs have found this supervision especially important since, in such old fabrics, many unexpected features are brought to light in the course of the work. Designs must very often be revised to take account of these newly discovered facts. Although above-grade structures are normally examined by the architectural staff, archaeologists are called in whenever their expertise is needed.

The way in which this program has been related to the building industry is extremely interesting. Basic construction is all done by special companies, each of whom bids on, and then works under contract to, the Institute. However, these companies furnish only straight building labor—structural steel and concrete workers, masons and carpenters, electricians, plumbers, and steam fitters. But the restoration of preindustrial architecture involves all the old crafts of construction, interior decoration, and cabinetmaking. Such skilled craftspersons are supplied by another national agency, especially set up for this purpose in 1952: the Center of Applied Arts. It has succeeded in organizing craftspersons in metal, glass and mosaic; in wood and stone carving and metal casting; in ornamental plasterwork and *sgraffito*; in leather, fabric, and tapestry—all these and others—into a network of ateliers.

These ateliers are placed under the supervision of professionally trained people, graduates either of the Academy of Art of of one of several schools of applied art. Many of them have previously completed their apprenticeship in the craft. Inside the atelier, however, the traditional relationship between master and apprentice is maintained.† Many of these crafts were on the verge of extinction, and a national census was made to locate older craftspersons and recruit them for the new program. It is these ateliers, under the direction of the Center for Applied Arts, which handle all handicraft and decorative art in the restoration projects. The work is done under

*The preservation movement has a long tradition in the country. The first Commission for the Registration and Conservation of Monuments of Architecture was established in Vienna on December 31, 1850. The first magazine on the subject, *Památký Archeologiké (Archaeological Monuments),* was published in Prague in 1854, earlier than similar ones published in Vienna (1856) and Switzerland (1866).

†The aim here is reminiscent of the Bauhaus: to break down the barriers between theory and practice, artist and artisan, classroom and shop, bringing technical expertise to the one and artistic literacy to the other.

contract, either in the workshop or on the site, depending upon the nature of the task. Ornamental plaster and fresco restoration is obviously done in situ, while stained glass or tesserae would be done in the atelier.

These ateliers are not limited to the restoration or reproduction of historic prototypes, however. They are encouraged also to execute work for contemporary architects and designers. Individual members are encouraged to design and execute work on their own. The center now has a chain of shops where such crafts are displayed and periodic exhibitions of atelier activities held; these give ample proof of both the aesthetic maturity and the excellent technique of the craftspersons. Thus this program, initiated to facilitate preservation work, is simultaneously being used as the material basis for the regeneration of handicraft and artisanship.

The theoretical principles which guide the Czech program of restoration are exceptionally interesting. In the first place, as in western Europe, a hierarchy of values has been established against which the value of the individual monument or work of art can be assessed. The first and highest category is that of monuments which are absolutely unique and irreplaceable, either artistically or historically or (as often happens) both. Under such a heading would come Hradčany in Prague, the Westminster-cum-Windsor of Czech history, or the fortress city of Tábor, capital of the utopian Hussite Republic of the fifteenth century, or Karlsteyn Castle.

A second category, by far the largest, would include those buildings which are valuable artistically but without any special historical significance. If these date from romanesque or early gothic periods, they are obviously more precious than baroque, rococo, or neoclassic structures, which still exist in great numbers. Such buildings may be preserved in toto, inside and out. It is much more likely that they will be modified internally to meet modern requirements. Even then, however, important interior features (a fine stairway, unusual vaulting, a painted ceiling) will be preserved. Since all Czech towns and cities have large undisturbed districts of such old buildings, whole streetscapes and districts are being restored. This will sometimes extend to an entire town, as in the case of Telč.

Another category of monuments will be preserved because of historical associations, irrespective of intrinsic aesthetic merit. Such would be the birthplace of a national hero or the site of some important event. Cultural and technical developments will also be thus memorialized. For example, as a result of the reorganization of agriculture on a cooperative basis and the parallel mechanization of farm work, the Czech village is undergoing a rapid evolution, both cultural and physical. Old modes of life and work will soon be modified beyond recognition; they are already beginning to assume a protohistorical significance. Hence certain characteristic villages are being selected for "preservation." What is envisaged here is a kind of living museum, a cross between Colonial Williamsburg, the Farmers Museum of Cooperstown, and the Skansen-type museums of Scandinavia.

They will remain living communities, employing old crafts and processes, to preserve as accurate a record of the precommunist village life as possible.*

The subjective factor in restoration work can, of course, never be completely eliminated. Any really old building in Bohemia or Moravia will confront the restorationist with an embarrassingly rich sequence of stylistic forms from which to choose. The Czechs are well aware of what they call "Viollet-le-Ducism" (i.e., the renovation of a building according to some purely personal image of its "golden" period), and the government agencies have adopted rigorous procedures to make certain that factual reasons exist for each decision. Thus a complete day-by-day log is kept on all buildings undergoing restoration. All important decisions as to what to keep or what to discard are the subject of staff discussion and approval. Important design changes are sometimes made necessary by unanticipated conditions. Since this log is photographic as well as written, it constitutes a valuable part of the record for future students and curators.

Such a policy is not always easy. For example: many of the greatest gothic churches were "baroque-ized" (as the Czechs say) by the Jesuits after the Counter-Reformation. To modern taste, their original form would often be more appealing that these later remodelings. Also, these would have originally been Hussite churches, traditional centers of resistance to both the German-language monarchy and the Jesuit order. Hence, leaving them in their baroque dress often strains modern Czech sentiments, aesthetically as well as patriotically. Nevertheless, it is only in cases like that of Emäus Monastery in Prague (1347), a splendid hall church which was gutted by fire bombs in the last days of World War II, that the opportunity is taken to strip off the remains of later improvements and restore the building to its original state.

The reconstruction of vanished buildings is, in principle, frowned upon. This is in contrast to Polish policy, where entire districts of historically important buildings have been reconstructed, at least externally, to their pre-Hitler state. The Czechs understand Polish motivations, but, since they themselves have sustained few such losses, they are not confronted with this type of problem. There is only one such reconstruction: that of the long-vanished Bethlehem Chapel of John Huss in Prague's Old Town. This lone example is rationalized as being perhaps defensible because that church played such a pivotal role in the struggle against German domination. But I was assured that such reconstructions are not apt to be repeated. As a matter of fact, Czech preservationists share the general European distrust of reconstructions. It is based on long European experience, of which

---

*Ideological motives, i.e., to demonstrate improved conditions of life under the new system, are doubtlessly involved in the creation of these museum villages. But since they preserve folkloristic, preindustrial village life, they have another kind of didactic significance as well.

the reconstruction of the Stoa of Attalus in the Athenian Agora by the American School is merely the last (Fig. 9.8). Most European restorationists are also extremely critical of the Williamsburg Restoration for the same reason.★

The Czech experts are opposed to faked antiquity in the new elements or members of a restored building. A new beamed ceiling, a rebuilt masonry wall, or a new ornamental stucco ornament is always obviously new. Where old and new materials meet, the line of demarcation is always clearly indicated. In masonry, for instance, the brick or the bond or the mortar color will be changed. In an all-of-a-piece structure, like the Baroque church of St. Nicholas in Malá Strana, this policy leads to surprising results. Here, the frescoes have all been beautifully restored, the cut stone washed down, the imitation marble cleaned and polished, the gold leaf reburnished. The result is dazzling: one can see the pink, lavender, green, and gilt polychromy of the elder Dientzenhofer, much as he left it in 1713. This same delicious palette can be seen in the sparkling pastel stucco façades of the town square in Telč.

In reality, the problem of a restoration looking too new is quickly resolved by two factors: the climate and the coal smoke of the cities. Both are extremely hard on the exterior stucco, which, ever since the first importation of Italian architects in the seventeenth century, has been the universal surfacing of Czechoslovak architecture. Unless it is annually refurbished, it begins to stain, craze, and flake off. These factors combine to keep Czech streetscapes low in key, *triste,* and a little shabby.

The problem of integrating old and new buildings has serious implications for town planning. The Institute has a fixed rule against a new building's being designed in a period style. On the other hand, it recognized the urbanistic importance of maintaining some sort of visual congruity between old and new. This criterion is, however, easier to formulate than to meet. Four national architectural competitions have been held for the design of a new Town Hall for Prague. The former building, a nineteenth-century gothic revival structure, was destroyed in the battle of Prague in May 1945. The site faces historic Old Town Square. It is flanked by the Clock Tower of the original late-medieval Town Hall, already restored, and faces the gigantic façade of the gothic Týn Church. Elsewhere around this square are a baroque church; several *fin-de-siècle* office buildings and apartments; two rococo palaces and a range of Renaissance and baroque town houses. Clearly, the "systematization" of this complex will be no easy task.

★This feeling was so strong at the Second International Congress of Architects and Technicians of Historic Monuments (Venice, May 25–31, 1964) that it found the following expression in Art. 14 of the Charter: *Tout travail de reconstruction devra être exclu à priori; seule l'anastylose peut être envisagée, c'est à dire la recomposition des parties existantes mais démembrées.* This charter was, in turn, the basis for the organization of the International Council on Monuments and Sites in Cracow, Poland, June 20–25, 1965.

The same kind of problem faces the preservationists in the restoration of historic towns. Simultaneously with the restoration of valuable buildings, hundreds of others which do not meet sanitary minima in terms of light, air, access, and so on, will be demolished. This, of course, further aggravates the existing housing shortage. New units can be placed in the center, thus raising the problem of old and new; but another possibility is to build entirely new communities around the old center. One such example is the little provincial center of Mladá Boleslav, which is the site of the huge Škoda motor works. Here a modern center for 15,000 people, consisting of apartments, shops, schools, and sports facilities, has been built adjacent to the old center. The architectural design of the new complex (which, in this post-Stalin era, resembles modern architecture everywhere) makes a pleasant foil against which to view the old center, and vice versa.

Thus, all in all, the Czechs are well along on a comprehensive program of preservation and restoration of their artistic heritage which will add measurably to the cultural resources of the nation. For all the obvious differences between their social system and ours, this is a program from which we could learn a great deal.

POLAND: PHOENIX FROM THE FLAMES

The end of World War II confronted many devastated cities in Europe and Asia with a problem: what to do about the relics of their past in rebuilding for the future. The experience of these cities—London, Coventry, and Rotterdam; Warsaw, Leningrad, and Hiroshima—is not without lessons for us who live elsewhere. For the uncontrolled erosion of peacetime construction threatens to wreak as much damage on the cities of the world as did the mindless violence of war. To the citizens of these phoenix cities, the war made diamond-clear one fact which is often befogged in peace, namely, that the past is, in many real ways, the only material out of which we can build the future. The protection of historic districts, buildings, and works of art was thus not merely the task of museologists and antiquarians. It was seen as the responsibility of every citizen who draws his sustenance, spiritual as well as economic, from the city.

With each city, of course, the problem varied. The old center of Rotterdam, completely leveled by high explosives, has been completely rebuilt along modern lines. London, heavily but spottily damaged by fire and blast, has tended to erect new buildings among the old within an essentially undisturbed street pattern. Coventry has entirely replaced its fire-swept business district with a remarkable new traffic-free commercial center. And instead of rebuilding its gutted cathedral, it has made the empty shell into a walled garden and built a splendid modern church along the axis of the transepts.

19.5 *Warsaw's return to life after World War II* required curatorial intervention at every level: preservation, consolidation, restoration, reconstruction. Wartime damage was so extensive (some 88 percent of the building stock was uninhabitable at war's end) that removal of rubble alone constituted an immense logistical problem (*1, 3*). With few buildings intact and most in ruins, site clearance had to precede new construction; and site clearance, in turn,

had to be accompanied by salvage archaeology. As a result of long and sometimes heated discussions, the decision had been made to return the historic center of the city to something of its prewar physiognomy. Old street patterns would be preserved; prewar building masses and street profiles would be reestablished; historically and artistically significant buildings such as the palaces along Nowy Świat Street would be restored to their original appearance (2).

3

4

Leningrad has restored the rococo palaces along the Neva to their nine-teenth-century splendor. Of prewar Hiroshima, nothing remains but a twisted steel skeleton at "point zero" of the world's first atomic attack.

The special character of Poland's program for the reconstruction of its artistic and historic monuments derives from the special circumstances of its history, particularly the period of the Nazi occupation from 1939 to 1945. Many of its greatest cities, including Warsaw and Gdańsk (Danzig), and many of its villages were all but destroyed, their art looted, and their historic buildings burned. Of course, other countries in Europe, including Germany herself, also endured great destruction. But no European city saw such coldly calculated demolition as Warsaw. It was the subject of four overwhelming attacks: first, in September 1939; then in the Battle of the Ghetto in 1943; again, in the Warsaw Uprising in 1944; and finally, in the Battle of Liberation of 1945. The naval and aerial bombardments of Gdańsk destroyed some 75 percent of the medieval center of that great Hanseatic seaport, and laid waste one of the largest concentrations of late-gothic buildings in existence. Hence, the postwar problem in Poland has more often been reconstruction than mere preservation or restoration.

The question of how these cities were to be rebuilt was the subject of long and intensive discussion among Polish architects and town planners. Warsaw presented an especially complicated problem, psychologically as well as physically. As the historic capital of Poland and the center of Polish resistance, Hitler had ordered (in a famous telegram which now hangs in the Historical Museum) that it be leveled to the ground like Carthage and replaced by a small garrison town (the plan of which also hangs in the museum). The Poles felt that this barbarous act left them no possible choice but to reconstruct at least the Stare Miasto, the medieval walled center of the city, as it had been before the war. One cannot help feeling that they acted correctly: certainly, today, even members of the Polish architectural avant-garde who opposed the reconstruction at the time are agreed that the decision was correct.

The reconstruction of these historic areas is substantially complete. Elsewhere, in towns and villages which escaped destruction, the conservation of isolated buildings and complexes goes on apace. Here the problem is the more conventional one of preservation or restoration. The ancient city of Krakow, for example, escaped with little damage heavier than rifle fire. (The Nazis had systematically mined and wired it for demolition, but a lightning encirclement by Russian troops foiled this act of vandalism.) As a result, an artistic and historic treasure trove remains intact. Like many provincial centers in the old Austro-Hungarian Empire, Krakow saw little development during the eighteenth and nineteenth centuries. There were few of the urbanistic improvements that marked Vienna: long stretches of Krakow's medieval fortifications, for example, still encircle the city. As a result, there are whole areas of the old center that offer a comparatively

19.6. *The Stare Miasto—1,000-year-old center of Warsaw*—was the center of Polish resistance during World War II and therefore the special object of Nazi wrath. Today the Municipal Museum has on display two significant documents: a telegram from Hitler ordering that it be leveled to the ground (as the Romans did Carthage); and a set of plans by the German army for replacing it with a small fortified military base (like a Roman *castrum*). The decision to rebuild the Stare Miasto was thus as much ideological as architectural or urbanistic. Destruction was so complete in Zamkowy Square (*1*) that not a single habitable building remained. Thus the restored square, today, is the end result of a long and complex program of restoration. Interestingly enough, this quarter, with its medieval texture of narrow streets and densely built-up precincts, is one of the city's most popular. Like many ancient Hanseatic towns, it is a more sophisticated response to the Baltic climate (short cool summers, long cold winters) than the new districts.

379

1

2

19.7 Gdańsk once possessed one of the Baltic's largest and finest concentrations of late-gothic brick architecture. This urban fabric was savagely mauled during World War II. As in War-saw and most other Polish cities, the decision was made to restore the historic core and build a ring of new microcommunities around the periphery. Thus the great central square has been completely restored with its soaring brick town hall and multicolored burghers' town houses (*1,2*). The Cathedral of St. Mary had stood in a densely built-up precinct of gothic houses. Both were gutted by fire (*3,4*); both have been either restored (*5*) or replaced by abstract versions of the historic originals (right, *5*). The precincts around the cathedral have been completely rebuilt so that views of the church like that in (*5*) are no longer possible. Thus today the historic core of Gdańsk presents a (somewhat idealized) image of its appear-ance in the 1500s and 1600s.

undisturbed chronology of styles, from romanesque to late-eighteenth-century rococo.

The care of all artistic and historic monuments in Poland is entrusted to the Ministry of Culture and Art. In this ministry there is a department which has jurisdiction over all museums and monuments. National programs and criteria for preservation work have been established by this central body, which has also drawn up an inventory of all such monuments and a schedule for undertaking rebuilding or repair. But the actual work is handled by regional offices.

Once a building has been declared a national monument, it cannot be altered by the owners without the permission of the national office. This, of course, is standard procedure in most countries where such agencies exist, as in France and Italy. But a peculiarity of Polish preservation work is that a building cannot be restored or reconstructed until a "client" is found to use it. Such a client may be a municipal agency, a school or museum, a national corporation, or a housing cooperative. An empty building in urgent need of physical repairs will be made weatherproof without having a client, but the interior will not be rebuilt or remodeled without one. However, national monuments in private ownership that are in urgent need of attention may be restored with government funds if the owners cannot afford to do it themselves. Many churches have been restored in this fashion.

Actually, no habitable building goes long untenanted. It is difficult for a westerner to visualize how precious enclosed space still is in a country like Poland. On the one hand, it lost millions of square feet of buildings in the course of six years of occupation and war. On the other, housing needs have increased enormously, as has the need for factory and office space. Because of such absolute scarcity, the restoration and reconstruction of old buildings become much more feasible, economically, than they otherwise might be.

This policy leads to a certain amount of adaptation and alteration of historic buildings, which might disturb the purist from the west. For example, the interiors of buildings which are located in old districts, but which have, themselves, no prime importance either artistically or historically, are rebuilt along modern lines. The Poles point out that they would not want a landscape full of museums (like so many of the National Trust houses in Britain) even if they could afford them. Their policy, they claim, has the virtue of introducing life and movement into districts which might otherwise be dead. One has only to visit the Independence Hall district of Philadelphia, or the Mall in Washington, after dark to see the validity of their thesis.

In Polish architectural circles, one hears many complaints about the low level of craftsmanship in the building industry. And it is very obvious, even to the visitor, that the workmanship in *new* construction leaves much to be desired. Be that as it may, there is little evidence of poor workmanship in Polish *preservation* work. Here, the quality ranges from good to superlative. This may be partly because, in nationally significant edifices like St. John's Cathedral or the Wilanów Palace, the government was willing to concentrate funds and people on the project. This was clearly the case in the rehabilitation of the National Opera House in Warsaw. An enormous enlargement of an old neoclassic building of the early nineteenth century, it will be not only the most complete opera plant in the world, but also one of the best built.

But another reason for the generally high level of preservation work is the fact that it involves workers in many old-time luxury crafts which are no longer in demand in modern architecture: workers in marble, iron, and ornamental plaster; craftsmen in stained glass, and in wood and stone carving; gilders and painters. Since these skilled craftsmen are usually older men, few of them have been absorbed into the new industries. As in other Communist countries, such men have been sought out, organized into cooperative ateliers, and given jobs that derive from the preservation program.

Whatever the explanation, the restoration of such buildings as the Lazienki and Wilanów palaces in Warsaw is technically immaculate and visually dazzling. In them, the Polish experts faced a characteristic spectrum of problems. The Lazienki, small and all of a piece, was gutted by Nazi demolition squads. Built by King Stanislas II Augustus in the last quarter of the eighteenth century, this elegant little rococo building stood in a downtown park and had long been open to the public. Hence it was possible and proper to restore it to its original state. That state was scintillating. Although designed by an Italian, Merlini, in the French manner, it bears the unmistakable brio and elegance of Polish taste. The architecture itself is fairly sober, but in the decoration—in the chocolate rocaille bathroom, the blue and white delft tile boudoir, the pink and green marbelized rotunda, and the grotesque sculptures of the ballroom—one sees the wit and exuberance that marks the Pole.

The Wilanów Palace is a great château begun in 1677 and continuously lived in, altered, and redecorated until World War II. Deterioration of the physical fabric was due more to poor construction and simple neglect than to wartime damage. Since Wilanów had been designated as a museum of interior design and the decorative arts, the decision was very wisely made to restore different rooms or suites of rooms to different styles or periods. This has not always been easy, for it offers an embarrassment of riches: even minor rooms turn out to have several layers of frescoes, each of which is interesting historically if not artistically. The experts' problem is to decide at which layer to halt.

And, like many seventeenth- and eighteenth-century palaces, including Versailles itself, Wilanów turns out to have been very shoddily built. The

1

2

3

19.8 *Adaptive use was often the only way* in which the Poles could justify the enormous expenditure required for the restoration of their very large stock of monumental buildings. They have shown great ingenuity in inserting a variety of new institutions into old vessels. One of the principal beneficiaries of this policy has been the national museum system. Thus a large late-gothic, brick-built monastery in downtown Gdańsk has been modified to house the Pomorski Museum with its internationally significant collection of gothic painting and sculpture (*1,2,3*). In Warsaw, the Lazienki Palace has been restored as a museum of baroque and rococo decorative arts. (*4,5*). Extensive conservation was required in both buildings. In the Pomorski, only simple neglect had to be corrected. But the Lazienki had been systematically vandalized, and its furnishings stolen, by retreating German armies. Illustrative of this damage was the postwar condition of a little dressing room (*4*); and illustrative of the expertise of Polish conservators is the little rococo room in restored state (*5*).

4

5

restorers found startling structural weaknesses from foundations to attics; the whole fabric has had to be reinforced with new members in steel, concrete, or wood as circumstances required.

The museum offers a fascinating picture of almost three centuries of the domestic life of the Polish aristocracy. It is surprising, in this connection, to find the communist countries lavishing so much attention—and all of it sympathetic—upon the re-creation of the homes of the old aristocracy. The results are misleadingly amiable. For to display these old palaces without all the squalid dependencies upon which they rested is to present as incomplete a picture of serfdom as do our bowdlerized restorations at Mount Vernon and Monticello, where the odious facts of slavery have been virtually expunged from the picture. However, to give a more balanced picture of peasant life in the old days, several outdoor museums of the Skansen type are under construction. The traditional houses, mills, barns, and chapels of the region will be assembled in a park, to give a picture of the life of the common people. There are also in preparation several so-called museums of work where various industries, such as the ancient salt mines of Silesia, will be re-created. (In addition, it should be pointed out that a vast program for the protection of the traditional arts and crafts of the common people is under way. One of the world's greatest libraries of folk music has been created in Warsaw, a network of regional ethnographic museums has been established to display all the folk arts of each region, and a broad program for the regeneration of the crafts and the integration of the craftsperson into modern life is being carried out.)

Most Polish conservators follow the accepted international practice of insisting that a clear and visible distinction must always be maintained between original and new tissue in the fabric of a restored building. One outstanding exception is the fourteenth-century Collegium Maius in Krakow, which now houses a new university museum. Although the restorer, Dr. Karol Estreicher, insists that he disapproves of Viollet-le-Duc, a detached observer can scarcely fail to see certain resemblances between the work of the two men.

Dr. Estreicher thinks that distinctions between old and new tissue are of interest only to experts, and that such information is much better preserved in the archives than in the building itself; he believes that the restorer should use all his talent to create a convincing picture of the selected period. It must be admitted that the half-finished restoration of Collegium Maius offers persuasive support for his argument. The completed galleries afford an ingratiating background for the university collection of paintings, objets d'art, and furniture. Since the collegium had been gutted by fire during World War II, he had nothing but an empty roofless shell to work with. And since the building was to be rebuilt as a museum (it had previously been used for classes), certain liberties had to be taken. The restorer's approach in this case may be defensible, but as a general policy for conservation it is clearly hazardous—one that is certain to cause trouble for future conservators and curators.

But the aspect of Polish conservation work which is at once the most impressive and the most controversial is the *reconstruction* of vanished buildings. In Warsaw the whole of the medieval center has been rebuilt in facsimile, as has the mile-long stretch of Krakowskie Przedmiescie and Nowy Swiat that runs along the bluffs above the Vistula River. In Gdańsk one of the three medieval enclaves has been reproduced in this way, including many of the old port buildings, the City Hall, the Cathedral of St. Mary, and numerous gothic monuments which lie outside this area. These reconstructions have been the subject of many polemics, abroad as well as inside Poland. Generally speaking, the younger architects, artists, and intelligentsia have been opposed. Even the architect who was in charge of the Stare Miasto reconstruction confesses that he had private reservations about it at the time.

Events have fully confirmed the validity of the policy. The reasons for its success, however, are not primarily aesthetic: they are political, patriotic, and emotional. Observers from the west must see the documentary evidence—photographs and films, many of them prepared by the Germans themselves—to have any comprehension of conditions in Warsaw immediately before and after liberation. The city had been reduced to a lunar wasteland. The destruction involved not only buildings, streets, and utilities but all cultural artifacts: even monuments of national heroes like Copernicus, Chopin, the nineteenth-century poet Mickiewicz, and Poniatowski, Napoleon's general, had been destroyed. In a very real sense, such political destruction left only one political response: complete restoration. Above and beyond that, in the first years after the war, living under conditions of incredible hardship, the people of Warsaw needed psychological security as much as physical shelter. The restoration of familiar streetscapes and beloved landmarks was thus a matter of fundamental importance to the restoration of the life of the city.

Even today, with the city largely rebuilt and tens of thousands of new apartments in new neighborhoods on both banks of the Vistula, the Stare Miasto is a favorite neighborhood for artists and professional people. It has the most active nightlife in the capital. Aside from historic associations, the narrow, picturesque old streets and cozy little squares of the quarter apparently afford a more hospitable setting for street life than the spacious avenues and extensive parks of the new city.

In Gdańsk, the reasons for restoring the old quarters were perhaps more archaeological than ideological. The city never had a significance in Polish history comparable to Warsaw's, and its destruction was almost incidental to military logistics. As an important seaport, it was a target for air attack, and much of the destruction came from allied bombs. On the other hand, the great churches, burghers' houses, guildhalls, and warehouses, done in the fantastic brick gothic idiom of the Hanseatic League, were perhaps more significant architecturally than anything in Warsaw. So here again, the decision was made to reconstruct at least part of the city in facsimile. In both cities, these facsimile reconstructions are largely exterior. The main intent is to restore the streetscape. Except for monumental public buildings, the interiors have been replanned and rebuilt along quite modern lines, with all modern amenities, including district heating. (Both of these cities have giant thermoelectric plants that furnish heat, light, and power to the entire town. An admirable system which all but eliminates the heavy coal smoke that is the curse of northern Europe. Ultimately it will be used in all Polish towns.)

Of course, the greater part of both cities has been rebuilt along contemporary town-planning principles, with wide streets, lavish park and green spaces, modern boulevard and highway systems, zoned land use, and so on. But in such brand-new cityscapes, handsome as they often are, isolated old buildings of no special artistic merit achieve great visual and emotional significance. Such landmarks help visitors in orienting themselves; to the natives, they are cherished mementos. In Warsaw, for example, a lightly damaged (and mediocre) rococo church was bodily moved some 50 yards to make way for the widening of a street. And a battle-scarred fragment of the Unknown Soldier's Tomb, of no intrinsic merit in itself, has been carefully worked into a landscaped park.

In the restoration or reconstruction of historic buildings, the Polish conservationists, like such experts everywhere, often face the necessity of deciding to what stage of its history a given structure should be "returned." In the case of Warsaw's eighteenth-century Church of the Sisters of the Holy Sacrament, which had been built as a unit and never subsequently altered, reconstruction posed no problems. But sometimes, in old and complex structures, the decisions are surprising. For example, in Warsaw's St. John's Cathedral, the flamboyant gothic facade (late, but wonderfully picturesque) was not reconstructed: instead, a much earlier and more severe stepped gable was re-created. When it comes to making such decisions, the Poles seem always to have extensive documentation at hand. And this is all the more remarkable in view of the ravaged museums, libraries, and archives of World War II. In Warsaw proper, architectural students at the polytechnic had for years been required to make measured drawings of old buildings in the Stare Miasto; these largely survived. This type of work was carried on, all during the Nazi occupation, by the Underground University, which also laid the basic outlines of the new plan of Warsaw. Among the most useful documents in the reconstruction of Warsaw (as also in Dresden) were the paintings of Bernardo Belotto, who worked in Warsaw in the

19.9. *The decision to conserve* these sixteenth-century mural paintings in the Polish cathedral at Oliwa was based on several considerations. They are a very rare art form for the Baltic area; they are artistically important features of the apse of the church; and they celebrate some of Poland's earliest kings. The church itself had been unroofed by German fire bombs in World War II, exposing the murals to the weather. Ironically, when the conservators started to work on the murals, they found they had been overpainted to represent the Teutonic Knights, leaders of that earlier German invasion of Poland!

1760s–1770s. His views of various sites have proved so accurate that they are used by conservationists as guides to vanished monuments (Fig. 13.10).

The work of restoring Poland's historic monuments is today, largely complete. And the visitor from the west can only marvel at the scope of this work and praise it for its uniformly high quality. A past so cherished will offer valuable guidelines to future action, not only in Poland but elsewhere in the world.

20

Preservation in the Third-World Countries: The Case of Africa

There is little time for the present in Africa and none at all for its past. Everywhere in the new African states, one meets historians, economists, dancers, town planners, ethnographers, and engineers whose daily assignment it is to move from a primitive-preliterate-colonial past into an industrialized future—and to do it directly, with no intermediate present. Often, the new African societies literally cannot afford the contemporaneous, common-sense way of doing things. They are, for instance, leaping directly from bush trail and dugout canoe to jet planes. This reliance on airplanes is leading to a "point civilization" that poses a serious threat to a balanced and rational development of the continent. African planners are well aware of this danger, but often the conditions of African life permit no alternative.

There are young African historians who hold the first university chairs of national history in their nation's history. They are expected to teach the history of their countries. But there are no written histories or textbooks and there is no literature. In some of the new countries, the written record begins in the nineteenth century. Prehistory in Kenya, for example, means before 1890! These young scholars, trained in historiography in western universities, are therefore compelled to write the histories of their respective fields at the same time that they teach them. On weekends and vacations, they head for the bush with camera, notebook, and tape recorder. There, in villages, they interview the village historians—elderly keepers of the oral tradition who are almost certainly the last generation of their species. The knowledge they hold, not only of the remote past but also of the recent past, is priceless. (In a society without written records, these men are the depositories of the genealogies of local kings, of the metes and bounds of tribal lands, of the proper ritual for community celebrations.) The oral histories are often astonishingly long—in Uganda, they encompass the reigns of more than 30 kings—and they are rich in significant detail for the social

391

historian. But they are completely encapsulated. Their chronology is local, without a casual cross-reference to external cultures. Only an occasional reference to eclipse or earthquake offers some chance of calibrating the local sequence of events with those of the world outside.

Nevertheless. the African historians hope to push the written record back at least to the opening of the sixteenth century by using these oral traditions. It will require a staggering amount of work on their part. Hundreds, even thousands, of village historians must be interviewed. The tapes must be transcribed, then translated from the dialect into French or English, the two languages of scholarship in sub-Saharan Africa. Only then can these local histories be interpreted, analyzed, and recast in modern form. The capstone of this colossal task of compiling a history of all Africa which will be comparable in scope and accuracy to western historiography will probably be the Encyclopedia Africana. This project was begun under the editorship of the late, great Afro-American W. E. B. Dubois.

The problem is also difficult for historians and preservationists of art and architecture. The durability of the art forms of the African past depends on the material out of which they are fabricated and the climate in which they occur. The mud architecture of the dry Saharan regions lasts almost indefinitely; a peasant's hut may collect the dust of centuries. And fragile funeral wreaths of herbs and flowers survive in Egyptian tombs for millennia. But in equatorial Africa, heat, humidity, bacteria, and insects combine to limit the life of all organic materials—e.g., wood, fabric, and leather—to a few decades. Thus even monumental architecture and sculpture are tragically short-lived. How great is the loss caused by this equatorial attrition can be clearly seen in the magnificent fragments which survive in the museums of Ghana, Nigeria, and Uganda. From the great bronze-encrusted doors and portrait sculpture of Benin and Ife we get a glimpse of a splendid plastic tradition. But these metal masterpieces constitute only rare landmarks in the vast terra incognita of African art. The voids in between must be filled in by patient research on the part of historian, archaeologist, and ethnographer—an immense task that is scarcely under way. And here, as in social historiography, isolation from the main world currents imposes certain limitations. Because of them, the African art histories are apt to be more typological than chronological.

In architecture, the problem is somewhat easier. Because of the climate, the Saharan mud architecture and the wood and stone architecture of the Ethiopian highlands survive fairly well. And this is very fortunate, for these areas afford some of the most beautiful as well as the most functional folk architectures of the world. Equatorial Africa also abounds in an astonishing and beautiful variety of architectural forms, but they are highly transient. Even the great royal tombs of Uganda are built entirely of straw (including the arch ribs which support the thatched roofs) and must be reconstructed every 20 years.

Since this vegetable-fiber architecture is so well adapted to the tropical climate, and since the raw materials are cheap and plentiful, one would expect to find a great demand in present-day Africa for modern chemicals that would render these fibers resistant to flame, rot, and vermin. But it is a typical third-world paradox that, instead, thatch is everywhere being replaced by corrugated metal. Made of either galvanized steel or (increasingly) aluminum, these shiny new roofs wink up at one's plane all across the continent. Expensive, ugly, and hellishly hot, they nevertheless have the prestige of modernity. They are longer-lived and more trouble-free than the traditional thatch, and they mark the owner as up-to-date. Thus do climate and technology, either singly or in combination, work to obliterate the wonderful folk architecture of Africa.

This high mortality rate of the artifacts of material culture is one reason for the visual poverty of the average village. To casual visitors from the west there is a startling lack of that magnificent religious and funerary art which they have seen in the museums. Even the simplest tools, utensils, and furniture of daily life seem nonexistent. But the ethnographer will explain that appearances are somewhat deceptive here, and that the lack of visual art forms is more than made up for by a wealth of poetry, song, and dance. Normally inaccessible to the outsider, these are the chief vehicle of African creativity.

But these "invisible" forms of art are not immune to civilization, either, and will require protection if they are to survive. Radio penetrates everywhere. Cheap tabloids follow literacy. The shoddiest of all movies (mostly American, alas) dominate the motion picture screens of the towns. Patriotic Africans are much disturbed by this cultural erosion. In both Nigeria and Ghana, one hears concern expressed about the vulgarizing impact of Afro-American jazz upon indigenous music.

The poets and novelists face another sort of problem. Generally speaking, they aspire to write on African themes for a mass African audience. But that audience scarcely exists as yet: the illiterate herders and peasants are still the captives of the oral tradition. Hence the paradoxical situation in which African writing is better known in Paris or London than in the author's own country. This creates an ambivalence of which the writers are uncomfortably aware. They are confident that a pan-African audience will sooner or later emerge; meanwhile, they have to act as though it already existed.

With independence, the people of dozens of African states have stepped through the looking glass. Issues which were literally matters of life and death before liberation seem now to have evaporated. Even in Algeria and Kenya, where the battle for independence assumed murderous dimensions, one hears little talk of those days and sees little evidence of them. In Nairobi, where only a few years ago the white planters wore side arms in the main streets and the natives were herded into "protective" villages, the visitor today sees both sides placidly riding the same buses, drinking in the same bars, attending the same schools. The traumatic experiences of the past undoubtedly left wounds, but these appear to be healing with astonishing rapidity. Instead, a whole new range of problems now become apparent. Having won that so-desired future, the new countries suddenly discover an unexpected importance in the past. As long as they were colonial pawns, the prestige of western culture held unchallenged ascendancy. In the colonialist capitals, the small African elite modeled its life after western prototypes (importing canned American goods, for instance, or performing Noël Coward comedies in their amateur theatricals). But with independence, a profound shift in taste and life-styles has set in. All over Africa today, new idioms in dress, decor, cuisine, and protocol are being evolved before one's eyes.

Their past confronts Africans with all sorts of challenges. The reevaluation of their own folklore was inevitable, since it represents a resource of both cultural and economic value. But its exploitation and development is fraught with great danger for both folk art and folk artist, as many Africans are well aware. Ethnographers, art historians, and museum curators are exploiting this field for the loftiest reasons. But folklore is also a valuable tourist asset (along with scenery and wild animals) because it attracts hard currency to the unbalanced economies of the new countries. How to make use of it without corrupting it is a delicate problem in cultural engineering and one for which there is not much precedent. The commercialization of traditional sculpture is already far advanced. At every airport and every big hotel, a curio shop sells inept mass-produced imitations of the masks, idols, and totems of the various tribes. And the European sections of the big cities are crisscrossed with peddlers of "antique" sculptures (occasionally really antique), some of them from half a continent away. No one seems to know exactly how this trade developed. It obviously shows the presence of alert entrepreneurs (white and black) responding on a local level to a new tourist demand for curios. And it obviously poses a clear threat to the survival of one of the richest and most varied plastic idioms on earth. This type of commercial degradation of native traditions is the most apparent, but it is merely symptomatic of the general impact of modern industrial society upon all form of preindustrial art and artisanship. Even under the best circumstances, the results can be unfortunate.

All serious observers realize that the local governments must intervene if all these forms of folk art are to be saved from the certain annihilation which otherwise awaits them. At the same time, it is difficult for these new countries, beset by so many more urgent problems, to give effectual help. Even in the remotest bush, the economic base of the village artist-artisan is being radically altered. With the decline of paganism and the spread of secular culture, the demand for ritual and funerary art declines. Traditionally, all this art was commissioned piece by piece, and the identity of the artist was usually well known. Robbed of patronage, the artist becomes a simple craftsperson. Wood carvers become carpenters or cabinetmakers. Metal-workers become blacksmiths. And the decay of the idiom proceeds at an accelerated pace. Thus, all folklore, traditional arts and crafts, and historic architecture are in a perilous state.

Actually, three interrelated but separate cultural tasks are involved here: (1) preservation of the artist-artisan; (2) preservation of the craft or metier; and (3) preservation, physically, of examples of traditional forms of the art. The ethnographic museum is the proper vehicle for the last. Craft schools and apprenticeship training programs can accomplish the second. But only a comprehensive program for state-subsidized and protected workshops and retail outlets can save the craftsperson and attract a new generation. Without help, handicraft production cannot be expected to survive the naked competition of modern mass production. But as far as the author knows, no African state has yet been able to launch such a program.

Many African universities now have advanced institutes for national studies and are carrying on impressive work in music, literature, history, and the visual arts. At the universities of Ife and Ibadan in Nigeria, a group of devoted scholars are working directly with folk artists in the villages, subsidizing their work and displaying and selling it in the cities. Here, too, are the *mbari* (literally, "creation") clubs, aimed at establishing centers of artistic activity in the rapidly growing towns. New trade and craft schools are springing up everywhere.

The attitude of the young western-trained professional artist toward all this cannot be other than complex. As one teacher on a Ghanaian art faculty has put it, "In speaking of a contemporary art in Africa, distinction must be made between 'contemporary art in Africa,' 'contemporary African art,' and 'art in contemporary Africa.'" Thus, in the galleries and museums of the African capitals, as well as in the homes and conversations of the intelligentsia, modern European painting and sculpture enjoy much the same prestige as in Paris or Milan. The abstract expressionist school of New York is well known in the art schools and studios of Uganda and Ethiopia. Returning home from years of subsidized study in the schools and studios of Europe and America, the African artist feels impelled to teach western theories and techniques. Hence, professional work in the galleries and student work in the art schools often seem very familiar to the visitor from the west.

Fortunately, there is another side to the picture, for the pressure of African reality is very evident in the subject matter, if not the style, of much contemporary African painting and sculpture. In the new monumental architecture of government buildings, museums, and universities the demand is for an art that deals in intelligible terms with African experience. Naturally, individual response to this demand varies widely. One can meet an impassioned young Ugandan painter who believed that the development of a national artistic idiom was a patriotic duty and a prosperous Ethiopian artist whose work, which ranged from society portraits to stained glass for Coptic churches, would have found a ready market in Manchester, England, or Kansas City. The issue is anything but resolved.

The posture of young architects or city planners is much the same. In Europe and America, they have seen in operation those technological processes which promise escape from the hunger, disease, and squalor that characterize the existence of so many of their countrypeople. Very often the landscapes of their childhood, whether jungle life or urban slum, have become the hated symbol of life under colonial rule. Hence their receptiveness to our criteria of modern architecture and urbanism: for these young people, they have come to symbolize physical comfort, security, cleanliness, abundance. The unfortunate fact that American cities so seldom, or so unevenly, accomplish all this often escapes them. The glass-skinned skyscraper and shadeless street, the outward-looking house and open lawn, the wasteful automobile and sprawling suburb: all these are imported carte blanche.

The power of modern industrial technology is so great that, in purely formal terms, these African facsimiles can be quite as well built as their western prototypes. But operationally, the results are often quite grotesque. Thus one sees cities of half a million where traffic jams are caused by the private cars of a minuscule elite and fantastically long queues wait for a few decrepit busses. Picture windows confront shadeless deserts. Air conditioners go mad in glass-walled skyscrapers in the Nigerian rain forests. Everywhere, one sees heat-holding pavement instead of heat-deflecting foliage, open space where common sense dictates cover, transparency where opacity is the first requirement of comfort.

It is precisely the task of the young African architect to avoid this mistake—to isolate the good from the bad, and the obsolete from what is still viable in his tradition. One hears the "open plan" and transparent wall of modern architecture praised by young intellectuals in this part of the world because, for them, it symbolized the liberation of the Moslem family from the crippling confinement of harem, purdah, and feudal relations generally. The fact that the desert sun, dust, and searing winds beat in through these newly opened walls did not disturb them. It was, they insisted, a small price to pay for the new social perspectives opened up.

But it must be perfectly clear to the outside observer that, in order for the new African architecture and urbanism to accomplish its minimum objectives, it must return to an attentive examination of its precolonial origins. Two factors make this inevitable. On the one hand, even under the most favorable economic and technical conditions imaginable, it will be decades before Africa will have achieved the technological basis for western architecture. And long before this is achieved, it will have become apparent that the western prototype, whether in individual buildings or in whole cities, is ill adapted to Saharan or equatorial Africa. The profoundly anti-popular, antifunctional character of the new African cities is already sufficient proof of this.

Nationalism always carries the germ of xenophobia. But this danger, in the field of art and culture at least, does not seem to me very great in Africa today. Most young African intellectuals and artists have been trained in western centers and have returned from this experience with a viewpoint of artistic and cultural possibilities that, if anything, is too cosmopolitan rather than too parochial. At the same time, their newfound national consciousness and patriotism leads them to a growing interest in precolonial folklore of their own cultures. Under the circumstances of rapid industrialization, this new "artistic patriotism" seems to me to serve a useful function. At the very least, it interposes some barriers to the ruthless demolition of all preindustrial monuments and arts and crafts. At the best, it could result in an integration of primitive and postindustrial aesthetics to create new artistic idioms of unique value and worldwide significance.

The two tendencies—a fascination with the whole apparatus of western technology and a growing understanding of the significance of their own past—create an ambivalent situation. The result is that western and African modes of expression—in costume and cuisine, architecture and art, music and dance—coexist and compete. It would be hazardous indeed for an outsider to predict the outcome of this complex situation.

Only modern knowledge, modern science, modern technology, can give Africa the abundance and well-being it desires. But these forces can never be more than fertilizing agents and catalysts, acting on African resources, human and material. The African's greatest single resource for building their artistic and cultural future is their own indigenous past.

21

Preservation in Tomorrow's World

It is safe to assume that every independent nation in the world today is committed, at least in principle, to the theory that the protection of the national artistic and historic heritage is a responsibility of the state.* The extent to which this commitment is discharged varies so widely from one nation to another that no summary is possible. In most countries, legislation does exist at the national level; but this legislation varies so widely in scope, funding, and enforcement as to defy any but the loosest generalization. Typically, such legislation is modeled after the French precedent which, as early as 1834, had established the national institution now called Le Services des Monuments Historiques. In most countries, again following the French precedent, similar institutions will ordinarily be under the jurisdiction of one of the Ministries, usually Cultural Affairs or Education.

All these agencies operate under legislation which establishes their jurisdiction, powers, funding, and organizational structure. Here again French precedent is dominant, especially the concept that such an agency will also have jurisdiction over the national system of museums and archaeological sites. The concept is entirely logical since the heritage *in toto* consists of artifacts which differ principally in size and environmental context. As might be expected, exceptions to this highly centralized administrative set-up occur in nations with a federated political structure—notably, the United States, Great Britain, the Federal German Republic, and the U.S.S.R. In countries of this latter political structure, separate legislation

*This author has no first-hand experience with preservation in the Middle East, China, or the Indian subcontinent. Moreover, the specialized literature on the art, architecture, and archaeology of these vast regions of the world is very inadequately represented in even the largest libraries of the West. And even when some of this literature is found, much of it has not been translated from its original language. The closest approach today to a truly international source of information on the current status of preservation in a given country would probably be found at UNESCO in Paris. In Paris also, ICOMOS has recently established a Documentation Center. Ultimately, its up-to-date records will be computerized for quick retrieval.

and agencies may coexist at national, regional, and municipal levels. There may also be a mix of public and private agencies at work (as in Great Britain and the United States), with overlapping and/or conflicting powers and jurisdictions.

The powers and funding of these agencies also vary enormously from nation to nation. In the socialist countries, where private ownership of land has been eliminated or greatly restricted in extent, control of many of the most important monuments and sites is already vested in the nation. This greatly simplifies their curatorial management (e.g., the reconstruction of Warsaw and Leningrad after World War II). It is also true, as we have seen, that preservation activities are generously funded in many socialist nations.

Among nonsocialist countries, the power of national preservation agencies varies widely. In France and Italy, these powers are comprehensive and tend to be more or less continuously broadened. However, funding does not necessarily keep abreast of legal power. For example, the Italian Soperintendenza dei Monumenti has perhaps the most complete control over Italy's artistic and historic heritage of any country in the world. There are whole sections of the nation in which even the smallest alteration to building or landscape must have the approval of the Soperintendenza. Unfortunately, however, this power to control the fate of the privately owned heritage is not matched by corresponding funds to permit either the government or the private owner to make necessary repairs. Grants, loans, and technical assistance to owners of listed monuments are totally inadequate. This often guarantees the ultimate disappearance of such buildings through decay, since the owners either cannot or will not make the investment necessary for their preservation.

It was to break such a tyrannical deadlock that the French government passed the so-called Malraux Laws, which began in 1966. This new legislation created a whole system of grants-in-aid, low-interest loans, tax abatements, rent increases (French rents had generally been frozen at the 1919 level), and technical assistance to enable private owners to rehabilitate listed properties. The consequences of this new policy are seen in every town in France, most dramatically perhaps in Le Marais district in Paris. A similar qui-pro-quo arrangement seems inevitable for any nation which is seriously committed to preserving its cultural heritage, and such a policy is, in fact, being adopted piecemeal in Holland, Great Britain, and the United States.

Only one generalization is possible as to the actual amount of restoration and preservation work going on around the world: nowhere does it reach optimal levels, either quantitatively or qualitatively. It is almost certainly highest in countries which suffered the most severe damage in World War II: England, both Germanies, Italy, Poland, and Russia. However, Czechoslovakia has perhaps the most comprehensive and competent program of any country in the West, even though it suffered scarcely any damage at all in World War II. The preservation movement has flowered spec-

tacularly in the United States in the last decade, changing the whole climate
of public opinion in the process. Nevertheless, our per capita national
expenditure would probably stand at about the level of Ecuador's or
Nepal's.★

Since Greece and Asia Minor are, so to say, the birthplace of modern
archaeology, a vast literature is generally available on their sites and monuments. But perhaps just because of the attention focused on their antiquities, little preservation work has been done on urban centers. (In Athens,
for example, the Plaka is usually regarded as merely a contemporary obstacle to the further excavation of the ancient Agora which lies below it.) This
same emphasis on antiquities is perhaps also the reason why so little preservation work has been done on folk and vernacular architecture generally.

In Central and South America, a somewhat analogous situation
obtains. Most Latin American countries have fairly comprehensive national
legislation, based again on the French tradition. But with the exception of
Mexico, the laws are poorly or not at all enforced and the agencies woefully
underfinanced and understaffed. In all these countries, the cultural heritage
is stratified: there are modern urban centers which tend to destroy everything in the path of their expansion; a wealth of towns and villages dating
from post-Columbian times dispersed across the countryside; and beneath
them all—especially in Mexico, Guatemala, and Peru—the vast pre-
Columbian remains of the great Aztec, Mayan, and Incan civilations.

The restoration and preservation of all these varied riches confronts the
developing nations with problems of enormous complexity. International
cultural tourism has been responsible for what preservation has been
accomplished there. (It is wholly due to tourism that the great sites on the
Yucatan peninsula are being freed of the jungle, with archaeology and
reconstruction of the major monuments being carried on.) But such tourism is here, as elsewhere, a double-edged sword. Not only does it expose
the artifacts to the attrition of honest tourists; it simultaneously exposes
them to the depredations of international art thieves. Although most of
these countries have strict regulations against the unlicensed exportion of
antiquities, a large trade goes on nevertheless.† Unless the rich nations of
the world (and the rich people in those nations) take their responsibility in

★The history of the American preservation movement has been best summarized by
Charles B. Hosmer, Jr., in *Presence of the Past,* New York, Putnam, 1965, which carries the story
up to the establishment of Colonial Williamsburg, and in *Preservation Comes of Age . . . 1926–
1949,* Charlottesville, Univ. Press of Virginia, 1981. The current status of American preservation is most comprehensively covered in *Monumentum,* vol. XIII, 1976, which is the organ of the
International Council of Monuments and Sites in Paris. The specific role of the national
government has been summarized by Robert R. Garvey and Terry Brust Morton in *The United
States Government in Historic Preservation,* Washington, D.C., 1975, pp. 3–37.

★The situation was so serious internationally that the International Council on Museums
and the International Council of Monuments and Sites joined to prepare an international
convention which all nations were urged to join.

this thievery more seriously than they have to date, the trade in stolen art will probably continue unchecked like the opium trade.

CONSERVATION AND CULTURAL SURVIVAL

The situation is perhaps more desperate in the third world. As we have seen in the section on Africa, many factors conspire to make this so. Most countries of the dark continent are just now emerging into nationhood. Aside from economic and political problems of staggering complexity, most of these new countries are the prisoners of a cultural ambiguity. While they may be committed to political independence from the West (and the East too, for that matter), they are also obsessed with the prestige of the new, the modern, the contemporary. They identify their emergence into modern statehood with the adoption of contemporary cosmopolitan life-styles.

This identification of modern technology with improved living conditions, this equating of change with progress, has had the disastrous consequence of casting into opprobrium all traditional practice, all conventional wisdom, and all preindustrial artifacts. Ironically, this devaluation of traditional art and architecture by the indigenous population occurs just at the time when its prestige is at an all-time high among cosmopolitan collectors, connoisseurs, and dealers. Thus the native heritage is subjected to two forms of attrition—neglect and abuse by the local decision makers and rapacious purchase or theft by foreigners. The consequences are appalling, not merely for the local culture but for world culture as a whole.

But the importance to these countries of their traditional architecture and town planning extends far beyond the touristic significance of isolated or discrete monuments of national or international repute. The whole physical fabric of city and village, gardens and farmlands which is the setting for national life is at risk. At an international conference called by the Aga Kahn in Istanbul in 1978, the special aspects of this problem for the Moslem world were discussed. In the summary report—appropriately called *Conservation as Cultural Survival*—the Aga Kahn observes:

> The degree to which modern buildings, constructed by Muslims and primarily for the use of Muslims, should incorporate design disciplines and aesthetic considerations which are specifically Islamic remains unclear. In what way should they, or can they, become intrinsically different from those architectural styles adopted by other societies and other faiths in non-Muslim parts of the world?
>
> I am not speaking here of factors such as climatic conditions, physical environment or the availability of land. Any moderately competent architect would take these limitations into consideration during the design stage of his project. I am looking for something much harder to define. It is an

evocation partly of our faith, partly of our culture, partly of our history and partly of our aspirations. Our history is firmly rooted, our culture evolving and our faith strong and permanent; surely these have an impact on our modern lives and sensibilities. Should they not be reflected in a happy and harmonious way in our buildings, in the different environments which make up the cities, towns and villages of modern Islam?*

THE CULTURAL ROLE OF THE
PRESERVED MONUMENTS

Organized society has always recognized the educational role of historic sites and monuments. Thus, for millennia, we have had shrines, sanctuaries, and points of pilgrimage; battlefields and places of martydom— whose sites where the traditional values of the society were preserved and celebrated. Sometimes the reason was *patriotic:* Tabor, the fortified Utopia of the Hussites; the battlefields of Borodino or Waterloo; the Place de la Bastille in Paris; Independence Hall in Philadelphia. And sometimes the motivation was *literary:* Plutarch's Fountain of the Vaucluse, Shakespeare's birthplace, the tomb of Rousseau.

Contemporary activity in historic preservation has enormously extended the number of monuments in all such categories, and modern cultural tourism has enormously increased the volume of visitors to them. Until the very recent past, however, this vast and growing interest in historic preservation has taken the form of *some* people visiting the habitats of *other* people. Too often, the "native inhabitants" are, on their own terrain, merely passive spectators of the touristic process. The governmental institutions which are so admired internationally for their preservation and restoration activities may discourage or actually exclude participation by the local citizenry. This contradiction accounts for much of the Venetians' discontent with the institutionalized preservation of Venice and for complaints from former inhabitants of the historic quarters of London and Charleston, who find themselves being displaced by the "gentrification" of their habitats.

Institutional response to this phenomenon, in such cities as Bologna and in the Marais district in Paris, is encouraging in the sense that it shows at least a recognition of the problem. Historic preservation has been traditionally characterized as "elitist," but this viewpoint is being modified as wider sections of the population begin to understand the cultural values of their own habitat and to demand a role in the formulation of plans for its preservation. This development should by no means be regarded as unde-

---

*Opening remarks, His Highness The Aga Kahn in *Conservation as Cultural Survival,* Proceedings of Seminar 2, Istanbul, Turkey, 1978, p. XI.

sirable (even if it poses new and not always easy problems for the professional). To the contrary, it presents an unparalleled opportunity to correct some of the sense of alienation which is so characteristic of modern society. It affords the opportunity for the citizens to regain a sense of identity with their own origins of which they have often been robbed by the sheer process of urbanization.

It is apparent that citizens all over the world are beginning to understand this dialectic. This is proved by the spectacular growth of such organizations as the National Trusts of Great Britain and the United States. It is proved in the U.S.A. by the successes of hundreds of local, and often spontaneous, actions to preserve threatened landmarks or historic districts. What this process demonstrates is that *the very struggle to save a bit of their local habitat is itself an important educational experience for citizens.* Their understanding of its importance is deepened by their participation in the act of saving it.

Professional preservationists too often assume that the average citizen becomes interested in a monument only *after* it has been conserved. The facts are quite otherwise, as has been proved by recent campaigns to save two of Great Britain's great cathedrals—those of Coventry and York. The decision to involve the public in the actual process of conservation by keeping the churches open throughout the work was extremely successful. Not only were millions of pounds raised, but the two great monuments were converted into two of the nation's most important pilgrimage sites: millions now visit them annually where only thousands did before.

This is fully confirmed by experience in the United States, where thousands of individual buildings and hundreds of historic districts are now being preserved, restored, and returned to viability. Although national and local institutions are essential to the process, the new and critically important factor is citizen participation. Nowhere is the educational value of historic preservation more apparent than in such activities. For the battle to save the habitat must parallel the battle to save the inhabitants of that habitat. These are, in fact, two complementary aspects of the battle to save the built world.

Notes

Chapter 2

[1] *Geschichte der Kunst des Altertums* was published in Dresden in 1764.

[2] *The Antiquities of Athens* was published in several volumes at London between 1762 and 1787.

[3] Theodore de Bry, a Flemish engraver, bought Le Moyne's watercolors from his widow and published them in Frankfurt in 1591 under the title *Brevis narratio eorum quae in Florida America*.

[4] Part of these drawings were published by De Bry in 1590; so great was the success of the venture that it went through some 17 printings in four languages by 1620.

[5] Osvald Sirén cites two French works as specially influential: *Lettres édifantes et curieuses, écrites des missions étrangères,* first edition in 34 vols., Paris, 1717–1976; and *Memoires concernant l'histoire, les sciences, les arts, les moeurs, les usages, etc., des Chinois. Par les missionaires de Pékin,* first edition in 17 vols., Paris, 1777–1814.

[6] *Description de l'Egypte* was published by the Commission des Monuments de l'Egypte between 1808 and 1830 in some 38 volumes of text and illustrations.

[7] Sir Banister Fletcher's *History of Architecture on the Comparative Method* quite accurately reflected the British Empire's view of the world. First published in 1896, its sixteenth edition (1954) still found it possible to devote 860 of its pages to the "historical styles"—i.e., Egyptian to American—and the remaining 76 to the "nonhistorical styles"—i.e., Chinese, Indian, Japanese, Middle American, and Saracenic! Prehistoric architecture is allotted three pages in this edition, primitive and folk building none at all.

[8] "If we compare the form of the newly invented machine with the perfected type of the same instrument, we observe, as we trace it through the phases of improvement, how weight is shaken off where strength is less needed, how functions are made to approach without impeding each other, how straight becomes curved, and the curve is straightened, till the straggling and cumbersome becomes the compact, effective and beautiful engine." (*Form and Function: Remarks on Art by Horatio Greenough,* Berkeley, 1947, p. 59.) For a more extended treatment of the evolution of Greenough's remarkably prescient theories on functionalist design in the era of modern industrialism, see Fitch, *Architecture and the Esthetics of Plenty,* New York, 1961, pp. 46–64.

[9] *Houses and House—Life of the American Aborigines,* Washington, 1881.

[10](Paris, 1875); published in English the following year under the title *Habitations of Man in All Ages* by Osgood, Boston, 1876.

[11]Even the avant-garde discovery of African Negro art, which shook Paris around 1907 and influenced such painters as Pablo Picasso, was prepared for by the arts-and-crafts and folkloristic movements. So, too, at a later date would be the immense success of Art of the South Seas, an exhibition of preponderantly ethnographic material presented by the Museum of Modern Art in New York City, January–May 1946, and the foundation of New York City's Museum of Primitive Art in 1957.

[12]See Fitch, *American Building; The Historic Forces That Shaped It*, Houghton Mifflin, Boston, 1966, pp. 60–73.

[13]Pausanias, probably a native of Lydia, apparently completed his great travelogue of the Greek world before A.D.180.

[14]See Fitch, "A Funny Thing Happened on our Way to the Eighties," *Journal of the American Institute of Architects*, Washington, Jan. 1980, vol. 4, no. 1, pp. 66–68.

Chapter 3

[1]Harry M. Weese, *Journal of Architectural Education,* vol. 29, no. 4, 1976, p. 15.

[2]Richard G. Stein and Associates and the Center for Advanced Computation, University of Illinois. The study was performed under ERDA Contract No. EY-76-S-02-2791, Washington, D.C., 1976.

[3]Ibid, p. 92.

[4]Richard G. Stein and Partners, Architects, *Proposal in Response to Department of the Interior* RFP 14-01-0001-77-R-25, August 1977.

[5]L. S. Stavrianos, *Promise of the Coming Dark Age,* Freeman and Co., San Francisco, 1976.

[6]E. F. Schumacher, *Small Is Beautiful,* Harper & Row, New York, 1975.

[7]Christopher Alexander et al., *The Oregon Experiment,* Oxford University Press, New York, 1975, pp. 68 ff.

[8]*The Costs of Urban Sprawl,* U.S. Government Printing Office, Washington, D.C., 1976.

[9]*The New York Times,* July 13, 1975, p. 14.

[10]Ibid., p. 25.

Chapter 5

[1]Abel Wolman, "The Metabolism of Cities," *Scientific American,* vol. 213, no. 3, September 1965, p. 180.

[2]Samuel Rosen et al., "Presbycusis Study of a Relatively Noise-Free Population in the Sudan," *Annals of Otology, Rhinology and Laryngology,* vol. 71, no. 3, 1965, pp. 732–733.

[3]The complexity of central-city functions and the dangers of oversimplified solutions to them have been the source of increasing interest to many observers. Jane Jacobs has dealt at length with some aspects of the problem in two books, *The Death*

and Life of Great American Cities, New York, 1959, and The Economy of Cities, New York, 1969. Louis Winnick, the economic historian, has described the city as man's greatest invention—a labor-saving device for helping man to overcome his two great limitations: "the friction of distance" and "the affliction of uncertainty." The city, he points out, overcomes these by affording economic man three advantages: *proximity* to goods and services; *predictability* of supply due to duplication; and *option*, i.e., a range of choice within a given category. Winnick, "The Economic Functions of the City, Yesterday and Tomorrow" in *Urban Problems,* Columbia University, Academy of Political Science, New York, 1960.

[4] *Urban Conservation in Europe and America: Planning, Conflict and Participation in the Inner City,* published jointly by the American Academy in Rome and the Istituto di Urbanistica, University di Roma, 1977, pp. 15–16.

[5] The methodology employed at Split is outlined by Tomislav Marasovic in *Urban Conservation in Europe and America,* pp. 65–85.

[6] P. L. Cervellati and R. Scannavini, eds., *Bologna: politica e metodologia del restauro nei centri storici,* Bologna Società editrice II Mulino, 1973.

[7] Thomas R. Angotti and Bruce S. Dale, "Bologna, Italy: Urban Socialism in Western Europe," *Social Policy,* May–June 1976, pp. 1–7.

[8] "Resolution of July 11, 1969, at Second International Conference, Oxford, England," International Council of Monuments and Sites, Palais de Chaillot, Place du Trocadero, Paris, 1969.

[9] *Decisions and Resolutions,* International Congress of Architects and Technicians of Historic Monuments, Venice, May 31, 1964, Document no. 1, pp. 4 ff.

Chapter 6

[1] Actually, this building was destroyed by fire in 1747 and replaced with a later one. But long research revealed that there was little archival material on the second building, while there was massive data on the first. *Official Guidebook of Colonial Williamsburg,* Dietz Printing Company, Williamsburg, 1951, p. 20.

[2] According to Marcus Whiffen, the fortunate researcher was Mary Goodwin: *The Public Buildings of Williamsburg: Colonial Capitol of Virginia,* Colonial Williamsburg, 1958, p. 205.

[3] The literature on conservation of art works is large, complex, and rapidly expanding. So far, however, there is no satisfactory comprehensive text on architectural conservation per se: thus, for analogues, we must turn to the publications of art conservators. Two comprehensive studies are *Proceedings, New York Conference on Conservation of Stone and Wooden Objects,* International Institute of Works of Historic and Artistic Value, London, 1971, and *Preservation and Conservation: Principles and Practices,* Proceedings of the North American Regional Conference, Williamsburg and Philadelphia 1972, Preservation Press, Washington, D.C., 1976.

[4] The complexity of conservation suggests the need for specialized training in the field. Academic training is discussed in Chapter 18.

[5] See Harold Tarkow, "The Characterization and Preservation of Wood," in *Preservation and Conservation,* pp. 101–128.

[6]Cf. *Proceedings, New York Conference on Conservation of Stone and Wooden Objects,* op. cit. See also Duval Cravens, "Soil Fumigants: Advances in Protecting Wood from Decay," *Technology and Preservation,* Boston, no. 4, 1977, pp. 22–25.

[7]An excellent survey of traditional American masonry—together with a description of indigenous stones, quarrying methods, and construction techniques—is to be found in Harley McKee, *Introduction to Early American Masonry,* The National Trust for Historic Preservation and Columbia University, Washington, 1973. See also Cornelia Brook Gilder, *Property Owners' Guide to the Maintenance and Repair of Stone Buildings,* Preservation League of New York State, Albany, 1977.

[8]Theodore H. M. Prudon, "The Cleaning of Historic Masonry Surfaces," paper read at annual meeting, Association for Preservation Technology, Halifax, N.S., Sept. 1974.

[9]John Mason Dixon, "Technics: terra cotta restoration," *Progressive Architecture,* Stamford, Conn., Nov. 1977, pp. 98–101.

[10]Robert A. Bell, "Shotcrete Restoration of an Historic Landmark," *Concrete Construction Magazine,* Chicago, Ill., 1974, pp. 161–163.

[11]The Cast Iron Society of America, 44 West Ninth Street, New York, N.Y. 10011. See also Margot Gayle, *Cast Iron Architecture in New York,* Dover Publications, New York, 1974.

[12]See Bainbridge Bunting, *Early Architecture in New Mexico,* University of New Mexico Press, Albuquerque, 1976.

[13]James R. Clifton, "Adobe Building Materials: Properties, Problems and Preservation," *Technology and Conservation,* Cambridge, spring 1977, pp. 30–34. This paper includes a short but valuable bibliography of periodical materials on the subject.

Chapter 7

[1]This was the theme of a conference held in Williamsburg and Philadelphia in September 1972, whose proceedings have now been published: *Preservation and Conservation: Principles and Practices,* The Preservation Press, Washington, D.C., 1976.

[2]See Anders Franzen, "Ghost from the Sea: The Warship *Vasa,*" *National Geographic,* vol. 121, no. 1, Jan. 1962, pp. 42–57.

[3]Ray Winfield Smith, "Computer Helps Scholars Re-create an Egyptian Temple," *National Geographic,* vol. 138, Nov. 1970, pp. 634–655.

[4]*The New York Times,* Feb. 22, 1976, p. 23. See also Donald B. Redford, "Recon-

Chapter 8

[1]Advisory Council on Historic Preservation, *Adoptive Use: A Survey of Construction Costs,* Washington, D.C., vol. 4, no. 4, June 1976.

Chapter 9

[1] According to Dr. Nicholas Platon, head of the Greek Archaelogical Service, "more damage has been done in the last 20 years than in the previous 20 centuries. The main problem is that polluted air (from automobile exhausts, and oil burners) contains sulfur, and sulfur combines with water to form sulfuric acid. The acid then turns the marble of the monuments to gypsum, a powdery substance that can be worn away by rain, wind, or even casual rubbing." *The New York Times,* Oct. 30, 1976, p. C25.

Chapter 11

[1] Samuel Dornsife, Introduction to *Exterior Decoration,* The Philadelphia Athenaeum, 1975.

[2] This is the thesis of Mario Praz's well-known book *An Illustrated History of Furnishings from the Renaissance to the Present,* George Braziller, New York, 1964. Since many of his illustrations are in color, Praz's book is especially useful. Unfortunately for Americans, however, the subject matter is exclusively European.

Chapter 12

[1] The best survey of preelectrical lighting fixtures (candles, rushlights, oil lamps, and gaslights) is to be found in L. S. Russell, *A Heritage of Light,* University of Toronto Press, Canada, 1968.

Chapter 13

[1] *Preservation and Enhancement of the American Falls at Niagara: Interim Report to the International Joint Commission,* American Falls International Board, Buffalo, N.Y., Dec. 1971.

[2] Loraine E. Kuck, *The Art of Japanese Gardens, John Day, New York, 1941.*

[3] Cf. Dorothy Burr Thompson, "Ancient Gardens in Greece and Italy," *Archaeology*, New York, vol. 4, no. 1, Spring 1951, pp. 41–47.

Chapter 15

[1] Salvage archaeology is now an integral part of American policy, confirmed by legislation and rulings which make it mandatory on any construction project involving Federal funding. See Robert D. Cunningham, "Impact of Another New Archaeology," *Journal of Field Archaeology,* vol. 1, no. 314, 1974 pp. 365–369.

[2] The best American monograph to date is by Perry E. Borchers, *Photogrammetric Recording of Cultural Resources,* Office of Archaeology and Historic Preservation, National Park Service, Washington, D.C., 1977.

[3] Two excellent introductions to archaeology are to be found in James Deetz, *Invi-*

tation to Archaeology, Natural History Press, Garden City, N.Y., 1967; and Ivor Noel Hume, *Historical Archaeology,* Knopf, New York, 1969.

⁴David M. Hart, *Technical Handbook for Historic Preservation,* National Park Service, Washington, Dec. 1975, pp. 1–2.

⁵From a lecture delivered at the Historic Preservation Division, Columbia University Graduate School of Architecture and Planning, New York, March 1976.

Chapter 16

¹J. Henry Chambers, A.I.A., *Cyclical Maintenance for Historic Buildings,* Interagency Historic Architectural Services Program, Office of Archaeology and Historic Preservation, National Park Service, U.S. Department of the Interior, 1976.

²Ibid.

³Walter R. Fischer, "Fire Safety Systems: Protecting Our Treasures from Threat of Fire," *Technology and Conservation,* Fall 1976, pp. 14–15.

⁴Ibid, pp. 15–16.

⁵Ibid, p. 16.

Chapter 18

¹*Report of the Study Committee on Architectural Conservation,* National Conservation Advisory Council. Published under the auspices of The Smithsonian Institution, Washington, D.C., 1977.

²Ibid., p. 7.

³Ibid., p. 23.

⁴Ibid., p. 33.

Chapter 19

¹Article 15, para. 2, Constitution of the C.S.S.R. Official English translation, Orbis, Prague, 1964.

Illustration Credits

2.1. (*1*) View from the Proposed Private Apartment from Humphry Repton. Designs for the pavilion at Brighton, London, 1808. (*2*) Longwood. Photograph by author.

2.2. (*1*) "View of the Eastern Patio of the Parthenon." From James Stuart and Nicholas Revett, *The Antiquities of Athens*, vol. 2, London, 1825. (*2*) "Etruscan Art." From *Geschichte der Kunst des Altertums*, Dresden, 1764.

2.3. (*1 and 2*) Reproduced in Stefan Lorant, *The New World*, New York, 1946, from Theodore de Bry, *Brevis narratio eorum quae in Florida America*, Frankfurt, 1590.

2.4. *Le Hameau*, Versailles, Robert Mique, architect, c. 1770. Photograph by author.

2.5. (*1*) "The First Hut." (*2*) "House of the Primitive Inhabitants of the Upper Indus." Both from Eugène Viollet-le-Duc, *Histoire de l'habitation humaine, depuis les temps histoiques jusque à nos jours*, Paris, 1879.

2.6. All drawings from Fitch and Branch, "Primitive Architecture and Climate," *Scientific American*, Dec. 1960, pp. 128–33, copyright © 1960 by Scientific American, Inc. All rights reserved.

4.1. Popular housing in Bologna. Photographs courtesy Bruce Dale.

5.1. (*1*) *Plan of New Orleans* by Jacques Tannessee, 1817. Courtesy Bureau of Governmental Research, New Orleans. (*2*) View of Jackson Square from southwest c. 1940. Author's collection, photographer unknown.

5.2. The Malá Strana with Hradčany Castle in background, Prague. Photograph by author.

5.3. Photographs and drawing courtesy Quebec Ministry of Information.

5.4. (*1*) Aerial view of Paris, c. 1735. Courtesy Musée de la Ville de Paris. (*2 to 6*) Photographs by author.

5.5. (*1 to 5*) All documentation courtesy Dr. Tomislav Marosovic, Chief of Historic Preservation Department, Dalmation Urban Planning Office, Split.

6.1. (*1*) Aerial view of temple complex of Ise Naiku, Japan. (*2*) General view, newly duplicated Treasure House at Ise. Both photographs copyrighted, The Mainichi Newspaper, Tokyo.

6.2. (*1 to 4*) Engraving, sketches (by architects Jan Pokorny and Robert Burley), and photograph, from the Collection of the South Street Seaport Museum.

6.3. The bedroom of Franklin Delano Roosevelt at Hyde Park. Photography courtesy the National Park Service.

6.4. (*1 to 11*) All photographs of Mount Vernon courtesy Mount Vernon Ladies' Association.

6.4. (*14*) Print of Banquet Hall, *Godey's Lady's Book*, April 1860. (*15*) Photograph courtesy Mount Vernon Ladies' Association.

6.5. The East Front of Monticello. Photograph by author.

6.6. (*1, 3 to 13*) All visual materials courtesy Colonial Williamsburg Foundation. (*2*) *The Frenchman's Map,* c. 1753, courtesy Swem Library, College of William and Mary.

6.8. Independence Hall, 1965–66. All documentation courtesy National Park Service. Photographs by George Eisenman, 1965–66.

6.9. "Conservation of Wooden Structures," by Theodore Prudon, APT Bulletin, vol. 7, no. 1, 1975, pp. 4–11.

6.10. (*1*) Iolani Palace, Honolulu. Palace under wraps. Photograph courtesy of The Friends of Iolani Palace. (*2*) The Palace after fumigation. Photograph by Ronald Melichar.

6.11. Restoration of the Woolworth Tower, New York City.
Photographs courtesy E. D. Ehrenkrantz and Associates, architects of the restoration.

6.12. Unity Temple, Oak Park, Ill., 1906. Frank Lloyd Wright; Robert A. Bell, restoration architect. Photographs: (*1*) Courtesy The Frank Lloyd Wright Home and Studio Foundation, Oak Park, Ill.; all others courtesy Robert A. Bell Architects, Ltd.

6.13. The first cast-iron house, erected 1848–1949. Tinted lithograph by Ackerman courtesy Museum of the City of New York. All photographs courtesy Preservation Department, Graduate School of Architecture, Planning and Preservation, Columbia University.

6.14. Restored facade, ZCMI Department Store, Salt Lake City. All photographs courtesy Stephen T. Baird, restoration architect.

6.15. Grand Opera House, Wilmington, Del. Stephen T. Baird, restoration architect. Photographs by Lubitsh and Bungatz.

6.16. (*1*) Palace of the Governors, Santa Fe, N.M. Photograph by Wayne Andrews. (*2*) Mud Masonry Village, Algeria. Photograph Musée de l'homme, Paris.

6.17. Church on Jeszno Street, Warsaw. Photographs courtesy Polish Ministry of Culture, Warsaw.

6.18. Dutch House, c. 1720, old Bethpage Village, Nassau County, N.Y. All photographs courtesy Old Bethpage Village Restoration.

6.19. Fifteenth-century church at Most, Czechoslovakia. All photographs courtesy *Technology and Conservation Magazine,* Boston.

6.20. The Museum of Lifesaving, Race Point, Mass. Photographs courtesy National Park Service.

7.1. Cathedral of Burano and Doumo of Pienza, Italy. All materials courtesy Soc. An Fondedile.

7.2. Restoration of York Minster, York, England. Fielden and Mawson, restoration architects; Ove Arup, consulting engineers. All documentation courtesy the architects.

7.3. State House Restoration, Springfield, Ill. Ferry and Henderson, architects for the restoration. Photographs by Orlando R. Cabanban, courtesy the architects.

7.4. The Chicago Stock Exchange Building, reconstituted entrance portal. Photograph courtesy the Art Institute of Chicago.

7.5. Reconstituted Church of St. Mary Aldermanbury, Fulton, Mo. Photographs courtesy Museum of the City of London.

7.6. Penn Mutual Insurance Complex, Philadelphia.
Mitchell/Giurgola Associates, architects. Photographs by Rollin R. LaFrance, courtesy the architects.

8.1. Market Street Restoration Agency, Corning, N.Y. Courtesy Market Street Restoration Agency, Douglas A. Loescher, Executive Director.

8.2. Baltimore City Hall. Architectural Heritage Inc., and Meyers, D'Aleo and Patton, Inc., architects for the restoration; Rita St. Clair Associates, interior design. Documentation courtesy

Office of the Mayor. Photographs *3, 5, 6, 8,* and *9* by George Cserna; others by Charles L. Hammond, Jr.

8.3. Restoration for adaptive use, Monastery of St. Agnes, Prague. Documentation courtesy Czechoslovak Ministry of Information.

8.4. The Faneuil Hall Marketplace, Boston. Benjamin Thompson Associates, architects for the restoration. All visual materials courtesy Benjamin Thompson and Associates, architects and planners.

8.5. Terminal Station, Chattanooga. Designed 1909 by Donn Barber. Adaptive restoration by Chattanooga Choo-Choo, Inc. Photographs by author.

8.6. The Swan Hotel, Lavenham, England. Photograph by author.

8.7. Sveti Stefan Island Resort, Yugoslavia. Photograph by author.

9.1. "The "Etruscan" Warrior. All rights reserved, The Metropolitan Museum of Art, New York. Photograph courtesy the Museum.

9.2. United States Mint, San Francisco. Alfred B. Mullet, architect. Walter M. Sontheimer, restoration architect. Photographs by Douglas C. Leslie, courtesy Dark Horse Productions. All rights reserved.

9.3. The "1876" Exhibition, Arts and Industries Building, Washington, D.C. Robert M. Vogel, exhibit curator. Photographs courtesy The Smithsonian Institution. Engraving (*1*), *Scientific American,* Dec. 23 and 30, 1876, p. 28.

9.4. New Temple Plaza, Salt Lake City. Fowler/Ferguson/Kingston/Ruben, architects for the Hotel Utah additions. Photographs courtesy LSD Public Communications.

9.5. The Bank of California complex, San Francisco. Anshen and Allen, architect. Photographs courtesy the architects.

9.6. Wall painting at 114 Prince Street, New York City. Richard Haas, artist. Photographs by Joel Witkin, courtesy Public Art Fund Inc.

9.7. Casa Italiana, Columbia University, New York City. Photographs by author; sketch by Cleo Rickman Fitch.

9.8. Reconstructed Stoa of Attalus, the Agora, Athens. Photograph by the author.

9.9. Replication of Greek Revival Farmhouse, Shelburne, Museum, Shelburne, Vt. Photograph courtesy the Museum.

9.10. Replication of the Parthenon Nashville. Photograph by the author.

9.11. Villa Vizcaya, Miami, Fla. Photographs courtesy Vizcaya Museum and Gardens.

9.12. The William Randolph Hearst Estate Museum, San Simeon, Calif. Photographs courtesy California Department of Parks and Recreation.

10.1. The Chicago Stock Exchange Building, Chicago, 1894. Louis Henri Sullivan, architect. John Vinci, conservation architect. Photograph courtesy the Art Institute of Chicago.

10.2. Skansen Museum, Stockholm; established 1891 by Artur Hazelius. All documentation courtesy Skansen.

10.3. Old World Wisconsin, Eagle, Wis. William H. Tishler, landscape architect. All documentation courtesy the architect.

10.4. Khizi Island Museum, Lake Onega, Karelia, U.S.S.R. The National Museum of Art and Architecture of the Karelian S.S.R. Photographs courtesy Intourist.

10.5. Aerial view of Mystic Seaport Museum, Mystic, Conn. Photograph copyright © the Mystic Seaport Museum, Inc. All rights reserved.

10.6. Old Sturbridge Village, Sturbridge, Mass. Photograph courtesy the Museum.

10.7. New Salem Village, Ill. Photograph courtesy Illinois State Division of Parks.

10.8. Old Bethpage Village, East Meadow, L.I., N.Y. Photograph courtesy Nassau County Museum.

10.9. Plimoth Plantation, near Plymouth, Mass. All Photographs courtesy Plimoth Plantation.

13.1. Yosemite National Park, Calif.; Grand Canyon National Park, Ariz. Photographs courtesy the National Park Service.

13.2. Proposed Preservation and Enhancement of the American Falls at Niagaga: Interim Report to the International Joint Commission. Photographs courtesy U. S. Army Corps of Engineers.

13.3 Grand Colonnade on the Island of Philae, Lake Nasser, Egypt. Photograph by Laurenza. © Unesco 1988. Reproduced by permission of Unesco.

13.4. (1) The Palm Stove, Kew Garden, London, 1845. Decimus Burton, architect. Photograph by author. (2) The Enid A Haupt Conservatory, New York Botanical Garden, The Bronx, William R. Cobb of Lord and Burnham Co., architect. Edward Barnes, architect for the restoration. Photograph courtesy the Library, New York Botanical Garden, Bronx, New York. (3) *Salle d'hiver, les Jardins des Plantes,* Paris, 1834. (4) Phipps Conservatory, Druid Park, Baltimore. (5) Conservatory, Sunset Park, San Francisco, 1897. Photographs courtesy Billie Britz.

13.5. (1) Villa at Tivoli, engraving by Duperac (1753). Courtesy Print Collection, Miriam and Ira D. Wallach Division of Art, Prints and Photographs, The New York Public Library, Astor, Lenox and Tilden Foundations. (2) Photograph by the author.

13.6. The gardens at Versailles. André Le Nôtre (from 1661). (1) Aerial photograph, courtesy French Government Tourist Office. (2 and 3) Garden of Sanzenin Temple, Kyoto, and Katsura-kikyu, Kyoto: both photographs courtesy Japan National Tourist Organization.

13.7. Landscape archaeological excavations in Pompeii. Documentation courtesy Dr. Wilhelmina Jashemski, archaeologist. Photographs 1, 3, and 4 and roots on plan by Stanley A. Jashemski.

13.8. The Ramble, Central Park, New York, begun 1857. Frederick Law Olmsted and Calvert Vaux, architects. Task Force for the Ramble Restoration: Bruce Kelly, James Marston Fitch, and Philip Winslow. Lithograph courtesy the New-York Historical Society, New York. (2 to 4) courtesy Central Park Conservancy.

13.9. Monet's homeplace and gardens, Giverny, France. Gerald van der Kemp, director of restoration. Photographs courtesy Barnabas McHenry. Painting, *A Bridge over a Pool of Water Lilies,* signed and dated "Claude Monet 99." Courtesy The Metropolitan Museum of Art. Bequest of Mrs. H. O. Havemeyer, 1929. The H. O. Havemeyer Collection.

13.10. *The Gardens of the Palace at Wilanow* by Bernardo Bellotto, 1764. Courtesy Polish Ministry of Culture. Photograph by the author.

13.11. Mount Vernon Mansion and Home Farms, Mount Vernon, Va. All documentation courtesy Mount Vernon Ladies' Association.

13.12. Paca House, Annapolis. Restored by Historic Annapolis, Inc. Photographs courtesy Historic Annapolis, Inc.

13.13. Pliny Freeman Farm, Old Sturbridge Village, Sturbridge, Mass. Photographs courtesy Old Sturbridge Village.

14.1. The Cathedral, Coventry, England. Sir Basil Spence, architect. Photographs by author.

14.2. Side aisle of the Chapel at Fountains Abbey, Yorkshire, England. Photograph by the author.

14.3. Abraham Lincoln Memorial Shrine, Hodgenville, Ky. Photographs by Jack Boucher and Allan Rhinehart courtesy National Park Service.

14.4. New Shelter at the Imperial Villa at Piazza Armerina. Documentation from *L'archittetura* (Rome).

14.5. Interpretation Center, Dinosaur National Monument, Utah. Anshen and Allen, architects. Photographs by Art Hupy.

14.6. Franklin Court, Independence Hall National Monument, Philadelphia. Venturi, Rauch, and Scott Brown, Inc., architects and planners; John Milner, Associates, preservation architects. Photographs: (*1, 3, and 6*) George Eisenman of Dillon & Co.; (*8 and 9*) Richard Freer. All courtesy National Park Service.

14.7. The theater at Epidaurus, Greece, c. 350 B.C. Photograph by Hirmer Fotoarchiv-München.

15.1. Canadian Inventory of Historic Buildings. Forms courtesy Canadian Inventory of Historic Buildings, National Historic Parks and Sites Directorate, Environment Canada—Parks.

15.2. Examples of photogrammetric recording courtesy UNESCO, Paris.

15.3. Photograph courtesy the National Park Service.

17.1. The Apothecary Shop, Shelburne Museum, Shelburne, Vt. Photograph courtesy the Museum.

17.2. Historical Research Center, Lejre, Denmark. All documentation courtesy Royal Danish Ministry of Foreign Affairs.

17.3. Asa Knight Store from Dummerstown, Vt., c. 1837, as restored by Old Sturbridge Village. Photographs by Donald F. Eaton courtesy Old Sturbridge Village.

17.4. Photographs courtesy Plimoth Plantation.

19.1. (*1 and 2*) Tábor; (*3*) Telč; (*4*) Slavonice. All photographs courtesy Czechoslovak Ministry of Information.

19.2. (*1 and 2*) Strahov Monastery, Prague; (*3 and 4*) town house in Prague; (*5 and 6*) town house in Litoměřice. All photographs courtesy Czechoslovak Ministry of Information.

19.3. Gardens of the former Wallenstein Palace, Prague. Photograph courtesy Czechoslovak Ministry of Information.

19.4. (*1*) Church of St. George, Prague; (*2*) Church of St. Barbara, Kutná Hora; (*3 and 4*) Castle of Český Krumlov; (*5*) Billiard Room, Villa at Lednice; (*6*) President's Suite, National Theater, Prague. All photographs courtesy Czechoslovak Ministry of Information.

19.5. All photographs courtesy Polish Ministry of Culture.

19.6. Place Zamkowy, Stare Miasto, Warsaw. All photographs courtesy Polish Ministry of Culture.

19.7. City Hall Square, Cathedral of St. Mary, Gdańsk. All photographs courtesy Polish Ministry of Culture.

19.8. Pomorski Museum, Gdańsk; Lazienki Palace, Warsaw. Photographs courtesy Polish Ministry of Culture.

19.9. Mural paintings, Cathedral of Oliwa, Poland, sixteenth century. Photographs courtesy Polish Ministry of Culture.

Index

ABOUT THE AUTHOR

JAMES MARSTON FITCH is Professor of Architecture
Emeritus and Director Emeritus of the Historic Preservation
Program of the Graduate School of Architecture and
Planning at Columbia University. A well-known authority
in architecture for more than 40 years, and an international
leader in the preservation movement, he has published well
over 200 books, articles, reports, reviews, and other
communications both here and abroad. He has taught and
lectured widely, has studied preservation and restoration all
over the world, including Africa, the Middle East, and the
USSR, and has served as a consultant on a great many
historic preservation projects in the United States, the
Caribbean, and South America.